AF761485

V&R unipress

Schriften zum
Internationalen Privatrecht
und zur Rechtsvergleichung

Band 55

Herausgegeben im

European Legal Studies Institute /

Institut für Europäische Rechtswissenschaft /

Institut pour le droit en Europe

der Universität Osnabrück

von

Professor Dr. Dr. h. c. mult. Christian von Bar, FBA, MAE,

Professor Dr. Christoph Busch,

Professor Dr. Hans Schulte-Nölke, MAE, und

Professor Dr. Dr. h. c. Fryderyk Zoll

Bartosz Kucia / Elwira Macierzyńska-Franaszczyk /
Ewa Rott-Pietrzyk / Fryderyk Zoll (eds.)

Shaping the Status of Heirs by Contractual Components under the Polish and German Inheritance Law

Comparative Challenges and the Perspective of Approximation of Legal Systems

V&R unipress

Universitätsverlag Osnabrück

UNIVERSITÄT OSNABRÜCK

UNIVERSITY OF SILESIA IN KATOWICE

DEUTSCH POLNISCHE WISSENSCHAFTS STIFTUNG | POLSKO NIEMIECKA FUNDACJA NA RZECZ NAUKI

Bibliografische Information der Deutschen Nationalbibliothek
Die Deutsche Nationalbibliothek verzeichnet diese Publikation in der Deutschen Nationalbibliografie; detaillierte bibliografische Daten sind im Internet über https://dnb.de abrufbar.

Veröffentlichungen des Universitätsverlags Osnabrück erscheinen bei V&R unipress.

Projekt realizowany na Uniwersytecie Śląskim w Katowicach we współpracy z Uniwersytetem w Osnabrück. Project realized at the University of Silesia in Katowice in cooperation with the University of Osnabrück. Projekt realisiert an der Schlesischen Universität in Katowice in Kooperation mit der Universität Osnabrück.
Projekt wspierany przez Polsko-Niemiecką fundację na rzecz Nauki – nr projektu 2018-25. Gefördert aus Mitteln der Deutsch-Polnischen Wissenschaftsstiftung – Projekt Nr. 2018-25. This monograph is part of a project supported by the German-Polish Foundation for Science – Project No 2018-25.

The views and opinions expressed in this book are those of the authors, and do not necessarily reflect the opinions of editors or supporting entity.

Reviewers: Prof. Dr. Reiner Schulze (Westfälische Wilhelms-Universität Münster), Dr. hab. Jakub Biernat, Prof. KAAFM (Andrzej Frycz Modrzewski Kraków University)

© 2023 Brill | V&R unipress, Robert-Bosch-Breite 10, D-37079 Göttingen, ein Imprint der Brill-Gruppe (Koninklijke Brill NV, Leiden, Niederlande; Brill USA Inc., Boston MA, USA; Brill Asia Pte Ltd, Singapore; Brill Deutschland GmbH, Paderborn, Deutschland; Brill Österreich GmbH, Wien, Österreich)
Koninklijke Brill NV umfasst die Imprints Brill, Brill Nijhoff, Brill Hotei, Brill Schöningh, Brill Fink, Brill mentis, Vandenhoeck & Ruprecht, Böhlau, V&R unipress und Wageningen Academic.
Wo nicht anders angegeben, ist diese Publikation unter der Creative-Commons-Lizenz Namensnennung-Nicht kommerziell-Keine Bearbeitungen 4.0 lizenziert (siehe https://creative commons.org/licenses/by-nc-nd/4.0/) und unter dem DOI 10.14220/9783737015943 abzurufen. Jede Verwertung in anderen als den durch diese Lizenz zugelassenen Fällen bedarf der vorherigen schriftlichen Einwilligung des Verlages.

Druck und Bindung: CPI books GmbH, Birkstraße 10, D-25917 Leck
Printed in the EU.

Vandenhoeck & Ruprecht Verlage | www.vandenhoeck-ruprecht-verlage.com

ISSN 2198-7041
ISBN 978-3-8471-1594-6

Contents

List of Abbreviations

Legal Acts

ABGB	Austrian Civil Code of 1 June 1811 (Federal Law Gazette Part I, No 175/2021 with further amendments) – Allgemeines bürgerliches Gesetzbuch für die gesammten deutschen Erbländer der Oesterreichischen Monarchie vom 1. Juni 1811 (BGBl. I Nr. 175/2021 mit weiteren Änderungen)
APEM	Act on Assistance to Persons Entitled to Maintenance of 7 September 2007 (Journal of Laws of 2021, item 877) – ustawa z dnia 7 września 2007 r. o pomocy osobom uprawnionym do alimentów (Dz. U. z 2021 r., poz. 877)
BGB	German Civil Code (Federal Law Gazette of 2002, Part I, pages 42 and 2909; and of 2003, Part I, page 738) – Bürgerliches Gesetzbuch (BGBl. 2002 I S. 42 ber. S. 2909, und 2003 I S. 738)
BSHG	Federal Social Assistance Act in the version promulgated on 23 March 1994 (Federal Law Gazette of 1994, Part I, page 646 and page 2975) as amended by Article 4 of the Family Support Act of 22 December 1999 (Federal Law Gazette 1999, Part I, page 2552) – Bundessozialhilfegesetz in der Fassung der Bekanntmachung vom 23. März 1994 (BGBl. 1994 I S. 646, 2975) geändert durch Art. 4 des Gesetzes zur Familienförderung vom 22. Dezember 1999 (BGBl. 1999 I S. 2552)
Code of Obligations	Regulation of the President of the Republic of Poland of 27 October 1933 Code of Obligation (Journal of Laws of 1933, No 82, item 598) – rozporządzenie Prezydenta Rzeczypospolitej z dnia 27 października 1933 r. Kodeks zobowiązań (Dz. U. z 1933 r., nr 82, poz. 598)
Copyrights Law	Act of 4 February 1994 on Copyright and Related Rights (Journal of Laws of 2021, item 1062) – ustawa z dnia 4 lutego 1994 r. o prawie autorskim i prawach pokrewnych (Dz. U. z 2021 r., poz. 1062)

Decree on Succession Law	Decree of 8 October 1946 on Succession Law (Journal of Laws of 1946, No 60, item 328) – dekret z dnia 8 października 1946 r. Prawo spadkowe (Dz. U. z 1946 r., nr 60, poz. 328)
EPA	Act of 17 June 1966 on Enforcement Proceedings in Administration (Journal of Laws of 2022, item 479) – ustawa z dnia 17 czerwca 1966 r. o postępowaniu egzekucyjnym w administracji (Dz. U. z 2022 r., poz. 479)
Grundgesetz	Basic Law for the Federal Republic of Germany of 23 May 1949 (Federal Law Gazette of 1949, Part I, page 1) – Grundgesetz für die Bundesrepublik Deutschland vom 23. Mai 1949 (BGBl. 1949 I S. 1)
HG	Act on Homes for the Elderly, Residential Homes for the Elderly and Nursing Homes for Adults (Care Homes Act) of 7 August 1974 (Federal Law Gazette 1974, Part I, page 1873) last amended by Article 3, Sentence 2 of the Act of 29 July 2009 (Federal Law Gazette 2009, Part I, page 2319) – Gesetz über Altenheime, Altenwohnheime und Pflegeheime für Volljährige (Heimgesetz) vom 7. August 1974 (BGBl. I S. 1873) zuletzt geändert durch Artikel 3 Satz 2 des Gesetzes vom 29. Juli 2009 (BGBl. I S. 2319)
Insolvency Law	Act of 28 February 2003 on Insolvency Law (Journal of Laws of 2022, item 1520) – ustawa z dnia 28 lutego 2003 r. Prawo upadłościowe (Dz. U. z 2022 r., poz. 1520)
KC	Act of 23 April 1964 on Civil Code (Journal of Laws of 2022, item 1360) – ustawa z dnia 23 kwietnia 1964 r. Kodeks cywilny (Dz. U. z 2022 r., poz. 1360)
KPC	Act of 17 November 1964 on Code of Civil Procedure (Journal of Laws of 2021, item 1805) – ustawa z dnia 17 listopada 1964 r. Kodeks postępowania cywilnego (Dz. U. z 2021 r., poz. 1805)
Konstytucja RP	Constitution of the Republic of Poland of 2 April 1997 (Journal of Laws of 1997, No 78, item 483) – Konstytucja Rzeczypospolitej Polskiej z dnia 2 kwietnia 1997 r. (Dz. U. z 1997 r., nr 78, poz. 483)
KRO	Act of 25 February 1964 on Family and Guardianship Code (Journal of Laws of 2020, item 1359) – ustawa z dnia 25 lutego 1964 r. Kodeks rodzinny i opiekuńczy (Dz. U. z 2020 r., poz. 1359)
KUG	Act of 9 January 1907 on Copyright in Works of Graphic Art and Photography (Reich Law Gazette 1907, page 7) – Gesetz betreffend das Urheberrecht an Werken der bildenden Künste und der Photographie (Kunsturheberrechtsgesetz) vom 9. Januar 1907 (RGBl. 1907, S. 7)
PB	Act of 29 August 1997 on Banking Law (Journal of Laws of 2022, item 2324) – ustawa z dnia 29 sierpnia 1997 r. Prawo bankowe (Dz. U. z 2022 r., poz. 2324)

PPM	Act of 4 February 2011 on Private International Law (Journal of Laws of 2015, item 1792) – ustawa z dnia 4 lutego 2011 r. Prawo prywatne międzynarodowe (Dz. U. z 2015 r., poz. 1792)
SGB / SGB XII	Social Security Code of 27 December 2003 (Federal Law Gazette of 2003, Part I, page 3022) – Sozialgesetzbuch / Sozialgesetzbuch (SGB) Zwölftes Buch (XII) – Sozialhilfe (Gesetz zur Einordnung des Sozialhilferechts in das Sozialgesetzbuch vom 27. Dezember 2003 (BGBl. I S. 3022)
SKOK	Act of 5 November 2009 on Cooperative Savings and Credit Unions (Journal of Laws of 2022, item 924) – ustawa z dnia 5 listopada 2009 r. o spółdzielczych kasach oszczędnościowo-kredytowych (Dz. U. z 2022 r., poz. 924)
Succession Regulation	Regulation (EU) No 650/2012 of the European Parliament and of the Council of 4 July 2012 on the jurisdiction, applicable law, recognition and enforcement of decisions and acceptance and enforcement of authentic instruments in matters of succession and on the creation of a European Certificate of Succession (Official Journal of the European Union of 27 July 2012, L 201, p. 107)
ZPO	Code of Civil Procedure in the version promulgated on 5 December 2005 (Federal Law Gazette 2005, Part I, page 3202, rev. 2006, Part I, page 431 and 2007, Part I, page 1781) – Zivilprozessordnung in der Fassung der Bekanntmachung vom 5. Dezember 2005 (BGBl. I S. 3202, ber. 2006 I S. 431 und 2007 I S. 1781)
ZSPOF	Act of 5 July 2018 on the Succession Management of a Natural Person's Enterprise and other Facilitations related to the Succession of Enterprises (Journal of Laws of 2021, item 170) – ustawa z dnia 5 lipca 2018 r. o zarządzie sukcesyjnym przedsiębiorstwem osoby fizycznej i innych ułatwieniach związanych z sukcesją przedsiębiorstw (Dz. U. z 2021 r., poz. 170)

Periodicals and official publications

AcP	Archiv für die civilistische Praxis
BGBl.	Bundesgesetzblatt (depending on context: German or Austrian Federal Law Gazette)
Dz. U.	Dziennik Ustaw (Polish Journal of Laws)
DNotZ	Deutsche Notar-Zeitschrift
DPP	Demokratyczny Przegląd Prawniczy
FP	Forum Prawnicze
GSP	Gdańskie Studia Prawnicze
JW	Juristische Wochenschrift

JZ	JuristenZeitung
KPP	Kwartalnik Prawa Prywatnego
Mon. Praw.	Monitor Prawniczy
NJW	Neue Juristische Wochenschrift
NP	Nowe Prawo
NPN	Nowy Przegląd Notarialny
OER	Osteuropa Recht
OSP	Orzecznictwo Sądów Polskich
OSNCP	Orzecznictwo Sądu Najwyższego Izby Cywilnej, Pracy i Ubezpieczeń Społecznych
OSPiKA	Orzecznictwo Sądów Polskich i Komisji Arbitrażowych
Pal.	Palestra
PiP	Państwo i Prawo
PP UW	Przegląd Prawniczy Uniwersytetu Warszawskiego
PS	Przegląd Sądowy
PWPMEiP	Problemy Współczesnego Prawa Międzynarodowego, Europejskiego i Porównawczego
RabelsZ	Rabels Zeitschrift für ausländisches und internationales Privatrecht
Rej.	Rejent
RGBl.	Reichsgesetzblatt (German Reich Law Gazzette)
RNotZ	Rheinische Notar-Zeitschrift
RPEiS	Ruch Prawniczy, Ekonomiczny i Socjologiczny
SC	Studia Cywilistyczne
SPP	Studia Prawa Prywatnego
ZEV	Zeitschrift für Erbrecht und Vermögensnachfolge
ZNUJ	Zeszyty Naukowe Uniwersytetu Jagiellońskiego
ZNUJ PPWI	Zeszyty Naukowe Uniwersytetu Jagiellońskiego. Prace z Prawa Własności Intelektualnej
ZNUJ. Pr. Praw.	Zeszyty Naukowe Uniwersytetu Jagiellońskiego. Prace Prawnicze
ZNUJ PWiOWI	Zeszyty Naukowe Uniwersytetu Jagiellońskiego. Prace z Wynalazczości i Ochrony Własności Intelektualnej

Others

BGH	Bundesgerichtshof (Federal Court of Justice)
CEIDG	Central Register and Information on Economic Activity
Legalis	Legal information system C.H. Beck Polska
LEX	Legal information system Wolter Kluwer Polska
LG	Landgericht (Regional Court)
OLG	Oberlandesgericht (Higher Regional Court)
SA	Sąd Apelacyjny (Court of Appeal)
SN	Sąd Najwyższy (Supreme Court)

Textbooks, Systems of Law and Commentaries

M. Anders, B. Gehle (eds.), *ZPO Kommentar,* 2022	M. Anders, B. Gehle (eds.), *Beck'sche Kurz-Kommentare. Zivilprozessordnung mit GVG und Nebengesetzen,* München 2022
M. Balwicka-Szczyrba, A. Sylwestrzak, *Komentarz KC,* 2022	M. Balwicka-Szczyrba, A. Sylwestrzak (eds.), *Kodeks cywilny. Komentarz,* Warszawa 2022, LEX
G. Bieniek (ed.), *Komentarz KC, book 3,* vol. 2, 2011	G. Bieniek (ed.), *Komentarz do kodeksu cywilnego, Księga trzecia. Zobowiązania. Tom 2,* Warszawa 2011
W. Burandt, D. Rojahn (eds.), *Erbrecht,* 2019, 2022	W. Burandt, D. Rojahn (eds.), *Beck'sche Kurz-Kommentare, Erbrecht,* München 2019, 2022, Beck online
J. Ciszewski, P. Nazaruk (eds.), *Komentarz KC,* 2019, 2022	J. Ciszewski, P. Nazaruk (eds.) *Kodeks cywilny. Komentarz,* Warszawa 2019, 2022, LEX
E. Gniewek, *Komentarz KC,* 2011	E. Gniewek (ed.), *Kodeks cywilny. Komentarz,* Warszawa 2011, Legalis
E. Gniewek, P. Machnikowski (eds.), *Komentarz KC,* 2016, 2017, 2019, 2021	E. Gniewek, P. Machnikowski (eds.), *Kodeks cywilny. Komentarz,* Warszawa 2016, 2017, 2019, 2021, Legalis
J. Gudowski (ed.), *Komentarz KC,* vol. V, 2018	J. Gudowski (ed.), *Kodeks cywilny. Komentarz. Tom V. Zobowiązania. Część szczegółowa,* Warszawa 2018, LEX
J. Gudowski (ed.), *Komentarz KC,* vol. VI, 2017	J. Gudowski (ed.), *Kodeks cywilny. Komentarz. Tom VI. Spadki,* Warszawa 2017, LEX
M. Gutowski (ed.), *Komentarz KC,* vol. I, 2021	M. Gutowski (ed.), *Kodeks cywilny. Komentarz. Tom I. Art. 1–352,* Warszawa 2021, Legalis
M. Gutowski (ed.), *Komentarz KC,* vol. II, 2019	M. Gutowski (ed.), *Kodeks cywilny. Komentarz. Tom II. Art. 353–626,* Warszawa 2019, Legalis
M. Gutowski (ed.), *Komentarz KC,* vol. III, 2019, 2022	M. Gutowski (ed.), *Kodeks cywilny. Komentarz. Tom III. Art. 627–1088,* Warszawa 2019, 2022, Legalis
J. Gwiazdomorski, *Prawo spadkowe,* 1959	J. Gwiazdomorski, *Prawo spadkowe,* Warszawa 1959
J. Gwiazdomorski, *Prawo spadkowe,* 1968, 1985	J. Gwiazdomorski, *Prawo spadkowe w zarysie,* Warszawa 1968, 1985

M. Habdas, M. Fras (eds.), *Komentarz KC*, vol. II, 2018	M. Habdas, M. Fras (eds.), *Kodeks cywilny. Komentarz. Tom II. Własność i inne prawa rzeczowe (art. 126–352)*, Warszawa 2018, LEX
M. Habdas, M. Fras (eds.), *Komentarz KC*, vol. V, 2018	M. Habdas, M. Fras (eds.), *Kodeks cywilny. Komentarz. Tom V. Zobowiązania. Część szczegółowa (art. 765–921[16])*, Warszawa 2018, LEX
M. Habdas, M. Fras (eds.), *Komentarz KC*, vol. VI, 2019	M. Habdas, M. Fras (eds.), *Kodeks cywilny. Komentarz. Tom VI. Spadki (art. 922–1087)*, Warszawa 2019, LEX
W. Hau, R. Poseck (eds.), *BeckOK BGB*, 2020, 2021, 2022	W. Hau, R. Poseck (eds.), *BeckOK BGB (Beck'sche Online-Kommentare)*, München 2020, 2021, 2022
Jauernig, BGB Kommentar, 2021	R. Stürner (ed.), Jauernig *BGB: Bürgerliches Gesetzbuch Kommentar mit ROM-I-VO, Rom-II-VO, Rom-III-VO, EG-UnthVO/HUntProt und EuErbVO*, München 2021
K. H. Johannesen et al. (eds.), *BGB Kommentar*, 1974	K. H. Johannesen, R. Alff, W. Ballhaus, R. Weber, W. Dunz (eds.), *Das bürgerliche Gesetzbuch: mit besonderer Berücksichtigung der Rechtsprechung des Reichsgerichts und des Bundesgerichtshofes: Kommentar*, Berlin 1974
A. Kidyba (ed.), *Komentarz KC*, vol. III (zobowiązania część ogólna), 2014	A. Kidyba (ed.), *Kodeks cywilny. Komentarz. Tom III. Zobowiązania – część ogólna*, 2014, LEX
A. Kidyba (ed.), *Komentarz KC*, vol. III (zobowiązania, część szczególna), 2014	A. Kidyba (ed.), *Kodeks cywilny. Komentarz, Tom III. Zobowiązania – część szczególna*, 2014, LEX
A. Kidyba (ed.), *Komentarz KC*, vol. IV, 2012, 2015	A. Kidyba (ed.), *Kodeks cywilny. Komentarz, Tom IV. Spadki*, Warszawa 2012, 2015, LEX
P. Księżak, M. Pyziak-Szafnicka (eds.), *Komentarz KC*, 2014	P. Księżak, M. Pyziak-Szafnicka (eds.), *Kodeks cywilny. Komentarz. Część ogólna*, Warszawa 2014
Münchener Kommentar, vol. 1, 2006	F.J. Säcker (ed.), *Münchener Kommentar zum Bürgerlichen Gesetzbuch. Band 1: Allgemeiner Teil.* München 2006
Münchener Kommentar, vol. 1, 2018	C. Schubert (ed.), *Münchener Kommentar zum Bürgerlichen Gesetzbuch, Band 1. Allgemeiner Teil §§ 1–240, AllgPersönlR, ProstG, AGG*, München 2018
Münchener Kommentar, vol. 2, 2007	W. Krüger (ed.) *Münchener Kommentar zum Bürgerlichen Gesetzbuch. Band 2: Schuldrecht Allgemeiner Teil (§§ 241–432)*, München 2007

Münchener Kommentar, vol. 3, 2019	W. Krüger (ed.) *Münchener Kommentar zum Bürgerlichen Gesetzbuch., Band 3: Schuldrecht – Allgemeiner Teil II (§§ 311–432),* München 2019
Münchener Kommentar, vol. 4, 2019	H.P. Westermann (ed.), *Münchener Kommentar zum Bürgerlichen Gesetzbuch, Band 4. Schuldrecht – Besonderer Teil I §§ 433–534, Finanzierungsleasing, CISG,* München 2019
Münchener Kommentar, vol. 5, 2009,	M. Habersack (ed.), *Münchener Kommentar zum Bürgerlichen Gesetzbuch, Band 5, Schuldrecht, Besonderer Teil III, Allgemeiner Teil §§ 705–853,* München 2009
Münchener Kommentar, vol. 7, 2020	M. Habersack (ed.), *Münchener Kommentar zum Bürgerlichen Gesetzbuch, Band 7. Schuldrecht – Besonderer Teil IV §§ 705–853, Partnerschaftsgesellschaftsgesetz, Produkthaftungsgesetz,* München 2020
Münchener Kommentar, vol. 9, 2010	G. Schlichting (ed.), *Münchener Kommentar zum Bürgerlichen Gesetzbuch. Band 9: Erbrecht: §§ 1922–2385, §§ 27–35 BeurkG, Band 9,* München 2010
Münchener Kommentar, vol. 11, 2020	S. Kessal-Wulf, (ed.) *Münchener Kommentar zum Bürgerlichen Gesetzbuch: BGB. Band 11: Erbrecht, §§ 1922–2385, §§ 27–36 BeurkG,* München 2020
Münchener Kommentar, vol. 11, 2022	S. Kessal-Wulf, T. Fest (eds.) *Münchener Kommentar zum Bürgerlichen Gesetzbuch: BGB. Band 11: Erbrecht, §§ 1922–2385, §§ 27–36 BeurkG,* München 2022
K. Osajda (ed.), *Komentarz KC,* vol. 3, 2013	K. Osajda (ed.), *Kodeks cywilny. Komentarz. Tom 3,* Warszawa 2013, Legalis
K. Osajda (ed.), *Komentarz KC,* vol. II, 2017	K. Osajda (ed.), *Kodeks cywilny. Komentarz. Tom II. Własność i inne prawa rzeczowe,* Warszawa 2017, Legalis
K. Osajda (ed.), *Komentarz KC,* vol. IIIB, 2017	K. Osajda (ed.), *Kodeks cywilny. Komentarz. Tom IIIB. Zobowiązania. Część szczegółowa,* Warszawa 2017, Legalis
K. Osajda (ed.), *Komentarz KC,* vol. IVA, 2019	K. Osajda (ed.), *Kodeks cywilny. Komentarz. Spadki. Tom IVA,* Warszawa 2019, Legalis
K. Osajda, W. Borysiak (eds.) *Komentarz KC,* 2020, 2021, 2022	K. Osajda, W. Borysiak (eds.), *Kodeks cywilny. Komentarz,* Warszawa 2020, 2021, 2022, Legalis
K. Osajda, M. Domański, J. Słyk (eds.), *Komentarz KRO,* 2020	K. Osajda, M. Domański, J. Słyk (eds.), Kodeks rodzinny i opiekuńczy. Komentarz, Warszawa 2020, Legalis
Palandt BGB Kommentar, 2010	P. Bassenge et al., *Palandt Bürgerliches Gesetzbuch. Kommentar.* München 2010

Palandt BGB Kommentar, 2016, 2018	G. Brudermüller et al., *Palandt Bürgerliches Gesetzbuch. Kommentar*, München 2016, 2018
K. Pietrzykowski (ed.), *Komentarz KC,* vol. I, 2018, 2020	K. Pietrzykowski (ed.), *Kodeks cywilny. Tom I. Komentarz do art. 1–449*^{10}, Warszawa 2018, 2020, Legalis
K. Pietrzykowski (ed.) *Komentarz KC,* vol. II, 2011	K. Pietrzykowski (ed.), *Kodeks cywilny. Tom II. Komentarz do art. 450–1088,* Warszawa 2011, Legalis
K. Pietrzykowski (ed.), *Komentarz KC,* vol. II, 2015, 2021	K. Pietrzykowski (ed.), *Kodeks cywilny. Tom II. Komentarz do art. 450–1088. Przepisy wprowadzające,* Warszawa 2015, 2021, Legalis
K. Pietrzykowski (ed.), *Komentarz KRO,* 2021	K. Pietrzykowski (ed.), *Kodeks rodzinny i opiekuńczy. Komentarz,* Warszawa 2021, Legalis
Z. Resich et al. (eds.), *Komentarz KC,* vol. 1, 1972	Z. Resich, J. Ignatowicz, J. Pietrzykowski, J.I. Bielski (eds.), *Kodeks cywilny. Komentarz. Tom 1,* Warszawa 1972
Z. Resich, et al. (eds.), *Komentarz KC,* vol. 2, 1972	Z. Resich, J. Ignatowicz, J. Pietrzykowski, J.I. Bielski (eds.), *Kodeks cywilny. Komentarz, Tom 2,* Warszawa 1972
Z. Resich et al. (eds.), *Komentarz KC,* vol. 3, 1972	Z. Resich, J. Ignatowicz, J. Pietrzykowski, J.I. Bielski (eds.), *Kodeks cywilny. Komentarz, Tom 3,* Warszawa 1972
R. Schulze (ed.), *BGB Kommentar,* 2021	R. Schulze (ed.), *Bürgerliches Gesetzbuch. Handkommentar,* Baden-Baden 2021
E. Skowrońska-Bocian, *Komentarz KC,* 2011	E. Skowrońska-Bocian, *Komentarz do Kodeksu cywilnego. Księga czwarta. Spadki,* Warszawa 2011, LEX
Soergel BGB Kommentar: Erbrecht 1, vol. 21, 2002	J. Damrau (ed.), *Soergel Kommentar zum Bürgerlichen Gesetzbuch. Band 21. Erbrecht 1, §§ 1922–2063*, Stuttgart-Berlin-Köln-Mainz 2002
Soergel BGB Kommentar: Erbrecht 3, vol. 23, 2002	J. Damrau (ed.) *Soergel Kommentar zum Bürgerliches Gesetzbuch Bürgerliches Gesetzbuch mit Einführungsgesetz und Nebengesetzen: BGB*, Band 23: Erbrecht 3 §§ 2274–2385 BGB, Stuttgart 2002
Staudingers Kommentar, vol. 1, 2004	K.-H. Gursky, N. Habermann (eds.), *J. von Staudingers Kommentar zum Bürgerlichen Gesetzbuch mit Einführungsgesetz und Nebengesetzen. Buch 1, Allgemeiner Teil §§ 164–240*, Berlin 2004
Staudingers Kommentar, vol. 2, 2006	D. Reuter (ed.), *J. von Staudingers Kommentar zum Bürgerlichen Gesetzbuch mit Einführungsgesetz und Nebengesetzen. Buch 2, Recht der Schuldverhältnisse §§ 657–704 (Geschäftsbesorgung)*, Berlin 2006

Staudingers Kommentar, vol. 5, 2002, 2004	G. Otte (ed.), *J. von Staudingers Kommentar zum Bürgerlichen Gesetzbuch mit Einführungsgesetz und Nebengesetzen, Buch 5, Erbrecht §§ 1967–2063*, Berlin 2002, 2004
Staudingers Kommentar, vol. 5, 2006	G. Otte (ed.), *J. von Staudingers Kommentar zum Bürgerlichen Gesetzbuch, Buch 5, Erbrecht, §§ 2265–2338*, Berlin 2006
Staudingers Kommentar, vol. 5, 2010	G. Otte (ed.), *J. von Staudingers Kommentar zum Bürgerlichen Gesetzbuch mit Einführungsgesetz und Nebengesetzen, Buch 5, Erbrecht §§ 2346–2385 (Erbverzicht, Erbschein, Erbschaftskauf)*, Berlin 2010
Staudingers Kommentar, vol. 5, 2017	G. Otte (ed.), *J. von Staudingers Kommentar zum Bürgerlichen Gesetzbuch mit Einführungsgesetz und Nebengesetzen. Buch 5, Erbrecht. Einleitung zum Erbrecht; §§ 1922–1966 (Erbfolge)*, Berlin 2017
System prawa cywilnego, vol. I, 1985	S. Grzybowski (ed.), *System prawa cywilnego. Tom I. Część ogólna*, Wrocław 1985
System prawa cywilnego, vol. III, part 1, 1976	Z. Radwański (ed.), *System prawa cywilnego. Tom III. Część 1. Zobowiązania – część ogólna*, Wrocław 1976
System prawa cywilnego, vol. IV, 1986	J. St. Piątowski (ed.), *System prawa cywilnego. Tom IV. Prawo spadkowe*, Wrocław 1986
System prawa prywatnego, vol. 2, 2019	Z. Radwański, A. Olejniczak (ed.), *System prawa prywatnego. Tom 2, Prawo cywilne – część ogólna*, Warszawa 2019
System prawa prywatnego, vol. 3, 2020	E. Gniewek (ed.), *System prawa prywatnego. Tom 3. Prawo rzeczowe*, Warszawa 2020
System prawa prywatnego, vol. 5, 2013	E. Łętowska (ed.), *System prawa prywatnego. Tom 5. Prawo zobowiązań – część ogólna*, Warszawa 2013
System prawa prywatnego, vol. 7, 2011, 2018	J. Rajski (ed.), *System prawa prywatnego. Tom 7. Zobowiązania – część szczegółowa*, Warszawa 2011, 2018
System prawa prywatnego, vol. 10, 2009, 2013, 2015	B. Kordasiewicz (ed.), *System prawa prywatnego. Tom 10. Prawo spadkowe*, Warszawa 2009, 2013, 2015, Legalis
System prawa prywatnego, vol. 13, 2017	J. Barta (ed.), *System prawa prywatnego. Tom 13. Prawo autorskie*, Warszawa 2017
M. Załucki (ed.), *Komentarz KC*, 2020, 2023	M. Załucki (ed.), *Kodeks cywilny. Komentarz*, Warszawa 2020, 2023, Legalis

Introduction

This book is the result of comparative research conducted by an international research team led by Professor Ewa Rott-Pietrzyk (University of Silesia in Katowice) and Professor Fryderyk Zoll (University of Osnabrück, Jagiellonian University in Krakow). The volume collects deliverables from the Research Project funded by the Polish-German Foundation for Science (Deutsch-Polnische Wissenschaftsstiftung) under Project No 2018-25.

The idea of the book and its fundamental goal is to present a multifaceted comparative legal analysis of the German and the Polish inheritance law norms, as well as elements of the law of obligation, which impact the legal status of the heir (whether testamentary or intestate). The findings of undertaken analysis provide conclusions as to the grounds of approximation of national legal regimes and contain recommendations for national legislators, practitioners and institutions applying the inheritance law in cross-border inheritance cases.

Since the book provides a comparative perspective, the momentous role of Regulation (EU) 650/2012[1] must be recognized at the outset. It justifies the need to analyse the substantive norms of the German and Polish inheritance laws in this book. The concept of the Succession Regulation (including the liaison of the last habitual residence of the deceased and its impact on jurisdiction and the applicable law for succession cases), more often leads to a situation when the domestic court applies the provisions of a foreign succession law.[2] The general rule of the Succession Regulation, providing that the law applicable to succession as a whole is the law of the state in which the deceased had their habitual

1 The Succession Regulation, which came into force on 17 August 2015, except for Articles 77 and 78, which apply from 16 January 2014, and Articles 79, 80 and 81, which apply from 5 July 2012 (see Article 84 of the Succession Regulation).

2 It should be noted, however, that the Regulation does not cover, for example, property rights, interests and assets created or transferred other than by succession, for instance as gifts, joint ownership with a right of survivorship, pension plans, insurance contracts and arrangements of a similar nature (Article 1 section 2 point g of the Succession Regulation).

residence at the time of death,[3] is the source of a uniform conflict of laws regime in that field across the European Union (except for Ireland and Denmark[4]), including the succession of real estate located in different states[5] (at least when it comes to the Member States bound by the Regulation[6]). Under the provisions of the Succession Regulation, thus the law of one country (e.g. Polish Succession Law[7]) may be applicable to the succession of the whole estate, including real property located in another country (e.g. in Germany).[8] At the same time, an

3 See also: exceptions such as those provided for by Article 21 section 2 or Article 22 of the Succession Regulation.

4 At the moment, Ireland and Denmark should not be considered "Member States" subject to the Regulation, as those states have not adopted the Regulation and are not bound by it or subject to its application. See point 82 of the Preamble to the Succession Regulation. See also: A. Wysocka-Bar, *Prawo właściwe dla dziedziczenia według unijnego rozporządzenia dotyczącego spraw spadkowych,* KPP 2012, No 4, p. 899.

5 See P. Lagarde, in: U. Bergquist, D. Damascelli R. Frimston, P. Lagarde, F. Odersky, B. Reinhartz, *EU Regulation on Succession and Wills. Commentary,* Köln 2015, pp. 120 et seq.; J. Górecki, *Nieruchomość jako składnik spadku – uwagi na tle Rozporządzenia Parlamentu Europejskiego i Rady (UE) nr 650/2012,* in: A. Dańko-Roesler, A. Oleszko, R. Pastuszko (eds.) *Rozprawy z prawa prywatnego oraz notarialnego. Księga pamiątkowa dedykowana Profesorowi Maksymilianowi Pazdanowi,* Warszawa 2014, p. 115. See, however, Article 30 of the Sucession Regulation concerning possible special rules regarding the succession of immovable property in selected countries.

6 The fragmentation of succession statute (*dépeçage*), whereby the succession of movables is governed by the *lex domicilii* of the decedent at the time of death, and the succession of immovables is submitted to the *lex rei sitae* (the law of the country where the immovable property is located) is still a widespread legal principle among states from outside the European Union, as well as in various Bilateral Conventions (which is particularly significant in view of Article 75 of the Succession Regulation). The *dépeçage* rule binds in e.g., English law (see Pipon v. Pipon (1744) Amb 25; Nelson v Lord Bridport (1846) 8 Beav. 547; Re Aganoor's Trusts (1895) 64 LJ Ch 521; Re Hernando, Hernando v Sawtell (1884) 27 Ch D 284; see also: L. Collins (ed.), *Dicey, Morris and Collins on the Conflict of Laws,* London 2006, pp. 1238 and 1251) and Canadian law (J. Walker, *Halsbury's Laws of Canada. Conflict of Laws,* Markham 2011, p. 876). See also Article 37 section 1 and 2 of the Agreement between the Republic of Poland and Ukraine on legal aid and legal relations in civil and criminal matters, drawn up in Kiev on 24 May 1993, Journal of Laws of 1994, No 96, item 465.

7 It will not necessarily be a Member State law, as the law designated under Article 20 of the Succession Regulation applies regardless of whether it designates the Member State law. See M. Pazdan, *Statut spadkowy w świetle rozporządzenia spadkowego,* in: M. Pazdan, J. Górecki (eds.), *Nowe europejskie prawo spadkowe,* Warszawa 2015, pp. 94 et seq.; A. Wysocka-Bar, *Prawo ...,* p. 903.

8 For the sake of clarity of further argument, the issue of determining the applicable law for issues located outside the scope of the general inheritance statute will be omitted here. See, for example, matters concerning the substantive or formal validity of dispositions of property upon death via agreements upon death or other *mortis causa* instruments, including testaments (Articles 24–26 of the Succession Regulation), the formal validity of dispositions of property upon death (Article 27 and Article 75 sec. 1 of the Succession Regulation), validity as to the form of a declaration concerning an acceptance or waiver of inheritance (Article 28 of the Succession Regulation) and other issues defined in the Regulation, international conventions (Article 75 of the Succession Regulation) or domestic private international law being in force as

important innovation of the Regulation is its abandonment of the rule of exclusive jurisdiction in real estate succession cases,[9] which may be found in many domestic civil procedure regimes.[10] That innovation broadens the recognition of foreign succession judgments from Member States bound by the Sucession Regulation.[11] As a result, there will likely be more cases involving foreign succession judgments (or other official documents equivalent to them) from one Member State recognised in another Member State, also with the succession of real property.[12]

The presented framing of the research field stems from the need for a unique perspective on the legal regimes under study. It serves to verify the hypothesis that the law of succession and its legal constructs, which by their very nature constitute a mechanism for the succession of property rights, remain largely neutral to the general idea of the approximation of the private law of European countries. The book uses the method of simultaneously examining each of the analysed legal systems from (a) an internal observer perspective and (b) from a comparative perspective (that of an external observer). Such a multifaceted analysis allows the studied systems to be "superimposed" using carefully selected judicial and factual cases, with the intention of creating a unique picture of Polish and German law, providing a basis for identifying dissimilarities and similarities in the two legal systems and providing a starting point for the formulation of common references and recommended legal solutions.

far, as it remains in force taking into account the date of applying the Succession Regulation, or its scope (see, for example, Article 1 sec. 2 point f as to the formal validity of dispositions of property upon death made orally).

9 See Articles 4–19 of the Succession Regulation. As a rule, the courts of the Member State in which the deceased had their habitual residence at the time of death will have jurisdiction to rule on the succession as a whole (Article 4 of the Succession Regulation). There are, however, a significant number of exceptions to that rule (see Article 5 et seq.).

10 See Article 1146 § 1 point 2 in conjunction with Article 1110^2 KPC, which give way to the Regulation in its scope of application. See also: K. Weitz, *Jurysdykcja krajowa w sprawach spadkowych w świetle rozporządzenia spadkowego*, in: M. Pazdan, J. Górecki (eds.), *Nowe europejskie prawo spadkowe*, Warszawa 2015, pp. 36 et seq.; A. Wysocka-Bar, *Jurysdykcja krajowa sądów polskich a kolizyjna jednolitość spadku*, PWPMEiP 2016, vol. XIV, pp. 92–97.

11 See Article 39 of the Succession Regulation.

12 See Article 39 et seq.; see also: Articles 62–73 of the Succession Regulation introducing the European Certificate of Succession, which may be issued in the Member State whose courts have jurisdiction under Article 4, Article 7, Article 10 or Article 11 of the Succession Regulation, by the court or another appropriate authority for use by heirs, legatees having direct rights in the succession, as well as executors of wills or administrators of the estate who, in another Member State, need to invoke their status or to exercise their respective rights as heirs or legatees and/or their powers as executors of wills or administrators of the estate. The certificate is effective in all Member States, without any special procedures being required (Article 69 section 1).

Within the framework of this research topic, there are fields of interest selected in which firstly – despite the legal regulations being different (or even being absent altogether in either of the legal systems) – it is possible, against the background of the two compared systems of inheritance law of Poland and Germany, to achieve similar legal interpretation results and legal consequences. Secondly – there are legal institutions that, despite similar legal regulations in both legal systems, are interpreted and understood sometimes in very different ways. Those include, in particular, the legal institutions from the area of contract law (including succession to economic aspects of the right to image or claims for compensation for property damage after death, donations *mortis causa*, debt relief agreements in case of death, contracts of care, dispositions of a future right to succeed, or the right to a compulsory portion while the future decedent is still alive, management of the commercial enterprise and arbitration agreements), as well as legal acts from the area of succession law that have effects on the legal relations or actions related to death (including agreements on renouncing a compulsory portion or intestate / testate succession, or testamentary limitations of the division of the inheritance after the death of the deceased person).

The book is extremely timely. In recent years, we have seen an increase in the value of inheritances acquired across borders. In Germany, the percentage of inheritances worth more than $1 million increased from 1.72 million in 2009 to 1.96 million in 2014. According to estimates, by 2025 there will be about 14 million inheritance proceedings in Germany, with a total inheritance value of 4.6 billion euros.[13] Transitions in inheritance are also taking place in Poland, whose society is one of the fastest growing in wealth in the Central European region. The mobility of Europeans within the borders of the common market, the establishment of binational families and the acquisition of assets abroad all contribute to the growing importance of inheritance with a cross-border element. The problems observed in practice and the discrepancies existing in the studied area in the Polish-German cross-border perspective justify an analysis of the degree of compatibility of these two legal systems and an attempt to identify the common denominators of the German and Polish systems of succession law in assessing the legal status of the heir.

It is also worth mentioning that this book is devoted to areas of succession law that, from the perspective of Polish law, are deeply neglected. Agreements on inheritance exist in Polish law but only on the margin of the system. Thus, all dispositions upon death can be executed, by principle, only by through the last will, which is perceived as strictly unilateral legal act. The succession law provisions of the 1964 Polish Civil Code provide for a general prohibition of

13 See https://www.openpr.de/news/586862/Neuer-BBE-media-Branchenreport-Erbschaften-2011-bei-markt-studie-de.html (access: 12.12.2022).

agreements concerning the succession. Polish law also explicitly forbids joint wills.

Despite all these restrictions, agreements concerning succession law are present in Polish law. At the core of succession law there is an agreement on the renunciation of inheritance and a transfer of the already inherited estate agreement (as the only expressly admissible contracts concerning succession). There is also a discussion about donations in the case of death (*donatio mortis causa*), whereas in several agreements outside the succession law, like insurance contracts, agreements for a bank account, lease or employment contracts, there are certain effects upon death.

The picture set out above should lead to the very general observation that Polish succession law is characterised by its radical simplification, providing for very limited possibilities for the conditional appointment and the clear exclusion of the fideicommissum. This has its roots in the time when the current succession law was being drafted. Thus, it was adjusted to the historical and geopolitical reality of the 1960s in the People's Republic of Poland[14], which was a country of poor people and of estates having predominantly only a symbolic value. A sophisticated succession law was not an attractive option and the lawmaker performed its task in a way that was aimed to meet the peoples' needs at the time and for the anticipated future. Times have changed, however, and today there is a much higher accumulation of wealth leading to a drastically different situation. Consequently, the Polish succession law has become much less appropriate for the needs of succession planning in the much more complex economic and social reality.

The idea of this book is to look at the institutions of the system that have a much more sophisticated, or even oversophisticated, scheme. The German law of succession remains in a complicated relation with Polish succession law. The German BGB was undeniably one of the important sources of inspiration for Polish law, but this is probably less true in the case of the succession law than with regard to other areas of civil law. From the 1946 Decree on Succession Law through the first draft of the Civil Code and finally up to the current stage of the Civil Code, including its recent novelisations, e.g. the 2011 introduction of *legatum per vindicationem*,[15] the Polish succession law has even further diverged from the German model. One of the emblematic manifestations of this legislative phenomenon is the 2018 introduction of the succession manager of an individual's business. This is a peculiar institution of Polish law (different from the

14 Polska Rzeczpospolita Ludowa (PRL) was the official name of the state of Poland in the years 1952–1989.

15 The Act Amending the Civil Code and Certain Other Acts of 18 March 2011 (Journal of Laws of 2011, No 2011, item 458).

executor of a will[16]) designed to prevent the dismemberment of that asset, in the event of the business owner's death.[17]

Nevertheless, German law plays a very important role in the Polish legal doctrine of private law, and in the area of succession law it is not much different. The comparison embodied in this book tries to examine the extent to which the specific German institutions of succession law vary from those of Polish law, and whether Polish law provides any equivalents that may satisfy the interests that are well-served by the elaborate and complicated German succession law. It looks at whether German law – its jurisprudence and legal doctrine – may be used to solve similar problems under Polish law.

It seems justified to raise this question. Currently, against the background of the most recent changes to Polish succession law and the decisions of the Polish Supreme Court, there is a tendency to search for legal instruments allowing for a more flexible Polish succession law and a more precise planning of succession.[18] Significantly, this sometimes takes place with regard to legal instruments that were already in force in the Polish legal system, but which were abandoned by the legislator when the 1964 Polish Civil Code was enacted.[19]

In this book, we applied the method used in our previous project on the law of obligations and the resulting publication.[20] This book – like the previous one – is based on a unique and innovative research method of analysing carefully selected legal cases (resolved in the jurisprudence of both or only one of the compared countries) from the perspective of both the German and Polish legal systems. This book again refers to a set of judgments from various levels of the German courts, which are then analysed by Polish lawyers from the perspective of Polish law, or

16 See M. Pazdan, *Zarządca sukcesyjny a wykonawca testamentu*, in: A. Dańko-Roesler, M. Leśniak, M. Skory, B. Sołtys (eds.), *Ius es tars boni et aequi. Księga pamiątkowa dedykowana profesorowi Józefowi Frąckowiakowi*, Wrocław 2018, p. 892.

17 See the Act of 5 July 2018 on the Succession Management of a Natural Person's Enterprise, Journal of Laws of 2021, item 170 (ZSPOF). However, it has a broader goal and is not limited only to the sphere of inheritance law. It is, in fact, not only about the temporary management of a business after the business owner's death (Article 17 and Article 21 ZSPOF), but also introduces a general mechanism for the public law succession of heirs or legatees into concessions, permits, licences and authorisations arising from administrative decisions issued in respect of the deceased and which are required for the continuation of business (Article 42 ZSPOF).

18 About that tendency, see the resolution of SN of 17 March 2017, III CZP 110/16, OSNC 2017, No 12, item 134 with reference to the SN resolutions of 13 December 2013, III CZP 79/13, OSNC 2014, No 10, item 98, and of 18 July 2012, III CZP 46/12, OSNC 2013, No 3, item 29.

19 See for example the resolution of SN of 17 March 2017, III CZP 110/16, OSNC 2017, No 12, dealing with the case of an agreement to renounce the compulsory portion, known to § 2346 section 2 BGB as well as Article 10 § 2 of the Polish 1946 Decree on Succession Law.

20 See M. Jagielska, E. Macierzyńska-Franaszczyk, E. Rott-Pietrzyk, F. Zoll, G. Żmij (eds), *Limits of harmonisation and convergence. Dissimilarities within Similarities of Polish and German Contract Law*, Warszawa 2018.

at least applying Polish legal reasoning. This reveals the perspectives of two legal systems that have a lot in common, but which also differ from each other in many interesting ways. From the perspective of the succession law described in this book, it must be underlined that German and Polish laws are two extremely remote members of the same family. From a Polish perspective, the similarity of these two legal traditions comes from the core understanding of the German law, which has influenced Polish legal thinking in various ways. In the previous book we tried to show how apparent similarities between Polish and German law can in fact be very misleading and disguise fundamental differences. This book is different. It takes as its starting point German legal institutions that do not seem at all similar to the solutions adopted under the Polish succession law, but reveals "similarities in dissimilarities" showing how the outcomes of legal issues are often closer than they first appear.

The another innovative feature of this book is the perspective of an analysis, which recognizes the momentous influence that the law of obligations (especially contracts) has on inheritance law. Moreover, other comparative publications covering the German and Polish legal orders have not focused on formulating proposals for common German-Polish norms of inheritance law. A study of Polish and German law on these levels offers an important contribution to the achievements of national and European legal science, providing inspirations for national legislators of European Member States, also from the perspective of harmonisation to a limited extent (namely bilateral harmonisation).

Looking at what distinguishes this book from others on similar topics, several elements could be pointed out. Firstly, the method of simultaneous examining each of the analysed legal systems from an internal and external observer's perspective. The adopted methodology assumed the juxtaposition and discussion of national legal orders, including an analysis of points of convergence, dissimilarities, and the resulting consequences. At the same time, it is not a simple juxtaposition and description of the two legal orders under study. The book makes extensive use of the method of analysing judicial case law, in which a certain factual situation that is the source of legal issues of fundamental importance for the entire system of national inheritance law, its scope and principles (institutions), is subject to a detailed analysis and comparison from the perspective of the results from German and Polish laws. Such a multifaceted analysis allows the studied systems to be "superimposed" on each other, to create a unique picture of Polish and German law. Secondly, the book addresses the unique issue of the impact and role of contract law in inheritance law, which has not been so far subject to scientific research in full. Thirdly, the book goes thematically beyond the typical comparative approach, delving in detail into the legal issues studied and compared from the perspective of a specific legal case. Fourthly, the focus on individual legal cases (factual situations that have been the subject of court decisions) is a source of significant theoretical and practical knowledge and information for both courts and legal practitioners, as well as legislators, as it allows them to see the law in action from the perspective of both inheritance law systems. And finally, comparative studies covering the German and Polish legal orders have not focused on formulating proposals for common German-Polish norms of inheritance law. The results of the project will therefore be an important step for German and Polish science in identifying the bases and recommendations for the approximation of the legislation of the two countries.

The book includes contributions from the authors involved in the project. Witold Borysiak compares the rules on claims for compensation for property damage that resulted from the death of a business owner. He also looks at the question of image rights from the perspective of their post-mortem protection, as well as the right to demand the return of a donation after the donor's death. Katarzyna Południak-Gierz and Wojciech Bańczyk focus on the appointment of a successor in an agreement on social care, which is a test for the minimum requirements to qualify a statement as a disposition upon death. Those authors also analyse a conditional renunciation of inheritance, and a contract in favour of a third party with the effects depending on the death of one party and look for answer to the question of the revocation of a power of attorney in relation to a donation upon death. Aneta Żuradzka analyses aspects of the Berliner will and the scope of its binding power as a joint will. Wojciech Klyta considers the demands for a reform of joint wills made in the German doctrine and their relevance to the Polish legislator's perception of such wills. Bartosz Kucia deals with the specific nature of a conditional appointment of an heir, as well as the revocation of the right to be an heir based on a testament. He also looks at the impact of divorce and annulment of a marriage on the appointment of an heir. The various effects of the renouncing an inheritance are the subject of considerations by Paulina Gwoździewicz-Matan, who also looks into the impact of a hardship clause on the withdrawal of the donation upon death. Małgorzata Lubelska-Sazanów explores the effects of an arbitration clause in a testament. Her further commentary concerns a ruling on a contract with an obligation to transfer an asset arising from the family provision, while the descendant is still alive. The last piece by this author concerns the question of a business being a part of the estate, with Polish law containing specific solutions making this comparison particularly interesting. Mikołaj Pietrzyk analyses the rights of the executor of a will in terms of managing a commercial enterprise as a component of succession assets. Elwira Macierzyńska-Franaszczyk examines the admissibility and legal effectiveness of a division of the inherited estate in the event that the testator limited a division in the will, as well the binding effect of testamentary dispositions for an executor.

We hope that this book may enrich the Polish discussion on the development of succession law, but also may provide foreign readers with a broad insight in the two legal systems, which in the area of the succession law are based on quite different fundamental assumptions, but still end up being fairly close to each other. The publication's impact may be even more broad and signifficant. The presented conclusions regarding the practical problems of Polish and German succession law can be generalized and valuable outside these systems.

Katowice – Osnabrück, December 2022

Bartosz Kucia, Elwira Macierzyńska-Franaszczyk,
Ewa Rott-Pietrzyk, Fryderyk Zoll

Wojciech Klyta

§ 1 – Proposals for a reform of joint wills submitted in the German doctrine and the prohibition on joint wills in Polish law. Preliminary remarks

Comparative conclusion
The scale of the practical problems associated with the legal concept of a joint will and the efforts made in the case law of the German courts to uphold the ambiguous provisions contained in private wills lead to the conclusion that it is necessary to thoroughly reconsider the postulates raised in recent years, in academic publications and conference contributions, pushing the introduction of this legal institution into the regulations of the Polish Civil Code.

I. Analysis of the case under German law

The recent decision of the German Higher Regional Court (*Oberlandesgericht*) in Celle, issued on 7 July 2022 in case 6 W 77/22,[1] concerning the interpretation of the term "Berliner Will" (*Das Berliner Testament*), confirms the view expressed in the German doctrine that this type of joint will continues to enjoy considerable popularity.[2] At the same time, the ruling is an excellent illustration of numerous practical problems. Hence, the Higher Regional Court noted that, "although the term 'Berliner Will' does not have an unambiguous meaning, the wording in the joint will whereby 'the residual estate is to be inherited through the application of the institution of the Berliner Will (*man wolle den 'Restbesitz durch ein Berliner Testament vererben*) should be interpreted as the spouses expressing their intention to appoint each other to the succession, and at the same time appointing their joint children in equal shares as final heirs (*Schlusserben*) in the event of the death of the surviving spouse, as long as they have previously sought legal advice from a notary, who has then sent the testators an outline of the will, the content of which shows their will to testify jointly and their will to appoint the joint children of these spouses to the succession." The central issue decided by the OLG in Celle

1 OLG Celle judgment of 7 July 2022, 6 W 77/22, BeckRS 2022, 23292.
2 R. Kanzleiter, *Das Berliner Testament: immer aktuell und fast immer ergänzungsbedürftig*, ZEV 2014, No 5, p. 225 *et seq.*

was whether the declaration made on 11 February 2021 by the testator, and subsequently signed by his spouse in accordance with § 2247 section 1 and § 2267 sentence 1 BGB, constituted a joint will or merely a draft of it. It should be noted that in the latter case, the rules of intestate succession would come into effect. The testator died on 31 March 2021, i.e., shortly after making the will with the contested wording. It seems necessary to briefly indicate the circumstances preceding the moment when this peculiar declaration of a last will was made.

The testator, who was seventy-three years old and married, with three adult children, made a natural effort to regulate the order of his succession. To this end, on 31 August 2020, he and his wife went to a notary who explained to the couple the meaning of the term "Berliner will" and drafted an outline. The notary drew up a draft, which was then sent to them. However, the testator – contrary to his original intention to engage the services of a notary – executed a document in his own handwriting on 11 February 2021, subsequently signed by his wife, in which he used the phrase 'Berliner will' without providing for any further information relating to the order of succession. However, the document did include the phrases 'inherit' (*vererben*) and spousal estate (*Restbesitz*). It is also significant that this document was not called a 'will' by the testator. Furthermore, it should be noted that the document the testator sent afterwards to the notary also included the words 'yours sincerely', which could suggest that it was merely a draft will. The notary forwarded this will to the probate (estate) court in a letter dated 21 April 2021. Both the Court of First Instance (the probate court) and the Court of Appeal found that the spouses' declarations described above demonstrate a testamentary intention. It is therefore not merely a draft or outline of a joint will. It is interesting to note that the Higher Regional Court reached firstly to the principles of supplementary will interpretation. Accordingly, it was noted that a testamentary heir does not have to be identified in the will by explicitly mentioning their name. It is sufficient – according to the still current ruling of the German BGH of 14 July 1965 in case V BLw 11/65[3] – that there has been no arbitrary action by third parties in naming them. The principles of the benevolent interpretation of a will, as set out in § 2084 BGB, must also be taken into account. It must then be determined whether the result obtained by such an interpretation complies with the principle of specificity set out in § 2065 section 2 BGB. The purpose of this rule is to counteract the impermissible substitution of the testator by a third party.

The most interesting aspect of the court's decision, however, is the laconic consideration given by the court of second instance as a response to the allegations raised in the appeal against the decision of the court of first instance (*Amtsgericht Geestland*), and focused on the issue of the spouses' bond (*Bin-*

3 NJW 1965, H. 47, p. 2201.

dungswirkung) arising from the joint will. According to this court, the mere use of the phrase "Berliner will" by the spouses cannot prejudge whether the two wills are interdependent. The Higher Regional Court of Celle applied a combination of the provisions of § 2270 section 2 and 2270 section 1 BGB to decide this issue. Thus, if one of the spouses receives a benefit from the second spouse, and whilst, in the event the "benefited" spouse (*des Bedachten*) survives this second spouse the disposition is made in favour of a relative of this second spouse, it is to be assumed that the disposition of one of the spouses would not have been made without the disposition of the other one.

From a historical and comparative perspective, reference should be made to an earlier decision of the Polish Court of Appeal in Poznań of 3 January 1937, case ref. II CZ (x) 1034/36,[4] which also concerned the "Berlin will".

The considerations of the Higher Regional Court of Celle reflect the scale of the practical problems involved in drafting a Berliner joint will and illustrate the efforts made in the German case law to uphold ambiguous provisions in private wills. They may also provide a good introduction to further legal comparative considerations.

II. Consideration of the problem presented in the German case and its comparison with Polish law

In the earlier Polish doctrine,[5] an assumption was expressed – still also accepted now[6] – that differences in social and cultural conditions between various countries adopting succession law norms cannot constitute a barrier to comparative legal research. It seems that the comparative approach strongly represented in the Polish doctrine is also justified by the fact that contemporary Polish succession law is also based on Austrian and German[7] regulations in which joint wills have a very long tradition. It is worth noting the previous provisions of § 586 and § 1248 of the Austrian Civil Code (ABGB),[8] which were also the subject of

4 See Z. Stasiński (ed.), *Orzecznictwo Sądu Apelacyjnego w Poznaniu w Sprawach Cywilnych, Zażaleniowych za Lata 1920–1937*, Self-published 1937, item 320, pp. 223–224.

5 K. Przybyłowski, *Niedopuszczalność wspólnych testamentów*, SC 1963, vol. IV, imprint, pp. 3–26.

6 R. Zimmermann, *Testamentsformen: "Willkür" oder Ausdruck einer Rechtskultur?*, RabelsZ 2012, vol. 76, p. 485; R. Zimmermann, *Kulturelle Prägung des Erbrechts?*, JZ 2016, No 7, pp. 321–332.

7 J. Gwiazdomorski, *Prawo spadkowe*, 1959, pp. 16–17; see review by A. Ohanowicz, RPEiS 1959, No 3, pp. 191–194.

8 An excellent review of the positions presented during the codification work on the provisions of the Austrian Civil Code relating to joint wills was prepared by K. Przybyłowski, *Niedopuszczalność…*, footnote 45, p. 15.

interest of the Polish Supreme Court.[9] At the same time, it should be emphasised that the Austrian legislator, pursuant to the Act on the Reform of the Inheritance Law of 30 July 2015,[10] made some amendments to these regulations. As a result, the matter of joint wills was recently regulated in § 586 ABGB in a new wording composed of two editorial units. Firstly, the provision of § 586 section 1 ABGB incorporates the normative content of the former § 586 ABGB; secondly, the slightly amended content of the former § 1248 ABGB was inserted into § 586 section 2 ABGB.[11]

It is likely that the Polish prohibition on joint wills,[12] provided for in Article 942 KC, is an impetus for the search – undertaken by representatives of the Polish doctrine – for justification of this peculiar restriction of the freedom of testation.[13] The fruits of these are the first proposals made *de lege ferenda.*[14] In the course of this discussion, considerable attention is paid to the provisions of § 2265 et seq. BGB.[15] However, what is rarely recognised in this debate is that the "triad" characteristic of German inheritance law, consisting of a joint will taking the form of a private document including interdependent decrees, is a kind of rarity in legal parlance.[16] It should be noted that the complex norms provided for in German law were, as indicated above, also the subject of interest from the former Polish jurisprudence.[17]

9 See judgment of SN of 19 May 1938, C II 3009/37, Przegląd Prawa i Administracji, Lwów 1938, item 292, pp. 484–486.

10 BGBl. I No 87/2015; it should be noted that this provision applies – pursuant to § 1503 section 7 point 5 ABGB – to wills drawn up after 31 December 2016.

11 R. Welser, *Der Erbrechts-Kommentar §§ 531–824 ABGB*, Wien 2019, p. 118.

12 This prohibition was introduced into Polish law by the Decree on Succession Law, which entered into force on 1 January 1947; see F. Zoll's characterization of these norms, in: F. Zoll, *Intestate Succession in Poland*, in: K. G. C. Reid, M. J. De Waal, R. Zimmermann (eds.), *Intestate Succession*, Oxford 2015, pp. 298 *et seq.*

13 A. Paluch, *Gewährleistung oder Beschränkung der Testierfreiheit – Über die Unzulässigkeit der gemeinschaftlichen Testamente im polnischen Erbrecht*, OER 2016, No 2, pp. 217–225.

14 K. Osajda, in: K. Osajda (ed.), *Komentarz KC*, vol. IV A, 2019, p. 370. The author distinguished four trends of opinions expressed in the Polish doctrine of inheritance law. Thus: first, he pointed to the conservative trend emphasising the advantages of the currently existing prohibition on joint wills, then the author identified the assumptions of the minimalist trend turning for inspiration to the provision of the German Civil Code, another group is formed by the view that the legal figure of joint wills should be adopted into Polish law without any restrictions, and finally there is also a group of opinions whereby the problems created by joint wills can be solved through an interpretative approach. *Idem*, pt. 28–32, p. 370.

15 T. Jasiakiewicz, *Testament wspólny jako przedmiot regulacji w prawie polskim i niemieckim*, Toruń 2018, p. 20.

16 B. Strobel, *Bedarf das gemeinschaftliche Testament des deutschen BGB einer Reform?*, AcP 2021, vol. 221, No 3, pp. 400–402.

17 See judgment of SN of 14 June 1922, C 3/22, OSP 1921–1922, Yearbook One, item 599, pp. 516–518; this ruling proves that the provisions of the German Civil Code concerning joint wills were a source of certain difficulties for the Polish Supreme Court. Of purely historical value

It is worth noting that the legal instrument of the joint will is a subject of heated debate among representatives of modern German doctrine.[18] The source of the dispute is a joint will drawn up by spouses in private form (*gemeinschaftliche Testament in privatschriftlicher Form*). When making dispositions on death, testators usually do not have the requisite knowledge, nor are they aware of the consequences set out in § 2271 section 2 sentence 1 BGB.[19] This provision is an intrinsically imperfect attempt to normalise the complex intertwining of issues that arise under a joint will.[20] The contemporary scientific revival among representatives of the German doctrine is understandable in the context of the observation made years ago by E. Till, who noted: "*a result of the reception of Roman law in Germany was a combination of revocable Roman wills with German irrevocable inheritance contracts, a combination that, given the contradiction of elements, produced a half-way and indistinct institution, contradictory in itself.*"[21] This view was alluded to more recently by K. Muscheler, who argued that, in the context of the postulates of the politics of law, the legal instrument of a joint will should be rejected.[22] On the other hand, contemporary representatives of German literature[23] emphasise the dangers to freedom of testation[24] arising from the construction of handwritten joint wills.[25] B. Strobel has identified three main groups of proposals formulated in literature with a view to amending the German regulation on joint wills, each are supposed to be a panacea for those difficulties.[26] The most far-reaching postulate – in line with the K. Muscheler's opinion expressed above – aims at the complete abolition of joint wills in German law.[27] It is obvious that the codification of civil law is – like any human work – not

are also the statements of SA in Poznań, in which the desire to achieve legal certainty in the area of the construction of joint wills made by spouses, rooted in German law, is evident. See the decision of this court of 20 April 1932, II b(x) 35/32, regarding the remarriage clause published in *Orzecznictwo Sądu Apelacyjnego*, item 319, pp. 223–224.

18 I. Kroppenberg, *Ist unser Erbrecht noch zeitgemäß? Überlegungen zum zivilrechtlichen Gutachten des 68. Deutschen Juristentags in Berlin*, NJW 2010, No 36, pp. 2609–2612; R. Kanzleiter, *Empfiehlt es sich, das privatschriftliche gemeinschaftliche Testament abzuschaffen?*, ZEV 2011, No 1, pp. 1, 2; B. Strobel, *Bedarf…*, pp. 422–432.

19 B. Strobel, *Bedarf…*, p. 400.

20 K. Przybyłowski, *Niedopuszczalność…*, footnote 20, p. 9.

21 E. Till, *Prawo prywatne austryackie, tom VI, Wykład Austr. Prawa Spadkowego*, Lwów 1904, footnote 9, p. 136.

22 K. Muscheler, *Erbrecht. Band I*, Tübingen 2010, nb 2035, p. 1047.

23 B. Strobel, *Bedarf…*, pp. 420–421.

24 See in German doctrine: W. Schmitz, *Das Problem der Beschränkung der Testierfreiheit*, Berlin 1936, pp. 1–98.

25 G. Hosemann, *Von den Bedenken gegen das Testieren "im stillen Kämmerlein" – Die Geschichte des eigenhändigen Testaments in Deutschland, dargestellt aus Anlass des 200. Geburtstags des Badischen Landrechts*, RNotZ 2010, No 10, pp. 520 et seq.

26 B. Strobel, *Bedarf…*, p. 422.

27 *Ibidem*, pp. 422–424 and 432.

perfect.[28] However, the legislator's radical interventions in the traditional institutions of civil law are associated with numerous difficulties. The number of potential problems associated with the "surprise effect" for spouses[29] who have acted in reliance on a legal concept established in their minds for years is difficult to estimate.[30] Furthermore, a number of difficulties would arise from the introduction of a prohibition, hitherto unknown in German law (*captatoria institutio*),[31] as with the example of Article 635 of the Italian Civil Code.[32] Such an institution would have the effect of preventing the interdependence of two handwritten wills drawn up by spouses that are not considered joint.[33]

The essence of a further proposal is to abolish the form of a private will as an acceptable form for joint wills. However, such a legislative change would result in joint wills taking the form of an official document, and therefore becoming meaningless, since by concluding a contract of succession the spouses can exercise their freedom to testify to a much greater extent.[34]

A further group of inspiring suggestions, presented by the German legal doctrine and collated by B. Strobel,[35] while fairly abstract by nature so far, are also worth noting. It has been proposed, to introduce – varying in scale – restrictions on the interdependence of dispositions in joint wills.[36] These proposals may refer to the actual state of interdependence (*Tatbestand der Wechselbezüglichkeit*) or to the resulting effects (*Rechtsfolgen der Wechselbezüglichkeit*). The essence of the first variant is the demand to modify § 2270 section 2 BGB defining the presumption of interdependence, which in fact has a *quasi*-statutory function. In particular, many doubts are raised by the second alternative set out in this legal norm. Consequently, it is proposed that it should be repealed.[37] By contrast, the

28 J. Gwiazdomorski, *Prawo spadkowe*, 1959, p. 20.

29 It should be noted that, as a result of the amendment of § 1353 section 1 sentence 1 BGB – aimed at "opening up" marriage to same-sex couples – made by the Law of 20 July 2017 (BGBl. I S. 2787), which entered into force on 1 October 2017, the possibility of drawing up a joint will by partners in a civil partnership applies to this type of union concluded before 1 October 2017 and did not take advantage of the possibility of converting such a union into marriage, regulated by § 20 "a" of the German Civil Partnership Act; M. Schuhmann, in: W. Burandt, D. Rojahn (eds.), *Erbrecht*, 2022, § 2265, pt. 1.

30 K. Przybyłowski, *Niedopuszczalność…*, pp. 3–4; the author describes the effects in previous Polish inheritance law of the procedure of prohibiting joint wills.

31 K. Przybyłowski, *Niedopuszczalność…*, footnote 45, p. 15; A. Paluch, *Captatoria conditio: meaning and admissibility in the light of freedom of testation. Analysis of selected legislations of Western European countries*, Acta Iuris Stetinensis 2020, No 4, pp. 52–63.

32 An example of this type of regulation is provided by Article 635 of the Italian Civil Code; Royal Decree of 16.03.1942, Gazzetta Ufficiale Serie Generale No 262, as amended.

33 B. Ströbel, *Bedarf…*, pp. 423–424.

34 *Ibid*em, pp. 424–425.

35 *Ibidem*, pp. 425–431.

36 I. Kroppenberg, *Ist unser…*, p. 2612.

37 B. Strobel, *Bedarf…*, pp. 424–425.

second variant of this proposal refers in essence to the effects of the interdependence of testamentary provisions. In turn, it is divided into three specific groups, among which the most noteworthy are proposals for the complete elimination of the interdependency effects of the testamentary provisions currently set out in § 2271 section 1 BGB, or the introduction of certain restrictions related thereto.[38] A peculiar intermediate solution - also conceivable - is the adoption of a legal regulation that assumes the existence of interdependent provisions only if the spouses expressly decide.[39]

The short comments above, relating to the discussion on proposals involving the reform of the legal instrument of the joint will in Germany, undoubtedly demonstrate that "*the idea of law is a constant state of becoming.*"[40] Years ago, F.K. Fierich prescribed "*to take from foreign laws what is good in them, what is suitable for our relationships, to take after careful consideration* (...)."[41] As a result, before the Polish legislator takes a final decision concerning the further fate of the currently binding prohibition on joint wills, it must wait, bearing in mind the evaluation of this institution expressed years ago by E. Till,[42] for the results of the discussion in the German literature, which has been quoted here.

38 This idea was alluded to by § 393 of the Civil Code of 19 June 1975 in force in the German Democratic Republic, (GBl.I. 1975 No 27, p. 465).

39 R. Kanzleiter, *Empfiehlt...*, pp. 1–2.

40 R. von Ihering, *Walka o prawo*, transl. by A. Matakiewicz, Lwów 1875, p. 9.

41 F. K. Fierich, *Rzut oka na najważniejsze zadania prac kodyfikacyjnych. Wykład wygłoszony w Warszawie przy inauguracji Komisji Kodyfikacyjnej d. 10 listopada 1919 r.*, Przegląd Prawa i Administracji 1919, year XLIV, pp. 279–297.

42 E. Till, *Prawo....*, footnote 9, p. 136.

Aneta Żuradzka

§ 2 – *Berliner testament.* The admissibility of a waiver of inheritance by the final heir after the death of the first testator

Comparative conclusion

In the case of the Berliner Testament, two openings of the succession should be taken into account: the opening of the succession upon the death of the first testator, and the opening of the succession upon the death of the second testator. The opening of the succession, is, in the case of the final heir, only the death of the longer surviving spouse. Since the Polish courts and doctrine strictly adhere to the principle that an inheritance may be accepted or waived only upon the opening of the succession (upon the death of the testator), it may be presumed that if joint wills were admissible in Poland (though they are not), the Polish court, like the German court, would rule that the final heir may only reject the inheritance upon the death of the surviving spouse.

I. Analysis of an example case under German law

The subject under consideration by the BGH in the verdict of 8 October 1997 in case IV ZR 236/96[1] was the admissibility of a waiver of the inheritance by the final heir after the death of the first testator and before the death of the second testator against the background of the institution of the joint wills of spouses (*Berliner testament*).

The facts of the BGH judgment were as follows. On 27 March 1953, the claimant's father and stepmother (the father's second wife) drew up a joint matrimonial will (*Berliner Testament*), where they appointed each other the sole heirs and appointed the claimant to inherit from the longer surviving spouse.

The father died on 25 June 1953. After the death of the father of the then still minor claimant, her mother, as her statutory representative, applied for a judicial attestation of the acquisition of the estate in favour of the claimant by way of intestate succession. Then the joint wills of the spouses were opened. The application for judicial declaration of the acquisition of the estate submitted on behalf of the claimant was therefore rejected. On 20 March 1954, the mother of

1 NJW 1998, 543.

the minor claimant, as her statutory representative, presumably in order to receive a compulsory portion, waived the inheritance intended for the claimant in the joint wills. The guardianship court agreed to this. On 9 February 1988, the claimant's stepmother drew up a notarial will in which she appointed the defendants as her sole heirs to the inheritance. On 10 January 1992, the claimant's stepmother died. The claimant considered herself to be the final heir under the joint matrimonial wills of her deceased father and stepmother. The claimant asserted her rights against the defendants, whom the stepmother had appointed as her sole heirs in a notarial will draw up after the claimant's father died. The claimant referred to the ineffectiveness of the waiver of the inheritance made by her mother on her behalf.

The court of first instance – the Regional Court (*Landgericht*) – agreed with the claimant and determined that the claimant had become the sole heir of her stepmother. Following an appeal by the defendants, the court of second instance – the Higher Regional Court (*Oberlandesgericht*) – dismissed the claim in its entirety. Then, the claimant's cassation appeal was found justified by the BGH.

As the BGH pointed out in the grounds for its judgment, the heir can accept or waive the inheritance as soon as the succession has been opened. The opening of the succession, as provided for in § 1946 BGB, takes place, in the case of the final heir, only upon the death of the longer surviving spouse. Before that, the final heir retains a right to the succession, which they can renounce pursuant to § 2352 BGB, but they are not yet the heir and cannot therefore waive it.

In this respect, the legal situation of the final heir differs fundamentally from that of the subsequent heir (*Nacherbe*, § 2100 BGB) in the fiduciary substitution and the substitute heir (*Ersatzerbe*, § 2096 BGB) in the substitution of an heir. It is true that, in the case of a fiduciary substitution, the inheritance goes to the subsequent heir after another heir has already been the original heir. However, there is only one succession event that results in an initial succession and then in a subsequent succession. In addition, in the case of the substitution of an heir, it is possible that the substituted heir acquires the inheritance only after the person appointed before him has died and from the moment of the death of the testator – but with retroactive effect for this heir. The substituted heir then becomes the direct heir of the testator. Thus, even in the case of a substituted succession, there is always only one opening of the succession. Since § 1946 BGB only requires that the succession has been opened and not acquired in order for the inheritance to be waived, it is reasonable, as stipulated in § 2142 section 1 BGB, to allow a subsequent heir the right to waive the inheritance already upon opening the succession, as well as to allow this option to the substitute heir, even if the previously appointed heir is still alive and, under certain circumstances, there is no acquisition of succession at all by the substitute heir.

In the case of a *Berliner Testament*, upon the death of the spouse who dies first, the final heir obtains the legal position resulting from the surviving spouse being bound by mutual dispositions made in the joint wills to the final heir. In this regard, it is irrelevant whether this is an expectative or only a legally justified perspective of becoming an heir in the future. § 1946 BGB stipulates that the final heir can only waive the inheritance after succession has been opened and they have become an heir. However, this refers to the death of the longer surviving spouse.

Accordingly, in the case at hand, the waiver of the inheritance declared by the final heir after the father's death and before the death of the stepmother was therefore ineffective. Of course, although it would be desirable to clarify the question of inheritance as early as possible, it is not sufficient to declare a waiver of the inheritance that is in violation of § 1946 BGB as admissible before opening the succession. If the final heir wishes to receive a compulsory portion of the spouses' estate before the possibly still distant event of the death of the surviving spouse, and the surviving spouse is interested in relieving their obligations under the joint will by granting a recompense to the final heir in the form of the compulsory portion, the law provides for a suitable way in the form of an agreement to renounce the inheritance pursuant to § 2352 BGB.

Having presented the facts and legal problem of the ruling under review, it should be clarified that the institution of joint wills in German law is regulated in § 2265 to § 2272 BGB (*Title 8: Gemeinschaftliches Testament*). Under § 2265 BGB, the admissibility of joint wills is limited to spouses only. However, as of 1 October 2017, the possibility of same-sex marriages is allowed.[2] Before that date, legalised homosexual couples had the right to draw up a joint will pursuant to § 10 section 4 of the Act on Registered Life Partnerships of February 2001.[3]

Joint wills between spouses are of significant importance in practice. In Germany, spouses often use this institution, despite the fact that they also have the choice between an individual will as well as an agreement on succession (§ 2274 et seq. BGB), as well as a donation *mortis causa* (§ 2301 BGB). It is estimated that between a half and two-thirds of all wills made in Germany are joint wills between spouses.[4]

The legal nature of a joint will between spouses is not uniformly understood in German doctrine and case law. There are three approaches to the nature of the 'commonality' of a joint will: the objective theory, the subjective theory, and the intermediate theory. According to the objective theory, a joint will comprises two

2 See Part 1 Section 1 (1) of the Act of 20 July 2017 (Federal Law Gazette I p. 2787).
3 Federal Law Gazette of 2001, Part I, p. 266.
4 C.F. Nordmeier, *Zulässigkeit und Bindungswirkung gemeinschaftlicher Testamente im Internationalen Privatrecht*, Tübingen 2008, p. 1, and the estimates given in footnote 1.

statements of intent contained usually in a single document. The subjective theory holds that the feature of joint will arises from the subjective perception of the testators and from circumstances outside the will. According to the intermediate theory, the intention to testify jointly must be apparent from the dispositions made in the will. The view that the inclusion of the spouses' dispositions in a single document is not a necessary prerequisite appears to be correct, and that the decisive factor determining the existence of a joint will is the intention to testify jointly, as interpreted. However, the interpretation should also take into account circumstances that exist outside the will itself (the external context). It follows from the above that joint wills are admissible under German law in two forms: substantive (jointness in content) and formal (jointness in form). It is also important to note that, although the spouses make dispositions jointly, each of them acts unilaterally, so that there are always two dispositions on death[5]

Spouses may draw up a joint will in any form provided for in an individual will, i. e. as a holographic will, a notarial will or an extraordinary will. A joint will may also take a mixed form. A will can be drawn up in an extraordinary form, even if the requirements set out there are satisfied by only one of the spouses (§ 2266 BGB). The mixed form is, for example, found when one spouse draws up a will in holographic form and the other spouse makes a declaration before a notary.[6]

Life experience shows that spouses would not make a joint will if they expected the dissolution of the marriage. The German legislature has therefore decided that the annulment or dissolution of the marriage leads to the ineffectiveness of the joint will (§ 2268 section 1 BGB in conjunction with § 2077 section 1 BGB). The dissolution of marriage is equivalent to a situation in which the grounds for divorce were met at the time of the testator's death and the testator applied for divorce or consented to a divorce. The same applies if the testator was entitled to apply for the annulment of the marriage at the time of the testator's death and filed such an application during their lifetime. However, under § 2268 section 2 BGB, dispositions will remain effective to the extent that it can be assumed that the spouses would also have made them in this case.[7]

With regard to the content of the dispositions made, the doctrine distinguishes between three types of joint will. The first is the formal will (simultaneous, simple, externally joint, or *gleichzeitig, äusserlich*). This type of joint will is used when the spouses make use only of the privilege of the form. The dispositions of the testators are set out in a single will, but their content is not linked

5 A. Duda, *Wspólny małżeński testament w prawie niemieckim*, Jurysta 2004, No 4, p. 36.
6 *Ibidem*, p. 37.
7 W. Klyta, *Testamenty wspólne*, Rejent 2006, No 2, p. 107.

to one another. In practice this type of will is rare. The second type are reciprocal wills (*gegenseitig, reziprok*), in which spouses name each other as heirs. The making of one disposition is not, however, dependent on the making of the other. The third type are mutual wills (*wechselbezügliche Verfügungen*), which is where making a disposition by one spouse is conditional upon making a disposition by the other spouse. At the same time, the dispositions of the spouses must be so closely linked that one spouse's disposition could not be made without the other spouse's disposition. Only such dispositions as: the appointment of an heir, legacy and instructions may take the form of mutually dependent dispositions. It should be emphasised that these dispositions exist only jointly, and at the same time they lose their validity jointly. Pursuant to § 2270 section 1 BGB, the invalidity or revocation of one of the dispositions results in the ineffectiveness of the other. Mutual wills are generally reciprocal, but there may be reciprocal wills that are not mutual.[8] It is also possible for one spouse's disposition to be made conditional on the disposition of another spouse, without the disposition of the latter being made conditional.

In the case of formal and mutual joint wills, there is complete freedom to revoke dispositions made on an individual basis. The revocation of a reciprocal will is subject to certain rigours in order to protect the trust of the other spouse. The testator may revoke a mutually dependent disposition unilaterally during the lifetime of both spouses. To this end, the spouse must make a declaration on revoking the disposition with a notary and serve this declaration in the form of a notarial deed on the other spouse, so that the latter does not continue to feel bound by their mutually dependent disposition and may testify differently (§ 2271 section 1 BGB). In addition, the spouses may revoke their mutually dependent dispositions jointly without hindrance, for example by jointly withdrawing the notarial will from official custody.[9] If this is not the case, the surviving spouse will, in principle, be bound by their interdependent disposition, and to that extent their freedom to testify is limited. However, even then, the surviving spouse may revoke their interdependent disposition if the person to be benefited has committed an act justifying disinheritance. The surviving spouse may dispose of their property by *inter vivos* acts, with the restriction of dispositions made with the intention of causing harm to the beneficiary in the will. The most popular will, in practice, is the *Berliner Testament.* In Germany, the *Berliner testament* is a will in which the testators (spouses) designate each other

8 *Ibidem*, p. 109.

9 A. Duda, *Wspólny…*, p. 37.

as heirs and appoint a third person (last heir) as the heir after the surviving spouse.[10]

The construction of a *Berliner Testament* in German law is an alternative to the institution of fiduciary substitution,[11] where the testator may appoint their spouse as the preliminary heir (*Vorerbe*) and a certain third party as the subsequent heir (*Nacherbe*). Thus, the third person does not inherit on the basis of the dispositions of the longer surviving spouse, but is the heir of the testator who died in the first place. If there is any doubt as to whether the construction of the *Berliner Testament* or fiduciary substitution was used, then pursuant to § 2269 section 1 BGB it must be assumed that the *Berliner Testament* was drawn up. In other words, in the event of any doubt, the third party is not to be treated as the subsequent heir, i. e. the heir of the testator who died first, but as the heir of the longer surviving spouse.[12]

In the *Berliner Testament*, the possibility for the surviving spouse to dispose of the estate of the deceased spouse can be regulated in two ways – according to the sharing principle or the unity principle. According to the sharing principle, the surviving spouse is restricted in their ability to dispose of the property left by the deceased spouse and must retain the substance of the estate. By contrast, under the unity principle, the longer surviving spouse is not subject to restrictions on the disposal of the estate of the deceased spouse. The assets of the deceased spouse merge into one with the assets of the surviving spouse (there are no separate estates). After the death of the surviving spouse, a third party inherits the estate of the surviving spouse and the estate of the previously deceased spouse that is still part of this estate.[13] In addition, the *Berliner Testament* often contains a 'remarriage clause' (*Wiederheiratungsklausel*), whereby the spouses undertake that, in the event of remarriage, the surviving spouse will pass on all or part of the deceased spouse's estate to the third party, which is usually the deceased spouse's child.[14]

10 See A. Duda, *Wspólny…*, p. 38, K. Osajda, *Testamenty wspólne*, Warszawa 2005, p. 23 and 107 et seq.

11 On fiduciary substitution in German law see W. Borysiak, *Dziedziczenie. Konstrukcja prawna i ochrona*, Warszawa 2013, p. 358.

12 T. Jasiakiewicz, *Testament wspólny jako przedmiot regulacji w prawie polskim i niemieckim*, Toruń 2018, p. 31.

13 A. Duda, *Wspólny…*, p. 38.

14 W. Klyta, *Testamenty…*, p. 108.

II. Consideration of the problem presented in the German case and its comparison with Polish law

Joint wills are inadmissible under Polish inheritance law. According to the provision of Article 942 KC, "A will may contain the dispositions of only one testator."[15] It is inadmissible to merge the declarations of intent of two or more people in one will. The term "will" as used in the discussed provision means a document containing a statement of intent that constitutes a will. The prohibition in Article 942 KC thus applies to wills made in writing, provided under Articles 949, 950, 951 and 953 sentences 1 and 2 KC. It does not cover oral wills (oral statements of a last will, even if made simultaneously, remain independent wills) or a letter under Article 952 § 2 KC (constituting only a statement of knowledge about the contents of a will).[16]

In addition, Polish law adopts the rule that the legal situation of an heir must be clarified definitively at the moment of opening the succession. A manifestation of this rule is the provision of Article 962 KC prohibiting a conditional appointment to the inheritance. As a rule, in Polish inheritance law, reciprocity is

15 The Inheritance Law Team of the Codification Commission, operating until 2015 under the direction of Professor Maksymilian Pazdan, developed a draft amendment to the inheritance law in which joint wills of spouses were admissible, following the German model. See M. Pazdan, *Wybrane projektowane zmiany w prawie spadkowym*, in: *Nowy kodeks cywilny odpowiedzią na wyzwania współczesności – konferencja naukowa (Warszawa, 10 April 2015)*, Warszawa 2015.

16 See K. Przybyłowski, *Niedopuszczalność wspólnych testamentów*, SC 1963, vol. IV, pp. 18 et seq.; M. Pazdan, in: K. Pietrzykowski (ed.), *Komentarz KC*, vol. II, 2021, Article 942, pt. 2, Legalis; E. Skowrońska-Bocian, *Komentarz KC*, 2011, pp. 98 et seq.; K. Osajda, *Testamenty…*, p. 84; T. Jasiakiewicz, *Testament…*, Toruń 2018, pp. 59 et seq; J. Kremis, in: E. Gniewek, P. Machnikowski (eds.), *Komentarz KC*, 2016, p. 1728, pt. 4; P. Księżak, *Prawo spadkowe*, Warszawa 2017, p. 160, pt. 170; A. Paiąk-Kozub, *Testamenty wspólne w prawie polskim – uwagi de lege lata i de lege ferenda*, in: M. Fras, P. Ślęzak (eds.), *Prawo prywatne wobec wyzwań współczesności. Księga pamiątkowa dedykowana Profesorowi Leszkowi Ogiegle*, Warszawa 2017, p. 327; B. Kucia, in: M. Habdas, M. Fras (eds.), *Komentarz KC*, vol. VI, 2019, p. 257, pt. 2; K. Osajda, in: K. Osajda (ed.), *Komentarz KC*, vol. IVA, 2019, pp. 369 et seq; differently, however J. Gwiazdomorski, *Wykładnia przepisów o testamencie na tle uchwały składu siedmiu sędziów Sądu Najwyższego*, NP 1973, No 6, pp. 828 et seq, who takes a slightly different view of the essence of a joint will, stating that the dispositions of two or more persons are joined into a joint will by the joint act of executing the will, and thus also by drawing up a single joint document. He also consistently defends the position that a 'will' in the provisions of inheritance law has one meaning and refers exclusively to a legal act; J. Gwiazdomorski's view was supported by S. Wójcik, F. Zoll, *Testament*, SPP 2006, No 2, p. 93, and S. Wójcik, F. Zoll, in: *System prawa prywatnego*, vol. 10, 2009 (first edition), pp. 296–298, with the thesis that 'will' used in Article 942 means a legal act and not a document. Recently, however, S. Wójcik, F. Zoll, in: *System prawa prywatnego*, vol. 10, 2013 (second ed.), pp. 320–323, decided that their position in favour of a wide extension of the prohibition of Article 942 KC was too assertive. Therefore, the position of J. Gwiazdomorski does not find approval among representatives of the doctrine today.

excluded in the case of an appointment to the succession. An appointment to the succession cannot be made dependent on the effectiveness of another will (disposition). This is an absolute prohibition, regardless of whether we treat the nature of reciprocity as a condition or *causa*. These limitations do not apply, however, when reciprocity is clarified at the moment of opening the succession at the latest. Such a situation will occur when, at the time of opening the succession of the person who drew up the reciprocal will, it will be certain that the will upon which the validity of the reciprocal will was conditioned is valid. An examination whether this certainty exists should take place *in concreto*.[17]

The acquisition of succession occurs when the succession is opened (Article 925 KC), but is not definitive until the heir makes a declaration on accepting the inheritance (or circumstances arise that allow the assumption that the heir has made such a declaration[18]). At this time, however, the heir is the actual heir. A special situation exists in the case of the succession by a conceived but unborn child (*nasciturus*). The legal condition of "live birth" can only be ascertained when the child is born. Before that moment, the statutory representative of the *nasciturus* cannot make a statement about accepting or waiving the inheritance.[19]

A declaration on accepting or waiving the inheritance may only be made after the testator's death. It would be devoid of legal effects if made during their lifetime. In its resolution of 19 October 2018,[20] the Supreme Court held that filing a statement on waiving the inheritance by a person in relation to whom the time limit specified in Article 1015 § 1 KC has not yet started running is ineffective. The ruling raises doubts. Neither Article 1012 nor Article 1015 KC forces such a position. It seems that, when establishing the list of heirs is postponed (e. g. due to proceedings on declaring a candidate as an heir unworthy of inheritance, or proceedings on exclusion from the inheritance pursuant to Article 940 KC, or waiting for a *nasciturus* to be born), the likely heirs should be able to make the statement regulated in Article 1012 KC before the time limit for making such a statement starts running.[21] B. Kucia spoke in favour of admitting the declaration referred to in Article 1012 KC after opening the succession, but before the start of the time limit for the person making the declaration.[22] W. Borysiak is of a different opinion, pointing out that a person appointed to inherit in a further order cannot waive the inheritance "in advance", so to speak, even before they learn

17 M. Niedośpiał, *Swoboda testowania*, Bielsko-Biała 2004, pp. 134–136.

18 See Article 1015 KC.

19 G. Gorczyński, in: M. Habdas, M. Fras (eds.), *Komentarz KC*, vol. VI, 2019, p. 540, pt. 29.

20 Resolution of SN of 19 October 2018, III CZP 36/18, OSNC 2019, No 7–8, item 74.

21 M. Pazdan, in: K. Pietrzykowski (ed.), *Komentarz KC*, vol. II, 2021, Article 1012, pt. 2, Legalis.

22 B. Kucia, *Oświadczenie o przyjęciu lub odrzuceniu spadku w imieniu małoletniego*, in: M. Fras, P. Ślęzak (eds.) *Prawo prywatne wobec wyzwań współczesności. Księga pamiątkowa dedykowana Profesorowi Leszkowi Ogiegle*, Warszawa 2017, p. 226.

about an appointment to inherit and before the actual start of the deadline to accept or waive the inheritance.[23] This would be submitting a declaration of intent made on condition (that a given person will be appointed to inherit), which is clearly prohibited by Article 1018 § 1 KC. However, it must be considered whether this view will also be relevant if such a precautionary declaration of waiver of the inheritance (made in the form *ad solemnitatem*) is formulated unconditionally: e.g. "I waive the inheritance" (which is most often the case). Can it then be supplemented by interpretation with such an unspoken condition?

In Polish law, the statement in question may be made on behalf of an heir with limited legal capacity by a statutory representative. A statement made without the guardianship court's consent is invalid.[24] An exception to this is proposed with regard to a declaration on accepting an inheritance with the benefit of inventory, which does not require the guardianship court's consent.[25]

An agreement on renouncing an inheritance, in terms of Polish law, is an agreement by which a potential heir renounces the intestate succession of the decedent. The renunciation only covers intestate succession. Therefore, it does not exclude the testamentary succession of the renouncing person. A person who renounces the succession may inherit on the basis of a will drawn up both before and after the inheritance was renounced.[26] They may also become a testamentary legatee.[27] A *de lege lata* renunciation of testamentary inheritance would be invalid (Article 58 § 1 in connection with Article 1048 KC). An invalid agreement on the renunciation of testamentary inheritance is not subject to conversion to an agreement on the renunciation of intestate succession. If the agreement on the renunciation of inheritance covered both intestate and testamentary inheritance, we would have to deal with the partial invalidity of the agreement (i.e. to the extent of renouncing the testamentary inheritance).[28]

The renunciation of inheritance has legal effects at the time of the testator's death (the opening of the succession). The person who renounced the inheritance, or their descendants covered by the renunciation, are excluded from the inheritance as if they had not lived to see the opening of the succession. They are also not entitled to a compulsory portion from the testator.

23 W. Borysiak, in: K. Osajda, W. Borysiak (eds.), *Komentarz KC*, 2021, Article 1015, pt. 31, Legalis.

24 See resolution of SN of 24 June 1961, I CO 16/61, OSNCP 1963, No 9, item 187; ruling of SN of 27 May 1998, I CKN 181/97, not published; justification of the judgment of SA in Rzeszów of 6 December 2012, I ACa 337/12, Legalis No 744852; justification of the decision of SN of 25 February 2015, IV CSK 304/14, Legalis No 1203291; resolution of SN (7) of 22 May 2018, III CZP 102/17, OSNC 2018, No 12, item 110.

25 M. Pazdan, in: K. Pietrzykowski (ed.), *Komentarz KC*, vol. II, 2021, Article 1012, pt. 4, Legalis.

26 See resolution of SN of 15 May 1972, III CZP 26/72, OSNCP 1972, No 11, item 197.

27 M. Pazdan, in: K. Pietrzykowski (ed.), *Komentarz KC*, vol. II, 2021, Article 1048, pt. 6, Legalis.

28 G. Wolak, in: M. Habdas, M. Fras (eds.), *Komentarz KC*, vol. VI, 2019, Article 1048, pt. 1, LEX.

In Polish law, according to Article 963 KC, a testamentary heir may be appointed in case another person appointed as an intestate heir or testamentary heir does not want or is not able to be an heir (the substitution of an heir). A substituted heir, like any other heir, acquires the inheritance upon its opening (Article 925 KC). Circumstances excluding the effective appointment of an appointed heir occur before the succession is opened, or after it is opened but with a retroactive effect from that moment.[29]

Fiduciary substitution, whereby the testator obliges the heir to preserve the acquired inheritance and to leave it (in case of death or another event) to another person indicated in the will, is inadmissible under Polish law. Therefore, it is difficult to relate the institution of fiduciary substitution (*Vorerbschaft und Nacherbschaft*) from German law to Polish law. However, the provision of Article 964 KC does not provide for the sanction of nullity, but for the conversion of the fiduciary substitution into the substitution of an heir under Article 963 KC. In Polish law, a disposition in the will by which the testator obliges the heir to preserve the acquired inheritance and to leave it to another person only has the effect that this other person is appointed to the inheritance in case the heir does not want or is unable to be an heir. However, if it is apparent from the contents of the will or from the circumstances that the heir would not have been appointed without this limitation, the appointment of the heir is invalid.

III. Summary

In German law, the admissibility of joint wills is limited to spouses only. The institution of joint wills is regulated in § 2265 to § 2272 BGB. However, since 1 October 2017, the possibility of marriage between persons of the same sex has been allowed. In German law, joint wills are admissible in two forms: substantive (jointness in content) and formal (jointness in form). The spouses may draw up a joint will in any form provided for in an individual will, i.e. as a holographic will, a notarial will or an extraordinary will. The joint will may also take a mixed form.

Joint wills are inadmissible in Polish law. This prohibition is absolute in Polish law, regardless of the content of the disposition and the person of the testator. At the same time, the prohibition of Article 942 KC applies only to written wills, i.e. holographic wills (Article 949 KC), notarial wills (Article 950 KC), allographic wills (Article 951 KC), and wills made on board a ship or aircraft (Article 953 sentences 1 and 2 KC), but not to oral wills (Article 952 KC).

29 B. Kucia, in: M. Habdas, M. Fras (eds.), *Komentarz KC*, vol. VI, 2019, Article 963, pt. 7, LEX.

Due to the content of the dispositions made, joint wills in German law can be formal (simultaneous, simple, externally joint or *gleichzeitig, äusserlich*), mutual or reciprocal. Mutual wills are generally reciprocal, but there may be reciprocal wills that are not mutual.

In Polish law, simultaneous wills and mutual wills are permissible (as long as they are not made in the same document). Reciprocity, however, has been excluded. The provision of Article 962 KC prohibits a conditional appointment to the inheritance. Thus, the legal situation of an heir must be clarified definitively at the time of opening the succession. An appointment to the inheritance cannot be made conditional on the effectiveness of another will.

In German law, an agreement on the renunciation of inheritance can concern both an intestate succession and a testamentary succession.

In Polish law an agreement on the renunciation of inheritance concerns only a potential appointment to intestate succession and does not extend to testamentary succession. It is rightly argued in the doctrine that extending the possibility of renouncing the inheritance to testamentary succession is justified only in those legal systems where institutions creating an inheritance bond (e.g. joint wills or an agreement on succession) are allowed.[30] Thus, while in German law the possibility of renouncing testamentary succession is justified, in Polish law it is not, due to the inadmissibility of institutions creating an inheritance bond.

In German law, the heir can accept or waive the inheritance as soon as the succession has been opened. Opening the succession happens upon the death of the decedent. The heir may accept or waive the inheritance as soon as the devolution of the inheritance has occurred. In the case of a *Berliner Testament,* there are two openings of the succession (the opening of the succession upon the death of the first testator and the opening of the succession upon the death of the second testator). In the case of the final heir, the succession is opened only upon the death of the longer surviving spouse. Before that, the final heir has a right to the succession, which he can renounce pursuant to § 2352 BGB, but he is not yet the heir and cannot therefore waive it. However, in the case of a fiduciary substitution, there is always only one opening of the succession. In this respect, the legal situation of the final heir differs fundamentally from that of the subsequent heir (*Nacherbe*, § 2100 BGB) in the fiduciary substitution, and of the substitute heir (*Ersatzerbe*, § 2096 BGB) in the substitution of an heir. A subsequent heir and a substitute heir have the right to waive the inheritance already upon opening the succession.

Both joint wills and fiduciary substitution are inadmissible under Polish law, so it is difficult to transpose the problem that the BGH had to resolve directly into

30 W. Borysiak, in: K. Osajda, W. Borysiak (eds.), *Komentarz KC,* 2021, Article 1048, pt. 44, Legalis.

Polish law. It should be noted, however, that in Polish law (like under German law), a statement on accepting or waiving an inheritance can only be made after the testator's death. It would be devoid of legal effects if made during their lifetime. This leads to the view that, in a situation where establishing a list of heirs is postponed (e.g. due to the proceedings on declaring a candidate as an heir unworthy of inheritance, proceedings on exclusion from the inheritance pursuant to Article 940 KC, or waiting for a *nasciturus* to be born), the likely heirs should be able to make a statement on accepting or waiving the inheritance after opening the succession, but before the time limit for making such a statement starts running.

Since Polish courts and doctrine strictly adhere to the principle that the inheritance may be accepted or waived only once the succession has been opened (upon the death of the testator), it may be presumed that, if joint wills were admissible in Poland (which they are not), the Polish court, like the German court, would rule that the final heir may only reject the inheritance upon the death of the surviving spouse.

It may be expected that, if the Polish legislator had allowed joint wills, it would also have allowed the possibility of renouncing testamentary succession along the lines of the German solution. If it had allowed joint wills without allowing the possibility of renouncing testamentary succession, the final heir (if they wanted to claim the compulsory portion earlier) would not be able to renounce the testamentary succession earlier (before the opening of the succession) through an agreement with the future testator (i.e. the longer surviving spouse), since, in accordance with current Polish regulations, the heir can only renounce the intestate succession by virtue of such an agreement.

Aneta Żuradzka

§ 3 – Debt relief agreement effective *mortis causa* and a binding joint will

Comparative conclusion
A debt relief agreement *mortis causa* (even one on the basis of which a moral duty or a duty of decency would be fulfilled) entered into by the longer surviving spouse after the death of the first spouse violates the joint will drawn up by these spouses, and as such is invalid. However, depending on the circumstances of the case, the invalid debt relief agreement *mortis causa* can be considered to have been converted (§ 140 BGB) into a donation *inter vivos* (§ 2301 section 2 BGB). In contrast to German law, under Polish law, a debt relief agreement that is effective upon the death of the person releasing the debt is classified as a conditional and timely legal act *inter vivos*.
Thus, if joint wills were permissible in Poland (though they are not) and joint mutual wills had been drawn up, and the surviving testator then entered into a debt relief agreement having effect on their death, it could be assumed that the agreement would be considered a permissible legal action *inter vivos* and not in breach of the joint will.

I. Analysis of an example case under German law

The subject of the BGH judgment of 30 November 1977 in case IV ZR 165/76[1] was the problem of whether a person bound by a joint will may conclude a debt relief agreement effective *mortis causa*.

The facts of the BGH judgment were as follows. In 1933, spouses A (the husband) and B (the wife) made joint wills,[2] in which they appointed each other heirs and, on the death of the surviving spouse, their inheritance was to go to their sons C and D in equal shares. Son D died in the war leaving no descendants. The husband (A) died in 1939. In 1963, the wife (B) gave a loan of 55,000 German marks to persons E and F for the construction of a new house. In 1996, a mortgage was established on the property to secure this loan. On 27 June 1974, the wife (B) concluded an agreement on succession in the form of a notarial deed with

1 NJW 1978, 423.
2 You can read more about the institution of joint wills in German law in this monograph, in e.g. § 1 and § 2.

persons E and F. Under the agreement, spouse B, as a token of thanks to persons E and F for their care, decided that, upon her death, she would release persons E and F from the debt under the loan agreement and authorise them to cancel the mortgage if they continued to care for her and look after her late husband's grave, and later her grave. Persons E and F accepted the agreement. On 16 December 1974, spouse B died. Son C (the claimant) demanded that the court declare that the defendants (persons E and F) owed him the amount of the loan of 55,000 German marks. He pointed out that the agreement on succession was invalid (ineffective) because it contradicted the 1933 joint wills of the spouses, and was therefore contrary to § 2271 BGB. Defendants E and F argued that the provision of § 2271 BGB did not apply in this case (the binding of the joint will had been broken) because the surviving spouse, irrespective of the binding force of the joint will, was entitled to make dispositions if she fulfilled a moral duty or duty of decency thereby.

The BGH dismissed son C's claim but did not share the defendants' arguments (the BGH presented its own). The BGH held that the June 1974 agreement on succession breached the spouses' joint wills of 1933, and as such was invalid. Spouse B, after spouse A's death, was legally deprived of the possibility of revoking the testamentary disposition contained in the will by concluding an agreement on succession and making dispositions *mortis causa* by means of it. The defendants are wrong in arguing that the provision of § 2271 BGB does not apply in the present case (the binding of the joint will had been broken), because the surviving spouse, irrespective of the binding force of the joint will, is entitled to make dispositions of property on death if she fulfilled a moral duty or showed a consideration for decency. Dispositions *mortis causa* on the basis of which a moral duty or a duty of decency would be fulfilled are not excluded from the binding force of § 2271 BGB.

It should be noted that other provisions, such as § 1425 section 2 BGB, § 1641 sentence 2 BGB, § 1804 sentence 2 BGB and § 2113 section 2 sentence 2 BGB, establish exceptions in favour of legal actions on the basis of which a moral obligation or a duty of decency is fulfilled. In the provision of § 2271 BGB, the legislator has not provided for such an exception.

The vagueness of the grounds possibly permitting the breaking of the binding of a joint will would lead to considerable uncertainty as to the effectiveness of a joint will. Moreover, there is no need for such a breakthrough, since the intended purpose in such cases can be achieved by means of permissible legal actions *inter vivos*.

In this case, the possibility of using conversion into donation seems obvious. According to § 140 BGB, if a void legal transaction meets the requirements of another legal transaction, then the latter is deemed to have been entered into, if it may be assumed that the validity of the latter would have been intended if it had been kown that the primary transaction was invalid. The application of § 140 BGB is also permitted for dispositions in a last will.[3] The will of the decedent (spouse B) is clear from her agreement declaration.[4] She wanted to relieve the debt of persons E and F from the date of her death, so that persons E and F would not have to make any payments after that date. The will of the contracting parties must, as far as possible, be taken into account. The decedent (spouse B), had she known that the provisions of the agreement were invalid, would have wished the transaction to be *inter vivos.*

The invalid agreement on succession must therefore be considered to have been converted into a donation, with the result that the loan debt was extinguished upon the death of the decedent (spouse B) without any further legal action being required. This donation is subject to the provisions on donations *inter vivos* in accordance with § 2301 section 2 BGB.[5]

II. Consideration of the problem presented in the German case and its comparison with Polish law

Article 942 KC states, "A will may contain the dispositions of only one testator." Joint wills are therefore inadmissible in Polish inheritance law.[6] It is not permissible to merge declarations of intent of two or more people in one will. The term "will" means a document containing a declaration of intent that constitutes a will.[7]

3 See F.J. Säcker, R. Rixecker, in: *Münchener Kommentar,* vol. 1, 2006, p. 1749 and pp. 1756–1757, in: *Münchener Kommentar,* vol. 9, 2010, p. 975–980; decision of SN of 14 February 2013, II CSK 294/12, OSP 2014, No 1, item 3, p. 28.

4 The reasoning of the judgment shows that the court was closer to the concept of conversion as an interpretative method. See M. Bławat, *Konwersja nieważnych czynności prawnych,* Warszawa 2019, footnote 533, Legalis.

5 In the critical gloss on this ruling, it was pointed out that the fundamental problem in this case was not to determine the decedent's will (actual or hypothetical), but to decide on the legal effects of an agreement on succession that conflicted with a joint will previously made by the decedent together with her spouse and thus contradicted § 2271 BGB. The fact that the testator was bound by the joint will, on the other hand, precludes conversion in view of the meaning and purpose of that provision and the need for certainty and security of trade. See K. Tiedtke, *Die Umdeutung eines Vermächtnisses in ein Rechtsgeschäft unter Lebenden,* NJW 1978, No 51, pp. 2573–2574.

6 As on the proposed changes to the Polish inheritance law in this regard, see this monograph § 2, footnote 15.

7 The prohibition in Article 942 KC thus applies to wills made in writing: Articles 949, 950, 951 and 953 sentences 1 and 2 KC. It does not cover oral wills (oral statements of last will, even if simultaneous, remain independent wills) or a writing under Article 952 § 2 KC (constituting only a statement of knowledge of the contents of the will). More on this issue, see this monograph § 2, footnote 16, and the literature indicated there.

As the most serious objection justifying the inadmissibility of joint wills, representatives of the Polish doctrine point to the impossibility of reconciling joint wills with the fundamental principle of the free revocability of testamentary dispositions, which is absolutely binding under Polish law.[8] With the admissibility of joint wills, the principle of the freedom of the unilateral revocability of a will may be violated.[9] If we allow it in full, we are not protecting the testator's trust. If we restrict it, we violate a fundamental principle of succession law.

With regard to the revocability of joint wills, two periods need to be distinguished – during the lifetime of the testators and after the death of first of them. Revocation can take place either with or without the knowledge of the other testator (an inadvisable situation). Whereas after the death of one of the testators, their will may be disregarded by the surviving testator. According to A. Baziński, the rationale behind the prohibition of joint wills in Polish law is precisely the intention to prevent the intention of the deceased testator from being disregarded by the surviving testator. The surviving testator, after taking possession of the estate, could disregard the intention of the deceased testator, disposing of the deceased's assets in a manner contrary to their wishes, and thus nullifying the reasons and motives that had induced the deceased to draw up a joint will.[10] Faced with such difficulties, the Polish legislator rejected the institution of joint wills, seeing no satisfactory way out of this situation.[11]

De lege ferenda, arguing in favour of the legislator admitting joint wills in Polish law, it seems that a certain exception could be introduced in the scope of the principle of the free revocability of testamentary dispositions. As regards the risk of the deceased testator's will not being respected by the surviving testator, it would seem that protection against this risk could be provided by the introduction of an appropriate statutory regulation following the example of German law (§ 2271 BGB).

The question that needs to be answered is also whether it is permissible under Polish law to dispose *mortis causa* of individual assets included in the estate. The principle of the exclusive disposal of property *mortis causa* under a will does not apply to the disposal *mortis causa* of individual assets included in the estate. Contingent and timely legal actions that are to have effects post mortem do not violate Article 941 and Article 1047 KC if they do not concern the estate within the meaning of Article 922 KC, i. e. all property rights and obligations of a given person at the moment of their death, or a part thereof (understood in the

8 See M. Planiol, *Podręcznik prawa cywilnego [O darowiznach i testamentach]*, translated by: A. Słomiński, Warszawa 1922, p. 81; W. Chojnowski, *Prawo spadkowe*, Warszawa 1951, p. 108.

9 K. Przybyłowski, *Niedopuszczalność…*, footnotes 35 and 36, p. 12.

10 A. Baziński, *Prawo spadkowe*, Łódź 1948, p. 198.

11 K. Przybyłowski, *Niedopuszczalność…*, pp. 13–14.

agreement as a part of the estate), and secondly, if they are shaped as a legal action *inter vivos* rather than legal actions *mortis causa.*

The parties may give to their transaction some of the characteristics of a legal transaction in the event of death. The validity of an act concluded by the parties may depend on the death of one of the parties and their survival by the beneficiary of the contract. Such actions (e.g. a donation in the event of death, or a contract for the benefit of a third party in which the performance depends on the death of one of the parties to the contract), if they have the nature of legal actions *inter vivos*, are permissible under Polish law. In particular, the parties may conclude a donation agreement, the effectiveness of which will depend on the fulfilment of a condition precedent (which is the survival of the donor by the donee) or of an initial term (the death of the donor). Contingent and timely legal transactions *inter vivos* will also include the release from debt, which is effective upon the death of the person releasing the debt. Each time, however, it must be assessed whether such an agreement would be a circumvention of Articles 941 and 1047 KC.[12]

The provisions of Polish civil law – in contrast to the German civil law (§ 140 BGB) – do not provide for the institution of the conversion of legal actions. However, the supporters of this concept believe that it is a separate institution that is also in the Polish legal system. K. Gandor,[13] following the model of § 140 BGB, formulates the following prerequisites for the admissibility of the conversion of legal actions:
1) only an existing but invalid legal act may be the subject of conversion;
2) the invalid legal act should meet all the substantive requirements of a substitute legal act, i.e. a legal act having different effects or content from the invalid act, provided that it allows the practical aim to be achieved and does not go beyond the effects of the act being converted;
3) it may be presumed that the parties would have entered into the substitute legal act if they had known that the legal act they had entered into was invalid (known as the hypothetical will of the parties understood as corresponding to the "reasonable will of the parties").

When these conditions are met, conversion, i.e. the transformation of an invalid legal act into another, substitute, valid legal act, is allowed.[14] Justification for the conversion should be found in the rule of benevolent interpretation (*benigna interpretatio*). It consists in accepting, in the course of interpretation, the

12 W. Borysiak, in: K. Osajda, W. Borysiak (eds.), *Komentarz KC*, 2021, Article 1047, pt. 45–46, Legalis.
13 K. Gandor, *Konwersja nieważnych czynności prawnych*, SC 1963, vol. IV, pp. 69–70, 73 et. seq.
14 Z. Radwański, M. Gutowski, in: *System prawa prywatnego*, vol. 2, 2019, § 39, p. 23, Legalis.

meaning of a declaration of intent that allows the legal act to be upheld, rather than the meaning that would entail qualifying the act as invalid.[15]

If the content of the will remains unclear despite interpretative efforts, the principle of "benevolent interpretation" of the will (*interpretatio in favorem testamenti* – Article 984 § 2 KC) should be applied. Out of all the possible meanings, the one that allows the disposition to be maintained in force and gives it reasonable content should be applied. The role of the interpreter is to make sure that a testator who has taken on the task of drawing up a last will and has therefore made their decision unequivocally known in this respect, does not succeed based on the intestate succession, as this would be completely against their will.[16]

The rule of benevolent interpretation of a will has been repeatedly applied by the Polish Supreme Court. For instance, a resolution of the Supreme Court of 22 March 1971[17] has held that the invalidity of a will, as provided for in Article 951 KC, caused by the inclusion in it of the dispositions of two testators (Article 942 KC), does not constitute an obstacle to regarding the declarations of intent made by the testators as two separate oral wills.[18] If the prerequisites for drawing up an oral will have been met and its form observed, the joint protocol – drawn up pursuant to Article 951 § 2 KC and containing the dispositions of two testators – becomes a document of secondary evidentiary character only. If each testator made a declaration of their last will, then it means two separate wills were drawn up, each having an independent legal existence. Such separate wills do not cease to be wills, even if made simultaneously and linked in content. As is aptly assumed in the literature, there is then no conversion of the legal act. This is because we are still talking about the same legal act (will), but in a different permissible form.[19]

15 Z. Radwański, *Wykładnia oświadczeń woli składanych indywidualnym adresatom*, Wrocław 1992, pp. 118 et. seq.

16 See *Re Harrison* [1885] 30 Ch. D. 390.

17 See III CZP 91/70, OSPiKA 1972, No 2, item 26.

18 This thesis was repeated in SN resolution of 12 December 1972, III CZP 88/72, Legalis No 16777; in SN decision of 12 February 1997, II CKU 4/97, Legalis No 123619; and in SN decision of 24 March 1998, I CKU 6/98, Prokuratura i Prawo 1998, No 9, p. 27; see also the partially approving gloss by A. Mączyński, *Glosa do uchwały SN z 22 marca 1971 r. III CZP 91/70*, OSPiKA 1972, No 2, item 26, and fully critical commentary by J. Gwiazdomorski, *Wykładnia przepisów o testamencie na tle uchwały składu siedmiu sędziów Sądu Najwyższego*, NP 1973, No 6, pp. 822 et seq.

19 B. Kucia, in: M. Habdas, M. Fras (eds.), *Komentarz KC*, vol. VI, 2019, Article 958, pt. 4, LEX.

III. Summary

Given the prohibition on joint wills in Polish law, it is difficult to transpose the problem that the BGH had to resolve directly into Polish law. It should be noted, however, that in Polish law a debt relief agreement that is effective upon the death of the person releasing the debt is classified as a conditional and timely legal act *inter vivos* (in contrast to German law – as is apparent from the ruling under review).

Therefore, if joint wills were permissible in Poland (though they are not) and joint, mutual wills have been drawn up, and the surviving testator then entered into a debt relief agreement having effect on their death, it can be assumed that the agreement would be considered a permissible legal action *inter vivos*, and not in breach of the joint will.

Furthermore, although the provisions of Polish Civil Code, in contrast to the German Civil Code (§ 140 BGB), do not provide for the conversion of legal transactions, both the doctrine and the courts allow it under certain conditions. Therefore, even if one were to consider that such a debt relief agreement coming into effect upon death is invalid, given the principle of benevolent interpretation, it would have to be considered that an invalid debt relief agreement has been converted into a donation.

Similarly to German law, under Polish law the parties may conclude an ordinary donation agreement, the effectiveness of which will depend on the fulfilment of a condition in the form of the donor's survival by the donee, or the coming of an initial deadline, namely the death of the donor. Such an act should be classified in the group of legal acts *inter vivos.*[20]

20 See the resolution of SN of 13 December 2013, III CZP 79/13, OSNC 2014, No 10, item 98.

Bartosz Kucia

§ 4 – The appointment of an heir subject to the condition that the validity or effectiveness of the will is not contested

Comparative conclusion
German succession law allows a testator to appoint a testamentary heir (or a legatee) on the condition that the person for whom the benefit is provided does not contest the validity or effectiveness of the will (*Verwirkungsklausel, a forfeiture clause*). However, the scope of the permissible forfeiture clause excludes allegations against a will that are aimed at giving effect to the testator's true intentions (e.g. an objection about a lack of testamentary capacity or a failure to perform the testamentary formalities), provided they are raised on sufficiently weighty grounds – those allegations cannot deprive the heir (or legatee) of the benefit conferred by the will. By its very nature, the condition in question can only occur after the death of the testator and would therefore not be permissible under Polish law when it refers to the appointment of a testamentary heir (Article 962 KC) or a legacy *per vindicationem* (Article 981^3 § 1 KC). The rule would be different, however, in the event of a legacy *per damnationem* (Articles 975 and 981^3 § 2 KC), as that condition (whereby the validity or effectiveness of the will cannot be contested) should be accepted if it is possible to fulfil and does not violate mandatory provisions (*ius cogens*) or the principles of social intercourse (Article 94 KC).

I. Analysis of the case under German law

The analysed OLG Dresden judgment of 16 February 1999, 7 W 1571/98,[1] raises issues of great importance from the perspective of the principle of testamentary freedom. It concerns a legal institution that allows the testator to have a significant impact on the fate of their estate beyond the mere determination of the persons to whom the estate is to be devoted in the will. Indeed, through appropriate (conditional) testamentary clauses, the testator may attempt to achieve specific goals, e.g. minimising the likelihood of future disputes under the will, while at the same time influencing a certain attitude of the beneficiaries of the estate after death.

1 NJW-RR 1999, 1165.

The facts surrounding the OLG Dresden judgment of 16 February 1999 included a will in which the testator allocated the inheritance to his children: two of them legitimate and one illegitimate. At the same time, he acknowledged his paternity of the latter in the will and granted him all his shares in a limited liability company (GmbH); while the mother of that child was granted a share of the capital in GmbH & Co. KG).

In Clause 7 of the will, which is essential for the outcome of the case, the testator stipulated that anyone who raised an objection or complaint against the will would be completely excluded from the inheritance (*"Sollte gegen mein Testament Einspruch oder Klage erhoben werden, so verfüge ich hiermit, daß diese Person von einem jeglichen Erbe meines Nachlasses ausgeschlossen wird"*).

In its decision, the court of first instance (*Landesgericht*) relied on the order of succession set out in the deceased's will, without considering Clause 7 and despite the legitimate children's attempts to challenge the validity of the will on the grounds of the testator's erroneous motivation (claimed to be the result of a mistake about the paternity of the last of the children).[2] The importance of taking these circumstances into consideration, however, was emphasised by OLG Dresden.

The presentation of the legal arguments invoked by the OLG Dresden to justify its ruling must be preceded by a remark of a procedural nature. The OLG emphasised that the viewpoints of the parties to the succession proceedings are not binding on the estate court, which should establish and consider the facts relevant to the case, even if they have not been invoked by the parties. In this regard, the estate court is not bound by the parties' assertions about the truth or falsity of a particular fact (*the principle of material truth*).[3] The court of first instance was therefore wrong to omit the relevant circumstances in its analysis that justified the application of the *Verwirkungsklausel.*

These procedural principles remain relevant under Polish inheritance procedure rules. Indeed, the estate court should determine the circle of heirs *ex officio* (Article 670 § 1 KPC) and is not bound by the legal assessment of the will provided by the parties to the proceedings.[4] This has significant consequences as, like in the German case, the Polish court should also examine, *ex officio*, the validity and effectiveness of the dispositions contained in the will (e.g. those bearing the condition of forfeiture clauses of the benefits of the estate), even if the parties have not invoked it.

---

2 The attempts to contest paternity were unsuccessful, as the court legally established after the testator's death that he was the father of his child born out of wedlock.

3 See judgment of OLG Dresden of 16 February 1999, 7 W 1571/98, NJW-RR 19999, 1165.

4 See e.g. decision of SN of 8 November 2012, I CSK 163/12, LEX No 1267159.

In its consideration of substantive law, the OLG Dresden referred to the position generally accepted under German law whereby it is permissible to draw up testamentary dispositions with the stipulation that anyone who opposes the testator's last will should receive nothing, or only a compulsory share (*Verwirkungsklausel*). At the same time, the court noted that it is necessary to determine the meaning of the expressions used in the clause in order to give the fullest possible expression of the testator's actual intention as expressed in the will (§ 2084 BGB). It is therefore necessary to ascertain the content of the condition set out in the will, including in particular which of the circumstances the testator has raised to the status of such a testamentary condition.[5]

In view of the general wording of the testamentary clause under consideration ("anyone who contests the will"), the court noted that if the interpretation of the will does not give rise to the conclusion that the testator gave the phrase a legal meaning, it would not be reasonable to restrict this condition only to cases of contesting the validity of the will by invoking the grounds regulated in § 2078 et seq. BGB. The phrase could then, in fact, be extended to cover all actions that, by their nature, could lead to the total or partial invalidity or ineffectiveness of the will, including objections in proceedings for a declaration of succession. In the circumstances of this particular case, this type of action has been understood to include the unjustified refusal to perform a legacy bequeathed to the mother of one of the heirs,[6] or – indirectly[7] – the initiation by other heirs of a case to establish the testator's paternity after the testator's death. The testator's extramarital son and his mother were subjected to harassment in that case, due to the (false) allegations made therein and the extent of the evidence adduced (the grounds for the judgment under discussion devote considerable space to this, giving it priority among the arguments referring to the application of the forfeiture clause in that case).[8]

5 Similarly, under Polish law, the stipulation of a condition or time limit must be made in the will itself, and not merely be apparent from the surrounding circumstances themselves, which would indicate the testator's wishes. See decision of SN of 14 October 1999, I CKN 147/98, LEX No 1216918.

6 See pt. bb) of the reasoning of the judgment of OLG Dresden of 16 February 1999, 7 W 1571/98, NJW-RR 1999, 1165 (1166).

7 Although court proceedings to establish paternity over one of the testamentary heirs may *prima facie* be unrelated to the inheritance case, this particular case was different. Indeed, with the possible denial of paternity, the other heirs seemed to infer that the testator had acted under the influence of a mistake as to motivation, which would have been relevant to the validity of the will. See pt. aa) of reasoning of the judgment of OLG Dresden of 16 February 1999, 7 W 1571-98, NJW-RR 1999, 1165 (1166).

8 It has been recognised in the doctrine of succession law that the imposition of a condition by the testator to induce the heir to perform a certain action or omission in the non-property sphere (e. g. to marry or not to marry) can be assessed *de casu ad casum* in light of § 138 I BGB. See D. Leipold, in: *Münchener Kommentar*, vol. 11, 2022, § 2074, pt. 23–25. In the circumstances

In the opinion of OLG Dresden, the condition contained in Clause 7 of the will came to be fulfilled also as a result of the allegation raised about the testator's mental health at the time the will was drawn up, despite a lack of relevant evidence, leaving it firmly in the realm of mere conjecture of the parties. Against the background of German law, it is recognised that allegations made against a will or its individual dispositions are not subject to a forfeiture clause if they are aimed at giving effect to the testator's true intent (e.g. an allegation of falsification of the will or lack of capacity to make a will intentionally or voluntarily) and are supported by relevant circumstances. In the court's view, however, this objection was raised not to protect the testator's actual wishes, but to prevent the disinheritance of part of his family. There were no legitimate reasons for raising it. It thus justified taking into account the condition excluding from the inheritance the heirs who contested the will.

II. Consideration of the problem presented in the German case and its comparison with Polish law

Although the need to grant the testator broad discretion to determine the fate of their estate after death is generally honoured by national legislators, no uniform normative model has so far been introduced in this regard, leaving the extent of the testator's discretion unevenly standardised. This also applies to the detailed, if not technical, legal aspects relating to the methods of appointing heirs and legatees, as well as to the drafting of the content of the will and the extent to which the testator can exert influence on the appointment of the heir, including the meaning of events occurring after death.

National legislators vary in their views on the permissibility of reserving a condition (term) in a will, including what are known as forfeiture clauses (*Verwirkungsklauseln*). This is because, on the one hand, they serve to limit post-mortem disputes about the validity and consequences of a will, while on the other hand they may be in conflict with the right to go to court[9] or other tenets of the rules on court proceedings (e.g. the duty of truthfulness of witnesses and parties to proceedings). This has prompted some legislators to introduce specific reg-

of this case, however, it was appropriate that the OLG Dresden did not carry out this assessment (although the condition included a prohibition on questioning the child's descent from the testator). See also: C.-H. Horn, L. Kroiß, *Testamentsauslegung. Strategien bei unklaren letztwilligen Verfügungen*, München 2019, § 17, pt. 4 (with the general opinion of forfeiture clauses as being in line with public policy within the meaning of § 138 I BGB).

9 As well as the right to invoke legal consequences occurring *ex lege* (e.g. the invalidity of the will due to failure to comply with the formalities or a lack of the required testamentary capacity). See also D. Leipold, in: *Münchener Kommentar*, vol. 11, 2022, § 2074, pt. 30.

ulations devoted to this matter. Thus, under the Nevada legislation – effective since 2009 – a 'no-contest clause' is regarded as one or more provisions in a will that express a directive to reduce or eliminate the share allocated to a devisee, or the distributions to be made to a devisee, if the devisee takes action to frustrate or defeat the testator's intent as expressed in the will, without regard to the presence or absence of probable cause for, or the good or bad faith of the devisee in taking the action prohibited by the no-contest clause (see § 137.005(1) and (9) Nevada Revised Statutes). The intention of the testator therefore plays a leading role, as a no-contest clause in a will must be enforced by the court because public policy favours enforcing the intent of the testator, even though this is not – like under German law – an absolute value.[10]

In contrast, no similar specific regulation is contained in German law, where the *Verwirkungsklauseln* are commonly allowed within the framework of the general norms devoted to reserving a condition (and term[11]) in a will. According to § 2075 BGB,[12] where the testator has made a testamentary gift subject to the condition that the person provided for refrains from doing or continues to do something for an indefinite period, then, if the ceasing or continuing is purely at the discretion of the person provided for, in the case of doubt it is to be assumed that the gift is to be dependent on the condition subsequent that the person provided for undertakes the action or refrains from it.[13] The general wording of § 2075 BGB proves that it is possible to render the effects of a testamentary disposition (appointing an heir or a legatee[14]) conditional on a future and un-

10 Not in every case will such a clause prove to be effective. This is the case if the devisee's legal action seeking to invalidate a will is instituted and maintained in good faith and based on probable cause, or when the devisee acts to enforce the clear and unambiguous terms of the will or any document referenced in or affected by the will, or to enforce the legal rights of that devisee. A non-contest clause in a will must not be enforced also when the devisee acted under coercion or undue influence, or the action was caused by the lack of sufficient mental capacity. See further: § 137.005 Nevada Revised Statute (added by Laws 2009, c. 358, § 8, as amended).

11 See D. Leipold, in: *Münchener Kommentar*, vol. 11, 2022, § 2074, pt. 10 (a testator may make their testamentary disposition contingent on a future, certain circumstance, stipulating either a beginning or an end date).

12 "*Hat der Erblasser eine letztwillige Zuwendung unter der Bedingung gemacht, dass der Bedachte während eines Zeitraums von unbestimmter Dauer etwas unterlässt oder fortgesetzt tut, so ist, wenn das Unterlassen oder das Tun lediglich in der Willkür des Bedachten liegt, im Zweifel anzunehmen, dass die Zuwendung von der auflösenden Bedingung abhängig sein soll, dass der Bedachte die Handlung vornimmt oder das Tun unterlässt*" (§ 2075 BGB).

13 See also § 2074 BGB: "*Hat der Erblasser eine letztwillige Zuwendung unter einer aufschiebenden Bedingung gemacht, so ist im Zweifel anzunehmen, dass die Zuwendung nur gelten soll, wenn der Bedachte den Eintritt der Bedingung erlebt.*" ["*If the testator has made a testamentary disposition subject to a condition precedent, then in case of doubt it is to be assumed that the gift is only to be made if the person provided for is living at the date when the condition is satisfied.*"]

14 See U. Czubayko, in: W. Burandt, D. Rojahn (eds.), *Erbrecht*, 2022, § 2074–2075, pt. 1.

certain event occurring after the testator's death (opening the estate).[15] In view of the statutory rule of interpretation adopted in this provision, in the event of any doubt, the condition of forfeiture should be regarded as a dissolving condition.[16]

In German jurisprudence, the interpretation of the general *Verwirkungsklauseln*, which do not refer to known legal constructions, raises considerable doubts (it is questionable, among other things, whether they refer only to actions in the course of court proceedings, or also to certain out-of-court activities). Although their generality may sometimes be a reason for their ineffectiveness, the prevailing view is that they are admissible.[17] The analysed judgment is an example of such a situation. This often leads to a broad understanding of the scope of the *Verwirkungsklausel* in the circumstances of a particular case,[18] which is supported by assumptions – not present under Polish law – as to the admissibility of an interpretation supplementing the content of the testator's last will and testament.[19]

Thus, the concept of a forfeiture clause is quite broad, based on the assumption that the effectiveness of a disposition is made conditional on a condition that may be shaped in many cases in a very general manner, depending on the wishes of the testator. The testator may therefore make the testamentary disposition conditional not only on the heir or legatee not contesting the validity or efficacy of the will (in full, in part, by invoking any or only specific grounds of invalidity or ineffectiveness etc.), but also on the omission of actions that would

15 See judgment of OLG Karlsruhe of 6 August 2004, 14 U 205/02, ZEV 2005, 256. See also: D. Leipold, in: *Münchener Kommentar*, vol. 11, 2022, § 2074, pt. 9; U. Czubayko, in: W. Burandt, D. Rojahn (eds.), *Erbrecht*, 2022, § 2074–2075, pt. 15.

16 See judgment of OLG Dresden of 16 February 1999, 7 W 1571/98, NJW-RR 1999, 1165; as well as C.-H. Horn, L. Kroiß, *Testamentsauslegung…*, § 17, pt. 4; D. Leipold, in: *Münchener Kommentar*, vol. 11, 2022, § 2074, pt. 30; U. Czubayko, in: W. Burandt, D. Rohahn (eds.), *Erbrecht*, 2022, § 2074–2075, pt. 15. By contrast, these clauses are recognised as variations of a resolutive condition by: T. Hoeren, in: R. Schulze (ed.), *BGB Kommentar*, 2021, § 2074–2076, pt. 5; R. Stürner, in: *Jauernig BGB Kommentar*, 2021, § 2074–2076, pt. 5.

17 W. Edenhofer, in: *Palandt BGB Kommentar*, 2010, p. 2265; D. Leipold, in: *Münchener Kommentar*, vol. 11, 2022, § 2074, pt. 31 and 33.

18 This is the case, for example, in the event of an out-of-court refusal to perform a testamentary legacy, or a procedural defence to that claim that has proven to be unfounded. See D. Leipold, in: *Münchener Kommentar*, vol. 11, 2022, § 2074, pt. 33 and 36.

19 The need for supplementary interpretation in the present case is pointed out by: W. Litzenburger, in: W. Hau, R. Poseck (eds.), *BeckOK BGB*, 2022, § 2074, pt. 2 and 5, distinguishing the motives of specific testamentary dispositions from conditions in the technical legal sense. On the need to distinguish between a condition and the mere motives of a specific testamentary disposition, see the decision of SN of 14 October 1999, I CKN 147/98, LEX No 1216918 and M. Pazdan, in: K. Pietrzykowski (ed.), *Komentarz KC*, vol. II, 2015, p. 1070.

undermine the economic substance of the disposition (e. g. by refusing to execute a will or a testamentary legacy).[20]

The potestative nature of the condition[21], constituting an immanent component of the *Verwirkungsklausel*, does not by itself affect the effectiveness of the testamentary clause;[22] nor would it be an obstacle to this type of clause under Polish law, which in principle accepts the construction of a potestative condition (*conditio potestativa, Potestativebedingung*)[23] against the background of a general regulation devoted to the condition (Articles 89 et seq. KC).[24]

These remarks are largely only of theoretical value in the current legislative framework, as the Polish Civil Code imposes certain restrictions on the possibility of rendering the effects of a testamentary disposition subject to a condition (term) that would or would not occur ("arrive") after the testator's death – it is allowed more broadly only in the case of an legacy *per damnationem* (Articles 975

20 U. Czubayko, in: W. Burandt, D. Rojahn (eds.), *Erbrecht,* 2022, § 2074–2075, pt. 6, citing the judgment of OLG Karlsruhe of 6 August 2004, 14 U 205/02, ZEV 2005, 256.

21 A potestative condition is characterised by the fact that it makes the effects of a legal act dependent on an event that relies on the conscious behaviour of the parties to the legal act [e. g. J. Zawadzka, *Warunek w prawie cywilnym,* Warszawa 2012, p. 133, 149; B. Swaczyna, *Warunkowe czynności prawne,* Warszawa 2012, pp. 71–72] or an interested person [Z. Radwański, in: *System prawa cywilnego,* vol. I, 1985, p. 540; M. Pazdan, in: K. Pietrzykowski (ed.), *Komentarz KC,* vol. I, 2020, Article 89, pt. 9]. The interested person in this sense (but naturally not a party to the legal act involving the will) may in this case be the heir or legatee to whom the condition under consideration would be addressed. However, the possibility of applying a condition of a mixed nature, depending not only on the interested party actions but also on other circumstances, cannot be excluded in advance.

22 D. Leipold, in: *Münchener Kommentar,* vol. 11, 2022, § 2074, pt. 30 and U. Czubayko, in: W. Burandt, D. Rojahn (eds.), *Erbrecht,* 2022, § 2074–2075, pt. 10 (who further notes that such clauses will not violate § 2065 section 1 BGB if a specific interest in their formulation can be attributed to the testator and while he was not careless as to whether the event in question occurs).

23 This view can now be regarded as well-established in case law. See J. Zawadzka, *Warunek…,* p. 135; Z. Radwański, in: *System prawa cywilnego,* vol. I, 1985, p. 540, as well as e. g. the resolution of seven Judges of SN of 22 March 2013, III CZP 85/12, OSNC 2013, No 11, item 132; judgment of SN of 26 September 2007, IV CSK 118/07, OSP 2008, No 12, item 125; as well as decisions of that Court of 5 March 1999, I CKN 1069/98, OSNC 1999, No 9, item 160 and 11 December 2015, IV CSK 405/15, LEX No 2160209.

24 On the other hand, the condition in question should be distinguished from a reservation (*"conditio") si voluero,* which, under Polish law, is not a condition in the technical-legal sense (Article 89 KC), as the binding effect of the legal act itself (or even its conclusion) is dependent solely on the wishes of a party to that act. For more on this legal concept see Z. Radwański, in: *System prawa cywilnego,* vol. I, 1985, p. 541; J. Zawadzka, *Warunek…,* p. 147 et seq. A testator's last will is binding regardless of the wishes of the heir or legatee concerned, and, for this reason alone, the forfeiture clause in question cannot be qualified as *si voluero* reservation. It is, however, a separate question as to whether the testator has expressed in his will a firm intention to dispose of property in the event of death, which is relevant as to whether, in fact, a legal action was made. See decisions of SN of 18 March 2008, IV CSK 490/07, LEX No 1422066 and 22 December 1997, II CKN 542/97, OSNC 1998, No 7–8, item 118.

and 981³ § 2 KC), and not in the case of the appointment of an heir or a legacy *per vindictionem* (Articles 962 and 981³ § 1 KC).[25]

The decisions of Polish courts do not tend to deal with the problem of forfeiture clauses, so the starting point for further considerations must be an analysis of the content of the relevant statutory provisions, which do not – like under German law – provide for an explicit regulation devoted to this particular type of testamentary clause. The general provision of Article 962 KC deems it impermissible to make the appointment of an heir subject to a condition (term) that would (or would not) come into existence after the death of the testator.[26]

There is no doubt that Article 962 KC covers the cases of positive testamentary dispositions (establishing an heir). There is also a persuasive view on the need to refer to that provision in the case of negative wills (dispositions), where the statutory heir is excluded from the inheritance – with the simultaneous appointment of another person to the inheritance (in the role of a testamentary heir) or even without the positive appointment of an heir (in which case the statutory inheritance excluding the omitted heir occurs).[27] According to the opposing view, the exceptional nature of the provision precludes the application of Article 962 KC to negative wills (dispositions).[28] Approval of the second view could lead, however, to the recognition that a conditional negative disposition is admissible without any limitations (within the general regime of Article 89 et seq. KC), which would lead to a systemic inconsistency in the institution of appointing an heir to the inheritance in a broader dimension, taking into account both titles of appointment to the inheritance.[29] I advocate the first view. This issue is not merely theoretical and becomes significant in the case of a will under which

25 Except in the case of an 'ordinary' substitution (Article 963 KC).

26 Similarly, in the case of a legacy *per vinditationem* (Article 981¹ § 1 KC), albeit with the possibility granted by Article 981¹ § 2 KC to convert an invalid legacy *per vindicationem* into legacy *per damnationem*. See also B. Swaczyna, *Warunkowe ...*, Chapter III, § 5, pt. 4; S. Wójcik, F. Zoll, in: *System prawa prywatnego*, vol. 10, 2015, p. 481; P. Księżak, *Zapis windykacyjny*, Warszawa 2012, p. 63; E. Niezbecka, in: A. Kidyba (ed.), *Komentarz KC*, vol. IV, 2015, Article 981³, pt. 4 (who is perhaps too restrictive in stipulating that the exclusion of this legal effect must be expressly stated in the will).

27 S. Wójcik, F. Zoll, in: *System prawa prywatnego*, vol. 10, 2015, p. 440; M. Pazdan, in: K. Pietrzykowski (ed.), *Komentarz KC*, vol. II, 2021, Article 962, pt. 7; M. Zelek, in: M. Gutowski (ed.), *Komentarz KC*, vol. III, 2022, Article 962, pt. 6.

28 K. Osajda, in: K. Osajda, W. Borysiak (eds.), *Komentarz KC*, 2022, Article 962, pt. 5, Legalis.

29 Against this view, it can be argued that Article 962 KC refers to the reservation of a condition or time limit only when appointing a testamentary heir. This is rightly considered by K. Osajda. K. Osajda, in: K. Osajda, W. Borysiak (eds.), *Komentarz KC*, 2022, Article 962, pt. 5. However, it should be noted that by means of a negative will, the future testator shapes the circle of his heirs generally (it is questionable to what extent the testamentary succession regime comes into play in this situation). Therefore, it is justified to recourse to Article 962 KC (at least *per analogiam*).

the testator – upon the statutory heir questioning the validity or efficacy of the will – made the exclusion of the latter from the statutory inheritance conditional.

Irrespective of the view adopted, the imperative nature of the relevant statutory provisions precludes depriving the heir of the compulsory portion (provided, of course, that the heir is among the circle of people entitled to the compulsory portion pursuant to Article 991 KC).[30] A similar approach is adopted under German law in the case of clauses concerning the forfeiture of an interest conferred by a will, in the event that, in addition to this interest, the heir or legatee also claims a compulsory portion.[31] Indeed, under Polish law, deprivation of the benefit of the estate does not affect the right to a compulsory portion.[32]

Article 962 KC sets out the general rule that the reservation of a condition (term) when appointing a testamentary heir is deemed to be non-existent (not executed).[33] Consequently, an heir who is appointed to the estate in a will on condition that he does not challenge in the future the validity or effects of the will (the will in which he is appointed or another will of the testator) is appointed to

30 A separate issue remains the effectiveness of disinheritance (Article 1008 KC), made by the testator under a condition of the validity or effectiveness of the will not being challenged. This is especially true in cases of an unjustified contestation of the will, e. g. for harassment, which can intuitively be seen as behaviour contrary to the principles of social intercourse (Article 1008 point 1 KC). By its very nature, this type of situation can only arise after the will has been drawn up, or even after the inheritance has been opened, whereas, according to the well-established doctrinal position, the reason for disinheritance should exist at the time the will is executed. Disinheritance subject to the occurrence of certain events is therefore not possible. See J. Gwiazdomorski, *Prawo spadkowe,* Warszawa 1968, p. 315; E. Skowrońska-Bocian, *Testament w prawie polskim,* Warszawa 2004, p. 158; P. Księżak, *Zachowek w polskim prawie spadkowym,* Warszawa 2010, p. 186.

31 D. Leipold, in: *Münchener Kommentar,* vol. 11, 2022, § 2074, pt. 31 and 44, who points out the contradiction of such a condition with § 2305–2307 BGB. See, however: R. Kanzleiter, *Verwirkungsklausel zu Lasten eines Erben, dem ein belasteter Erbteil in Höhe des Pflichtteils (oder weniger) zugewendet ist?,* DNotZ 1993, No 12, p. 781 and F. Lübbert, *Verwirkung der Schlußerbfolge durch Geltendmachung des Pflichtteils,* NJW 1988, No 43, p. 2708.

32 A claim for a compulsory portion is payable to the extent that the beneficiary has not received it either in the form of a gift made by the testator, or as an appointment as an heir or legatee (Article 991 § 2 KC).

33 This rule does not apply if the occurrence or non-occurrence of a condition, or the advent of a time limit, occurred before opening the estate (Article 962 sentence 3 KC). See also J. Zawadzka, *Warunek…,* p. 284, who recognises that, in such a case, there can be no question of a condition within the strict meaning of Article 89 KC, since dispositions limited by this type of reservation take effect only from opening the estate. Similarly: S. Wójcik, F. Zoll, in: *System prawa prywatnego,* vol. 10, 2015, p. 481. However, a juxtaposition of the stipulated condition (time limit) with the date of drawing up the will (undertaking of the legal act) would lead to a different conclusion. The counterpart of Article 962 sentence 3 KC was not contained in Article 104 § 1 of the Decree on Succession Law, which was limited to the norms currently reflected in Article 962 sentences 1 and 2 KC. See, however: J. Gwiazdomorski, *Prawo spadkowe,* 1959, pp. 335–337, who advocated that restrictions on the conditional or time-limited appointment of an heir did not apply to events that occurred before opening the succession.

the inheritance unconditionally.[34] However, we should ask whether this provision would always prevent the intended purpose of a testator who, for some reason (usually to prevent post-mortem disputes over the will) stipulated such a condition. The starting point here is the legal norm whereby, if it follows from the content of the will or the circumstances that, without such a reservation (condition), the heir would not have been appointed, the appointment of the heir is invalid (Article 962 sentence 2 KC). In this case, depending on the individual circumstances, the testator's intention may be viewed either in general[35] or – which will not be wholly excluded – as a variant (depending on whether or not the condition eventually occurred), but the testator's perspective at the time the will was drawn up[36] must always be adopted. As a rule, a testator who has stipulated such a condition does not wish to appoint to the succession an heir who, after the succession is opened, challenges the validity or effect of the will. As a rule, therefore, the appointment will turn out to be invalid and the intended purpose of the forfeiture clause will be achieved.[37] In the event that the heir does not contest the will, it may be difficult to establish whether or not the testator intended to appoint him to the succession (and thus the disposition appointing the heir to the succession will be valid and unconditional and the stipulated condition deemed to be non-existent). On the other hand, the testator's general intention (not taking into account the variants mentioned above) will tend to make it impossible to achieve the purpose of the forfeiture clause (since, depending on the will of the testator, even if the heir does not contest the will, their appointment may turn out to be invalid, just as, in the final analysis, the testator may have intended to appoint the heir to the inheritance even despite contesting the will, and therefore the appointment is unconditional within the meaning of the first sentence of Article 962 KC). It has been (rightly) accepted that the intention of the testator in the cases given must be determined both on the basis of the content of the will and also taking into account any surrounding circumstances.[38]

34 E. Skowrońska *Z problematyki powołania spadkobiercy w testamencie,* Pal. 1993, No 1–2, p. 8; S. Wójcik, F. Zoll, in: *System prawa prywatnego,* vol. 10, 2015, pp. 439–440.

35 See J. Gwiazdomorski, *Prawo spadkowe,* 1968, p. 153, who recognises the need to assess how a testator would act if confronted with the following options: either the given heir's appointment is considered unconditional and indefinite, or it must be renounced altogether.

36 See e.g. J. Kuźmicka-Sulikowska, in: E. Gniewek, P. Machnikowski (eds.), *Komentarz KC,* 2021, Article 962, pt. 2 (at the time when the reservation is made).

37 The invalidity of a disposition appointing an heir may in turn result in the invalidity of the entire will (Article 58 § 3 KC).

38 See decision of SN of 29 June 2012, I CSK 575/11, LEX No 1216833, as well as: E. Skowrońska, *Z problematyki…,* p. 8; M. Pazdan, in: K. Pietrzykowski (ed.), *Komentarz KC,* vol. II, 2021, Article 962, pt. 2; B. Swaczyna, *Warunkowe…,* p. 173; P. Księżak, *Prawo…,* p. 247; A. Sylwestrzak, in: M. Balwicka-Szczyrba, A. Sylwestrzak (eds.), *Komentarz KC* 2022, Article 962, pt. 3; K. Szpyt, in: M. Załucki (ed.), *Komentarz KC,* 2023, Article 962, pt. 2. In favour of the need to take into account all the circumstances existing at the date of the will, on the other hand:

As was pointed out in the reported decision of the OLG Dresden of 16 February 1999, 7 W 1571/98, the purpose of a forfeiture clause generally consists in strengthening the will (by discouraging a person interested from contesting the will) and preventing post-mortem disputes between people close to the testator.[39] However, such clauses are not accepted to the extent that their effect would be to deny interested persons the right to invoke mandatory rules (e. g. on the form of a will or the capacity to make a will).[40] The forfeiture clause, therefore, does not have the effect of depriving the beneficiary of the benefit under the will when the clause is itself successfully challenged (also as part of a will that has been challenged in its entirety) or when the successfully raised invalidity of the will is limited to the other parts of the will or other wills of the testator in question.[41] At the same time, the right of the parties to have access to court requires that the forfeiture clause to be limited to cases of reprehensible,[42] groundless attempts to challenge the validity or efficacy of a will – the view that the *Verwirkungsklauseln* does not cover cases where the objections to a will are legitimate by nature[43] and

---

M. Zelek, in: M. Gutowski (ed.), *Komentarz KC,* vol. III, 2022, Article 962, pt. 3; J. Ciszewski, J. Knabe, in: J. Ciszewski, P. Nazaruk (eds.), *Komentarz KC,* 2019, Article 962, pt. 5 and: J. Kremis, in: E. Gniewek, P. Machnikowski (eds.), *Komentarz KC,* 2016, Article 962, pt. 2 (with reference to the relationship between testator and testamentary heir). The primacy of subjective criteria (the intention of the testator) over the objectifying criterion of a rational testator is advocated by S. Wójcik, in: *System prawa cywilnego.* vol. IV, 1986, p. 231; S. Wójcik, F. Zoll, in: *System prawa prywatnego,* vol. 10, 2015, p. 440; J. Kuźmicka-Sulikowska, in: E. Gniewek, P. Machnikowski (eds.), *Komentarz KC,* 2021, Article 962, pt. 2.

39 U. Czubayko, in: W. Burandt, D. Rojahn (eds.), *Erbrecht,* 2022, § 2074–2075, pt. 15 and C.-H. Horn, L. Kroiß, *Testamentsauslegung...,* § 17, pt. 1.

40 D. Leipold, in: *Münchener Kommentar,* vol. 11, 2022, § 2074, pt. 35 and 37. A contrary view could lead to an abuse of the clause in a manner contrary to its purpose. It would therefore not be acceptable for a clause to attach a negative effect, for example, to a plea raised (successfully) to the invalidity of a will made under the influence of a stranger, allocating half the inheritance to that person and half to one of the testator's several children, who acted in collusion with him, for whom the disposition was made conditional on raising objections as to the validity of the will.

41 D. Leipold, in: *Münchener Kommentar,* vol. 11, 2022, § 2074, pt. 37–38; C.-H. Horn, L. Kroiß, *Testamentsauslegung...,* § 17, pt. 18; W. Edenhofer, in: *Palandt BGB Kommentar,* 2010, p. 2265.

42 Acting knowingly against the will is sufficient: judgment of BayObLG of 21 February 1962, BReg. 1 Z 85/61, BayObLGZ 1962, 47(57) and judgment of OLG Stuttgart of 31 July 1997, 19 U 214/96, BeckRS 2010, 27946; and even more so – malicious actions: judgment of OLG Celle of 9 March 1995, 22 U 73/94, BeckRS 1995, 30885338. See also: T. Hoeren, in: R. Schulze (ed.), *BGB Kommentar,* 2021, § 2074–2076, pt. 5; R. Stürner, in: *Jauernig BGB Kommentar,* 2021, § 2074–2076, pt. 5; U. Czubayko, in: W. Burandt, D. Rojahn (eds.), *Erbrecht,* 2022, § 2074–2075, pt. 15. See also C.-H. Horn, L. Kroiß, *Testamentsauslegung...,* § 17, pt. 15–16, who recognise the need to weigh up the 'subjective element'.

43 See judgment of OLG Braunschweig of 13 January 1976, 2 Wx 30/75, OLGZ 1977, 188.

are the expression of a diligent effort on the part of the interested party[44] (even if they do not ultimately lead to a determination that the will is invalid or does not have a specific effect). Such a rule seems therefore to be well-established in German inheritance law.

The provision of Article 962 KC takes precedence over the regulation of Article 94 KC.[45] As a result, and quite unexpectedly, the general and flexible Polish regulation may therefore lead to results that are much more far-reaching than those under German law (which draws attention to cases of limited effectiveness of the *Verwirkungsklausel*, where the heir or legatee covered by it challenges the validity or effectiveness of the will with good reason, in order to give effect to the true intention of the testator[46]). These latter circumstances are irrelevant from the point of view of Article 962 KC, as the testator is not allowed to effectively appoint an heir subject to a condition that would come into effect after the testator's death (as would be the case of the *Verwirkungsklausel*) – as mentioned before, a condition of this kind would be regarded as unreserved under Polish law, or the disposition appointing the heir would be invalid.

It seems, however, that the view taken under German law is defensible under Polish law in the case of a legacy *per damnationem* made under the condition (usually resolutive) that the legatee does not contest the validity or efficacy of the will.[47] In this case, Polish law allows for a legacy to be made under a condition (term), even if it concerns events that may occur after the opening of the inheritance (Article 975 KC). However, this does not imply granting unfettered discretion to the testator. On the contrary, a condition of this kind is subject to review under Article 94 KC. In particular, the hypothesis of this legal norm would cover a condition that, according to the intention of the testator, would prevent

44 See R. Stürner, in: *Jauernig BGB Kommentar*, 2021, § 2074–2076, pt. 5, who notes the need to consider on a case-by-case basis whether a beneficiary's particular conduct was reasonable. See also § 138 section 1 BGB.

45 Similarly, against the background of Article 981^3 KC. Compare: S. Wójcik, F. Zoll, in: *System prawa prywatnego*, vol. 10, 2015, p. 481. An impossible condition, as well as a condition contrary to the law or to the rules of social intercourse, entails the invalidity of the legal act when it is suspensive (precedent); it is deemed not to have been stipulated when it is resolutive (Article 94 KC). Similarly under German law: W. Flume, *Allgemeiner Teil des bürgerlichen Rechts. Zweiter Band. Das Rechtsgeschäft*, Berlin-Heidelberg 1992, pp. 691–692; D. Leipold, in: *Münchener Kommentar*, vol. 11, 2022, § 2075, pt. 8 and W. Litzenburger, in: W. Hau, R. Poseck (eds.), *BeckOK BGB*, 2022, § 2074, pt. 25–28.

46 See R. Stürner, in: *Jauernig BGB Kommentar*, 2021, § 2074–2076, pt. 5; U. Czubayko, in: W. Burandt, D. Rojahn (eds.), *Erbrecht*, 2022, § 2074–2075, pt. 15. See also: A. Wacke, *Rechtsfolgen testamentarischer Verwirkungsklauseln Anwachsung oder Ersatzerbschaft?*, DNotZ 1990, No 7, p. 404, who observes that the forfeiture clause will not extend to an heir who is in dispute about the meaning of the testator's last will.

47 Also, when pursuant to Article 981^3 § 2 KC, an invalid legacy *per vindicationem* has the legal effect of a legacy *per damnationem*.

the interested legatee from deriving legal consequences from events rendering the will invalid (or ineffective) by operation of law itself,[48] provided that the interested legatee's allegations are made in good faith.[49] Unfounded allegations made in a conscious manner, on the other hand, could fall within the scope of an effective forfeiture clause. This seems, moreover, to coincide with the general normative tendency, which assumes that anyone who abuses their rights, including in procedural terms, does not deserve legal protection (see Article 5 KC and Article 3 KPC[50]).

III. Summary

Restrictions on the possibility of subjecting the appointment of a testamentary heir to a condition or time-limit (term) from the outset has been negatively assessed in Polish legal literature,[51] which perceives that there are no sufficiently important social or systemic reasons in favour of this solution. Maintaining the prohibition on a condition (time limit) relating to events occurring after death is dictated solely by the need to avoid difficulties in the normative regulation of this legal institution, and the otherwise necessary complexity of the legal status of heirs and the property they inherit.[52] In this context, however, calls for a change in the law by extending the freedom of testation in this particular situation are

48 The same would have to be recognised in the case of civil procedure regulations imposing, for example, an obligation on a party or witness to give evidence (Article 261 § 1 and, of relevance in the case of a party, Article 233 § 2 KPC), to provide the truth (Articles 268 and 304 KPC) or to produce a document (Article 248 § 1 KPC).

49 Under Article 7 KC, good faith is to be presumed. The extensive case law explaining the concept of good and bad faith generally refers to the state of consciousness of a person assessed in light of the circumstances of a particular case, including the fulfilment of the duty to exercise due care. Indeed, bad faith involves the holder becoming aware of information that, reasonably assessed, should give rise to a reasonable suspicion that they are not entitled to a particular right (or, in the case under consideration, an allegation). See e. g. the judgment of SN of 15 February 2017, II CSK 157/16, LEX No 2254784 (against the background of a case concerning the claims of the owner of an asset against its possessor).

50 Under Article 3 KPC, parties and participants in proceedings are obliged to perform procedural acts in accordance with good practice, to give explanations as to the circumstances of the case truthfully and without concealing anything, and to present evidence.

51 Against the background of § 104 Decree on Succession Law, see M. Lisiewski, *Ograniczone prawa spadkowe* DPP 1947, No 8, p. 14; F. Zoll, A. Szpunar, *Prawo cywilne w zarysie,* Kraków 1948, pp. 76–78 and J. Gwiazdomorski, *Prawo spadkowe,* 1959, pp. 333–334 (who notes that the prohibited purpose could be achieved by the testator by charging the heir appointed unconditionally and without time-limit with a corresponding testamentary legacy), and after Article 962 KC has come into force: J. Gwiazdomorski, *Prawo spadkowe,* 1968, p. 27.

52 J. Gwiazdomorski, *Prawo spadkowe,* 1968, p. 27.

formulated cautiously.[53] It would seem that the problems mentioned on this occasion (including as regards the point in time at which the estate was acquired and the state of uncertainty persisting after death) would be less relevant if forfeiture clauses were allowed for the appointment of heirs, particularly when it comes to clauses sanctioning allegations made in bad faith as to the validity of the will. This uncertainty as to the fate of the decedent's estate is, however, somewhat inherent in the nature of succession proceedings, in which the validity of the will is often called into question (e.g. with regard to its form or whether it was drawn up in a state of unconsciousness or freedom). Introducing a forfeiture clause concept could even lead to its mitigation. However, it is open to debate whether it should be more broadly permissible to make the appointment of an heir subject to a condition or time limit that would apply to events occurring after the testator's death.

53 See E. Skowrońska, *Z problematyki…*, pp. 8–9; S. Wójcik, F. Zoll, in: *System prawa prywatnego*, vol. 10, 2015, p. 439. However: F. Błahuta, in: Z. Resich et al. (eds.), *Komentarz KC*, vol. 3, 1972, p. 1889, who perceives the solution adopted in Article 962 KC as justified, although severe from the point of view of the interests of heirs.

Wojciech Bańczyk / Katarzyna Południak-Gierz

§ 5 – Appointment of an owner of a care home as an heir in a handwritten contract of care

Comparative conclusion

The analysed judgment of a German court contained three problems: the admissibility of appointing an heir in a handwritten contract of care, treated as if it was a will; the prohibition on an owner of the care home of benefiting from the estate; as well as the validity of a will drafted by a person with dementia.

The Polish and German legal systems both treat the first and the third problems comparably, based on general rules on wills. At the same time, German law prohibits a will in favour of an owner of the care home in which the testator is given care, which is a result available in Polish law only based on the general rules on the invalidity of wills drafted in a state excluding conscious or free decision-making and an expression of intent on the side of the testator.

I. Analysis of an example case under German law

According to the analysed judgment of 28 January 1998 in case 1 ZBR 162/97,[1] due to the lack of available places in a care home *(Pflegeheim)*, the owner of this institution offered to house the deceased in her private house, for a monthly payment of DM 2,500. Shortly after, on 19 December 1989, a contract of care was drafted, according to which the deceased appointed the owner of the care home as the sole heir in exchange *(als Gegenleistung)* for the services of care *(versorgen)*. This contract was handwritten by the deceased and was signed by both her and the owner of the care home. The deceased was a widow and had no children. After the deceased's inheritance was opened, the owner of the care home demanded the attestation of the acquisition of the estate in her favour (as an heir). The siblings and nieces of the deceased opposed this, arguing in favour of statutory inheritance due to the lack of a valid – in their opinion – disposition *mortis causa*.

1 BayObLGZ 1998, 22.

Among the parties arose a conflict as to the classification of the handwritten contract as a will.

Firstly, it was discussed whether the handwritten contract should be seen as an inheritance contract *(Erbvertrag)*, and therefore invalid due to form deficiency (§ 2276 section 1 BGB states that a contract of inheritance may only be made by being recorded by a notary in the presence of both parties). The contractual nature of the legal act of 19 December 1989 raised no doubts, since it was clear that the deceased appointed the owner of the care home as her heir, whereas the owner of the care home undertook an obligation to take proper care of the deceased. At the same time, the court, following the doctrine, underlined that inheritance contracts typically do not impose obligations *(schuldrechtliche Verpflichtungen)* between the parties. Instead, such contracts aim at binding the deceased with the disposition *mortis causa* to the favour of the counterparty *(Bindung des Verfügenden zugunsten des Vertragsgegners)*, preventing the deceased from disposing of their estate otherwise *(nicht anderweitig letztwillig verfügen zu können)*.[2]

Furthermore, introducing a link between the appointment of an heir and that heir providing care to the deceased could reflect the conditional character of the appointment of an heir. Such a disposition should be understood as having been made under a dissolving condition *(auflösende Bedingung)*, which is commonly used to ensure care *(Pflege)* over the testator.[3]

Although the document was called a contract, this does not affect the analysis of its actual legal nature. In this regard, the actual intent *(wirkliche Wille)* of the deceased should be given priority over the literal meaning *(buchstäblichen Sinn)* of the wording used (§ 133 BGB). It is undisputed in the German judicature that a will does not need to be called a will. It can be even called a power of attorney for example. What matters is whether the document's content expresses the intention of testation (*Testierwilllen*).[4]

The additional signature of the owner of the care home did not affect the handwritten form of the statement of the deceased. As the court noted, it served to confirm the obligation of care of the owner of the care home, which was

2 The judgment cites the commentary of Palandt. Alike e.g. on lacking a relation of duty (Leistung) and counter-duty (Gegenleistung) e.g. W. Litzenburger, in: W. Hau, R. Poseck (eds.), *BeckOK BGB*, 2021, § 2274, No 6.

3 The judgment cites prior jurisprudence of BayObLG and commentary of Leipold in this context. At the same time, this judgment is cited in this context by R. Stürner, in: *Jauernig BGB Kommentar*, 2021, § 2074–2076, No 6. Also, on the meaning of testamentary condition to ensure care towards the testator e.g. W. Litzenburger, in: W. Hau, R. Poseck (eds.), *BeckOK BGB*, 2021, § 2075, No 1.

4 Judgment of BayObLG from 12 December 2000, 1 Z BR 136/00, No 2.c.

important for the deceased. Consequently, the fact that the document was signed by the owner of the care home had no impact on the validity of the will.

Another issue is a prohibition on testation in favour of a care home. This conclusion calls for a consideration of the prohibition from § 14 section 1 and § 14 section 5 HG which makes it inadmissible for a care home, care manager or care home employee to benefit other than by remuneration. This also precludes testation in their favour.

At the same time, the qualification as a care home, as in § 1 section 1 HG, does not depend on the number of residents. The smallest care homes *(Kleinstheime)* with one or two residents, are covered by this definition as well. A private house *(Privathaus)* can be considered a care home as long as it has the following characteristic – its residents may change at any time, and the care is not provided only to a particular person. This differentiates care homes from family care *(Familienbetreuung)* or care based on another personal relation *(Betreuung aufgrund eines sonstigen persönlichen Bezugsverhältnisses)*, where the care is offered to a particular person only, and it matters to the person taking care who the person cared about is. Among other things, this regulation protects the people in care from abuses by the care home and its managers or employees. It also protects their freedom of testation.[5]

Subsequently, the court referred also to the testamentary capacity of a person with dementia. According to the medical examination mentioned in the analysed case, at the moment of testation the testator suffered from mental disorders and dementia, which impaired, but not necessarily excluded her free will. However, a will may not be drafted by a person who, due to a pathological mental disturbance *(krankhafter Störung der Geistestätigkeit)*, mental deficiency *(Geistesschwäche)* or derangement of the senses *(Bewusstseinsstörung)*, is unable to understand the meaning of the produced statement of intent, or to act based on their understanding (§ 2229 IV BGB).

In that case, it is possible that the testator's free will is impaired but not excluded due to a partial mental insufficiency *(partielle geistige Insuffizienz)*. The will drafted in such a state is valid as long as the mental insufficiency of the testator has not affected the particular disposition *mortis causa*.[6] Still, the requirements that the testator needs to fulfil in order to be able to validly draft the will should be lower than regarding undertaking lifetime activities, since a will is often drafted by people of weaker mental condition due to age or health.[7] The

5 G. Müller-Engels, in: W. Burandt, D. Rojahn (eds.), *Erbrecht*. 2019, § 14, No 8.

6 P. Sticherling, in: *Münchener Kommentar*, vol. 11, 2020, § 2229, No 25; a similar judgment of BayObLG from 31.01.1991, BReg. 1 a Z 37/90, No 2.c

7 I. Kroppenberg, *Ist unser Erbrecht noch zeitgemäß? Überlegungen zum zivilrechtlichen Gutachten des 68. Deutschen Juristentags in Berlin*, NJW 2010, No 36, p. 2609.

courts of lower instance should, however, develop appropriate evidentiary proceedings to address such matters.

II. Consideration of the problem presented in the German case and its comparison with Polish law

Polish law does not oppose the classification of a handwritten contract as a will. Even a document that is not intended as a will may be considered as such, provided that it represents the intent of disposition *mortis causa*, and it is produced in the form required by law in the case of a will. This view has been presented regarding the banking account disposition *mortis causa* (Article 56 of the Polish Banking Law), which may also be seen as a will[8] if it meets the requirements of a will. In addition, it is irrelevant whether the technical language of succession law was adopted, e.g. whether a "donation"[9] or "decision as to division of wealth"[10] are explicitly described as testamentary, as long as they reflect the intention to dispose of property *mortis causa*.

On the contrary, the will may contain statements that are not testamentary (e.g. establishing the testator child's tutor, accepting paternity, etc.).[11] These do not need to be made in the form of a will, since the rules on wills do not apply to them.[12] In addition, even the invalidity of a will should not affect the validity of such statements included in it, provided that the conditions of their validity stemming from separate provisions are met.[13]

It could be concluded that, whenever there is an intention to dispose *mortis causa*, and it was expressed in a form required for the validity of a will, such an expression of intent may constitute a valid will[14] It is not important whether a document was intended to be a will.

During an assessment whether an expression of intent should be considered a will, it should not matter if it contains some additional elements that are not required for the will, e.g. that it contains statements from anyone other than the testator, or that it is addressed to a third person. The presence of such elements

8 R. Wiśniewski, *Charakter dyspozycji wkładem oszczędnościowym w myśl art. 37 Prawa bankowego*, NP 1983, No 7–8, p. 69.

9 B. Kucia, in: M. Habdas, M. Fras (eds.), *Komentarz KC*, vol. VI, 2019, Article 959, pt. 8, LEX.

10 Judgment of SN of 10 January 2018, I CSK 177/17, Legalis No 1733693.

11 E. Skowrońska-Bocian, *Testament w prawie polskim*, Warszawa 2004, pp. 187–189.

12 Against, in favour of analogy e.g. of Article 948 KC – L. Kociucki, in: K. Osajda, M. Domański, J. Słyk (eds.), *Komentarz KRO*, 2020, Article 149, pt 16, Legalis.

13 A. Mączyński, *Dziedziczenie testamentowe w prawie prywatnym międzynarodowym*, Warszawa-Kraków 1976, p. 61; S. Wójcik, F. Zoll, in: *System prawa prywatnego*, vol. 10, 2015, p. 359.

14 W. Bańczyk, P*ozaspadkowe sposoby kształtowania następstwa na wypadek śmierci – o przełamaniu monopolu prawa spadkowego*, Kraków 2021 (unpublished doctoral thesis), p. 1043.

should affect the will only exceptionally, e.g. when they suggest that the testation process was disturbed. For instance, adding the signature of another person next to the signature of the testator may on the one hand confirm the actual intent of testation, but on the other, it may suggest that the other person influenced the testation process. If the third person did indeed influence the testation process by limiting the conscious or free decision-making and expression of intent of the testator, then that would lead to the invalidity of the will (Article 945 § 1 point 1 KC).

In the doctrine it is mentioned that a person drafting a notarial will should meet a notary alone, with no third parties (e.g. family members) present.[15] Following this statement, if the handwritten will is signed by the testator and someone else, this might suggest a far-reaching influence of that other person, at least raising doubts as to the validity of the will due to the lack of conscious or free decision-making and expression of intent on the side of the testator. The impact of this other person should, however, be assessed on a case-by-case basis, based on a prior analysis of the circumstances in which the will was made. Nevertheless, in some situations, the presence and involvement of a third party in the testation process, as expressed by them signing the will, may be sufficient for the factual presumption (Article 232 KPC) that the testator made the will while not being sufficiently conscious, in a state excluding free decision-making and an expression of intent, consequently leading to the invalidity of the will, unless proven otherwise. Such a presumption is made if the content of the will suggests that the third party who signed it had an influence on the content (e.g. when the disposition *mortis causa* is made in favour of that person).

Such a presumption could not be made in the analysed case. The signature of the owner of the care home was not a manifestation of her influence over the testator, but appeared on the document rather due to the influence of the testator over the owner of the care home. It was the testator who wanted to bind the owner of the care home with the obligation to take care of the testator by means of the will in the favour of the owner of the care home.

In Polish law, there is no detailed prohibition of testation in favour of a care home, as in German law. Even more generally, there is no prohibition on testation in favour of specific groups of subjects, including those potentially exerting a particular influence on the testator. Nevertheless, all situations in which the testator was in a state excluding their conscious or free decision-making and expression of intent would lead to the invalidity of the will (Article 945 § 1 point 1 KC). This is the case, for example, when a person loses the internal feeling of freedom of one's action under mental coercion, in particular under the dominant

15 T. Sokołowski, in: M. Gutowski (ed.), *Komentarz KC*, vol. II, 2019, Article 944, pt 7, Legalis.

influence of suggestion.[16] An example of this would be a situation where the testator followed someone's suggestion as to the content of the will.[17] Still, a free choice of the testator needs to be fully excluded[18] (and not only limited) in order to cause the invalidity of the will.

Following those observations, a will in favour of a care home under Polish law may be invalid, but only under general rules on the invalidity of will drafted in a state impeding conscious or free decision-making and an expression of intent. This may take place when a testator who is in a care home and under the influence of its staff testates in their favour. However, given that a free-willed testation in favour of a care home is highly atypical, but the possibility of a care home influencing the testator to draft a will in its favour is substantial, a factual presumption in favour of a state excluding conscious or free decision-making and an expression of intent on the side of the testator may be applied (Article 232 KPC).[19]

Still, the issue of the testamentary capacity of a person with dementia has a specific regulation in Polish law. As mentioned above, but in a different context, Article 945 § 1 point 1 KC regulates the invalidity of a will whenever it is drafted in a state excluding conscious or free decision-making and an expression of intent. This provision, unlike its equivalent in the general part, does not give the examples of such states. The provision of the general part (namely Article 82 sentence 2 KC) provides the following examples of states excluding conscious or free decision-making and an expression of intent: mental illness, mental retardation, or other mental disorder (including temporary). However, whenever analysing the scope of Article 945 § 1 point 1 KC, the example indications from Article 82 sentence 2 KC should be taken into consideration.[20] At the same time, it should be noted that, under the inheritance law provision, the scope of situations

16 Judgment of SN of 14 December 2011, I CSK 115/11, ONSC 2012, No C, item 61, p. 82; see also the similar judgment of SN of 14 June 2012, I CSK 564/11, Legalis 524822; W. Bańczyk, *Granice uwzględniania woli testatora z zaburzeniami psychicznymi w polskim prawie spadkowym*, Białostockie Studia Prawnicze 2017, No 4, p. 160; J. Pionkowski, *Nieważność testamentów osób wykazujących zaburzenia psychiczne*, NP 1963, No 2, p. 187; K. Osajda, in: K. Osajda, W. Borysiak (eds.) *Komentarz KC*, 2020, ed. 26, Article 945, pt 16, Legalis; E. Skowrońska-Bocian, *Testament…*, p. 40; J. Wierciński, *Brak świadomości albo swobody przy sporządzaniu testamentu*, Warszawa 2013, pp. 218–221.

17 Judgment of SN of 22 January 1974, III CRN 326/73, OSNCP No 11, item 199; J. Kremis, J. Kuźmicka-Sulikowska, in: E. Gniewek, P. Machnikowski (eds.), *Komentarz KC*, 2017, Article 944, pt. 9, Legalis; P. Księżak, *Prawo spadkowe*, Warszawa 2017, p. 163.

18 Judgment of SN of 21 April 2004, III CK 523/02, Legalis No 123626.

19 In the same way, an unnatural disposition may indicate an unconscious decision-making or expressing statement of intent, but does not preclude it – B. Kucia, in: M. Habdas, M. Fras (eds.), *Komentarz KC*, vol. VI, 2019, Article 945, pt. 10, LEX; J. Wierciński, *Brak…*, p. 207.

20 S. Wójcik, F. Zoll, in: *System prawa prywatnego*, vol. 10, 2015, p. 351.

causing the invalidity of a legal act is broader than under the general civil law provision.[21]

In particular, mental disorder and dementia are undeniably included in Article 945 § 1 point 1 KC as potential grounds for invalidity, as mentioned in the even narrower Article 82 sentence 2 KC. If mental disorder and dementia actually excluded conscious or free decision-making and an expression of intent of the testator, her will would be invalid. Still, it should be taken into consideration that wills tend to be drafted by older people, suffering from various illnesses, since only then, feeling the approximation of death, might the testator be willing to dispose of their property *mortis causa.*[22]

III. Summary

Although Polish law contains no rules prohibiting testation in favour of care homes or their managers and employees (unlike German law), wills made in their favour can be invalidated based on general provisions on the invalidity of wills. This is the case if the will is drafted in a state excluding conscious or free decision-making and an expression of intent. In practice, when the choice of heir is not typical and there is a likelihood that the appointee influenced the testator, it can be presumed (a factual presumption, Article 232 KPC) that the testator was in a state excluding their conscious or free decision-making and their expression of intent.

At the same time, the issue of the validity of wills drafted in a state of dementia or the validity of wills drafted as contracts, but meeting the formal requirements of a will, and made with the intent to create dispositions *mortis causa*, is approached in the same way under both analysed legal systems. Similarly, such wills are invalid if – in a particular scenario – the conscious or free decision-making and expression of intent was excluded.

The fact that Polish law does not admit inheritance contracts does not affect the validity of legal acts being lifetime contracts that additionally express the intent to create dispositions *mortis causa.* In such cases, the will does not have to be called a will and may include elements that are not required by law. This leads to the conclusion that a will can be included in a contract, provided that this

21 M. Niedośpiał, *Testament. Zagadnienia ogólne testamentu w polskim prawie cywilnym*, Kraków-Poznań 1993, p. 39; T. Sokołowski, in: M. Gutowski (ed.), *Komentarz KC*, vol. II, 2019, Article 945, pt. 4, Legalis.

22 E. Skowrońska-Bocian, *Testament…*, p. 132; F. Zoll, *Czy odwołalność testamentu zawsze powinna być nieograniczona?*, in: M. Pecyna, J. Pisuliński, M. Podrecka (eds.), *Rozprawy cywilistyczne. Księga pamiątkowa dedykowana Profesorowi Edwardowi Drozdowi*, Warszawa 2013, pp. 554–555.

contract (or, more specifically, the statements of the deceased) expresses the intention of testation and is concluded in the form required to make a will.

Bartosz Kucia

§ 6 – The legal effect of dissolving or annulling a marriage on the appointment of an heir or legatee

Comparative conclusion

In its judgment of 16 February 2016 in case 20 W 322/14, the OLG Frankfurt a.M. held that the last will of a cohabitant, executed before entering into marriage, will not be subject to § 2077 BGB. This provision of law specifies that a testamentary disposition in favour of a spouse (or betrothed) is ineffective if the marriage is subsequently dissolved or annulled, or the testator has demanded its dissolution (or, in the case of a betrothed, the engagement has been broken off). The Polish succession law does not contain a similar statutory rule. However, similar circumstances may be taken into account under the general mechanism of the conditional appointment of an heir or legatee (to the extent permitted by Articles 962, 975 or 981^3 § 1 KC). In particular, it is possible to make the disposition subject to the condition that the marriage is actually concluded (condition precedent) and to make the disposition ineffective if the marriage is dissolved or annulled (dissolving condition).[1] Additionally, the general nature and scope of the regulation on testamentary conditions allows the effectiveness of a testamentary disposition to depend on whether or not an engagement or a *de facto* relationship (cohabitation) has been entered into or has broken off. However, if the condition is not stipulated in the will, the above circumstances will generally remain irrelevant to the effectiveness of the will. Nevertheless, the testator may have acted under the influence of a legally relevant mistake, e.g. by believing that the dissolution or annulment of a marriage (or breaking off the engagement or *de facto* relationship) after the execution of will renders a testamentary disposition ineffective (Article 945 § 1 point 2 KC).[2]

1 See also: §§ 2074–2076 BGB, as well as: W. Reimann, *Das Schicksal letztwilliger Zuwendungen an Schwiegerkinder nach Ehescheidung*, ZEV 2011, No 12, p. 636 (with reference to the example of a disposition in favor of the son-in-law, on the condition that he does not divorce his wife).

2 Compare with: § 2078 section 2 BGB.

I. Analysis of an example case under German law

The judgment of OLG Frankfurt a.M. of 16 February 2016 in the case 20 W 322/14[3] addresses a legal institution that can be perceived against the background of a broader range of issues related to the legal consequences of a subsequent change in circumstances for the validity and effectiveness of a testamentary disposition drawn up by the testator.

The facts of the case are not extensive, so it is worth selecting issues from the reasoning of the decision that would also be relevant and important when reviewing a similar situation under Polish law. At the same time, the nature of the dates of respective events leads to a general reflection that past events (in this case, a will preceding a marriage of many years) can affect the title of inheritance (and the group of heirs appointed) many years later.

The OLG Frankfurt a.M. judgment concerned a will drawn up on 4 January 1974, before the testator was married. While observing the formalities of the will, the testator appointed as his heir a person he subsequently married (in 1975). Their marriage was dissolved after more than 25 years (in 2001). After testator's death, his brother, claiming his status as an intestate heir, applied for a judgment confirming the acquisition of the estate. He argued that the testator had neither executed a will nor entered into an inheritance agreement and, moreover, that the testator had divorced. This application was subsequently granted by the probate court.

The testator's former wife, on the other hand, took the opposite position, citing that the divorce was amicable and that the former spouses had a friendly relationship thereafter. The testator's brother did not dispute this, but opposed the request of the testator's former wife. Given that the couple were already living together (residence and household) at the time the will was drawn up, the testator's brother argued that the testator should be deemed to have been engaged at the time of executing the will, and therefore the will should be adjudicated in accordance with § 2077 BGB.

The doubts that ultimately led the probate (estate) court to submit the case to the OLG Frankfurt a.M. for resolution involved the existence of a legal gap that would justify the application of § 2077 BGB also to the situation at hand (*per analogiam*).

According to the senate of the OLG Frankfurt a.M., the case involved an inheritance under a will dated 4 January 1974, which determined the order of inheritance, excluding the succession of the testator's brother under the rules of intestacy. At the same time, it was assumed that the testator had not revoked that will made before the marriage, and § 2077 BGB is not applied to wills made by

3 See ErbR 2016, ERBR 2016, 276.

cohabitants, even if they subsequently became engaged and married. Indeed, in the opinion of the OLG Frankfurt a.M., cohabitation similar to marriage does not yet justify the recognition of cohabitants as betrothed under German inheritance law (§ 1297 et seq. BGB).[4] By contrast, the court did not establish that testator and his former wife had engaged before the execution of the will in question. Thus, in the spirit of linguistic and systemic arguments, the interpretation of the provisions seem to support the decision taken, though there was no functional analysis of § 2077 BGB and no assessment of its relevance to the changing reality, within the framework of which premarital *de facto* cohabitation often strengthens the relationship between two people, while displacing the formal institution of engagement.

In view of the general exclusion of the applicability of § 2077 BGB to the case described above, the OLG Frankfurt a.M. did not consider whether the testator, despite the divorce, would have nonetheless formulated the relevant testamentary disposition in favour of his former spouse – a positive answer to that question would have been an additional argument for attributing the effect of the will, even if it fell within the hypothesis of § 2077 BGB.

At this point, and anticipating further discussion, it should be noted that the need to examine the testator's actual intention arises regardless of whether § 2077 BGB is applicable. This is because it is of vital importance in assessing the legal consequences that the testator attributed to the wording used in the will, especially whether he appointed an heir or a legatee under a specific condition as to the event. The absence of any consideration of this issue in the reasoning of the judgment in question may have been due to the fact that, in light of the evidence, the court found no grounds to assume that the testator's actual intention was different and, consequently, that his intention to maintain the testamentary disposition in favour of his former spouse, with whom he was subsequently in a friendly relationship, was unquestionable (which was also supported by the fact that the testator, despite this possibility, did not revoke the will). In particular, the heir was identified in the will only by name, surname, date of birth and address, and therefore without reference to her present or future role as a spouse. However, the above conclusions can be deduced from the entirety of OLG Frankfurt a.M.'s discussion, rather than the specific opinions formulated in the reasoning of the judgment under review.

4 Moreover, simply living together for many years without a specific intention to marry does not constitute an engagement. See D. Leipold, in: *Münchener Kommentar*, vol. 11, 2022, § 2077, pt. 15.

II. Consideration of the problem presented in the German case and its comparison with Polish law

Although the bulk of the analysis will focus on instances where the testator's marital status has changed as a result of divorce or annulment of marriage, the problem under analysis is part of a broader spectrum of issues concerning circumstances that occur after a will is executed, and often even after the testator's death (as in the case of a posthumous annulment of marriage, permitted under Articles 18 and 19 KRO) and their impact on the effectiveness of the will.

The legal issue presented to the OLG Frakfurt a.M. is of momentous practical importance, as it determines the extent to which the construct of the (*ex lege*) ineffectiveness of a testamentary disposition under § 2077 BGB will apply.[5] This involves depriving the effects of a testamentary disposition when the testator himself has not revoked the will, or even that part of the will. Thus, in the cases covered by the hypothesis of that provision, the testator does not have to revoke the will or make the appointment of an heir subject to a certain condition, such as divorce or annulment of the marriage. At the same time, the provision of § 2077 BGB is exceptional in its nature, which probably determines the interpretive emphasis placed within it. For it is not – in the case of the judgment in question – a general perception of cohabitation in the sphere of inheritance law, but an indication of the extent to which it is possible to attribute certain consequences (in this case, consisting in depriving a testamentary disposition of its effectiveness) to the silence of the testator (who did not revoke the will). At the same time, the case of a will made during cohabitation is considered here only in a specific situational context, taking into account the fact of subsequent marriage.

The normative background for this legal issue is provided by the provision of § 2077 BGB.[6] Under this provision, a testator's testamentary disposition[7] in fa-

5 The provision applies to both the appointment of an heir (*Erbeinsetzung*) and a legatee (*Vermächtnis*). See U. Czubayko, in: W. Burandt, D. Rojahn (eds.), *Erbrecht*, 2022, § 2077, pt. 2.

6 See § 2077 BGB: "*1. Eine letztwillige Verfügung, durch die der Erblasser seinen Ehegatten bedacht hat, ist unwirksam, wenn die Ehe vor dem Tode des Erblassers aufgelöst worden ist. Der Auflösung der Ehe steht es gleich, wenn zur Zeit des Todes des Erblassers die Voraussetzungen für die Scheidung der Ehe gegeben waren und der Erblasser die Scheidung beantragt oder ihr zugestimmt hatte. Das Gleiche gilt, wenn der Erblasser zur Zeit seines Todes berechtigt war, die Aufhebung der Ehe zu beantragen, und den Antrag gestellt hatte.*
2. Eine letztwillige Verfügung, durch die der Erblasser seinen Verlobten bedacht hat, ist unwirksam, wenn das Verlöbnis vor dem Tode des Erblassers aufgelöst worden ist.
3. Die Verfügung ist nicht unwirksam, wenn anzunehmen ist, dass der Erblasser sie auch für einen solchen Fall getroffen haben würde."

7 This provision also applies to a joint will (§ 2268 BGB), an inheritance contract (§ 2279 section 2 BGB) or a donation *mortis causa*, but not to a donation with reservation of death, which is qualified as an *inter vivos* legal action under German law (§ 2301 section 1 BGB). See also: G. Schlitt, *Das Erbrecht in der Ehekrise*, ZEV 2011, No 12, p. 96. On the qualification of

vour of his spouse[8] is ineffective where the marriage is dissolved before the testator's death, as well as when the prerequisites for divorce existed and the testator had requested it or consented to the divorce at the time of the testator's death. The same rule applies when the deceased, at the time of his death, was entitled to request and had applied for the annulment of the marriage (§ 2077 section 1 BGB). In the same way, breaking off an engagement will render a testamentary disposition ineffective in favour of the person to whom the testator was engaged (§ 2077 section 2 BGB). However, in the given circumstances, a testamentary disposition is not ineffective if it can be established that the testator would have nevertheless drafted it (§ 2077 section 3 BGB).[9]

The legislative solution being analysed is dictated primarily by the need to protect the interests of heirs who would come to the inheritance in the absence of the appointment of a spouse (this is especially true in the case of intestacy). The idea is to prevent situations when the testator inadvertently, to the detriment of such heirs, failed to revoke their previous will. This type of legal solution generally corresponds to the prevailing social perception that in the event of divorce or the annulment of a marriage the need to appoint a spouse (now: former spouse) as heir ceases to exist. This, by the way, is also reflected in the regulations devoted to intestate succession and a compulsory portion of inheritance, which usually do not provide for entitlements for former spouses in this regard.

The subjective scope of § 2077 BGB is not uniformly understood. Some authors consider the need to interpret the relevant provision in light of social changes, where cohabitation sometimes approaches the relationship arising from engagement (which has been losing its importance in recent years). These authors allow the application of § 2077 BGB *per analogiam* to a testamentary disposition in favour of a cohabitant with whom the testator then entered into a marriage, despite a subsequent divorce or marriage annulment.[10] By contrast, the

donations see also: E. Drozd, *Darowizna na wypadek śmierci*, Rejent 1992, No 1, p. 75; J. Górecki, *Umowa darowizny na wypadek śmierci*, Rejent 2006, No 2, p. 30; W. Borysiak, *Dziedziczenie. Konstrukcja prawna i ochrona*, Warszawa 2013, p. 277; P. Zakrzewski, *Umowa darowizny na wypadek śmierci w prawie holenderskim, niemieckim i polskim*, in: A. Olejniczak, J. Haberko, A. Pyrzyńska, D. Sokołowska (eds.), *Współczesne problemy prawa zobowiązań*, Warszawa 2015, pp. 746–747.

8 The provision of § 2077 BGB also applies to partners in registered partnerships. See § 10 V LPartG. Compare to R. Stürner, in: *Jauernig BGB Kommentar*, 2021, § 2077, pt. 5.

9 Doubts have been raised in German literature about the legal nature of § 2077 BGB; the prevailing view is that it is a statutory rule of interpretation. See D. Leipold, in: *Münchener Kommentar*, vol. 11, 2022, § 2077, pt. 2–3; W. Reimann, *Das Schicksal…*, p. 637. The dispositive nature of the provision, however, is considered by T. Hoeren, in: R. Schulze (ed.), *BGB Kommentar*, 2021, § 2077, pt. 1.

10 See D. Leipold, in: *Münchener Kommentar*, vol. 11, 2022, § 2077, pt. 16. On the contrary: U. Czubayko, in: W. Burandt, D. Rojahn (eds.), *Erbrecht*, 2022, § 2077, pt. 20.

BGH decision of 3 May 1961[11] permitted the analogous application of Section 2077 of the BGB in the case of a will drawn up with the intention of entering into a future marriage (or at least an engagement). This intent of the deceased, however, was not recognised by the OLG Frankfurt a.M. in the judgment commented on here, noting that the purpose of drawing up the will in that very case was to secure the basis for the cohabitants' existence, not to regulate inheritance matters in the context of a future marriage. Such an unambiguous ruling may be questionable, especially if one considers the imminent entry into marriage after drawing up the will. Unanswered in the OLG Frankfurt a.M. judgment of 16 February 2016 is the extent to which the interpretation of § 2077 BGB in the circumstances of this case was influenced by the long-standing marriage between the testator and heir, and the subsequent continuing friendly relationship between the former spouses. However, the question seems legitimate. Interpretation with reference to the criterion of making a will with the intention of a future marriage or at least an engagement – which is not explicit in Section 2077 BGB and is difficult to comprehend – leads to a significant differentiation in the legal situation of co-habitants, with the situation of the cohabiting heir being more favourable if, at the time of making the will, they were not perceived as a future fiancé or spouse. This means that a weaker relationship with the testator is actually more beneficial, as a testamentary disposition in favour of a cohabitant will not lose its effectiveness, even if a subsequent marriage with the testator is later dissolved.

The functional argument formulated earlier, aimed at expanding the scope of application of § 2077 BGB (*ex lege* ineffectiveness of testamentary dispositions), given the current similar role of fiancé and cohabitant directly preceding the marriage, undoubtedly appeals to the imagination. However, it may lead to casuistic adjudications that are not supportive of achieving a position of legal certainty. Many problems have already arisen out of unanswered questions about the proper legal criteria, e.g. whether the cohabitation should be for a certain duration, or whether the mere initiation of a factual relationship is deemed sufficient. In the case of accepting a narrower interpretation, i.e. allowing only wills made with the intention of entering into a future marriage, it is not clear how this intention should be expressed and whether it should necessarily occur in the will containing the testamentary disposition being evaluated.[12]

---

11 FamRZ 1961, p. 366. The ruling is endorsed, among others, by R. Stürner, in: *Jauernig BGB Kommentar*, 2021, § 2077, pt. 7 as well as D. Leipold, in: *Münchener Kommentar*, vol. 11, 2022, § 2077, pt. 7.

12 This criterion is also used, for example, by the English regulation concerning the effect of marriage on a will, though with an explicit statutory requirement that this intention be included in the will. In principle, a will is revoked by the testator's marriage. However, where it appears from a will that, at the time it was made, the testator was expecting to be married to a particular person and intended that the will should not be revoked by the marriage, then the

It seems that these dilemmas could be avoided if § 2077 BGB is reinterpreted to determine the moment of relevance as to the position of the heir or legatee. The statutory provision does not exclude, *prima facie*, another interpretive hypothesis under which the heir or legatee obtains the status of spouse or fiancé after the will is executed. This interpretation may lead to solutions that are clearer for those involved. It can be assumed that the circumstances specified in § 2077 BGB (breaking off an engagement, divorce, annulment of a marriage or requesting a decree therefor) are so momentous that in many cases testators are generally not interested in appointing former spouses or fiancées to the inheritance, regardless of when the will was drawn up. So far, however, this provision seems to have been interpreted with reference to the status that the testamentary heir had at the time when the will was drafted (whether they were a spouse or fiancé at that particular moment),[13] although § 2077 BGB does not, presumably, provide any explicit interpretive guidance (other than ruling that it should be a disposition in favour of a spouse or fiancé, which could indicate the time when it was drafted, although it does not necessarily mean it).

As an aside, it should also be noted that, in a broader perspective, the analysed provision of § 2077 BGB results in a more favourable arrangement of the position of the cohabiting partner compared to that of the spouse, since its hypothesis does not cover wills made by cohabitants *sensu stricto*. Consequently, the cessation of the cohabitation does not, as a rule, affect the effectiveness of testamentary dispositions in favour of the cohabitee (unless the testator included an appropriate condition).

The presented interpretative dilemmas do not generally occur against the background of the Polish Civil Code, since it does not contain an equivalent of § 2077 BGB[14] and there was no equivalent in the Decree on Succession Law of 1946. The issue has also not been given much space in the Polish doctrine,[15]

will will not be revoked by marriage to that person. See § 18(1) and (3) Wills Act 1837 (1837 c. 26).

13 See D. Leipold, in: *Münchener Kommentar*, vol. 11, 2022, § 2077, pt. 7; U. Czubayko, in: W. Burandt, D. Rojahn (eds.), *Erbrecht* 2022, § 2077, pt. 2.

14 The provision of § 2077 section 1 sentences 2 and 3 BGB brings to mind Article 940 KC, providing for the exclusion of a spouse from intestate succession in the event that the testator died in the course of a divorce or separation suit and demanded that it be pronounced due to the fault of the excluded spouse. However, the Polish regulation does not apply to an appointment to the inheritance under a will and does not affect the circle of beneficiaries under it.

15 A. Dyoniak, *Dziedziczenie testamentowe rozwiedzionego małżonka*, RPEiS 1988, No 3, p. 55 *et seq.*

though the importance of the analysed legal institution is shown by its pervasiveness among the legal orders of other countries, among other things.[16]

It could be argued that this legal situation is an expression of a broader legislative concept in which – in order to ensure flexibility in the legal regulation on wills – the need for specific regulation of the legal status of various categories of persons with regard to the testamentary regime is not recognised, including in particular spouses, fiancés or cohabitants. Consequently, while the annulment of a marriage, or a divorce or separation will affect the circle of intestate heirs (see Articles 931 and 935^1 KC in conjunction with Article 61^4 KRO) and those entitled to a compulsory portion (Article 991 § 1 KC), those events will not, by operation of law, render ineffective a will drawn up with the (former or separated) spouse in mind. Thus, the absence of a specific regulation devoted to the issue at hand does not necessarily imply the absence of a position of the Polish legislature itself. On the contrary, in terms of the German model, the Polish Civil Code reverses this rule, by assuming that marriage annulment, divorce and separation do not *ex lege* affect the effectiveness of a previously made will, unless the testator has decided otherwise.

Under Polish law, a testator can decide whether the annulment of marriages (divorce or separation) will affect the effectiveness of an earlier will (in full or with respect to certain dispositions). In particular, the testator can revoke a previously made will (Articles 946–947 KC). Similar consequences can be reached by appointing a spouse as an heir[17] subject to a dissolving condition of: the annulment of marriage, divorce, separation, the initiation of proceedings in these cases, or even the cessation of cohabitation (Article 962 KC).[18] There is no obstacle to the

16 Under English law, divorce or the annulment of marriage does not revoke a will. However, this does not mean that these events are indifferent to the effectiveness of the will. However, under section 18 A (1) Wills Act 1837, when a decree of a court of civil jurisdiction in England and Wales dissolves or annuls testator's marriage, any property which, or an interest in which, is devised or bequeathed to the former spouse shall pass as if the former spouse had died on that day. As a consequence, the former spouse is treated as a person who did not survive the testator and may not inherit after him; but the testator may decide otherwise in the will. This is also the case in American and Australian regulations, see e. g. laws of California [§ 6122 Cal. Prob. Code (*California Probate Code*), enacted by Stats.1990, c. 79 (A.B.759), § 14 as amended], Georgia [§ 53-4-49 Ga. Code Ann. (*Georgia Code Annotated*), enacted by Ga. L. 1996, p. 504, § 10], South Australia (§ 20 A Wills Act 1936, Gazette 14.12.1993 p 2965 as amended) or New South Wales (§ 13 Succession Act 2006 No 80 as amended).

17 These comments should also be applied to a legacy *per damnationem* (Article 975 KC) as well as legacy *per vindicationem* (Article 981^3 KC).

18 In view of the requirement in Article 962 KC (as well as in Article 981^3 KC) that the condition be fulfilled before opening the inheritance (the death of the testator), it is questionable whether this effect would also occur in the case of a marriage annulment after the testator's death (which is exceptionally accepted by Articles 18 and 19 KRO). This is because such an annulment has an *ex tunc* effect with regard to the moment when the marriage bond ceases, though with regard to the relationship of the spouses to their respective children and property

condition referring to other events, such as the existence of a certain de facto relationship characteristic to cohabitation.

On the other hand, cases where the testator did not revoke the will and did not stipulate an appropriate condition in the will can be a source of considerable interpretative dilemmas. This is especially true in the case of wills that specify the person of the heir or legatee with reference to his or her status as a spouse ("*I appoint my spouse X.Y. to the entire estate*"). It is not possible to refer in these cases to Article 931 or 940 KC (there is no legal gap justifying *analogiae legis*) or to Article 58 § 2 KC (the appointment of a divorced or separated spouse to the inheritance is not necessarily contrary to the principles of social intercourse).[19] Due to the provision of Article 1047 KC (prohibition on contracts regarding an inheritance after a living person), it would also not be possible to regulate this issue in an agreement between spouses, such as a matrimonial property agreement.[20]

What remains to be considered, however, is whether the desired result can be achieved by interpreting the will (Article 948 KC), or by referring to the concept of a mistake (Article 945 § 1 pt 2 KC). The scope of application of these provisions does not overlap and it is usually possible to assess the validity of a will from the point of view of a mistake only after determining the meaning of its contents.[21]

If the testator did not include an explicit disposition in the will to conditionally only appoint the spouse to the inheritance, careful interpretive efforts (Article 948 KC) can sometimes lead to the ineffectiveness of that disposition. However, this will not always be possible. The interpretation of a will should aim towards the truest implementation of the testator's intention. In turn, if the will can be interpreted in multiple ways, the interpretation that allows the testator's dispositions to be upheld and given reasonable content should be applied. It is crucial, however, that the content of the declaration of intent made by the testator, despite its vague or clumsy wording, is the only subject to interpretation; it will not, therefore, lead to the amendment of the will or supplementing it with

relations between the spouses, it is effective *ex nunc*, since the provisions on divorce are then applied accordingly (Article 21 KRO).

19 See also: A. Dyoniak, *Dziedziczenie…*, pp. 57–58.

20 This conclusion requires no further justification in the case of appointing an heir. However, in the case of a legacy that by its nature does not refer to all or part of the inheritance and does not shape the order of succession, similar conclusions may be justified with reference to Articles 972 and 981^5 KC (leading to the application of provisions on the appointment of an heir accordingly). Polish law also does not provide for the possibility of revoking or amending a will by contract (Article 941 KC). It is not clear whether a contract that is invalid due to a violation of Article 1047 KC could, using the conversion mechanism, be considered a unilateral legal act resulting in the revocation of a will (Article 946 KC).

21 Compare to: A. Dyoniak, *Dziedziczenie…*, p. 62.

provisions not contained therein.[22] An obstacle to the latter procedures, moreover, is provided by the provisions on testamentary formalities, required *ad solemnitatem* (Article 958 KC).

The interpretation of the will may also lead to the determination of the testator's actual will in a negative way, by assuming that the testator, in his will, did not include certain situations,[23] and so there is no basis for attributing to his last will the effect of appointing a spouse on condition.

Although the presented position is already well-established in Polish jurisprudence, in particular circumstances the demarcation between supplementing a last will on the one hand and determining the meaning of a disposition already expressed in the will, on another hand, sometimes raise doubts, especially when the last will can be interpreted in different ways (Article 948 § 2 KC). This is especially true when the testator – in the situation discussed in this paper – appoints an heir or a legatee with reference to their marital status or similar terms.

Indeed, if the testator did not explicitly refer to the word "condition," is it necessary to *a priori* exclude the possibility of attributing a conditional nature to the testamentary disposition? On 29 July 2020, the District Court of Elbląg considered this legal issue in the case I Ca 170/20.[24] Under a will drawn up in the form of a notarial deed, the testator appointed his wife ("my wife, J.H.") to the entire estate. The marriage between the testator and the future heiress was subsequently dissolved. The appellant argued that the overall circumstances of the case required the assumption that the testator would not have appointed J.H. as a testamentary heir if he had known that she would not be his wife on the date of his death. However, this position did not find approval from the courts of either instance. The District Court pointed out that the interpretation of a will cannot aim to give it a meaning contrary to its literal wording and cannot lead to modification of the will's content. The will described the heir by name, and used the phrase "spouse", remaining appropriate to the heir's status at the time. In the

22 See judgments of SN of 15 March 1963, III CR 131/62, OSNC 1964, No 2, item 39; and of 18 February 1999, I CKN 1002/97, LEX No 521803; as well as SN decisions of 12 October 2001, V CKN 503/00, OSP 2002, No 11, item 141 or of 6 May 2005, II CK 676/04, LEX No 603159. See also: Z. Radwański, *Wykładnia testamentów*, KPP 1993, No 1, p. 23; M. Pazdan, in: K. Pietrzykowski (ed.), *Komentarz KC*, vol. II, 2015, p. 1033. In contrast, under German law, citing § 133 BGB: W. Reimann, *Das Schicksal…*, p. 636 (who also considers a change in circumstances after the exection of will but before the opening of the inheritance) and the judgment of BayObLG of 10 April 1991, FamRZ 1991, 1234. On the contrary, against the background of § 2077 BGB: T. Hoeren, in: R. Schulze (ed.), *BGB Kommentar*, 2021, § 2077, pt. 11.

23 Cf. the decision of SN of 6 December 2002, IV CKN 1587/00, LEX No 1162961 (the Court established that the testator did not express his intention to uphold the will previously revoked).

24 LEX No 3274435.

opinion of the District Court, the will did not contain any additional references to the effect that the testator would only have appointed his wife to the inheritance if the marriage relationship had continued on the date of the opening of the inheritance. Consequently, the testator did not draw a condition in accordance with Article 962 KC (it could not be inferred from the mere use of the term "wife" in the will).

The cited court's decision, although convincingly reasoned, should be read as a ruling in the circumstances of a specific case, taking into account in particular the fact that the will was drawn up in the form of a notarial deed (Article 950 KC[25]) and that the testator did not decide to revoke it, although several years had passed since the divorce. However, it is possible that the outcome would have been different under other circumstances, in particular, if the will had only been drawn up in the testator's own handwriting (Article 949 KC).[26]

Indeed, when interpreting a will, it is the viewpoint (exclusively) of the testator that is decisive, as in accordance with § 2077 section 3 BGB.[27] The interpretation of the last will should ensure the truest possible embodiment of the intention that the testator nevertheless expressed in his will (not his general intention only). This supports the view that the decisive factor here is the intention that he had at the time when he executed the last will.[28] Thus, with respect to this moment, it must be assessed whether he intended his disposition to become ineffective in the event of a change in his marital status.

When interpreting a will, a momentous role is played by various external circumstances of which the testator was aware, even if not mentioned in the will, such as the testator's habits and views, his relations with other people, motives, behaviour and statements of the testator[29] (the latter may be taken into account when interpreting a will, but are not the subject of the interpretation, since that

25 The notary shall satisfy himself that the persons participating in the notarial deed understand the content and meaning of the deed accurately, and that the deed is in accordance with their intention (Article 94 § 1 sentence 2 and Article 87 § 1 point 2 of the Act of 14 February 1991, Notary Public Law, Journal of Laws of 2022, item 1799).

26 The jurisprudence of Polish courts provides examples of favorable interpretation of very imprecise wills. See e.g. the decision of SN of 22 Decebmer 1997, II CKN 542/97, OSNC 1998, No 7–8, item 118 (a last will giving the property "as a donation").

27 On the necessity of taking into account the hypothetical intention, if the interpretation of the will does not allow to determine the actual intention of the testator: D. Leipold, in: *Münchener Kommentar*, vol. 11, 2022, § 2077, pt. 25 *et seq.*

28 K. Osajda, in: K. Osajda, W. Borysiak (eds.), *Komentarz KC*, 2022, Article 948, pt. 34.

29 See, among others, the decisions of SN: of 13 February 2001, II CKN 378/00, LEX No 550937; of 14 July 2005, III CK 694/04, LEX No 604040; of 6 October 2016, IV CSK 825/15, LEX No 2191475, as well as M. Rzewuski, *Wykładnia testamentu a okoliczności zewnętrzne towarzyszące testowaniu*, PS 2015, No 1, p. 107.

subject is the will only[30]). The reason why the testator appoints his spouse to inherit is generally (but not exclusively) the family bond that unites them, which ceases in the event of a divorce or the annulment of the marriage (and is significantly weakened in the event of separation). This may argue for the need to interpret the will taking into account the motives of the testator in establishing his spouse as an heir.

The opinions of German doctrine on the basis of § 2077 section 3 BGB remain largely consistent with the Polish approach – for example, the existence of an intention to appoint an heir in the situation referred to in § 2077 BGB may be documented by drawing up a will during a marital crisis, leading to a divorce.[31] On the other hand, the mere fact of maintaining correct or even friendly relations after the divorce will not necessarily still support the establishment of intention to uphold the appointment of the heir.[32] Similarly, the fact of remarriage between the testator and the former spouse should be assessed (although against the background of § 2077 section 3 BGB there is also a view that this provision should not be applied at all in that case[33]). In summary, it is therefore necessary to assess the circumstances of the specific case.

Consequently, it must be assumed that the above interpretive efforts are aimed at establishing testamentary intent at the time the will was made. A change in circumstances after the will was already made cannot, in itself – if it was not taken into account by the testator – justify the peculiar updating of the will by adjusting it to the changed circumstances.[34] Following this line of reasoning, the rules on the interpretation of wills also do not allow the substitution of a divorced spouse who is mentioned in the body of the will as a person appointed to the inheritance, with a spouse from a subsequent marriage (which may seem the case if the testator had limited himself to the term: "spouse", unless the testator used a condition referring to later events).[35]

On the other hand, it does not seem that a particular interpretive result should be determined by circumstances such as guilt in the breakdown of marital re-

30 See, for example, the decision of SN of 28 October 1997, I CKN 276/97, OSNC 1994/4/63, and the judgment of SN of 5 September 2008, I CSK 51/08, LEX No 465963.

31 See D. Leipold, in: *Münchener Kommentar,* vol. 11, 2022, § 2077, pt. 25.

32 See K. Tappmeier, *Erbeinsetzung und Bezugsberechtigung des Ehegatten aus einer Kapitallebensversicherung nach Scheidung der Ehe,* DNotZ 1987, No 12, pp. 716–718, with critical dogmatic reservations about the § 2077 BGB. On the other hand, the omission of the fact of the subsequent reconciliation of the spouses seems to be strongly advocated by U. Czubayko, in: W. Burandt, D. Rojahn (eds.), *Erbrecht,* 2022, § 2077, pt. 21.

33 Possible scenarios are considered in detail by: D. Leipold, in: *Münchener Kommentar,* vol. 11, 2022, § 2077, pt. 29. See also: K. Tappmeier, *Erbeinsetzung…,* p. 716.

34 See, accurate opinion in: K. Osajda, in: K. Osajda, W. Borysiak (eds.), *Komentarz KC,* 2022, Article 948, pt. 34.

35 A. Dyoniak, *Dziedziczenie…,* pp. 62–63; K. Tappmeier, *Erbeinsetzung…,* p. 719.

lations (this is because of the principle of the free revocability of a will, as provided for in Article 943 KC, even if it were to lead to harm to the family; for in such a case, the effects of the will would be corrected by the institution of a compulsory portion).

In its judgment of 16 February 2016, 20 W 322/14, the OLG Frankfurt a.M. found no basis for assuming that the will was made under the influence of a mistake relating to motive (§ 2078 section 2 BGB). On the other hand, the need to consider this issue, in the case of a marital crisis (or even a general change in the situation of the testator), when the hypothesis of § 2077 BGB has not been fulfilled, was pointed out in the German literature.[36] It should be noted, however, that § 2078 section 2 BGB expressly allows a mistake regarding the expected course of future affairs, such as the duration of marriage or cohabitation.[37]

In turn, the jurisprudence of the Polish courts excludes prima facie the possibility of invoking a mistake as to future events, if they are not covered by the content of the executed legal act.[38] However, it should be noted that the relevant rulings are generally formulated against the background of the general regulation of a mistake, under which it is required that the mistake be rational and relate to the content of the legal act (Article 84 KC). On the other hand, the supreme value reflected in the regulation of defects in declarations of intent in wills is the intention of the testator (Article 945 § 1 KC). This is reflected in the liberalisation of the statutory prerequisites for a legally relevant mistake in the case of last wills: there is no requirement for it to be reasonable, nor does it have to relate to the content of the last will (Article 945 § 1 point 2 KC). Indeed, any mistake that resulted in the making of a will (and is therefore, from the point of view of the testator's subjective perception, momentous) is legally relevant.

Thus, a mistake in the case of a will may relate to a circumstance constituting the motive of the testator's action, even if it was not even covered by the content of the legal act. Whether it should be encountered here a mistake as to the motive only,[39] or rather a mistake on the part of the testator as to the assessment of the

36 See e.g. D. Leipold, in: *Münchener Kommentar*, vol. 11, 2022, § 2077, pt. 4, 6; W. Reimann, *Das Schicksal…*, p. 638 and the judgment of BGH of 2 April 2003, NJW 2003, 2095.

37 D. Leipold, in: *Münchener Kommentar*, vol. 11, 2022, § 2077, pt. 16.

38 See the judgment of SA in Szczecin of 7 May 2015, I ACa 703/14, LEX No 1785310, with a ruling that a mistaken assessment of both current and future circumstances, not covered by the content of the legal act performed, does not constitute a mistake as to the content of the legal act. See also, for example, the judgments of SN of 8 September 2017, II CSK 845/16, LEX No 2350002 and 16 November 2018, I CSK 568/17, LEX No 2578185.

39 See A. Dyoniak, *Dziedziczenie…*, p. 61, and B. Lewaszkiewicz-Petrykowska, *Wady oświadczenia woli przy sporządzaniu testamentu*, in: B. Kordasiewicz, E. Łętowska (eds.) *Prace z prawa cywilnego wydane dla uczczenia pracy naukowej Profesora Józefa Stanisława Piątowskiego*, Wrocław 1985, p. 208 (recognising that a legally relevant mistake may relate to future circumstances).

legal consequences of a particular testamentary disposition[40] (e.g. when the marriage will be dissolved or annulled), remains a different matter. Therefore, it seems possible to consider as invalid a will made under the influence of the testator's mistaken belief that divorce will cause the *ex lege* revocation of a will that provides for the benefit of the spouse (Article 945 § 1 point 2 KC).[41] The legal effect of a mistake on the part of the testator would be that the disposition made for the benefit of the spouse would be invalid. If, without the invalid disposition, no will would have been made at all, then the entire will would be invalid (Article 58 § 3 KC).

III. Summary

The development of jurisprudential practice against the background of Polish inheritance law raises questions about the shape of future Polish inheritance regulations. It seems that there is currently a social need that may justify the introduction into the Polish Civil Code of a regulation governing the impact of a marriage annulment, divorce and separation on the last will, for which the model could be § 2077 BGB – taking into account, however, the interpretative reservations mentioned above, and omitting the regulation devoted to fiancé (which is not regulated in the current Polish law).[42] With regard to court proceedings in the above cases (initiated but not concluded during the testator's lifetime), Article 940 KC could be a model for future regulation. It is worth noting here that § 2077 BGB employs the construction of the ineffectiveness of a testamentary disposition ("*eine letztwillige Verfügung* [...] *ist unwirksam*"). This approach would also be appropriate within the framework of Polish inheritance law, which – unlike some *common law* jurisdictions – is not familiar with the concept of an *ex lege* revocation of a will, identifying it instead only with a legal action (although doubts arise as to whether it is a juridical action *mortis causa* or it has an

40 See judgments of SN of 14 January 2009, IV CSK 358/08, LEX No 603181, and of 9 August 2018, V CSK 435/17, LEX No 2531715 – general rulings relevant to wills.

41 This allegation was also raised before the court of first instance in a case settled by final decision of the District Court in Elbląg of 29 July 2020, I Ca 170/20, LEX No 3274435, mentioned above. However, a legally significant mistake was not demonstrated (Article 945 § 1 point KC), and the court's findings as to that issue were not subsequently the subject of an appeal plea.

42 Similarly, the question of introducing an instrument governing the effect of a conclusion of marriage on the effectiveness of previous testamentary dispositions or even the entire will remains open. This institution can be found in some common law systems. See the laws of England and Wales (§ 18 Wills Act 1837), Oregon (§ 112.305 Oregon Revised Statues, Laws 1969, c. 591, § 44 as amended) and Kansas (§ 59-610 Kansas Statutes Annotated, Laws 1939, ch. 180, § 46, when the testator is married and has a child by birth or adoption).

immediate effect upon revocation[43]). In any case, possible changes in the legal regulations in this area require an in-depth analysis, since the current flexible regulation of the Polish Civil Code has its own value, which is difficult to undermine.

Finally, it should be noted that a similar interpretative issue may also arise in the case of other legal institutions, such as a disposition *mortis causa* of a deposit on an account.[44] The relevant statutory regulation is silent on this subject. It seems that a solution should be sought against the background of the statutory provisions on the permissible content of such dispositions (subjectively limited to spouses and others). Therefore, if, at the time of the account holder's death (the time when the disposition takes effect), the designated person was not among those entitled under the law (e.g. they had ceased to be the account holder's spouse), the disposition would have to be considered invalid (*ius cogens*). This seems to be supported by the *mortis causa* nature of this type of disposition. However, these reservations are not without doubt and should be explicitly regulated by law.

43 Compare the resolutions of SN of 30 January 1963, III CO 42/62, OSNC 1964, No 1, item 4 and of 29 May 1987, III CZP 25/87, OSNC 1988, No 9, item 117. See also: Ł. Żarnowiec, *Odwołanie testamentu w polskim prawie spadkowym*, Rej. 2011, No 12, p. 127.

44 See Article 56 of the Banking Law (FB) and Article 14 section 1 point 2 of the Law on Cooperative Savings and Credit Unions (SKOK).

Elwira Macierzyńska-Franaszczyk

§ 7 – The testamentary exclusion of the division of the inherited estate

Comparative conclusion
According to German and Polish law, a right of a testator to include in their will a disposition limiting the division of the estate is not contrary to the law and falls within the freedom to testate. Nevertheless, when assessing the legal effectiveness of such a testamentary disposition, it must be borne in mind that, at the stage of dividing the estate, both the German and the Polish legislators granted a strong primacy to the intentions of the heirs before the intentions of the testator.

I. Analysis of an example case under German law

The main issue related to the law of succession examined by the BGH in case V ZR 130/61[1] was the admissibility and legal effectiveness of a division of the inherited estate in the event that the testator limited a division in his will. Against this background, several secondary issues emerged, including the binding effect of testamentary dispositions for an executor and the effectiveness of legal acts completed by the preliminary heir (*Vorerbe*) towards the subsequent heir (*Nacherbe*).

As outlined in the verdict, according to several last wills left by the testator (S), the estate was inherited by his children – the son (W), the daughter (E) and granddaughter (I). One of the wills included an instruction limiting the temporary admissibility of the division of the inherited estate. After the testator's death in 1924, the estate was managed by the executor of the will appointed by the testator. In 1930, the testator's son (W) and his wife (M) concluded a loan agreement with the community of heirs, in the amount of DM 25,000. The repayment of the loan was collateralised by a mortgage established on the private property belonging to borrowers (W and M). In the same year, the executor, acting with the consent of all heirs, sold the inherited estate asset. The act was

1 BGH judgment of 25 September 1963, V ZR 130/61, NJW 1963, 2320.

considered as equal to the partial division of the estate. The amount of money from the division was divided among all the heirs apart from W. The amount due to W was deducted from the debt resulting from the loan agreement, up to the whole amount of the loan. In 1952, W and M concluded an additional agreement with the executor to clarify the legal status of the mortgage. Under this agreement, the parties confirmed the transfer of the mortgage to W in accordance with § 1172 section 1 BGB, and its conversion into a land debt entitled to W against his wife M, pursuant to § 1177 BGB. When W died in 1955, his only heir was his wife M, who died one year later. The executor of M's will sold the property burdened with the land debt. Shortly after that, the executor of M's estate raised an allegation against the executor of S's estate and I (the successor of S), arguing that the land debt was improperly established in 1952 and was invalid due to an error. In 1957, the claimants filed a lawsuit against the land purchasers (defendants) for the forced execution of the purchased property up to the amount of the land debt, to which they were entitled. They justified their demand by their entitlement to the share of S's estate, including the right to the land debt against M. According to them, W was appointed the heir of S only conditionally, as the preliminary heir (*Vorerbe*), and was obliged to transfer S's inheritance to the claimants. Subsequently and with reference to the main claim, the claimants also questioned the effectiveness of the partial division of S's estate, due to its inadmissibility caused by S's testamentary disposition, limiting the division of the inherited estate and preventing its divisions, including that of 1930. Since a division was not allowed, it was not possible to deduct the loaned amount from the amount received as consideration of the division. As a result, the debt that arose in 1930 still exists and charges M's estate, purchased by the defendants.

The first and second instances courts settled that, although the claimants are the subsequent heirs (*Nacherben*) of S's estate, there are no grounds to claim the invalidity of the partial division of the estate when the legal act was made by the executor together with the heirs or preliminary heirs of the inherited estate. The agreement regarding the division of the estate conducted with the participation of the preliminary heirs and the executor was valid and did not violate the testamentary limitation of the division of the estate (§ 2044 BGB). The subsequent contractual deduction (§ 387 BGB) of the loan due to S's estate from the amount due to W according to the division of the estate was also valid. In conclusion, the courts stated that the testamentary limitation of the partition does not preclude the effectiveness of disposing of inherited assets made by all heirs, or by the executor together with the heirs. The BGH agreed with the stance presented by the appeal court and confirmed that the participation of the executor together with all preliminary heirs in the legal act removes the obstacle to the division constituted by the testator's disposition. In this case, the taken legal act did not require the presence of subsequent heirs for its legal effectiveness.

Explaining the adopted position, the BGH clarified that the limitation of the division of the estate made by the testator in the will (§ 2044 BGB) may be slightly different in nature. When the aim of the ban is to protect against disputes among heirs that could arise out of dividing the estate, the disposition should be treated as precluding the admissibility of a request for a court division imposed by the individual heir (§ 2042 section 1 BGB). However, this will not prevent a unanimous division resulting from a joint request of all co-heirs. Such a division would not be treated as contrary to the intention of the testator. In some circumstances, the testamentary limitation of dividing the estate may express the unanimous and firm intention of the testator and prohibit the division even in the event of the joint heirs' request. Nevertheless, in these cases, the testamentary exclusion of the division does not have a normative, judicial or official (authoritative) nature (§§ 134–136 BGB). The source of it is the testator's legal act (§ 137 BGB). Therefore, it may only oblige heirs to refrain from disposing of the estate, but not prevent them from doing so. The violation of this ban does therefore not affect the effectiveness of legal acts performed by the heirs.

Under German law, it should be admitted that the way of regulating the co-ownership of the inherited estate is not aimed at maintaining the persistence and indivisibility of the inheritance, but rather at allowing the division.[2] The provision of § 2042 section 1 BGB constitutes a general ability of each co-heir to request a partitioning of the inherited estate at any time, unless § 2043 to 2045 BGB provide otherwise. The request for a division of the estate can be limited as a result of the following situations: a testamentary disposition (§ 2044 BGB), an agreement between co-heirs (§ 2042 section 2 BGB in conjunction with § 750 section 2 and § 750 section 3 BGB), an inability to determine shares that will be attributed to heirs due to the expected birth of a co-heir or due to a decision regarding adoption or its cancellation, or an expected establishment of a foundation (§ 2043 sections 1 and 2 BGB).

The testamentary limitation on dividing the estate included in the testator's will, which was an element in the case at hand, is based on § 2044 BGB. According to § 2044 section 1 BGB, the testator may limit a division with regard to particular goods contained in the estate, or the whole estate; or make the partitioning dependent on a notice period. The provision of § 2044 section 2 sentence 1 BGB stipulates that the testator's disposition ceased to be effective thirty years after the devolution of inherited estate. Unless the testator provides in the will that it remains effective until the occurrence of a determined event relating to a co-heir or until the devolution of inheritance in the event of the subsequent succession (*Nacherbfolge*) or legacy.

2 K. Muscheler, *Erbrecht. Band II*, Tübingen 2010, p. 2040; O. Werner, in: *Staudingers Kommentar*, vol. 5, 2002, § 2044, pt. 10, p. 660.

The testator may provide a broader or narrower effect of the limitation of the estate division established pursuant to § 2044 BGB. In its essential form the disposition included in the will, may exclude the right of each heir to demand individually the division of the inherited estate. But the testator may make the effectiveness of the division request dependent on the sum of estate shares attributed to heirs demanding the division.[3] The testamentary disposition may also directly exclude the admissibility of the division in the case of the unanimous request of all heirs.

According to the German doctrine, a testamentary limitation of dividing the estate may take the legal form of a testamentary legacy (§§ 2147–2191 BGB) or an instruction (§§ 2192–2196 BGB), and the decision on which form will apply is determined separately in each specific case.[4] However, a more detailed position as to the legal nature of a testamentary disposition limiting the division in favour of each heir can also be found in the literature. Such a disposition can be interpreted as a testamentary instruction (§ 1940 BGB, *Auflage*), a simple legacy (§ 2147 BGB, *Vermächtnis*) or a preferential legacy (§ 2150 BGB, *Vorausvermächtnis*). A contrary opinion was also expressed whereby the testamentary limitation of division constitutes a particular type of testamentary disposition that is neither a legacy nor an instruction;[5] in addition, an analogy to a legacy or instruction will be excluded.[6] Nevertheless, the prevailing view presented in the doctrine about a testamentary limitation of a division, as provided in § 2044 BGB, recommends interpreting the legal nature of the disposition as a testamentary instruction in the meaning of § 1940 BGB). Adopting this view, instead of following the qualification as a bequest, results in essentially distinct legal consequences. A violation of the instruction may, at most, lead to claims stipulated by the law of obligation vested in the entities entitled according to § 2194 BGB.[7]

3 An example can be a reservation made by the testator whereby the division should be allowed in the event of a request by the majority of successors, for example – see RGZ 110, 270 JW. 1925, 2120.

4 O. Lange, L. Kuchinke, *Erbrecht. Ein Lehrbuch*, München 2001, § 44 II 3 a; O. Werner, in: *Staudingers Kommentar*, vol. 5, 2002, § 2044 pt. 5, p. 658.

5 A qualification of the exclusion of the division as a legacy is excluded due to its purely obligatory nature and the inability to apply all the provisions governing a legacy to such an exclusion, e.g. § 2180 BGB referring to the acceptance and waiver of the legacy – see T. Kipp, H. Coing, *Erbrecht*, §116 IV 3 a, p. 631; K. Muscheler, *Erbrecht….*, p. 2055. An ambiguous position has been taken by T. Weckbach, *Die Bindugswirkung von Erbteilungsverboten*, Berlin 1987, p. 34. What prevents the exclusion of the division from being interpreted as a testamentary instruction is the lack of the obligation to perform. It would also be doubtful whether the disposition considered as an instruction would be subject to the provision of § 749 sections 2 and 3, § 750–751 BGB, which under § 2044 section 1 sentence 2 BGB are applicable to the exclusion of the division – see K. Muscheler, *Erbrecht…*, p. 2055.

6 K. Muscheler, *Erbrecht…*, p. 2057.

7 Compare BGHZ 37, 147 NJW 62, 1344.

According to this provision, the execution of the testamentary instruction can be demanded by an heir, a co-heir or anyone who would directly benefit from the exemption of the person charged with the instruction. If an enforcement of the instruction lies in the public interest, it can be demanded by the responsible public authority. With regard to the legal effects of the discussed testamentary limitation of the division, the dominant view is that its legal consequences will be limited to an obligatory limitation on demanding the division of the estate, effective against each heir separately.[8] The indicated effect can also be perceived as an obligation on each heir to refrain from requesting the division and remain in the community of heirs. The literature has also emphasised the subjective effect of the disposition, whereby the testamentary limitation of the division leads to each heir's right to avoid the demand of the division by the other heirs.[9] Regardless of the adopted interpretation, the testamentary exclusion of division forces each heir indicated in the will to refrain from requesting the division and prevents the effectiveness of such a request in the event of objections, even if submitted by a single heir.

Additionally, the content of § 2044 section 1 BGB should be borne in mind, as this points to the respective application of § 749 sections 2 and 3 BGB which state that the right to demand the division can be allowed if there is a compelling reason to do so; an agreement (e. g. an agreement among heirs) contrary to this entitlement is void. Because the disposition included in the testator's will results only from a unilateral legal act and has no normative, judicial or administrative nature (§§ 134–136 BGB), it cannot deprive the heirs of the right to dispose of the estate or items thereof (cf. § 137 BGB). According to § 2044 BGB, the testator making an exclusion on dividing the estate is an effective obstacle to implementing the division of the estate at the request of selected heirs, although the division of the estate at the joint request of all the heirs is allowed. Only in particular circumstances, as mentioned before, may such a division give rise to the heirs' liability under the law of obligation against the authorised entity indicated in § 2194 BGB.[10]

A division made by the heirs against the intentions of the testator constitutes a violation of the testamentary disposition, but does not result in the invalidity of the legal act.[11] A testamentary exclusion of a division has neither obligatory (*schuldrechtliche*) nor in rem (*dingliche*) effectiveness, therefore legal acts resulting in each of these effects can be valid.[12] Such a division would tend to be

8 T. Weckbach, *Die Bindungswirkung…*, p. 64.

9 K. Muscheler, *Erbrecht…*, p. 2052; O. Werner, in: *Staudingers Kommentar*, vol. 5, 2002, § 2044 pt. 6, p. 658.

10 See the verdict BGHZ 37, 147, NJW 62, 1344.

11 T. Kipp, H. Coing, *Erbrecht…*, § 116, IV 3 c.

12 O. Lange, L. Kuchinke, *Erbrecht…*, § 44, II 3 a, p. 1141.

interpreted not as a violation of a testamentary disposition or violation of the heirs' obligation to refrain from the division, but as an expression of each heir's decision to waive their right to exercise the avoidance of the division.[13]

In principle, a testamentary limitation of the division does not prevent heirs from concluding agreements on disposing of estate items. However, the division will not be allowed despite the heirs' consent in the event of appointing an executor for the purpose of exclusively administering the estate, or under the stipulation that the executor will continue administering despite the other obligations incumbent on the executor (*Dauervollstreckung*, § 2209 BGB). If an executor is appointed, the heirs are removed from the administration of the estate, which is entrusted to the executor (§ 2205 sentence 1 and § 2211 section 1 BGB), with an exception as to items excluded from the executor's administration (§ 2208 BGB). In such cases, the heirs' right to dispose of the estate item is limited to the extent of the administration rights afforded to the executor.

Another question refers to the effect of the testamentary limitation of a division on the executor's rights (or their limitation or possible waiver). According to the notion of the court, as presented in the case at hand, the testamentary limitation of the division is also binding on the executor. Therefore, the executor will not be entitled to undertake legal action in order to perform the division, nor to agree to the division or even the disposition of individual items of the estate in the case of objection from at least one of the heirs. In that case, the division may be performed only jointly by the executor and all the heirs. The opposite approach – prohibiting the division – would ultimately be contrary to § 137 BGB. If the inheritance division results not from a testamentary legacy or instruction, but from an order prohibiting the dissolution of co-ownership (*negative Teilungsanordnung*) it will be binding also on the executor, as it stipulates § 2216 section 2 sentence 1 BGB.

In some cases, it might be problematic to distinguish the testamentary limitation of the division from the testamentary limitation of the sale of the estate or an item thereof. The second situation can be interpreted as a testamentary order in the meaning of § 2192 BGB, the non-performance of which gives rise to the liability for damages to the extent indicated in § 2194 BGB. In the German doctrine, it has been pointed out that, while the testamentary limitation from the sale of a particular asset will result in its exclusion from division, the pure testamentary limitation of the division cannot result in the prohibition on disposing of items.[14]

The limitation of the division made in the will also raises a question related to the effectiveness of the division carried out by the preliminary heirs (*Vorerben*)

13 K. Muscheler, *Erbrecht...*, p. 2052.
14 K. Muscheler, *Erbrecht...*, p. 2047.

with respect to the subsequent heirs (*Nacherben*). The results of such a legal act should be assessed according to § 2113 and § 2120 BGB. Pursuant to § 2113 section 1 BGB, in the event that a subsequent succession occurs, the disposition by the prior heir of the estate being the part of inheritance is ineffective only if it defeats or adversely affects the right of the subsequent heir. The consent granted by preliminary heirs is, in principle, sufficient for the valid disposal of movable or immovable items of the estate. The effectiveness of the legal action is not limited due to the appointment of an executor, if the executor was empowered to act in the name of the preliminary heirs and the subsequent heirs.[15]

II. Consideration of the problem presented in the German case and its comparison with Polish law

The testamentary exclusion of the admissibility of the division has not been provided for in the catalogue of testamentary dispositions regulated by Polish law. In general, the Polish legislator did not provide for any separate type of testamentary disposition that could serve a testator intending to legally influence the future division of an estate inherited by the successors, in particular to limit the division of the estate or oblige the heirs to maintain the co-ownership of the estate against their wishes, or to influence the way or results of the division in a binding way. The testamentary dispositions settled in the Polish Civil Code, such as a positive or negative appointment of heirs, a legacy or a vindicative legacy, allow a *mortis causa* distribution of an estate or of its separate items to be planned, but not to influence the division directly. Among the provisions of Polish succession law, there are no provisions equivalent to § 2044 BGB, which would directly refer to or allow the testamentary exclusion of the division.

The impact of the testator's intentions expressed through the will regarding the manner of dividing the estate, or its temporary or subjective limitations, gives rise to controversies in the Polish doctrine and jurisprudence. It should be clarified, however, that under Polish law the division of an inherited estate included in the last will of the testator, or performed by the executor, or agreed with the future testator during his lifetime, are not legally effective in the sphere of the division of the inherited estate.[16]

In Polish law, like in German law, the transitional nature of the co-ownership of the inherited estate is emphasised.[17] The provisions of law do not impose any

15 NJW 1963, 2320.

16 A. Stempniak, *Autonomia i integracja postępowań działowych w prawie polskim*, Warszawa 2017, pp. 130–137.

17 J. Gwiazdomorski, *Prawo spadkowe w zarysie*, 1985, p. 198.

obligation on the unanimously acting heirs' to consider or to follow the dispositions of the testator directing them about the division or interfering into its eligibility.[18] The right to demand the division of the estate is vested in the heirs, who also retain a considerable degree of freedom in selecting the appropriate mode and the scope of the division. Pursuant to Article 1037 § 1 KC, the division of an estate may be the result of an agreement between all the heirs, or a decision of the court. The division agreement depends on the decision of all the heirs and does not require the court's approval. In addition, the joint application of the heirs requesting a court decision will constitute the binding basis for the court to issue a division decision according to the unanimous intentions of the heirs, even if it disregards the testator's intention concerning the limitation of the division.

As indicated above, the co-ownership of the inherited estate arose between the co-heirs. Pursuant to reference in Article 1035 KC, the co-ownership of inherited estate and the division of the estate are governed by the general provisions on co-ownership in fractional shares and its termination, but applied appropriately and with observing the law of succession. The material scope of the reference in Article 1035 KC to the general provisions includes the appropriate application of the provisions of Articles 210–212 KC and of Articles 220–221 KC. If the estate includes a farm, Articles 213–218 CC will apply appropriately, according to the reference included in Article 1070 KC.[19]

Pursuant to the dominant view presented by the doctrine, the limitation of the right to demand a division can result from the stipulation made by the testator in a valid last will containing the disposition limiting the division of the whole estate, an indicated part of it or just certain items, directed towards all or selected heirs, or from the legal action undertaken by the heirs after the testator's death.[20]

As a result of the reference, included in Article 1070 KC, to an assessment of the admissibility and legal effectiveness of the limitation of the right to request the division of the inheritance, the appropriate application of Article 210 KC should be considered, despite whether the limitation results from a unilateral or multilateral legal action. The provision of Article 210 § 1 KC stipulates that the right to demand the cancelation of co-ownership may be precluded through a legal action for up to five years. This five-year period may be extended by another

18 Comp. T. Felski, *Wpływ woli testatora na sposób podziału majątku spadkowego*, Pal. 1994, No 38/12, p. 5.

19 Comp. J. Gwiazdomorski, *Prawo spadkowe*, 1985, p. 197.

20 See J. Gwiazdomorski, *Prawo spadkowe*, 1985, p. 201; E. Gniewek, w: *System prawa prywatnego*, vol. 3, 2020, p. 462, pt. 152; K. Górska, in: E. Gniewek, P. Machnikowski (eds.), *Komentarz KC*, 2021, Article 210, pt. II.1; J. Kremis, w: *System prawa prywatnego*, vol. 10, 2015, p. 956.

five years; but whether it may subsequently be renewed again is disputable.[21] If the period of a testamentary limitation is for longer than five years, then the period will be automatically reduced to five years. The temporary nature of the limitation indicated in Article 210 § 1 KC will be applied as appropriate to a testamentary limitation for longer than five years counted from the moment the will became legally effective (the moment of opening the estate).

Pursuant to Article 210 § 1 sentence 2 KC, the exclusion of the right to demand a partitioning must result from a legal action. Although the Polish legislator did not specify the legal nature of this action, nor the parties participating in it, it has been pointed out in the literature that it may, but does not have to, take the form of an agreement.[22] And in practice the legal action undertaken by the co-owners usually takes the form of an agreement.[23] An agreement between co-owners does not require all the co-owners to participate in order to be considered valid. The contractual exclusion of the right to demand the division of an inheritance may result from an agreement concluded by all or some of heirs.[24] The co-heirs concluding an agreement should, however, have reached a consensus regarding the temporary exclusion of the right to demand the abolition of the co-ownership. The binding effect of the agreement is limited to those co-owners who participated in the legal action and their successors.[25] Any heirs who did not conclude the agreement have the right to claim its division and are allowed to request it before the court. As a result, the division of the estate may be ordered, despite of the existence of an agreement excluding its division.[26] Nonetheless, the applicability of Article 210 § 1 in conjunction with Article 1035 KC as grounds for the contractual exclusion of the division of inherited estate by co-heirs remains debatable.[27]

---

21 A disputable issue is the number of subsequent five-year period by which the exclusion of the request to abolish the co-ownership can be extended. See e.g. P. Księżak, in: K. Osajda, W. Borysiak (eds.), *Komentarz KC*, 2020, ed. 26, Article 210, pt. 18; K. Górska, w: E. Gniewek, P. Machnikowski (eds.), *Komentarz KC*, 2021, Article 210, pt. II.4; M. Grochowski, *Artykuł 210 § 1 k.c. – jako regulacja dyspozytywna*, Pal. 2017, No 1–2, p. 153.

22 G. Karaszewski, w: M. Balwicka-Szczyrba, A. Sylwestrzak (eds.), *Komentarz KC*, 2022, Article 210, pt. 5.

23 J. Ignatowicz, in: Z. Resich et al. (eds.), *Komentarz KC*, vol. 1, 1972, p. 542.

24 See K. Szadkowski, in: M. Gutowski (ed.), *Komentarz KC*, vol. I, 2021, Article 210, pt.II.2; E. Gniewek, in: *System prawa prywatnego*, vol. 3, 2020, p. 462, pt. 152; K. Górska, in: E. Gniewek, P. Machnikowski (eds.), *Komentarz KC*, 2021, Article 210, pt. II.1; A. Wąsiewicz, *Powstanie, istota i zniesienie współwłasności ułamkowej*, Poznań 1965, p. 234.

25 E. Skowrońska-Bocian, M. Warciński, w: K. Pietrzykowski (ed.), *Komentarz KC*, vol. I, 2018, Article 210, pt. 3.

26 P. Księżak, w: K. Osajda (ed.), *Komentarz KC*, vol. II, 2017, Article 210 KC, pt. 11.

27 See K. Grzegorczyk, K. Osajda, w: K. Osajda, W. Borysiak (eds.), *Komentarz KC*, 2022, Article 1035, pt. 33 i 35–36.

Similarly questionable is the admissibility of the testamentary limitation on the division of an estate.[28] In the Polish doctrine, there are diverging views on the legal admissibility or effectiveness of testamentary dispositions regarding the division of the estate. These views can be applied analogically to the testamentary disposition limiting the division. The most extreme opinions either definitively reject the possibility of the testator's disposition having an impact on the division,[29] or take the contrary position, approving not only the admissibility of those dispositions, but even their binding nature.[30] According to one minor view, testamentary dispositions regarding a division are allowed and legally binding on the heirs and on the court in division proceedings.[31] The majority of the doctrine, however, adopts a compromise view whereby the testamentary disposition regarding the division is allowed, but is not legally binding, though it should be followed by the heirs, and even considered by the court in the estate division proceedings,[32] particularly in the absence of the heirs unanimous application.[33]

The last of the above views may support, to some extent, an assessment of the testamentary disposition limiting the admissibility of the division of the estate. This assumes, that the testator has the right to include in their will a disposition limiting the division of estate, which is not contrary to the law and falls within the freedom to testate. However, an assessment of the legal effectiveness of the testator's disposition must take into account the fact that, at the stage of dividing the estate, the Polish legislator prioritised the wishes of the heirs over the intent of the testator.[34]

According to Article 1037 § 1 KC, the inherited estate may be divided under an agreement concluded by all the heirs or under a court decision at the demand of any of the heirs.

The testamentary limitation of the division will not prevent the heirs from concluding an agreement on division. The validity of the contract will also not impact the appointment of the executor, who is not the party of the estate division agreement and has no right to object to the heirs' unanimous desire to

28 See e.g. J. St. Piątowski, B. Kordasiewicz, *Prawo spadkowe*, Warszawa 2003, p. 122.

29 J. St. Piątowski, B. Kordasiewicz, *Prawo…*, p. 125.

30 J. Biernat, *Z problematyki tzw. testamentu działowego w polskim prawie spadkowym*, PS 2005, No 4, p. 158–159; P. Księżak, *Zapis windykacyjny*, Warszawa 2012, p. 28.

31 M. Niedośpiał, *Testament. Zagadnienia ogólne testamentu w polskim prawie cywilnym*, Kraków - Poznań 1993, pp. 102–104; M. Niedośpiał, *Swoboda testowania*, Bielsko-Biała 2004, p. 122.

32 J. Gwiazdomorski, *Prawo spadkowe*, 1985, p. 90 and p. 222; T. Felski, *Wpływ…*, p. 6; S. Wójcik, in: *System prawa cywilnego.* vol. IV, 1986, p. 495; see also SN judgment of 3 October 1980, III CRN 80/8, OSN 2–3, No 1981, item 45.

33 According to the dominant view, the dispositions of the testators should be taken into account exclusively in the proceeding before the court and only in the absence of a compliant application of heirs - alike: J. Biernat, *Z problematyki…*, pp. 37–40.

34 See A. Stempniak, *Autonomia…*, p. 129.

divide the estate. Regardless of the unanimity or non-unanimity of the heirs' intentions as to the division, its scope or form, each of the heirs has the right to demand the division of the inherited estate before the court (Article 1037 § 1 KC). This entitlement vests individually in each heir, regardless of their share in the inheritance. An heir interested in the division of the estate may demand the division of the entire estate, or, if there are important grounds, a partial division limited to specific components of the estate or up to the value of the indicated share.[35] The right to demand the division of the estate is a statutory right of each heir that has priority over the testator's wishes expressed through testamentary dispositions. It is recognised as a fundamental right of co-heirs. None of the co-heirs can waive their right to demand a division in a legally effective way, since it would infringe Article 57 § 1 and 2 KC.[36]

The heirs can submit a joint application to the court unanimously or accept the division plan proposed in an application submitted by another heir. Pursuant to Article 688 KPC in conjunction with Article 622 § 2 KPC, in proceedings involving the division of an estate the court is guided, first and foremost, by a unanimous application of the heirs, unless the proposed mode of division is contrary to the law or the principles of social coexistence, or grossly violates the interests of any entitled person. However, the jurisprudence indicated that, in case of a unanimous application of all the heirs, the court is not allowed to reject the application only because the particular interest of one of the heirs would cause the application to be rejected.[37] The testamentary limitation or temporary exclusion of the division of the estate is not binding for the court preceding the division application. It may, however, constitute "other circumstances", within the meaning of Article 682 KPC, that may affect the court's decision by adjudicating the division of the estate.

It must be borne in mind that any circumstances limiting the availability of the estate division and resulting in a court decision dismissing the application are exceptional by nature. It should be emphasised also that, in principle, the court is not bound by testamentary dispositions limiting the division of the estate.[38] This covers testamentary dispositions specifying the form of the division as well as the dispositions limiting or temporarily restricting the division. As indicated in the literature, if the heirs do not make a unanimous application otherwise, the court may respect the intent of the testator as to the method of the division but will only

35 J. Gwiazdomorski, *Prawo spadkowe*, 1959, p. 220.

36 J. Kremis, in: *System prawa prywatnego*, vol. 10, 2015, p. 956.

37 See judgment of SN of 18 August 1964, III CR 87/64, OSNCP 1965, No 3, item 50 with the gloss of W. Siedlecki, OSPiKA 1965, No 9, item 200.

38 See T. Felski, *Wpływ…*, p. 6; see also verdict of SN of 14 April 2021 r., II CSKP 16/21, Legalis 2692140; K. Osajda, in: K Osajda, W. Borysiak (eds.), *Komentarz KC*, 2022, Article 1037, pt. 20.

exceptionally uphold the testator's disposition temporarily limiting the division.[39]

Furthermore, the court must careful assess all circumstances of a testamentary disposition impacting the admissibility of the estate division in terms of its compliance with the law, the principles of social coexistence and the possible impact on the individual situation of every heir, e. g. provoking an escalation of conflicts among the heirs, leading to harm, causing discrimination or a socially or morally negative mutual dependence among heirs, or even preventing the resolution of a bond of solidarity among heirs. In this context, a moral and social assessment of the testator's right to impact the position of the heirs should also be carried out. On the other hand, the legitimacy of maintaining the estate community, due to the interests of particular heirs (e. g. minor or disabled heirs) or protecting the complexity of particular property items (e. g. an enterprise), must be taken into account.

In order to carry out an assessment of the justifiable impact of the testator's intention to the estate division, it is worth brief referencing the applicability of Article 5 KC in cases relating to the division of estate. The first sentence of Article 5 KC states that no one can exercise their right in a manner contradictory to its social and economic purpose or the principles of social coexistence. Pursuant to the opinion presented in the doctrine and the jurisprudence, dismissing a demand for the division of property based on Article 5 KC may be justified only in exceptional circumstances where it is considered incompatible with the principles of social coexistence.[40] In relation to the division of the inherited estate, the jurisprudence clearly denied the applicability of Article 5 KC as a ground to dismiss a demand for a division.[41] The Polish Supreme Court stipulated that the right of the heirs to demand the division of the inherited estate should be seen as a statutory, elementary right to terminate the co-ownership of the estate, which by its nature is impermanent and temporary, and each of the co-heirs should take this into account.[42]

39 See F. Błahuta, in: Z. Resich et al. (eds.), *Komentarz KC*, vol. 3, 1972, pp. 1856–1857; S. Wójcik, in: *System prawa cywilnego*, vol. IV, 1986, p. 228.

40 K. Krziskowska, D. Łobos-Kotowska, M. Stańko, in: M. Habdas, M. Fras (eds.), *Komentarz KC*, vol. II, 2018, Article 210, nb. 3, the resolution of SN of 24 January 2007, III CZP 117/06, LEX No 209071, the judgment of SN of 26 October 2017, II CSK 7/17, LEX No 2427134.

41 Judgment of SN of 6 June 2002, I CKN 249/00, LEX No 55559; judgment of SA in Łódź of 17 April 2013, I ACa 1424/12, LEX No 1313330.

42 See the resolution of SN of 18 April 1990, III CZP 15/90, OSNCP 1990, No 10–11, item 137.

Małgorzata Lubelska-Sazanów

§ 8 – Possibility to submit all future disputes arising from a will to arbitration by a unilateral decision of the testator

Comparative conclusion
Whereas under German law the testator is allowed to include an arbitration clause referring to issues falling within the scope of freedom to testify in their will, under Polish law this is not admissible since arbitration clauses may only be included in contracts. Therefore – unlike in German law – under Polish law it is not possible to include any arbitration clause at the unilateral decision of a testator in a will.

I. Analysis of an example case under German law

The analysis is based on the facts from the German Federal Court of Justice (BGH) judgment of 16 March 2017 in the case I ZB 49/16,[1] on the possibility to submit all future disputes arising out of or in connection with a will, including possible rights and claims to compulsory portion by a unilateral decision of a testator.

On 25 May 2010, the father of the parties (the Father) died. In his notarial will of 8 April 2004, he made his daughter (the Daughter) the sole heir. In his last will, he also ordered that "all disputes arising out of or in connection to his will, from his will and beyond that, as well as in reference to the course of succession after him and to the possible rights and claims to compulsory portions, should be decided by an arbitral tribunal in accordance with the rules of the Arbitration Court of German Notaries (the Arbitration Court)."

After the Father's death, the mother of the parties (the Mother) filed a case for a compulsory portion against the Daughter in a public court. The court of first instance (*Landesgericht,* LG) forwarded the case to the court of second instance (*Oberlandesgericht,* OLG). After examining the facts of the case, the OLG stated that the arbitration clause included in the Father's will was binding and instructed the Mother to initiate arbitration proceedings. The Daughter's brother

1 ZIP 2017, 1736.

(the Brother) then brought an arbitration claim for a compulsory portion of EUR 5937.50 plus interest against the Daughter in the Arbitration Court.

The Daughter stated that she could not afford the costs of the arbitration proceedings and legal representation. Since the Brother also refused to cover these costs, the Arbitration Court ordered the Daughter to apply to the state court to confirm that the arbitration proceedings are not possible. The Daughter applied to the OLG, which determined that the Daughter was not insolvent, thus the arbitration proceedings were possible. As a result, the Arbitration Court issued a judgment and ordered the Daughter – as the Father's sole heir – to pay EUR 5937.50 plus interest to the Brother as his compulsory portion. At the same time, the Arbitration Court instructed the parties that they are entitled to file objections within two weeks. The Daughter filed an objection, but she submitted it by fax, causing it to be rejected by the Arbitration Court.

In the end, however, the OLG rejected the application for a declaration of enforceability and nullified the arbitration award. Thus, the OLG stated that the arbitration award went against § 1059 section 2 subsection 2 (a) ZPO and the case was inadmissible for arbitration proceedings since the right to a compulsory portion could not have been submitted to arbitration by a unilateral decision of the testator. The OLG stated also that the Arbitration Court had disregarded the Daughter's right to be heard by holding her objection as inadmissible. The objection filed by the Brother was not successful.

This case was analysed to answer the question whether – under the German and Polish legal systems – succession issues, including possible rights and claims to compulsory portions may be submitted to arbitration proceedings by a unilateral decision of the testator in his will or not.

In the case at hand, the OLG made two important legal statements. Firstly, it confirmed that only a state court may decide whether a certain case in a specific situation is eligible for arbitration. Secondly, it confirmed that – since the purpose of arbitration clauses is to express the parties' consent to settle all disputes arising between them by arbitration – the testator, as a third party is not entitled to order in a will that a dispute concerning a compulsory portion, i. e. a dispute between two different parties, must be resolved by arbitration.

The OLG's reasoning behind the decision to reject an arbitration award was based on the legal provision of § 1059 ZPO. According to § 1059 ZPO, there are only two cases where the court may file a reversal of an arbitration award – firstly, if the court determines that the subject matter of a dispute is not eligible for arbitration, and secondly if the court determines that the recognition or enforcement of the arbitration award would lead to a result contrary to public order. In the BGH case at hand, it was not the parties who decided to settle all future disputes arising between them by arbitration, but a third person – the testator. The arbitration clause in the will may, however, refer only to those issues that fall within the scope of freedom to testify. Therefore, since allowing the testator to decide about the compulsory portion is not permissible, the subject matter of a dispute was not eligible for arbitration according to § 1059 ZPO section 2 subsection 2 (a). The point of view that – in general – a claim for a compulsory portion may constitute the subject of arbitration by virtue of an agreement between the parties, but a dispute over a compulsory portion claim cannot effectively be the subject of a testamentary order, has also been confirmed by the BGH in a number of cases.[2]

At the same time, in the case at hand, the OLG stressed that the solution would have been different if the parties themselves had decided that the arbitral tribunal will resolve possible future disputes arising between them with reference to a compulsory portion. Thus, according to § 1030 section 1 ZPO, any claim under property law may become the subject matter of an arbitration agreement. However, it refers only to agreements made between the parties to these future arbitration proceedings. In this sense, the concept of property rights should be understood broadly, as it encompasses claims that are either derived from property rights or are aimed at services of a specific value.[3] Hence, claims under property law in the meaning of § 1030 ZPO also include claims to compulsory portions.

The possibility to decide in one's will that an arbitral tribunal will rule on possible future disputes arising in connection therewith is a result of freedom to testify. Still, it is obvious that this is limited to the scope of legal issues falling within the scope of the testator's power. Therefore, the BGH admitted that the right to a compulsory portion is not an expression of the freedom to testify, but rather an inevitable result of his decision to exclude a certain person from his will.

Nevertheless, in this particular case, the BGH stated that the defendant, i. e. the Daughter, could not file a petition for the reversal of the arbitration award, since she invoked the arbitration clause included in her Father's will herself. Therefore, she tacitly accepted the testator's choice to settle the disputes concerning a compulsory portion to be resolved by arbitration.

Still, summing up, the German legal system allows arbitration clauses to be included in the will, though they cannot exceed the scope of freedom to testify.

2 See, e. g. BGH case of 12 October 2016 – V ZB 178/15, NJW 2017, 1112.

3 So M. Anders, in: M. Anders, B. Gehle (eds.), *ZPO Kommentar*, 2022, ZPO § 1059 Aufhebungsantrag, pt. 15a. With reference to an ineligibility for arbitration under German law, see also e. g.: BGH, Beschl. v. 16 March 2017 – I ZB 49/16 (OLG München), NJZ 2018, 3.

II. Consideration of the problem presented in the German case and its comparison with Polish law

In order to compare the admissibility of submitting all future disputes arising out of a will, including disputes concerning a compulsory portion under the German legal system with its admissibility under the Polish legal system, it is necessary to take into account the following legal rules.

First of all, it must be noted that, according to Article 1161 KPC,[4] in order to bring a dispute before an arbitration court, the parties must conclude an agreement specifying the matter at issue, or the legal relationship from which a dispute arose or could arise. The examination of whether it is possible to bring a dispute before an arbitration court on a ground different than a partial agreement (especially arising from a last will) follows below.

Under Polish law, a will may include various types of regulations, including: the appointment of an heir, a legacy, a legacy *per vindicationem* (often referred to as *legatum*), a disinheritance, granting a foundation, the appointment of a guardian for a minor, testamentary instructions, etc. According to Article 982 KC, when making a testamentary instruction in the will, the deceased may impose on a heir or a legatee the obligation to act in a specific way, or refrain from acting, but without making anyone a creditor.[5] Hence, an arbitration clause – as a claim not connected with property laws – may be understood as such a testamentary instruction.

However, it must be stressed that, under Polish law, a failure to comply with a testamentary instruction does not lead to any sanctions in relation to the burdened person. The instruction may involve property or non-property rights.[6] It is commonly accepted that an instruction cannot lead to an heir's obligation that could be analogous to an obligation *sensu stricto*.[7] Hence, it is a natural obligation (*obligatio naturalis*).[8] This means that the testamentary instruction does not impose legal, but only moral obligation on the burdened person.[9] Additionally, the instruction is invalid if it is impossible to execute, contrary to the law (which

4 See Article 1161 KPC.

5 Article 982 KC.

6 E. Skowrońska-Bocian, *Komentarz KC*, 2011, p. 166; A. Dyszlewska-Tarnawska, in: M. Habdas, M. Fras (eds.), *Komentarz KC*, vol. VI, 2019, Article 982, p. 452.

7 J. Kremis, in: E. Gniewek, P. Machnikowski (eds.), *Komentarz KC*, 2016, p. 1801, pt. 4; A. Dyszlewska-Tarnawska, in: M. Habdas, M. Fras (eds.), *Komentarz KC*, vol. VI, 2019, Article 982, p. 452.

8 This is also the opinion of SN of 19 April 2002, III CZP 19/02, OSP 2003, No 10, item 123.

9 See M. Pazdan, in: K. Pietrzykowski (ed.), *Komentarz KC*, vol. II, 2021, p. 898. *See also:* J. Kremis, in: E. Gniewek (ed.), *Komentarz KC*, 2011, p. 1788. However, some representatives of the Polish doctrine represent the opinion that the order might be executed by filing a claim, for this see P. Księżak, *Żądanie wykonania polecenia*, PS 2006, No 4, p. 49.

would be the situation in the German case at hand), is intended to circumvent it or is contrary to the principles of social coexistence.[10]

Nevertheless, significantly, an arbitration clause has a contractual character and the expression of one's last will is a unilateral legal action. Therefore, *de lege lata* it is not possible to consider the inclusion of an arbitration clause into one's will as legally admissible under Polish law. Thus, such a testamentary provision would bind two parties to an agreement (i. e., an arbitration clause) they did not make. In the Polish Supreme Court verdict of 13 July 2011,[11] the court confirmed that the fact that a solidarity debtor has concluded an arbitration agreement does not impact other solidarity debtors. The same applies to a partner in a general partnership (*spółka jawna*), who is not bound by an arbitration agreement made by this partnership. In the conclusions of the ruling in this Polish Supreme Court case, the court expressed a legal rule whereby an agreement to resolve all future claims in front of an arbitration tribunal in a contract is applicable only to the parties to that contract. Thus, a contradictory situation would abuse the constitutional right to be judged by a state court.

The case cited above has been considered by representatives of the Polish doctrine. In a gloss to the Polish Supreme Court cited above,[12] the authors admitted that the possibility of being bound by an arbitration clause by a partner in a general partnership does not abuse the constitutional right to be judged by a state court.[13] Thus, according to W. Kurowski and J. Zrałek, the constitutional right to be judged by a state court is also granted by an arbitration court. Hence, a choice between a state court and an arbitration court is not a choice between a "rule" and its "exception", but rather a choice between two equal but different axiologies of using the law.[14] Still, whereas this point of view could be applicable to partnerships, it is not acceptable to apply it to arbitration clauses included by a testator in a will.

Another issue would be in the case of legal succession under a general title, i. e. in a case of succession expressly provided for in the law.[15] Thus, under Polish law, a succession under a general title is a situation where, by force of one legal event, all rights and obligations are transferred from one entity to another. In the Polish

10 See J. Knabe, in: J. Ciszewski, P. Nazaruk (eds.), *Komentarz KC*, 2022, Article 982, pt. 6.
11 Judgment of SN of 13 July 2011, III CZP 36/11, Legalis No 344783.
12 *Idem.*
13 W. Kurowski, J. Zrałek, *Związanie osoby trzeciej skutkami zapisu na sąd polubowny (głos w dyskusji na przykładzie dłużników solidarnych)*, in: A. Dańko-Roesler, A. Oleszko, R. Pastuszko (eds.), *Rozprawy z prawa prywatnego i notarialnego. Księga pamiątkowa dedykowana Profesorowi Maksymilianowi Pazdanowi*, Warszawa 2014, pp. 469–479.
14 *Idem.*
15 With reference to the fact that a general succession should be expressly provided for in the law and it should not be merely presumed, see the ruling of SN of 25 June 2008, III CZP 45/08, LEX No 393765.

literature, the issue of extending the binding scope of an arbitration clause in the case of an event resulting in succession under a general title does not raise any questions in reference to its admissibility.[16] Hence, already in 1920s the Polish Supreme Court underlined that "an arbitration clause binds only the parties and their successors."[17] Still, an event resulting in succession under a general title is a legal situation different to that of a last will (where the testator may not include an arbitration clause that would be legally binding on his heirs).

III. Summary

Summing up, including a testamentary order in the form of an arbitration clause (no matter whether within the scope of freedom to testify or not) would not be admissible under Polish law. Additionally, even if it was admissible, it would only impose a moral (not legal) obligation on the heirs.

The legal admissibility of arbitration clauses has been the subject of scholarly considerations under both the Polish and German legal systems. The German courts represent the opinion that it possible to include an arbitration clause in a will, though only with reference to issues falling within the scope of the freedom to testify.[18] On the other hand, the Polish courts,[19] as well as representatives of the Polish doctrine,[20] agree that the submission of future claims arising out of a will by the testator to be decided by arbitration court is inadmissible.

16 See Ł. Błaszczak, M. Ludwik, *Sądownictwo polubowne (Arbitraż)*, Warszawa 2007, p. 127; R. Kulski, *Umowy procesowe w postępowaniu cywilnym*, Warszawa 2006, pp. 251–252; K. Potrzobowski, W. Żywicki, *Sądownictwo polubowne*, Warszawa 1961, p. 30; M. Pacocha, *Związanie podmiotów trzecich umową arbitrażową*, Warszawa 2019 (unpublished doctoral thesis), available at: https://www.wpia.uw.edu.pl/uploads/media/5ee21d2dc7731/zwiazanie-podmiotow-trzecich-umowa-arbitrazowa.pdf?v1 [last access: 17.12.2021].

17 Judgment of SN of 19 February 1929, III R 116/29, Przegląd Prawa i Administracji 1929, item 119, See also: judgment of SN of 8 February 1937, C. III. 1254/35, Zb. Orz. 1938, No I, item 44. Cited after: M. Pacocha, *Związanie…* [last access: 17.12.2021].

18 See the case at hand, i.e. BGH case of 16 March 2017 – I ZB 49/16 (OLG München), NJOZ 2018, 3 and the BGH case of 12 October 2016 – V ZB 178/15 NJW 2017, 1112.

19 E.g. judgment of SN of 13 July 2011 r, III CZP 36/11, OSNC 2012, No 3, item 31.

20 See M. Pazdan, *Bezskuteczność lub nieważność zapisu na sąd polubowny w prawie polskim*, in: P. Nowaczyk, S. Pieckowski, J. Poczobut, A. Szumański, A. Tynel (eds.), *Międzynarodowy i krajowy arbitraż handlowy u progu XXI wieku. Księga pamiątkowa dedykowana doktorowi habilitowanemu Tadeuszowi Szurskiemu*, Warszawa 2008, p. 121; P. Wrześniewski, *Charakter prawny zapisu na sąd polubowny*, Warszawa 2010; A. Franusz, *Arbitraż testamentowy jako specyficzna forma zapisu na sąd polubowny*, in: J. Olszewski (ed.), *Arbitraż i mediacja. III Ogólnopolska Konferencja Naukowa. Nałęczów Zdrój 8–10 Maja 2009*, Rzeszów 2009, p. 59 et seq. In general to the applicability of arbitration clauses to third parties, *see also:* G. Suliński, *Osoba trzecia w arbitrażu handlowym*, Warszawa 2018; A. Budniak-Rogala, *Charakter prawny zapisu na sąd polubowny w postępowaniu cywilnym*, Wrocław 2015.

The provisions of the Polish and German Civil Codes and Codes of Civil Procedure lead to similar legal solutions with reference to the inadmissibility of submitting all future disputes arising in reference to compulsory portions. Therefore, the judgment of the Polish court issuing a decision in the state of facts presented in the BGH case of 16 March 2017 – I ZB 49/16 (OLG München), would be similar to the opinion of the Federal Court of Justice – at least in reference to the main question of the case at hand, i. e. whether it is admissible for the testator to submit all future disputes arising out of his last will, also in reference to compulsory portions, to arbitration. However, the Polish legal system seems to be more conservative than the German one concerning the general admissibility of submitting future disputes to arbitration in a will.

Whereas under German law the testator is allowed to include an arbitration clause referring to issues falling within the scope of freedom to testify in a will, under Polish law it is not admissible since arbitration clauses may only be included in contracts. Therefore, under Polish law it is not possible to include an arbitration clause providing that an arbitral tribunal will decide any possible future disputes arising between the heirs with reference to the compulsory portion by the unilateral decision of a testator in the will.

Bartosz Kucia

§ 9 – The renunciation of an inheritance under a will

Comparative conclusion

Under German law (§ 2352 BGB), a testamentary heir or legatee may, in a contractual agreement with the testator (the future bequeather), renounce the benefit accruing to them under the will (or the succession agreement).[1] A contractual renunciation of the right to an inheritance in respect of both the intestate title or the testamentary appointment to inheritance was permissible under Polish law in the previous legislative framework (§ 10–14 of the Decree on Succession Law of 1945[2]). When the Civil Code of 1964 came into force, the application of this institution was limited to intestate succession only (Article 1048 KC), while in the jurisprudence of the Polish Supreme Court, it was also allowed – despite the lack of any explicit statutory regulation – to limit the agreement to the right to just the compulsory portion.[3] The fact that notarial form is reserved in each of these cases demonstrates the significance of the legal effects of these agreements (§ 2348 BGB, Article 10 § 2 of the Decree, Article 1048 KC).

1 T. Große-Boymann, in: W. Burandt, D. Rojahn (eds.), *Erbrecht*, 2022, § 2352, pt. 3 (the rule concerns a will that has already been drawn up).

2 Journal of Laws of 1946, No 60, item 328.

3 See resolution of SN of 17 March 2017, III CZP 110/16, OSNC 2017, No 12, item 134 with academic glosses of: P. Księżak (Rejent 2017, No 9, p. 124), P. Bender (Rejent 2018, No 5, p. 65), T. Jasiakiewicz (OSP 2018, No 9, item 86), T. Justyński (OSP 2018, No 11, item 109). In contrast, this possibility was allowed *expressis verbis* in Article 10 § 2 Decree on Succession Law and § 2346 II BGB. This rule was reintroduced into the Polish succession law recently under Article 129 pt. 12 of the Act of 26 January 2023 on Family Foundation (Journal of Laws of 2023, item 326) which added § 2 to the Article 1048 KC. Under the new provision the contractual renunciation of inheritance may be limited to the right to a compulsory portion in whole or in part. Importantly, however, the legislature has thus cut through the doctrinal dispute over whether only a part of the compulsory portion may be renounced.

I. Analysis of the case under German law

The commented decision of the BGH of 24 October 1973, IV ZR 3/72[4] is a goldmine of legal issues in the field of agreements for the inheritance after a living person (the future bequeather). It also interprets the concluded settlement (the agreement) in order to determine whether it includes a renunciation of the right to inherit on the basis of a (joint) will drawn up by the testators.

The background to the settlement under assessment concerns a joint matrimonial will drawn up in 1944, in which the spouses appointed each other to the inheritance and appointed three of their joint children as the heirs, after the spouse who would die later. The inheritance included a built-up property that had been destroyed during the Second World War and was subsequently rebuilt using funds of two of the testators' children (acting as claimants), though this issue remained in dispute in the case. In 1959, the parties to the dispute concluded a settlement agreement in which the fact that expenses had been incurred was acknowledged (§ 1 of the settlement agreement) and, in order to settle their mutual claims, the defendant (the daughter of the testators) transferred her share of the inheritance (to which she was entitled as subsequent heir and the heir of her mother) in equal shares to her two siblings (the claimants) for the price of DM 4,000, payable in instalments (§ 2 of the settlement agreement). In the crucial § 3 of the settlement agreement, the defendant renounced the right of intestate succession of her previously deceased father and her mother, to which the latter (also a claimant) agreed. The settlement agreement turned out to be the cause of a dispute that arose 10 years later, when the defendant – invoking the invalidity of the 1959 settlement – did not consent to the donation of the real property to the two remaining siblings by the parties' mother.[5]

The court of first instance (LG) upheld the claim to determine the validity of the 1959 settlement agreement, while the *Oberlandesgericht* amended the judgment under appeal and dismissed the claim, declaring the settlement agreement to be invalid under § 312 section 1 BGB, as the defendant could not dispose of her share in her mother's inheritance during the latter's lifetime. In the *Oberlandesgericht's* opinion, the invalidity of this provision of the settlement agreement resulted in the invalidity of the entire settlement agreement (§ 139 BGB). The invalidity of § 2 did not allow the interpretation that the renouncement of the intestate succession contained in § 3 also covered the appointment to the estate under the will.

In the opinion of the BGH, which examined the appeal against the OLG decision, the possibility that an invalid settlement agreement could be deemed

4 NJW 1974, 43.

5 BGH judgment of 24 October 1973, IV ZR 3/72, NJW 1974, 43 (43–44).

another valid agreement (§140 BGB), in particular an agreement for the renunciation of the defendant daughter's testamentary succession in favour of her siblings (§ 2352 BGB), was not considered in the circumstances of the case. That matter should have been determined in accordance with the intention of the parties at the date of the settlement (which they would have done if they had known that the agreement was invalid), and not by the position already expressed in the course of the subsequent court dispute. According to the findings previously made by the OLG, it was undisputedly the intention of the parties to the settlement agreement that the defendant should renounce all rights to inherit from her parents, which strongly favours the mentioned legal concept.[6]

For this purpose, after the death of her father (in 1949), the defendant transferred her share of his inheritance, falling to her as his testamentary heir, to her siblings. This agreement was judged by the BGH to be admissible, contrary to the agreement made during her mother's lifetime to dispose of the share falling to the defendant after her under the joint will.[7] The effect of the defendant's siblings alone inheriting their mother's estate could, however, have been achieved by an agreement that the defendant would renounce – in favour of her siblings (the beneficiaries) – the inheritance under the joint will, which was also drawn up by and accepted by her mother. In the BGH's persuasive opinion, an agreement of this kind is permissible and constitutes a variant of an agreement to renounce the inheritance as long as the beneficiaries come to the inheritance.[8]

II. Consideration of the problem presented in the German case and its comparison with Polish law

The interpretation of the law presented in the commented decision of the BGH of 24 October 1973, IV ZR 3/72, would not find grounds in the current Polish law provisions, though – despite the lack of a general legal norm – a mechanism of converting an invalid legal act into another valid legal act in compliance with the intentions of the parties to that act (*konwersja*) is commonly recognised.[9] The

6 The BGH even noted that, in light of the circumstances of the case, it can be assumed by the parties involved – as reasonably thinking people – that they would have agreed such a renunciation of the right to inherit in order to achieve the economic success they were striving for, which was the only thing that mattered to them. See BGH judgment of 24 October 1973, IV ZR 3/72, NJW 1974, 43 (45).

7 BGH judgment of 24 October 1973, IV ZR 3/72, NJW 1974, 43 (44).

8 This effect could only occur if the share covered by the renunciation did not fall to the waiving defendant's descendants pursuant to § 2069 BGB, which, however, did not apply in this particular case. See further BGH judgment of 24 October 1973, IV ZR 3/72, NJW 1974, 43 (44).

9 See K. Gandor, *Konwersja nieważnych czynności prawnych*, SC 1963, t. IV, pp. 27 et seq.

current Polish inheritance law does not allow the conclusion of an agreement on the disposal (sale, donation, etc.) of an inheritance (estate) during the testator's lifetime (Article 1051 KC),[10] nor does it recognise an agreement on the renunciation of inheritance under a will to be concluded during the testator's lifetime. Such an agreement would be invalid under Polish law due to the prohibition in Article 1047 KC on agreements on the succession of a living person (*ius cogens*).[11] However, an exception to the above rule is provided for in Articles 1048–1050 KC, under which an agreement to renounce inheritance is limited to the intestate title to inheritance only.[12]

If, pursuant to the rules of private international law, a Polish court were to decide on a case in which the provisions of German law were applicable to a renunciation agreement under a will or an succession agreement (see Articles 5–7 and 9 of the Succession Regulation),[13] there should be no reason for interference from the public policy clause (Article 35 of the Succession Regulation).[14] This thesis is supported by the analysis of the provisions of Article 21 and Article 64 of the Constitution of the Republic of Poland. In light of these provisions, although the legislator is obliged to provide individuals with appropriate instruments enabling them to regulate their property affairs in the event of death, the Constitution leaves the freedom to choose what kind of instruments should be introduced into the statutory law.[15] In the case at hand, it would also be unjustified to consider Article 1047 KC an overriding mandatory provision.

It is worth noting at this point that an agreement on renouncing (the right[16] to) an inheritance, whether under a will or intestate, was allowed in Polish law under

10 See also: W. Chojnowski, *Prawo spadkowe,* Warszawa 1951, p. 39.

11 See W. Borysiak, *Konstrukcja czynności prawnych mortis causa,* PP UW 2006, No 2, p. 12; E. Drozd, *Darowizna na wypadek śmierci,* Rejent 1992, No 1, p. 79. The principle of a closed catalogue of legal transactions *mortis causa* (*numerus clausus*), which is unscripted in Polish law, does not seem – in the absence of an express statutory provision to the contrary – to allow for agreements between the testator and the future legatee (*per damnationem or per vindicationem*) to renounce a testamentary legacy either.

12 W. Hans, *Umowy dotyczące spadku,* np. 1967, No 2, p. 244; F. Błahuta, in: Z. Resich et al. (eds.), *Komentarz KC,* vol. 3, 1972, p. 1988–1989. In the course of drafting the Civil Code, there was talk about abandoning the institution in question altogether, but it was retained eventually. See J. Gwiazdomorski, *Prawo spadkowe,* 1959, p. 76.

13 See Article 25 of the Succession Regulation, as well as: A. Wolak, *Umowa zrzeczenia się dziedziczenia w polskim prawie cywilnym,* Warszawa 2016, pp. 60 et seq.

14 Thus, against the background of the previous legal framework: M. Pazdan, *Umowa o zrzeczenie się dziedziczenia w polskim prawie prywatnym międzynarodowym,* NP 1975, No 5, p. 665; J. Kosik, in: *System prawa cywilnego,* vol. IV, 1986, p. 582.

15 See the judgment of the Constitutional Tribunal of 31 July 2001, P 4/99, OTK 2001/1/5.

16 This wording (referring to a subjective right of a person) was abandoned in the currently applicable Article 1048 KC, as the previous terminology had come under criticism; see J. Gwiazdomorski, *Prawo spadkowe,* 1959, p. 74, footnote 18.

the previously binding Articles 10–14 Decree on Succession Law.[17] It may have taken place pursuant to an agreement concluded in the form of a notarial deed (*ad solemnitatem*) between the future deceased and the future heir renouncing the inheritance (Article 10 § 2 Decree on Succession Law). The renunciation of inheritance could have only take the shape of a contract concluded with the future deceased; a contract for inheritance with another person was invalid.[18] According to this statutory regulation, the future heir did not inherit because of the renunciation;[19] however, the agreement on renouncing the inheritance would only have been effective to the extent that the renouncing future heir had actually been appointed to the inheritance. The heir inherited, however, even if he or she had entered into a contract renouncing the inheritance by virtue of a will, in the event that he or she was appointed to inherit on the basis of a will made after the renunciation (Article 11 § 1 Decree on Succession Law).

Under the 1946 Decree on Succession Law, a contractual renunciation of the right to an inheritance in favour of another person was allowed, though in the event of doubt it was construed as a renunciation subject to a condition that another person came to the inheritance (Article 13 Decree on Succession Law).[20]

17 This decree is now largely of historical value. It has become inoperative with the entry into force of the Civil Code on 1 January 1965. According to the intertemporal norms, it would have to be applied only to successions of anyone who died while it was in force (Article LI of the Act on Introductory Provisions of the Civil Code of 23 April 1964, Journal of Laws of 1964, No 16, item 94), although the law in force at the time when these declarations were made (Article LII) would apply to agreements on the renunciation of inheritance, as to the capacity of individuals, the form and any defects in their declarations.

18 A. Baziński, *Prawo spadkowe. Komentarz*, Łódź 1948, p. 55.

19 This effect was limited to the title to the estate covered by the renunciation only (Article 11 § 2 Decree on Succession Law), and within that scope merely the renouncer was treated as if he had not been alive at the time of opening the estate (Article 12 § 2 of the Decree). See also J. Gwiazdomorski, *Prawo spadkowe*, 1959, p. 78; A. Baziński, *Prawo…*, p. 63. The renunciation of the right to the intestate succession was in principle extended to the descendants of the renouncing party, unless otherwise agreed in the agreement (Article 12 § 1 of the Decree). In contrast, the current German law prescribes a basically identical rule that applies by virtue of the reference to § 2349 BGB (contained in § 2352 BGB) also to agreements on the renunciation of testamentary dispositions – in the previous legal regime, i. e. before 1 January 2010, though that effect was not acceptable, even by analogy. See S. Wegerhoff, in: *Münchener Kommentar*, vol. 11, 2022, § 2352, pt. 13.

20 See J. Pisuliński, *Umowa zrzeczenia się dziedziczenia na korzyść określonej osoby*, in: B. Jelonek-Jarco, R. Kos, J. Zawadzka (eds.), *Usus magister est Optimus. Rozprawy prawnicze ofiarowane profesorowi Andrzejowi Kubasowi*, Warszawa 2016, p. 172, as well as decision of SN of 20 March 1984, III CRN 35/84, OSNC 1984, No 10, item 184. The predominant opinion under the Polish Civil Code so far was that it is acceptable to conclude an agreement to renounce an intestate succession on the condition that another person comes into the inheritance, i.e. with the proviso that the renunciation would be ineffective if the designated person would not be willing or able to inherit. However, outside this framework, it is not legally permissible to designate in a renunciation agreement the person to whom the estate will devolve in lieu of the renouncer, as the agreement is not a title to the estate under the

A similar conditional agreement was accepted in the commented decision of the BGH of 24 October 1973, IV ZR 3/72, in the case of a renunciation agreement relating to the benefit under a will or succession agreement – despite the absence of an explicit statutory provision on this issue (the lack of reference in the relevant provision of § 2352 BGB to § 2350 BGB).[21]

III. Summary

An agreement to renounce a share in the decedent's estate or legacy plays a role under German law, especially in the case of dispositions that are not freely revocable, such as those arising from joint wills or inheritance agreements. The commented decision of the BGH of 24 October 1973, IV ZR 3/72, provides a convenient example of its application.[22] Only the introduction of these institutions into the Polish legal order would constitute systemic justification for the reinstatement of the agreements on renunciation of inheritance under a will. The niche for the application of the institution in question in the case of wills that cannot be revoked due to the testator's incapacity,[23] that is recognised in German literature, could instead be filled by alternative and simpler instruments (e.g. by allowing the revocation of a will before the court).

Polish succession law. See the resolution of SN of 5 February 1993, III CZP 10/93, OSNC 1993, No 9, item 147, as well as: W. Hans, *Umowy…*, p. 244; A. Oleszko, *Umowy dotyczące spadku w praktyce notarialnej*, NP 1977, No 6, p. 845; J. Kosik, in: *System prawa cywilnego*, vol. IV, 1986, p. 584; E. Skowrońska, *Glosa do uchwały Sądu Najwyższego z 5.02.1993 r., III CZP 10/93*, OSP 1994, No 5, item 83, p. 217–218; M. Pazdan, in: K. Pietrzykowski (ed.), *Komentarz KC*, vol. II, 2021, Article 1048, pt. 25–27; M. Pazdan, *Umowa o zrzeczenie się dziedziczenia w polskim prawie spadkowym*, Rejent 1997, No 4, pp. 192–193; I. Kozak, *Umowa o zrzeczenie się dziedziczenia*, PS 2004, No 11–12, p. 83; P. Księżak, *Prawo spadkowe*, Warszawa 2017, p. 471; A. Wolak, *Umowa…*, p. 150–151; W. Borysiak, in: K. Osajda, W. Borysiak (eds.), *Komentarz KC* 2022, Article 1048, pt. 66; J. Pisuliński, *Umowa…*, p. 174. On the contrary: J. Pietrzykowski, in: Z. Resich et al. (eds.), *Komentarz KC*, vol. 3, 1972, p. 1988. Article 129 pt. 12 of the Act on Family Foundation, reintroduced – by adding Article 1048 § 3 KC – a provision with wording similar to Article 13 Decree on Succession Law although unlike the latter provision, a contract for the renunciation of inheritance under a will is still not permitted under Articles 1048–1050 KC.

21 See also: J. Pisuliński, *Umowa…*, p. 171, footnote 34.

22 S. Wegerhoff, in: *Münchener Kommentar*, vol. 11, 2022, § 2352, pt. 2; T. Große-Boymann, in: W. Burandt, D. Rojahn (eds.), *Erbrecht*, 2022, § 2352, pt. 1.

23 S. Wegerhoff, in: *Münchener Kommentar*, vol. 11, 2022, § 2352, pt. 2. The renunciation agreement may then be concluded by his legal representative with the approval of the guardianship court (§ 2347 II BGB). See T. Große-Boymann, in: W. Burandt, D. Rojahn (eds.), *Erbrecht*, 2022, § 2352, pt. 6.

Paulina Gwoździewicz-Matan

§ 10 – Legal qualification of contributions related to a renunciation of an inheritance and/or a compulsory portion

Comparative conclusion
When legally qualifying a financial contribution related to the renunciation of an inheritance and/or a compulsory portion, the intentions of the parties concluding the contract (the future heir and the future testator) should be taken into account. It cannot be ruled out *a priori* that the contribution is free of charge. In these arrangements, it may be helpful to analyse the intentions of the parties as to the free of charge nature of the contribution, the circumstances of concluding the contract and its individual form, and whether the amount of the contribution approximately corresponds to the expected share of the inheritance, or whether it exceeds that share.

I. Analysis of an example case under German law

The issue of qualifying contributions related to the renunciation of an inheritance and/or a compulsory portion was the subject of the BGH judgment of 7 July 2015 in case X ZR 59/13.[1]

The judgment was issued based on the following facts. On 29 January 2008, an agreement was concluded between the father (the claimant) and a daughter from the first marriage (the defendant). The agreement was composed of several stages: an "indirect" real estate donation agreement (the transfer of money in order to purchase real estate and shares in two other apartments) (*mittelbare Grundbesitzschenkung*), where the parties agreed that the donated money was an indirect donation of real estate; then an inheritance contract (including giving the defendant shares in the co-ownership of apartments purchased with the donated funds) (*Erbvertrag*); and finally an agreement on renouncing statutory inheritance and a compulsory portion subject to the performance of the donation and inheritance agreement (*Erb- und Pflichtteilsverzicht*). The defendant initially lived with her daughter in the co-owned apartments (in which she had acquired shares). After two years, she moved in with her current husband. The claimant

1 NJW 2016, 324.

then cancelled the donation due to the blatant ingratitude of the defendant, consisting in concealing her financial situation. He argued that the defendant had not disclosed to him the maintenance payments from the father of the claimant's granddaughter and had thus simulated the need that prompted him to provide his daughter and granddaughter with housing and financial support. Moreover, in the claimant's opinion, the defendant made it impossible to rent an apartment under the contract, she was obliged to rent a flat to her father for thirty years) and prevented the claimant from contacting his granddaughter. The claimant demanded the return of the shares in ownership of the apartments, which he claimed to have given to his daughter (§ 530 BGB). The doubts arose out of the cancellation of the donation agreement to the remaining elements of a mixed agreement concluded in this way (or a bundle of agreements).

The court of first instance rejected the case, as did the court of second instance. The latter (OLG München) took the view that the agreement was mixed and could be classified as a mutual agreement. In the justification of its judgment, OLG München excluded the possibility of formulating a claim for the return of benefits on the basis of unjust enrichment due to the failure to achieve the purpose of the benefit. It assumed that the classification of the contributions to the defendant as donations were excluded, as the defendant had waived not only the compulsory portion, but also the statutory right of inheritance. However, the BGH judged otherwise. The BGH assumed that the renunciation of the compulsory portion is not consideration for the benefit made in connection with it, because – from the perspective of potential creditors' – the debtor only transfers the object from his assets, but does not acquire anything that the creditors can enforce. This position, taken in the context of assessing the *actio pauliana* (Anfechtungsgesetz), can be attributed a general value. A contract to waive an inheritance is often tied to another contract, such as a donation. However, this does not mean that the second contract should be considered dependent. Finally, the related contract is not treated as a *causa* of the inheritance renunciation contract. This is, at best, a motive for the conclusion of the inheritance waiver agreement, which cannot affect the validity of the agreement. On the other hand, the mutual influence of contracts on each other may result from contractual clauses agreed by the parties themselves.

II. Consideration of the problem presented in the German case and its comparison with Polish law

An inheritance renunciation agreement is how a potential heir waives their right to an inheritance. Practice shows that the renunciation of an inheritance is often "accompanied" by the conclusion of another agreement, such as a donation agreement, in favour of the renouncing party in which the renouncing party receives "remuneration" from the testator. Moreover, it is often done in the same notarial deed. Hence, one of the essential aspects of concluding an agreement to renounce an inheritance (or an agreement to renounce the right to a compulsory portion) is the issue of its connection with the other contract accompanying the renunciation. A detailed analysis of this issue of the commented judgment should be preceded by a few remarks.

Firstly, both legal systems allow for the conclusion of contracts renouncing an inheritance (Article 1049 KC and § 2346 BGB), which must be in the form of a notarial deed.[2] However, unlike the German regulation, the Polish Civil Code, at the time of writing this article[3], did not regulate the possibility of waiving only the right to a compulsory portion (discussed in § 13)[4] or the possibility of a partial waiver. In addition, under Polish law the agreement on renunciation of an inheritance is limited only to intestate succession.[5] Secondly, apart from the indicated catalogue of disputes in the context of Polish regulations, there are also differences in the legal nature of the agreement on renouncing an inheritance.[6] Under the German law, it may be classified as a reciprocal (§ 320 BGB, and that was the way followed by the court of second instance in the analysed judgment), payable and abstract contract.[7] In Polish law, it is not treated at all in terms of

2 See Article 1048 KC and § 2352 BGB.

3 According to the Act on Family Foundation of 26 January 2023, which came into force on May 22, 2023, waiving the right only to a compulsory portion is explicitly provided. See footnote 4, p. 149.

4 See also § 13 of this monograph.

5 There is no need to renounce a testamentary succession, as in Polish law a will may always be revoked by the testator (Article 943 KC). The inability to renounce a testamentary succession is justified by the fact that Polish law has no legal actions that create a legal succession (e. g. joint wills, inheritance agreements). This aspect is mentioned by W. Borysiak, in: K. Osajda (ed.), *Komentarz KC*, vol. IVA, 2019, pt. 44.

6 Both in Polish and German literature, it is assumed that an agreement on renouncing inheritance is not a binding agreement, because neither party to such an agreement undertakes to perform a service for the other party (see W. Borysiak, in: K. Osajda (ed.), *Komentarz KC*, vol. IVA, 2019, Article 1048, pt. 10; G. Schotten, in: *Staudingers Kommentar*, vol. 5 (§§ 2346–2385), 2010, p. 15.

7 A detailed analysis of the inheritance renunciation agreement in German law was made in Polish literature by J. Pisuliński, *Zrzeczenie się dziedziczenia w prawie niemieckim*, Rejent 1999, No 12; See also A. Oleszko, *Umowy dotyczące spadku w praktyce notarialnej*, NP 1977, No

contributing contracts (which is why it does not fall under the classification of abstract or causal contracts), and is not considered a mutual or payable agreement (unless the agreement and circumstances indicate such intent).[8]

In the analysed case – as pointed out by OLG München (the court of second instance) – the agreement between the parties, referred to in the notarised contract as an "indirect donation agreement", should not be qualified as a donation within the meaning of § 516 section 1 BGB.[9] "The defendant, by waiving inheritance, made a consideration in synallagmatic (equivalent) relation to the transfer of ownership of shares in the real estate in dispute. If the renunciation of the inheritance, as in the disputed case, is not made free of charge, but in return for consideration, then the renunciation of inheritance and this consideration are elements of a bilateral legal relationship / transaction, which in turn includes the testator's obligation to perform the mutual service. Such a legal act would be – unlike a legal act to perform an obligation [executing / disposing of a legal act] – a counter-contract within the meaning of §§ 320 et seq. BGB, which is carried out by two independent legal actions of performance of the obligation (agreement for the waiver of inheritance and mutual transfer of ownership).

"The issue of qualifying the waiver of inheritance or compulsory portion as consideration (*Gegenleistung*) in exchange for a donation is disputed in German literature. According to one of the views,[10] it is a contract for pecuniary interest, in which a distinction is made depending on whether the right to the inheritance or only the right to a compulsory portion has been waived. The calculation of the compulsory portion pursuant to § 2310 sentence 1 BGB is a pecuniary act, and in the latter case it is an unpaid legal act."[11]

OLG München (the court of second instance) shared this view in the analysed case. Some authors defend the view that, in the event of a renunciation of inheritance in exchange for another benefit, in principle, the payment of a legal transaction should be assumed, but that an evident disproportion between the mutual benefit and the expected inheritance share – a "mixed donation" (par-

6, p. 841. In German literature, cf. J. Damrau, in: Soergel, *Kommentar zum Bürgerlichen Gesetzbuch*, Band 9, Erbrecht, Stuttgart-Berlin-Köln 1992, p. 1861), and it is also stated that it may be based on a binding legal act (schuldrechtliches Grundgeschäft), see R. Stürner, in: O. Jauernig (ed.), *Bürgerliches Gesetzbuch*, München 1991, p. 1891 (quoted after M. Pazdan, in: *System prawa prywatnego*, vol. 10, 2015, p. 1139).

8 The view expressed by M. Pazdan, in: *System prawa prywatnego*, vol. 10, 2015, pp. 1138–1139. See A. Oleszko, *Umowy…*, p. 843.

9 This article reads: "A disposition by means of which someone enriches another person from his own assets is a donation if both parties are in agreement that the disposition occurs gratuitously."

10 See U. Simon, in: H.P. Westermann et al. (eds.), *Erman Bürgerliches Gesetzbuch. Band 2*, Köln 2014, § 2346, pt. 6.

11 See M. Zimmer, *Anmerkung zu BGH, Urteil vom 3. 12. 2008 –IV ZR 58/07*, NJW 2009, p. 1146.

tially paid, partially free of charge) should be accepted.[12] According to yet another approach, the legal classification should be decided on the circumstances of each individual case or the intention of the parties to the contract. Finally, some authors assume that consideration awarded in response to a renunciation of inheritance, without waiving any other obligations, is an objectively gratuitous donation of the testator to the relinquishing party.[13]

On the other hand, the BGH judgments qualifying this type of subsidy contain references to two types of situations. First, it was analysed whether these increases could be challenged under the act on *Actio pauliana* (Anfechtungsgesetz, Avoidance Act).[14] A waiver of a compulsory portion is not deemed consideration for a benefit made in connection with it, since, from the creditors' point of view, the debtor only gives away something already in its assets, but does not acquire anything that the creditors can enforce. Only when an equivalent value has objectively flowed into the debtor's assets are there any grounds to examine whether the parties involved viewed this as consideration, or whether the debtor's contribution was intended to be free of charge. A similar view on the inability of creditors to recognise a waiver of inheritance agreement as ineffective pursuant to Articles 527–534 KC was expressed in Polish literature.[15]

Secondly, the legal qualification of benefits made in connection with the waiver was analysed in terms of their impact on the claim to supplement the compulsory portion.[16] With regard to the question of whether compensation granted for a waiver of inheritance is subject to the augmentation of the compulsory portion according to § 2325 section 1 BGB, the BGH does not consider it decisive whether the mutual consideration is to be viewed as paid or unpaid. In any case, the augmentation of the compulsory portion is only subject to what goes beyond remuneration or adequate compensation for the waiver of inheritance. In order to decide whether this was the case, the person entitled to a compulsory portion could rely on the simplification of evidence recognised in the case law in connection with mixed donations, whereby a donation is to be

12 See J. Damrau, in: T. Soergel (ed.), *Bürgerliches Gesetzbuch mit Einführungsgesetz und Nebengesetzen: BGB*, Band 23: Erbrecht 3, § 2346 BGB, Stuttgart 2002, pt. 3; M. Zimmer, *Anmerkung…*, p. 1146.

13 G. Schotten, in: *Staudingers Kommentar*, vol. 5 (§§ 2346–2385), 2010, § 2346, pt. 124–140.

14 BGH, Urteil vom 28. Februar-1991 – IX ZR 74/90, BGHZ 113, 393.

15 See M. Pazdan, in: *System prawa prywatnego,* vol. 10, 2015, p. 1139. See also the foreign literature on this issue cited by the author: in Austrian law cf. F. Gschnitzer, Ch. Faistenberger, *Österreichisches Erbrecht*, Wien–New York 1983, p. 53; B. Eccher, in: M. Schwimann (ed.), *Praxiskommentar zum Allgemeinen Bürgerlichen Gesetzbuch, Band 3*, Wien 1989, p. 46. In German law, see J. Damrau, *Bürgerliches Gesetzbuch, Band 9, Erbrecht*, Stuttgart-Berlin-Köln 1992, p. 1861.

16 BGH, judgment of 3 December–2008 – IV ZR 58/07, NJW 2009, 1143, pt. 16.

presumed if there is an objective and significant disproportion between performance and consideration.[17]

As for the classification of the contract under Polish law, a contract on a waiver of inheritance is generally assumed to be independent by nature, even if the contract is combined with other contracts (e.g. with a donation contract). A renunciation of inheritance does not constitute a *causa* for the donation contract and does not replace the *causa* characteristic for this contract, even if – according to the intention of the parties – the donation is to constitute compensation for the renunciation of inheritance. The renunciation of inheritance then acts only as a motive for the donation contract.[18] In short, unless the parties have agreed otherwise, a donation may not be called into question merely because its motive to renounce an inheritance has failed. The donor (testator) may not demand the return of what was testified to the renouncing heir.

A suitable illustration here can be found in the judgment of the Provincial Administrative Court in Łódź in the judgment of 9 October 2007 I SA / Łd 692/07[19]. In this case, the tax authorities had interpreted the provisions of an agreement in terms of whether or not its subject was subject to inheritance and donation tax.[20] On the basis of the agreement, a mother transferred a certain amount of money to the joint property of her son and his wife, and the son renounced the inheritance from his mother. In the opinion of the tax authorities, the parties concluded a paid inheritance waiver agreement, which was invalid as it was not in the form of a notarial deed, as required by the law (Article 1048 KC). However, in the opinion of the Provincial Administrative Court examining the complaint, the contract comprised two legal actions: a donation agreement and an agreement on renouncing an inheritance. Due to the failure to observe the appropriate form, the son's declaration on the renunciation of inheritance is invalid and has no legal effects. However, as the court rightly assessed, this does not affect the validity of the remaining provisions of the contract, and therefore the performed donation contract remains valid. The son's obligation cannot be treated as equivalent to the donor's performance. It is unacceptable to interpret a legal transaction in which an invalid provision of a contract is treated as a condition for its conclusion.

17 BGH, NJW 2009, 1143, 17.

18 It may go beyond this role only if the parties introduce appropriate reservations to the donation agreement (e.g. a termination condition binding legal effects with the fact that the resigning heir did not survive the testator or was deemed unworthy). See, M. Pazdan, *System prawa prywatnego*, vol. 10, 2015, p. 1139.

19 LEX No. 437726.

20 According to the Succession and Donation Tax Law of 28 July 1983 (Journal of Laws 2021, item 1043).

There is also an opinion in the literature that it is possible to link a contract of inheritance waiver with another contract, if this is the parties' intention.[21] Therefore, in a situation where the future testator undertakes to make a gratuitous contribution to the other party (a statutory heir), who in turn undertakes to renounce the inheritance, then the provisions on obligations under mutual agreements should be applied accordingly (Articles 487–497 KC).[22] In each such case, the intention of the parties and the circumstances of concluding the contract should be examined, as was recommended by the BGH in the analysed judgment. As the BGH properly pointed out, the court of second instance had failed to determine the parties' intentions. It had relied solely on the fact that the defendant had waived not only the right to a compulsory portion, but also inheritance.

III. Summary

To sum up, the position adopted by the BGH should be assessed as being fully correct. As for the grounds for annulling the judgment and referring the case back to the court of first instance for reconsideration, the BGH rightly ordered that the specific circumstances accompanying the conclusion of the contract should be examined. In the opinion of the court, it was necessary to take into account, among other things, the fact that the notarial deed explicitly referred to the donation and that the waiver of inheritance was included only in the third part of the contract. In the opinion of the court, it is also important that the claimant's benefit was to be used only for a specific purpose (for the purchase of a flat): "This alone suggests that the claimant was not primarily interested in obtaining the waiver of inheritance by the defendant, but rather in transferring the defendant's property to support and protect her and her daughter in a difficult financial situation." The combination of the donation with the requirement to use the money to buy a living space also suggests that it is a donation. If the claimant was primarily interested in the renunciation of inheritance, it would have been more appropriate to make the contribution without any conditions.

21 This view was expressed by M. Pazdan, in: *System prawa prywatnego*, vol. 10, 2015, p. 1139; see also E. Rott-Pietrzyk, *Umowa o zrzeczenie się dziedziczenia – uwagi de lege lata i de lege ferenda*, Rejent 2006, No 3, pp. 105–119; G. Wolak in: M. Habdas, M. Fras (eds.), *Komentarz KC*, vol. VI, 2019, p. 860.

22 This view is criticised by W. Borysiak, in: K. Osajda (ed.), *Komentarz KC*, vol. IVA, 2019, Article 1048, pt. 18, who draws attention to the difficulties related to applying the provisions on withdrawal from the contract by a person who has renounced an inheritance, substitute performance or provisions on liability for damages under such contracts.

As the BGH noted, the parties did not consider the defendant's inheritance waiver as the main benefit for which the claimant's contribution would be due as consideration. The parties concluded an inheritance contract containing the claimant's clause in favour of the defendant in the second part of the contract, i.e. before the inheritance was renounced, and therefore the contract also includes a *mortis causa* disposition. Despite the renunciation of inheritance, the notarial agreement not only did not exclude the possibility of the defendant claiming an inheritance, but explicitly included this possibility. This could also indicate that the amounts awarded were not intended as remuneration for renouncing the inheritance, but that the waiver of the inheritance and the compulsory portion were only intended to serve as a compensatory measure.

Wojciech Bańczyk / Katarzyna Południak-Gierz

§ 11 – Inheritance renunciation contract conditional on the transfer of the future estate

Comparative conclusion
German law allows for a wide range of contractual arrangements affecting the future estate that, taken together, may help families reach harmony in post-mortem financial arrangements. This includes: the inheritance contract, the inheritance renunciation contract and the contract regarding the future estate between the future statutory heirs (which may be a condition of the inheritance renunciation contract as well as other benefits). Polish law allows only for the second of these contracts, namely the inheritance renunciation contract (which may be under a condition (including a benefit) that fulfils before the death of the person after whom the party to the contract was to inherit the estate, so may not regard a future estate). At the same time, even the available options of German law will not always solve the problem of family conflicts if not properly utilised, as the judgment shows.

I. Analysis of an example case under German law

According to the analysed BGH judgment of 23 November 1994 in case IV ZR 238/93,[1] three contracts were concluded between the family members, including two siblings being the only children of the deceased (later parties to the proceedings) and the deceased. Firstly, one of the siblings (later the claimant) and the deceased concluded a notarial inheritance renunciation contract (*Erbverzichtsvertrag*, § 2346 section 1 sentence 1 BGB). Secondly, immediately after, the other sibling (later the defendant) and the deceased concluded a notarial inheritance contract based on which the defendant became the sole heir (*Erbvertrag*, see § 2274 and subsequent BGB), but was burdened with two legacies in favour of the sons of the sibling (later the claimants). Thirdly, the siblings supposedly concluded also a third contract, this time an oral contract, regarding the future estate (*Erbschaftsvertrag*, § 311b section 5 sentence 1 BGB, earlier § 312 section 2 sentence 1 BGB) according to which the defendant was obliged to pay the claimant half of the value of the estate, diminished by the legacies in favour of

1 NJW 1995, 448.

her son. This is the only admissible type of contract regarding future estate in German law (which is generally prohibited, § 311b section 4 sentence 1 BGB, earlier § 312 section 1 BGB). In the case brought before court, the claimant demanded payment of the sum resulting from the third contract.

German law recognises many contracts influencing the creation of inheritance, most of which were used in the facts of the analysed case. Thus, German law favours the equal treatment *(Gleichbehandlung)* of statutory heirs to that extent that the deceased may achieve such equality in many ways under various contractual arrangements expressing his last will *(letzte Wille)* to fully consider the position of the statutory heirs versus their varied lifetime situations.[2] In particular, the deceased may conclude an inheritance renunciation contract (a statutory heir waives their status as an heir) and an inheritance contract (a person is granted the status of an heir). The reason behind such agreements may be, for example, a separate contract between the future statutory heirs regarding the future estate.[3]

All three types of contracts must be concluded in the presence of a notary.[4] This form requirement applies throughout the entire contractual combination of three contracts aimed at the creation of an inheritance.[5]

In particular, German law provides far-reaching requirements regarding the justification and form of the contract of transfer of future estate. Generally, a contract regarding the future estate of a still living third party is invalid (§ 311b section 4 sentence 1 BGB). The aim of this norm is to protect a future heir from reckless wealth disposal *(leichtsinnige Vermögensverschleuderung)*, and to protect the deceased from morally improper speculation *(sittlich verwerflich Spekulation)* on their death and from the subjective limitation of their testamentary freedom *(subjective Einschränkung der Testiersfreiheit)*.[6] The participation of the deceased in such a contract does not cure its invalidity,[7] though it could possibly

2 Judgment IV ZR 238/93, pt. 2a.

3 Judgment IV ZR 238/93, pt. 2a.

4 The form of notarial deed is required for both the inheritance renunciation contract (§ 2348 BGB), and for contract regarding future estate (§ 311b section 5 sentence 2 BGB), whereas, according to the first sentence of § 2276 section 1 BGB, the inheritance contract needs to be recorded by a notary in the simultaneous presence of both parties.

5 No 2.b of the justification of the analysed judgment.

6 See also in the doctrine M. Gehrlein, in: W. Hau, R. Poseck (eds.), *BeckOK BGB*, 2021, § 311b, pt. 46; S. Ruhwinkel, in: *Münchener Kommentar*, vol. 3, 2019, § 311b, pt. 122. Sometimes the judicature and doctrine underline mostly the protection from reckless wealth disposal and morally improper speculation – judgment of Bundesgerichtshof from 4 July 1962, V ZR 14/61, BGHZ 37, 319, No I; judgment of Bundesgerichtshof of 11 May 1988, IVa ZR 325/86, BGHZ 104, 279; A. Stadler, in: *Jauernig BGB Kommentar*, 2021, § 311b, pt. 57; M. Fries, R. Schulze, in: R. Schulze (ed.), *BGB Kommentar*, 2021, § 311b, pt. 35.

7 See also the judgment of Bundesgerichtshof from 11.5.1988, IVa ZR 325/86; S. Ruhwinkel, in: *Münchener Kommentar*, vol. 3, 2019, § 311b, No 137.

be argued that if that person is present during the conclusion of agreements regarding their future estate, they would be able to protect their own interests. In addition, it is irrelevant whether or not the aim of the contract was improper;[8] the contract is invalid even if its aim was commonly acceptable (e.g. achieving equality of heirs).[9]

At the same time, § 311b section 5 sentence 1 BGB allows for a contract regarding the estate to be concluded between the future statutory heirs. This is justified by the need to settle financial matters in advance.[10] Such a contract is allowed only exceptionally: if concluded between future statutory heirs including statutory heirs who waived their inheritance.[11]

Such contracts regarding the estate between the future statutory heirs must be concluded in the form of a notarial deed (§ 311b section 5 sentence 2 BGB). This requirement cannot be substituted by the participation of the deceased in the conclusion of the contract. The reason behind this is to ensure the professional advice of a notary. Such advice cannot be provided by the deceased, whose interests might contradict the interests of the parties to such a contract.[12] Even in the analysed case, the contract regarding the future estate is supposedly connected with the inheritance renunciation contract and the inheritance contract; it regards the future estate and regulates far-reaching rights and duties of the parties to this contract who need advice from a notary.

In addition, apart from argumentation based on the explicit wording of the applicable law, since this contract supposedly does not endanger the interests of the deceased (though such danger can appear in the context of the contract specified in § 311b section 4 BGB), it is irrelevant whether the deceased knew and approved the contract regarding the future estate. Thus, the validity of the contract of this type does not depend on its actual aim.[13]

In German law, an inheritance renunciation contract may be (and, in fact, often is) connected with granting a benefit *(Abfindung)* for the waiving party, and receiving such a benefit may be a condition of such renunciation. This economic justification of the inheritance renunciation contract may (but does not have to) take the form of a legal relation with the deceased.[14] In particular,

8 The judgment cites the commentary of Wufka, in: Staudinger in this context. See also M. Gehrlein, in: W. Hau, R. Poseck (eds.), *BeckOK BGB,* 2021, § 311b, pt. 50.
9 Judgment IV ZR 238/93, pt. 2b.aa.
10 A. Stadler, in: *Jauernig BGB Kommentar,* 2021, § 311b, pt. 63.
11 No 2.b of the justification of the analysed judgment. See also M. Fries, R. Schulze, in: R. Schulze (ed.), *BGB Kommentar,* 2021, § 311b, pt. 39; S. Ruhwinkel, in: *Münchener Kommentar,* vol. 3, 2019, § 311b, pt. 137; A. Stadler, in: *Jauernig BGB Kommentar,* 2021, § 311b, pt. 64.
12 Judgment IV ZR 238/93, pt. 2.b.bb.
13 Judgment IV ZR 238/93, pt. 2.b.aa.
14 Judgment IV ZR 238/93, pt. 2.a.

such a benefit could also be granted through a contract on the transfer of the future estate.[15]

As above, the inheritance renunciation may be conditional, and the condition may be fulfilled also after death of the deceased. In that case, the position of the waiving party is the same as for preliminary or subsequent heirship (*Vor-* or *Nacherbschaft*).[16]

Therefore, the validity of the contractual benefit arrangement *(Abfindungsvereinbarung)*[17] or the effectiveness of the benefit transfer *(Abfindungsleistung)*[18] may also be conditions of an inheritance renunciation contract. Such a condition does not have to result from the explicit wording of the inheritance renunciation contract: the contract may be interpreted as conditional (§ 133, § 157 BGB) even if the wording of the inheritance renunciation contract lays the groundwork for such an interpretation.[19] Thus, an inheritance renunciation contract whose wording does not give rise to an interpretation in favour of such a condition should never be deemed to be conditional.

The contract regarding the future estate in the analysed case could not have created exchange benefit contractual arrangement due to its invalidity as per lack of form. As a result, the condition of the effectiveness of the inheritance renunciation contract (if any was included: the inheritance renunciation contract appeared to lack even a starting point for an interpretation in favour of such a condition) is not fulfilled.

A condition for the transfer of the benefit in inheritance renunciation contracts can be shaped in two ways. Firstly, the benefit transfer itself may meet the condition. In such cases where a donation contract is invalid due to the form deficiency, making such a free of charge benefit may cure the donation according to § 518 section 2 BGB (by means of performance). Alternatively, a contractual benefit arrangement does not yet fulfil the condition of the benefit transfer. Secondly, the contractual benefit arrangement condition may be fulfilled when a valid contract is concluded: the actual performance of the obligations arising from this contract could be seen as irrelevant.

In the analysed case, if we assume that the inheritance renunciation contract was conditional, the condition was that a contractual benefit arrangement needs to be concluded (this understanding of the legal act at hand is justified given the

15 Judgment IV ZR 238/93, pt. 2b.bb.

16 W. Litzenburger, in: W. Hau, R. Poseck (eds.), *BeckOK BGB*, 2021, § 2346, pt. 45; S. Wegerhoff, in: *Münchener Kommentar*, vol. 11, 2020, § 2346, pt. 28.

17 S. Wegerhoff, in: *Münchener Kommentar*, vol. 11, 2020, § 2346, pt. 28.

18 W. Litzenburger, in: W. Hau, R. Poseck (eds.), *BeckOK BGB*, 2021, § 2346, pt. 45.

19 S. Wegerhoff, in: *Münchener Kommentar* vol. 11, 2020, § 2346, pt. 29; also on 133 and 157, but with no further-reaching demand of reference point W. Litzenburger, in: W. Hau, R. Poseck (eds.), *BeckOK BGB*, 2021, § 2346, pt. 45.

combination of contracts among the parties and the deceased). However, the contract regarding the future estate was invalid, and consequently the condition of the inheritance renunciation contract (if any) was not fulfilled. Though in that case, no such condition was effectively included.

II. Consideration of the problem presented in the German case and its comparison with Polish law

Polish law allows for a far narrower scope of admissible contracts influencing the creation of inheritance. Inheritance renunciation contracts are allowed under Polish law (Article 1048 KC). At the same time, they are the only admissible contracts regarding a future estate (Article 1047 KC). This prohibition renders the contracts concluded between future statutory heirs,[20] other than inheritance renunciation contracts, invalid. In particular, inheritance contracts are forbidden, and the status of an heir may only be granted by the statute or through a last will (Article 926 KC).

In particular, Polish law prohibits contracts on the transfer of a future estate. Such a broad prohibition on contracts transferring a future estate in Polish law is justified by the extensive protection of testamentary freedom of the deceased. As a result, the main role of the prohibition is to prevent the conclusion of an inheritance contract that could bind the deceased with an already made disposition *mortis causa.*[21] At the same time, it is supposed to minimise the risk that a person entitled to another's estate *mortis causa* would undertake some actions to cause the other's death.[22] No counter-interests are protected; for example, under Polish law, it is not possible to settle financial matters among close family members by concluding a contract similar to the one specified in § 311b section 5 sentence 1 BGB.

Despite the limited impact of contracts on inheritance under Polish law, inheritance renunciation contracts play an important role in practice. Under Polish law (as in German law), they are commonly connected with a contractual benefit, in order to achieve a just division of assets among family members.[23] This effect,

---

20 E. Skowrońska-Bocian, J. Wierciński, in: J. Gudowski (ed.), *Komentarz KC,* vol. VI, 2017, Article 1047, pt. 3, LEX.

21 W. Borysiak, in: K. Osajda, W. Borysiak (eds.), *Komentarz KC,* 2020, ed. 26, Article 1047, pt. 3, Legalis.

22 W. Borysiak, in: K. Osajda, W. Borysiak (eds.), *Komentarz KC,* 2020, ed. 26, Article 1047, pt. 4, Legalis; R. Longchamps de Berier, *Zobowiązania,* Lwów 1938, p. 148; M. Niedośpiał, *Czynności prawa spadkowego,* Przegląd Prawa i Administracji 1995, No XXXIII, p. 89.

23 Resolution of SN of 5 February 1993, III CZP 10/93, OSNCP 1993, No 9, item 147; A. Doliwa, in: *System prawa prywatnego,* vol. 10, 2015 p. 924–925; J. Kosik, in: *System prawa cywilnego,*

however, may not be achieved by concluding a contract regarding the future estate, but rather by donations, for example.

The relation of both such contracts (inheritance renunciation and benefit exchange for the waiving party) is often agreed as conditional.[24] The inheritance renunciation contract may be concluded on a condition, but the latter can only be fulfilled before the death of the person after whom the estate is inherited, so that at the moment of death it is certain who the heir is.[25] This reflects the limited admissibility of a condition in Polish inheritance law (according to Article 962 sentence 3 KC, the reservation of a condition made in the appointment of a testamentary heir will be considered non-existent unless the condition was satisfied or remained definitively unsatisfied before the death of the testator). In that case, the benefit being the condition of the inheritance renunciation contract will also have to be transferred at the moment of the death of the deceased at latest.

Furthermore, such a condition does not have to be included in the wording of the last will, but may be the subject of interpretation as long as the interpretation does not inadmissibly supplement the content of the last will.[26] The German argumentation in this regard is explicitly referred to in the Polish legal doctrine.[27]

vol. IV, 1986, p. 585; M. Pazdan, *Umowa o zrzeczenie się dziedziczenia w polskim prawie spadkowym*, Rejent 1997, No 4, pp. 185–186; J.St. Piątowski, B. Kordasiewicz, *Prawo spadkowe*, Warszawa 2011, p. 63; G. Wolak, *Umowa zrzeczenia się dziedziczenia w polskim prawie spadkowym*, Warszawa 2016, p. 16.

24 W. Borysiak in ed. K. Osajda, W. Borysiak (eds.), *Komentarz KC*, 2020, ed. 26, Article 1048, pt. 14–15, Legalis; M. Pazdan, *Umowa …*, p. 188.

25 J. Pisuliński, *Umowa zrzeczenia się dziedziczenia na korzyść określonej osoby*, in: B. Jelonek-Jarco, R. Kos, J. Zawadzka (eds.), *Usus magister est optimus. Rozprawy prawnicze ofiarowane Profesorowi Andrzejowi Kubasowi*, Warszawa 2016, p. 174–175; B. Swaczyna, *Warunkowe czynności prawne*, Warszawa 2012, p. 193; also W. Bańczyk, *Pozaspadkowe sposoby kształtowania następstwa na wypadek śmierci – o przełamaniu monopolu prawa spadkowego*, Kraków 2021 (unpublished doctoral thesis), p. 596. More generally, about an admissible condition – W. Borysiak, in: K. Osajda, W. Borysiak (eds.), *Komentarz KC*, 2020, Article 1048, pt. 14–15, Legalis; J. Ciszewski, J. Knabe, in: ed. J. Ciszewski, P. Nazaruk (eds.), *Komentarz KC*, 2019, Article 1048, pt. 7, LEX; A. Doliwa, in: *System prawa prywatnego*, vol. 10, 2015, p. 926; J. Kosik, in: *System prawa cywilnego*, vol. IV, 1986, p. 585; I. Kozak, *Umowa o zrzeczenie się dziedziczenia*, PS 2004, No 11–12, p. 79; K. Mularski, in: M. Gutowski (ed.), *Komentarz KC*, vol. III, 2019, Article 1048, pt. 11, Legalis; E. Niezbecka, in: A. Kidyba (ed.), *Komentarz KC*, vol. IV, 2015, Article 1048, pt. 7; J.St. Piątowski, B. Kordasiewicz, *Prawo …*, p. 64; E. Rott-Pietrzyk, *Umowa o zrzeczenie się dziedziczenia – uwagi de lege lata i de lege ferenda*, Rejent 2006, No 3, p. 114; G. Wolak, *Umowa …*, p. 150. Against J. Pietrzykowski in ed. Z. Resich et al. (eds.), *Komentarz KC*, vol. 3, Warszawa 1972, p. 1988; L. Stecki, in: J. Winiarz (ed.), *Kodeks cywilny z komentarzem*, Warszawa 1980, p. 903.

26 S. Wójcik, F. Zoll, in: *System prawa prywatnego*, vol. 10, 2015, p. 440; M. Zelek, in: M. Gutowski (ed.), *Komentarz KC*, vol. III, 2019, Article. 962, pt. 5, Legalis.

27 S. Wójcik, F. Zoll, W. Bańczyk, in: *System Prawa Prywatnego*, vol. 10 (IV edition – to be printed).

In conclusion, the contract concluded in the analysed case between the claimant and the defendant would be ineffective also if looked at from Polish law perspective. Firstly, such a contract would be invalid due to an infringement of Article 1047 KC (it is a contract regarding the future estate); secondly, a contractual provision according to which the inheritance renunciation contract becomes effective only if some event (condition) occurs after the death of the testator cannot be admitted, as under the Polish inheritance law the condition must refer to the event before the death of the testator.

III. Summary

The case touches upon the admissibility and effectiveness of a combination of contractual arrangements aimed at managing a future estate and future inheritance. Under German law, three types of inheritance-related contracts are allowed: an inheritance contract, an inheritance renunciation contract and a contract regarding the future estate between the future statutory heirs. The first two contracts may determine whether a person will have the status of an heir, whereas the third contract may be concluded to finalise financial settlements outside the inheritance, it may even be a condition of an inheritance renunciation contract.

Under Polish law, on the other hand, inheritance contracts and contracts regarding future estate are not allowed. Only an inheritance renunciation contract can be concluded. Such a contract can be linked with another transfer of property (but not being a contract regarding a future estate). The latter can be a condition of the effectiveness of the inheritance renunciation. Such conditions, however, are limited in comparison to the conditions under German law, as such a condition must be fulfilled before the death of the person after whom the contract party was to inherit the estate.

Małgorzata Lubelska-Sazanów

§ 12 – Disposing of a future right to succeed or a right to a compulsory portion while the future decedent is still alive

Comparative conclusion
The aim of this chapter is to compare the legal provisions, jurisprudence and doctrinal considerations regarding the possibility of disposing of a future right to succeed or a right to compulsory portions while the future decedent is still alive under Polish and German law.
Under German law, contracts relating to the estate of a third party who is still living, as well as contracts relating to a compulsory portion or a legacy from the estate of a third party who is still living, are void. However, this does not apply to contracts entered into between future heirs on intestacy relating to the hereditary share on intestacy, or the compulsory portion after one of them. Under Polish law, the future testator cannot agree with the future heirs on what assets will be allocated to them, and they cannot agree with the testator about the expected profits awaiting them after the testator's death (the only slight exception to this rule is an agreement on the renunciation of an inheritance). Thus, the German legal system contains a significantly broader scope of exceptions with reference to the invalidity of agreements on succession or agreements on compulsory portion after a third person who is still alive. Additionally, the institution of joint wills is popular in Germany and does not raise any ambiguities under German law, whereas in the Polish legal system, this institution does not exist.

I. Analysis of example case under German law

The foundations for the analysis come from two contradictory cases before the Federal Court of Justice. These are: the BGH case of 11 May 1988 - IVa ZR 325/86[1] and the BGH case of 16 May 1956 – IV ZR 339/55.[2] The main subject of consideration of the court in both cases was the interpretation of § 311b section 5 BGB. However, since the subjects of consideration in this Chapter are two different states of facts and two different points of view of the Federal Court of Justice concerning the legal problem of the admissibility of agreements on

1 NJW 1988, 2726.
2 NJW 1956, 1151.

succession, these cases will be presented separately. In each case, the presentation of the state of facts will be followed by the decision of the court and its argumentation. The facts of the cases will be presented exhaustively, i. e. going beyond the main legal question provided in the title above, so that other aspects of the case will be addressed as well.

First then, the German legal background will be provided and compared with the problem of the admissibility of agreements on succession referring to the disposal of a future right to succeed or a right to a compulsory portion while the future decedent is still alive under the Polish legal system. Finally, I will present the result, i. e. a hypothetical solution of these cases under the Polish legal system. However, the presentation of two cases of the Federal Court of Justice case under the frame of one legal problem arising on the problems connected with the interpretation of § 311b section 5 BGB meant it was necessary to slightly change the structure that has been previously applied in this book.

1. Disposal of a future right to succeed or a right to a compulsory portion while the future decedent is still alive under the German legal system – the reasoning of the BGH case of 16 May 1956 – IV ZR 339/55.

This part includes a presentation of the facts of the BGH case of 16 May 1956 – IV ZR 339/55 – concerning the joint will of the parents of the parties to the litigation, i. e. three sisters and a brother (jointly further referred to as the Parties). The father died in 1941, the mother (the Mother) in 1955. The parents – spouses – made a joint will, leaving each other the entire inheritance and providing that, at the time of death of the last living spouse, the full inheritance, i. e. the real estate and a brick factory, would become the property of the son (the Brother) – the defendant – with the obligation to pay a pension to each of his three sisters for the next 20 years.

The amount of the pension for each of the three sisters was established as 10% of the annual net income from the estate, but not less than RM 1,500 for the brick factory and RM 1,200 for the property for a period of 20 years.

In 1952, after the father's death, but while the Mother was still alive, the Parties concluded an agreement on succession providing that the Brother would be relieved from the debt, but would also waive any rights that could be inherited in the future from the Mother. In return, the Brother was obliged to pay DM 3,000 to each of his three sisters within the period of time from January 1950 to January 1963.

One of the sisters claimed that this agreement was invalid. Although the court of first instance (LG) agreed, the court of second instance (OLG) rejected the sister's appeal.

The LG confirmed that, according to section 4 of § 311 b BGB[3] an agreement on the estate is invalid. The same applies to an agreement relating to a compulsory portion or an agreement on succession after a third person who is still alive. However, according to the subsequent subsection of that section,[4] this does not apply to an agreement concluded between future heirs relating to the estate inherited in the form of intestate succession, or to the right to a compulsory portion after one of the parties to this agreement. Still, such contracts must be recorded by a notary.

Since the agreement concluded between the Parties concerned legacy, it did not constitute an exemption from the legal rule providing that a contract regarding succession after a third party who is still living is void, as contained in § 311b section 5 BGB. Whereas these exemptions refer to intestate succession and rights to a compulsory portion of one of the parties to the contract, the contract between the Parties in the case at hand concerned legacy. Since the provisions of § 311b section 5 BGB should be interpreted in a narrow sense, the contract was void.

According to § 2180 section 2 BGB,[5] a declaration to reject a will may be submitted only after the inheritance has arisen. Therefore, on 9 July 1952, any sort of obligation to refuse to accept a legacy in the event of the Mother's death was invalid under § 312 section 1 BGB. For this reason, the BGH agreed with the LG in Luebeck, which admitted that the sister's claim was admissible and decided that the contract between Parties was invalid.

2. Disposal of a future right to succeed or a right to a compulsory portion while the future decedent is still alive under the German legal system in the reasoning of the BGH case of 11 May 1988 – IVa ZR 325/86.

This part includes a description of the facts of the case and the reasoning of the court in the case of the BGH of 11 May 1988 – IVa ZR 325/86. The case at hand concerns a situation where the applicant's parents – her father, who died in early 1956 and her mother, who died on 23 July 1983 – drew up a joint will in 1952, leaving each other the entire inheritance. Three children – the applicant (further referred to as the Applicant) and her siblings (i. e. a sister – the Sister – and a brother – the Brother) were each left 1/3 of the total inheritance from the later deceased spouse.

3 See subsection 4 of section 311 b BGB as amended by Article 4 para. 5 of the Act of 1 October 2013 (Federal Law Gazette 2013, Part I, page 3719).

4 See subsection 5 of section 311 b of BGB

5 See subsection 2 of section 2180 BGB, according to which "the declaration may be made only after the devolution of the inheritance; it is ineffective if it is made subject to a condition or a stipulation as to time".

The inheritance mainly constituted land developed with a residential building. The Applicant acquired the Sister's share in the will in return for a payment of DM 9,000. On 29 November 1966, the Applicant also entered into an agreement in the form of a notarial deed with the Brother, providing that he will also "transfer" to the Applicant his future statutory share in the inheritance against payment of DM 9,000. The Applicant signed a declaration confirming that she had been instructed that the contract concluded before the notary was binding only between the parties and would become invalid if the Brother was excluded from inheritance. Following the Mother's death, the Applicant asked for the Brother's share in the will, as stipulated in the contract between them. The Brother's representative *in absentia* refused to comply with her request, stating that the contract of 1966 was invalid pursuant to § 312 section 1 (1) BGB (today: § 311b section 4 BGB)[6] as an agreement on the estate concluded while the future decedent was still alive. According to the representative *in absentia*, the exception of § 312 section 2 BGB (today: § 311b section 5 BGB), which allows contracts to be concluded between future legal heirs in terms of statutory inheritance share, could not apply in the case at hand, as it did not concern statutory inheritance but testamentary inheritance. As a result, the Applicant sued the public notary (the Notary) for damages that arose as a result of the contract she signed before the Notary being invalidated, rather than seeking to achieve the purpose intended by the parties, in particular to include the Mother in the contract. For this reason, the Applicant filed a claim against the Notary to compensate the damage resulting from the fact that she had not been notified about the invalidity of the contract that the Notary certified. The court of first instance and the court of second instance considered the claim justified. However, in the end the BGH accepted the defendant's argument, stating that the Applicant had not suffered any damage as the contract she had concluded with the Brother in the form of a notarial deed was applicable under German law.

According to the BGH, the contract concluded in 1966 between the heirs is formulated as an agreement on the estate within the meaning of § 2033 section 1 BGB, hence it could not be validly concluded at the time when the testator was still alive. The OLG found that it was an agreement on the estate concluded at the time when the testator was still alive in the meaning of § 312 BGB (§ 311b section 4 BGB) and that such contracts are permissible only under statutory exceptions. Thus, under § 311b section 5 BGB, this does not apply to a contract concluded between future heirs relating to the estate inherited in the form of an intestate

6 According to § 311b section 4 BGB "a contract relating to the estate of a third party who is still living is void. The same applies to a contract relating to a compulsory portion or a legacy from the estate of a third party who is still living".

succession, as well as the right to a compulsory portion after one of the parties to this contract. Still, such contracts must be recorded by a notary.

The only question that raised doubts was whether, in the presented facts, the contract actually concerned the part of the Brother's inheritance designated on the basis of the rules regarding intestate succession. In the opinion of both courts: the court of the first and second instances, i.e. the LG and the OLG, the case concerned part of the inheritance falling to the Brother on basis of a testamentary succession and such contracts are inadmissible due to the risk that could be associated with the fact of legal consent to their conclusion to the health and even the life of the testator.

However, the BGH also stated that – in the event that the testator draws up a will by dividing the estate in exactly the same way as indicated by the rules of intestate succession – there is no reason why the agreement between the future heirs should be declared invalid. Therefore, according to the court there is no reason why these grounds should be treated differently, thus the contract between the Applicant and the Brother in the form of a notarial deed was lawful.

3. Disposal of a future right to succeed or a right to a compulsory portion while the future decedent is still alive under the German legal system.

Under German law, spouses may legally structure joint wills under § 2269 BGB. If the spouses in such wills have directed that a legacy is to be performed after the death of the survivor, it is assumed that the legacy does not pass to the person provided for until the death of the survivor.[7] Additionally, a declaration on accepting a legacy can only be made after the devolution of the inheritance; it is ineffective if it is made subject to a condition or a stipulation as to time.[8]

Still, the common point of the considerations of the Federal Court of Justice in both cases remained the issue of the legal admissibility of agreements to the estate in light of the previously (i.e. at the time when the court related to its content in the cases at hand) applicable § 312 BGB. According to its counterpart today – § 311b section 4 BGB – an agreement relating to the estate of a third party who is still living is invalid. The same applies to an agreement relating to a compulsory portion or a legacy from the estate of a third party who is still living. The purpose behind the rules providing for the invalidity of the contract as a result of concluding an agreement relating to the estate of a third party who is still living is to avoid speculation regarding the death of the future decedent or attempts to influence his freedom to testify.[9] What is decisive in this situation is

7 Compare § 2269 section 2 BGB.
8 See § 2180 section 2 BGB.
9 M. Gehrlein, in: W. Hau, R. Poseck (eds.), *BeckOK BGB*, 2021, § 311b, pt. 46.

the knowledge of the contracting parties. Hence, § 311b section 4 BGB applies also where the decedent has already passed away, but the parties did not know about it the time of concluding the contract and provides that such a contract would also be invalid.[10] The reason is the purpose of this rule; aimed at protecting moral standards in contract law and avoiding speculation about the decedent's death between future heirs. An agreement between future heirs relating to the estate, as well as relating to a compulsory portion or a legacy from the estate of a third party who is still living is void, even if this third party – i.e. the future decedent – would also agree.[11]

This rule, however, does not apply in one case. The only exception is a contract concluded between future heirs in the case of intestate succession in relation to hereditary shares or compulsory portions. In this way, future family disputes arising in connection with the inheritance might be avoided.[12] Thus, with reference to intestate succession in relation to a hereditary share or a compulsory portion, the risk of immoral behaviour of future heirs is minimised and the advantages connected with the possibility of avoiding future family disputes seems to overcome this risk. Still, such a contract must be recorded by a notary.[13]

In both of these cases, future heirs entered into an agreement relating to the estate of a third party who was still living. In the first case (the BGH case of 16 May 1956 – IV ZR 339/55) the contract between the Parties concerned the legacy at the time the future decedent was still living, meaning the contract was invalid. However, the argumentation of the court was based on the fact that the provisions of § 311b section 5 BGB should be interpreted in a narrow sense. In the second BGH case of 11 May 1988 – IVa ZR 325/86 – the parties also concluded an agreement on the estate of a third party who was still living. However, the agreement actually concerned part of the Brother's inheritance designated on the basis of the rules regarding intestate succession. Thus, the BGH interpreted § 311b section 5 BGB in a broader sense than in the previous case, stating that where the testator draws up a will by dividing the estate in exactly the same way as indicated by the rules of intestate succession, there is no reason to declare the agreement between the future heirs invalid. In the case at hand, the BGH's broad interpretation of § 311b section 5 BGB allowed the agreement on the estate to be considered a contract on intestacy, i.e. as an exemption from the general inadmissibility of agreements on the estate between future heirs at a time when the future decedent is still alive.

10 W. Ballhaus, in: K. H. Johannesen et al. (eds.), *BGB Kommentar*, 1974, § 312a, pt. 2.
11 A. Stadler, in: *Jauernig BGB Kommentar*, 2021, § 311b, pt. 62.
12 M. Gehrlein, in: W. Hau, R. Poseck, *BeckOK BGB*, 2021, § 311b, pt. 46.
13 See § 311 b section 5 BGB.

II. Consideration of the problem presented in the German case and its comparison with Polish law

With reference to the differences and similarities that may appear as a result of comparing the state of facts and the state of law in these two cases under Polish and German law, two legal issues stood out. Firstly, it is important to note that both cases considered here address the issue of joint wills between spouses. Whereas this fact did not raise any ambiguities under German law, joint will is an institution that does not exist in the Polish legal system. Secondly, it was the main subject of consideration of the German Supreme Court in both cases, i.e. the problem of the admissibility of agreements on the estate between future heirs when the future decedent is still alive. Thus, whereas the first issue showed the differences between the Polish and German legal systems, the second one turned out to be a problematic issue also under German law.[14]

Regarding joint wills, it is Article 942 KC that provides explicitly that each will may include only dispositions of one decedent.

Concerning the admissibility of agreements on the estate between future heirs while the future decedent is still living, it is necessary to analyse Articles 1047 and 1048 KC. Article 1047 KC generally prohibits concluding contracts for inheritance after a person who is still alive.[15] This applies to contracts the subject of which is a potential inheritance, a share in an inheritance or an object forming part of an inheritance and which are concluded between: a living person and their potential heir, or a third party who would become an heir as a result of the contract [known as an inheritance contract], the potential heirs of a living person or a potential heir of a living person and a third party.[16] The sanction is the invalidity of the contract. Thus, under Polish law, the future testator cannot agree with the future heirs what assets will be allocated to them, and they cannot agree with the testator about the expected profits awaiting them after the testator's death. The only exception to that rule is an agreement on the renunciation of an inheritance that – also under Polish law – will be accepted if concluded in the form of a notarial deed.[17] According to Article 1048 KC, an agreement on the renunciation of inheritance is an agreement where the future heir waives their intestate statutory inheritance after a future decedent. Therefore, after concluding such an agreement, testamentary succession is still possible. The party

14 M. Denkinger, *Europäisches Erbkollisionsrecht-Einheit Trotz Vielfalt?*, Köln 2009, pp. 220 et seq.
15 See Article 1047 KC.
16 So M. Pazdan, in: *System prawa prywatnego*, vol. 10, 2015, pp. 1131–1132.
17 See Article 1058 KC.

that waives their intestate statutory inheritance may still be a testamentary successor or a legatee in the future.[18]

An agreement on the renunciation of inheritance produces legal effects only upon the death of the testator and is therefore a legal act with a *mortis causa* effect.[19] It is also assumed that it is a *sui generis* kind of contract, therefore it is not an obliging or disposable legal act, nor an incremental activity.[20] It is not an agreement that would exclude the possibility to conclude it by proxy.[21] There is no agreement in the literature as to whether and to what extent it is possible to limit the scope of an agreement on renunciation. It is quite commonly accepted that waiving a fraction of an inheritance or a share in the inheritance, as well as the right to a reserved portion, is admissible.[22] On the other hand, greater doubts are raised by the issue of giving up a separate inheritance (e.g. a farm, enterprise) or individual items included in an inheritance.[23]

It is explicitly allowed to conclude an agreement on renunciation between the testator and the future heir in course of intestate succession. However, it is also possible to conclude such agreement between the testator and the successor of his immediate intestate heir, but in this case the agreement may be concluded only after the immediate intestate heir's death.[24] Provisions of the Polish Civil code do not allow to conclude this contract for the benefit of a concrete des-

18 See E. Rott-Pietrzyk, *Umowa o zrzeczenie się dziedziczenia – uwagi de lege lata i de lege ferenda*, Rejent 2016, No 3, p. 109; M. Pazdan, in: *System prawa prywatnego*, vol. 10, 2015, pp. 1137–1136. The fact that an heir who waived their intestate statutory inheritance may still be a testamentary successor in the future has been confirmed by the Polish Supreme Court case already in 1972, see resolution of SN of 15 May 1972, III CZP 26/72, OSNCP 1972, No 11, item 197.

19 See e.g.: J. Biernat, *Umowa o zbycie spadku w polskim prawie spadkowym,* Warszawa 2021.

20 See M. Pazdan, in: *System prawa prywatnego*, vol. 10, 2015, pp. 1137–1138; J. Kuźmicka-Sulikowska, in: E. Gniewek, P. Machnikowski (eds.), *Komentarz KC*, 2021, Article 1048, pt. 1. See also: M. Pazdan, *Umowa o zrzeczenie się dziedziczenia w polskim prawie spadkowym,* Rejent 1997, No 4, pp. 184–196.

21 See E. Rott-Pietrzyk, *Umowa…*, pp. 110–111.

22 *So* e.g.: E. Skowrońska-Bocian, J. Wierciński, M. Pazdan, G. Wolak. See E. Skowrońska-Bocian, J. Wierciński, in: J. Gudowski (ed.), *Komentarz KC,* vol. VI, 2017, p. 433; M. Pazdan, in: *System prawa prywatnego*, vol. 10, 2015, p. 1143; M. Pazdan, in: K. Pietrzykowski (ed.), *Komentarz KC,* vol. II, 2021, Article 1048, pt. 29; M. Pazdan, *Umowa…*, p. 193; G. Wolak, *Umowa…*, pp. 300–308; G. Wolak, in: M. Habdas, M. Fras (eds.), *Komentarz KC,* vol. VI, 2019, Article 1048, pt. 45; J. Kuźmicka-Sulikowska, in: E. Gniewek, P. Machnikowski (eds.), *Komentarz KC,* 2021, Article 1048;. Differently e.g.: J. Górecki, W. Borysiak. See W. Borysiak, in: K. Osajda (ed.), *Komentarz KC,* vol. 3, 2013, pp. 1121–1132; J. Górecki, *Umowa zrzeczenia się dziedziczenia*, Rejent 2020, No 12, pp. 18–19.

23 E. Skowrońska-Bocian, J. Wierciński, in: J. Gudowski (ed.), *Komentarz KC,* vol. VI 2017, p. 433; *J. Górecki, Umowa…*, p. 19; G. Wolak, in: M. Habdas, M. Fras (eds.), *Komentarz KC,* vol. VI, 2019, Article 1048, pt. 58; M. Pazdan, in: K. Pietrzykowski (ed.), *Komentarz KC,* vol. II, 2021, Article 1048, pt. 30.

24 M. Pazdan, *Umowa…*, p. 196; E. Rott-Pietrzyk, *Umowa…*, p. 110.

ignated person, since it is not possible to indicate who will inherit instead of the renouncing heir.[25]

Under Polish law, the contract concluded by the testator's siblings while the testator was still alive in the facts presented in the BGH case IVa ZR 325/86, would also be invalid as it is not possible to conclude contracts between future heirs while the future decedent is still alive. In this case, the reason was that one of the testators – the mother – was still alive at the time her children concluded the agreement (although her husband was already dead). Additionally, the case involved a joint will of the spouses, which is an institution that does not exist in Polish law, therefore the outcome under the Polish legal system in this case would have to be the court ruling on the invalidity of the agreement on the estate between future heirs.

For the same reasons, the situation presented in the BGH case IV ZR 339/55 concerning an agreement about execution of a testamentary legacy between future heirs would also be inadmissible under Polish law.

Nevertheless, legal solutions recognised by the German legal system but not recognised by the Polish legal system, e.g. joint wills, may still apply to Polish citizens. Thus, the Polish legislator has since 2011 allowed a choice of the law applicable to succession issues, though always in a limited scope.[26] Since 2004, when the Republic of Poland became a Member State of the European Union, all the EU legislation is directly[27] applicable in Poland or is implemented into the national legal order (in the case of directives). Therefore, when Succession Regulation came into force, testators gained the freedom to choose the law for dispositions *mortis causa* (which they did not have before then, as the Polish Private International Law Act did not mention it).[28] The regulation allows Polish citizens to use the possibility to conclude inheritance contracts if this is allowed under the legal system of one the spouse's domestic law, thanks to the choice of laws. Thus, Article 25 section 3 of Succession Regulation provides that the spouses may choose the law applicable to their inheritance contract under the conditions set out in Article 22 of the Succession Regulation.

According to the basic rule provided in Article 21 § 1 of the Succession Regulation, if the testator did not make any choice of law, the law applicable to

25 E. Rott-Pietrzyk, *Umowa…*, p. 114.

26 A. Paluch, *Granice swobody rozrządzania majątkiem na wypadek śmierci w prawie polskim*, Warszawa 2021, p. 76.

27 See Article 288 of the consolidated version of the Treaty on the Functioning of the European Union, O.J. 326, 26.10.2012 (TFEU). Compare e.g.: D. Cahill, N. Connery, T. Kennedy, V. Power, *European Law*, Oxford 2011, p. 1987.

28 Still, before Succession Regulation came into force, the freedom to choose the law for inheritance cases became significantly more limited in relation to its scope granted by the Polish Private International Law Act. See M. Pazdan, in: *System prawa prywatnego*, vol. 10, 2015, pp. 1146–1147.

the succession is the law of the state of their habitual residence at the time of their death. At the same time, if the testator was married at the time of their death, it is just as important to consider the provisions of Polish Private International Law Act. Thus, according to Article 51 section 1–2 of the Polish Private International Law Act being a Polish national legal act referring to legal issues with an international aspect – the law applicable to the personal and property relations between spouses is their respective common national law, and in the absence of a common national law – the law of the state in which both spouses have their place of residence, and if they do not reside in the same state – the law of the country where both spouses have their habitual residence. The Polish Supreme Court, in a recent case from 2021, explicitly confirmed which choice of law rules are applicable to inheritance issues connected with decedents who died between 2011 and 2015, i.e. after the Polish Private International Law Act came into force but before Succession Regulation did.[29] Since the provisions of law may lead to the applicability of different legal systems to different issues connected with succession after the same testator, the choice of law in the will is always a wise decision of the testator concerning international property in the case of families with different habitual residence of their members.[30]

29 Decision of SN of 19 March 2021, III CSKP 69/21, OSNC 2021, No 11, item 76.
30 See also: A. Paluch, *Granice…*, p. 76.

Paulina Gwoździewicz-Matan

§ 13 – Agreement with the future testator to renounce a compulsory portion and its impact on the situation of third parties

Comparative conclusion
Waiving the right to a compulsory portion – as a right to a future, potential (and not already existing) source of income – cannot be considered detrimental to third parties, and thus contrary to morality, i. e. invalid. The admissibility of concluding an agreement to renounce a compulsory portion should be compatible with the way that the given legal system provides for calculating the amount of the inheritance share. It cannot be simply assumed that a compulsory portion derives from the right to an inheritance, and at the same time it cannot be considered that anyone renouncing the right to a compulsory portion should be treated differently from those renouncing the right to an inheritance (which are not taken into account when calculating the amount of the inheritance share), if it does not result directly from the legal provision.

I. Analysis of an example case under German law

An agreement to waive the right to a compulsory portion can serve as a good example of the issue of the freedom to testimony. While the institution of the compulsory portion itself is perceived as restricting the freedom in planning succession, the possibility of concluding an agreement to waive the right to a compulsory portion between the future heir and the future testator is already a tool that allows for a more flexible disposal of property. On the other hand, there is the question of the rights of third parties that could potentially be infringed upon. This issue was considered in the judgment of the BGH of 11 January 2011 in the case IV ZR 7/10[1].

The facts of the case are as follow. In 2006, the defendant and his wife made a joint will.[2] After the will was confirmed, three children (including a physically disabled daughter) made a renouncement, in a notarial form, of the compulsory portion of the first of the deceased – the mother who died the evening after the

1 See BGH judgment of 11 January 2011 – IV ZR 7/10, NJW 2011, 1586.
2 For the regulation of joint wills under the German law, see § 1, § 2 and § 3 in this monograph.

will was drawn up, and agreements were concluded to disclaim the compulsory portion. The children waived the compulsory portion in order to provide the father with financial security. It was agreed that the children should receive the parents' property only after the last deceased parent. As a result, the social assistance agency (the claimant, the "Agency"), which provided support for the disabled daughter, brought a claim against the still living father on the basis that the disabled daughter was entitled to the compulsory portion. The agency claimed that the daughter's waiver of the compulsory portion is contrary to morality (§ 138 section 1 BGB)[3] and was done deliberately in order to continue using the Agency's benefits. In the claimant's opinion, the waiver was done to prevent the Agency from accessing its entitlement to the compulsory portion, and this justifies the claimant's position that a contract was concluded at the expense of a third party. The claim was dismissed by the appellate court due to the fact that there was no violation of morality. In addition, the BGH accepted that a waiver of a compulsory portion by a benefit recipient is not an example of a legally inadmissible contract "at the expense of a third party," because the waiver of the compulsory portion does not impose any contractual obligations on the social assistance agency. In expressing this view, the BGH dismissed the former objections, according to which a contract renouncing an inheritance in the absence of an equivalent consideration could be treated as contrary to morality. As stated in the justification of the court, there is no legal basis in the Social Welfare Act (*Sozialhilfegezetzbuch*) to limit the rights of disabled persons to the tools the inheritance law offers. According to the principle of the autonomy of the will of civil law entities – everyone (regardless of whether they are disabled or not) can decide whether they want to inherit or obtain an inheritance grant from another person in a different way (known as the negative freedom of inheritance). The BGH further noted that the case law on the ineffectiveness of a waiver of maintenance in marriage and divorce contracts, which is detrimental to the social assistance agencies, cannot be appropriately applied to a renunciation agreement. Contrary to the right to maintenance, the right to a compulsory portion is not yet a certain – already existing – source of income.

3 This article reads: "(1) A legal transaction that is contrary to public policy is invalid. (2) In particular, a legal transaction is invalid by which a person, by exploiting the predicament, inexperience, lack of sound judgment or considerable weakness of will of another, causes himself or a third party, in exchange for an act of performance, to be promised or granted pecuniary advantages that are clearly disproportionate to the performance."

II. Consideration of the problem presented in the German case and its comparison with Polish law

Before we move on to an analysis of the judgment, it is first worth looking at the admissibility of concluding a waiver of a compulsory portion agreements under Polish and German law, though this issue itself was not dealt with by the court in its ruling. The differences in this respect boil down to the following issues: first, the admissibility of concluding an agreement on renouncing a compulsory portion, and second, the method of determining the amount of the inheritance share. According to Article 1048 KC, "An intestate heir may, by a contract with a person to whom they are to succeed, waive succession to that person. The contract should be executed in the form of a notarial deed."[4] The subsequent Article 1049 § 2 KC regulates the effects of such a waiver providing that "The waiving person, and their descendants covered by the waiver of succession, are excluded from succeeding as if they had not lived to the opening of the succession." However, these provisions concern an agreement on renouncing inheritance, while the issue of the admissibility of waiving the right to a compulsory portion itself is debatable. It is not expressed directly in the content of the provision (as it was, for example, in the Decree on Succession Law, which in Article 10 § 2 explicitly indicated the possibility).[5] The ruling of the Polish Supreme Court Civil Chamber of 17 March 2017 in the case II CZP 110/16[6] was supposed to dispel any doubts. According to the state of facts that was the basis for referring a legal question to the Supreme Court, a notary public refused to draw up an agreement on waiving a compulsory portion between a father and son, referring to Article

4 At the time of writing the article, this provision was amended by adding the following paragraphs: "§ 2. The renunciation of inheritance may be limited to the waiver of only the right to all or part of a compulsory portion. § 3. A renunciation of inheritance in favour of another person will be deemed a renunciation, in of the event of any doubt, provided that the person will inherit." See Article 129 of the Act on Family Foundation of 26 January 2023, adopted by the Sejm, amending the Civil Code of 23 April 1964 (Journal of Laws of 2022, items 1360, 2337 and 2339). The law came into force on 22 May 2023.

5 The article stated: "This renunciation [*of inheritance*] may be limited to the renunciation of the compulsory portion only".

6 Compare also the judgment of SN of 21 April 2004 (III CK 353/02 (not published), in which it was found admissible to renounce the inheritance of a fractional part of the inheritance, recognising that the Civil Code does not prohibit the conclusion of such an agreement; see also the judgment of the Constitutional Tribunal of 25 July 2013 (P 56/11) OTK-A Coll. 2013, No 6, item 85, which recognised Article 991 KC as compliant with the Constitution and indicated *expressis verbis* as admissible under Article 1048 KC using the *a maiori ad minus* reasoning, concluding an agreement for the waiver of the right to a compulsory portion. As for the decisions of lower courts, the judgment of the SA in Kraków of 30 December 2011, I ACa 1244/2011, LEX 1680464, also referred to further on (see footnote 37).

1047 KC,[7] which prohibits the conclusion of agreements involving the succession of a living person other than are expressly provided for in the KC. The need to conclude an agreement to renounce a compulsory portion was justified by the need to freely plan the succession due to the father's family business, which the testator wanted to leave only to one child. This is because the need to pursue claims for a compulsory portion in extreme cases may often lead to the collapse of an enterprise or a farm included in the estate, if the testator has no other property from which he could satisfy the heirs entitled to the compulsory portion.[8] A similar motivation lies at the basis of the German case being commented on. A comparable effect could not be achieved by concluding an agreement on the renunciation of inheritance, which is admissible under Polish law, because such an agreement would increase the potential compulsory portion claims of the other heirs. The Supreme Court expressed the view that concluding agreements to waive a compulsory portion was permissible.[9] It did not share the opinion that only what was explicitly regulated is allowed (regardless of what seems to be a closed catalogue of legal actions *mortis causa* in Article 941 and 1047 of KC).[10] Consequently, as noted in the literature,[11] the position of the Supreme Court could mean that it acknowledged the existence of the "principle of freedom of legal action *mortis causa.*" In the justification of the ruling, the argument *a maiori ad minus* is used (since the right to inheritance may be waived, the more so the right to a compulsory portion, which is "a derivative of the right to inheritance"). The court also underlined the need for such an instrument on the market to regulate family relations. Finally, it was pointed out that excluding the admissibility of the agreement to waive the right to a compulsory portion would violate the principle of freedom of testation. This ruling met with a great response and was commented on several times.[12] Among the critical voices, the most

7 The article states: "Subject to the exceptions provided for in this title, a contract concerning succession to a living person is invalid".

8 See, J. Pisuliński, *Zrzeczenie się dziedziczenia w prawie niemieckim*, Rejent 1999, No 12, p. 64.

9 However, the problem of the risk of non-uniform practice in this area (despite the ruling of the Supreme Court) was also noticed in the justification of the planned amendments of the KC, see footnote 3 and 18 and p. 53 of the Justification of the draft Act on Family Foundation.

10 As an example, the Supreme Court cites the institution of a negative will, which has not been regulated in Polish law, but its admissibility is nevertheless not questioned – because it has not been *expressis verbis* prohibited. On the negative will, see § 4. II in this monograph.

11 See T. Justyński, *Glosa do uchwały Sądu Najwyższego z dnia 17 marca 2017 r. III CZP 110/16, OSNC 2017/12/134*, OSP 2018, No 11, item 109; T. Jasiakiewicz, *Glosa do uchwały Sądu Najwyższego z dnia 17 marca 2017 r., III CZP 110/16, OSNC 2017/12/134*, OSP 2018, No 9, item 86, p. 9.

12 Critically: T. Justyński, *Glosa do uchwały SN z dnia 17 marca 2017 r., III CZP 110/16*, OSP 2018, No 11, item 109, pp. 3–8; T. Jasiakiewicz, *Glosa…*, p. 9; in favour: M. Komarowska, *Dopuszczalność umowy zrzeczenia się zachowku. Glosa do uchwały SN z dnia 17 marca 2017 r.*, Białostockie Studia Prawnicze 2017, No 4, pp. 293–303.

frequently mentioned argument is the argument from the historical interpretation: since in the current legal state the legislator did not mention a contract on waiving the compulsory portion, which means that it refrained from introducing it into the legal order. Moreover, it is argued that the law of inheritance should be clear and transparent, there should be no room for a broad interpretation and for "making the law of succession more flexible."[13] With all those critical arguments in mind, however, an agreement on renouncing a compulsory portion should be viewed as admissible,[14] due to its practical usefulness and economic importance, as well as the inability to achieve similar results with the support of other instruments.[15]

As for the regulation given in German civil law, the possibility of concluding a waiver of the right to a compulsory portion is expressly stipulated in § 2346 BGB "(1) Relatives and the spouse of the testator may renounce their right of intestate succession by contract with the testator. The person renouncing is excluded from intestate succession as though they were no longer alive at the time of the devolution of the inheritance; they do not have the right to a compulsory portion. (2) The renunciation may be restricted to the right to a compulsory portion." It should also be noted that the provisions of the BGB include several variants of contracts for the renunciation of inheritance: a contract for the renunciation of statutory inheritance (§ 2346 section 1 BGB), which may be limited to a waiver of the right to a compulsory portion (§ 2346 section 2 BGB)), and may only relate to a waiver of inheritance resulting from a will or an inheritance contract or to a legacy made in a will or inheritance contract in favour of the renouncing party (§ 2353 BGB).[16] This provision has no equivalent in Polish law. The Polish Civil

13 See T. Justyński, *Glosa…*, p. 9, where the author points out: "The law of inheritance, however, is maximum simplicity and certainty. Unlike law on obligations, where the parties create even a very complicated law (*lex contractus*) for themselves and only they have to obey it." On the similarities and differences in the scope of Polish and German obligation law, see, M. Jagielska, E. Macierzyńska-Franaszczyk, E. Rott-Pietrzyk, F. Zoll, G. Żmij (eds.) *Limits of harmonization and convergence. Dissimilarities within similarities of Polish and German contract law*, Warszawa 2018.

14 This view is prevailingly approved in Polish literature, see M. Pazdan, in: *System prawa prywatnego*, vol. 10, 2015, p. 1144: W. Hans, *Umowy dotyczące spadku*, NP 1967, No 2, p. 244; J. Kosik, in: *System prawa cywilnego*, vol. IV, 1986, p. 586; M. Pazdan, *Umowa o zrzeczenie się dziedziczenia w polskim prawie spadkowym*, Rejent 1997, No 4, p. 194; A. Doliwa, *Umowy dotyczące spadku*, SPP 2008, No 1, p. 137; E. Rott-Pietrzyk, *Umowa o zrzeczenie się dziedziczenia – uwagi de lege lata i de lege ferenda*, Rejent 2006, No 3, pp. 117–118; E. Niezbecka, in: A. Kidyba (ed.), *Komentarz KC*, vol. IV, 2012, p. 372; P. Księżak, *Zachowek w polskim prawie spadkowym*, Warszawa 2012, p. 130 *et seq.*

15 The adoption of the provision allowing for the conclusion of agreements for the waiver of compulsory share directly in § 2 of Article 1048 KC will eliminate these doubts.

16 A person who applies for the issue of a certificate of inheritance on the basis of a disposition *mortis causa* must specify the disposition upon which their right of succession is based, and

Code only provides for the possibility of waiving statutory inheritance. The possibility of renouncing testamentary inheritance (separately or together with the statutory inheritance) was allowed under the Decree of Succession Law (Articles 10 and 11).

When looking at the method of calculation the compulsory portion, the question of the admissibility of an agreement to waive the right to a compulsory portion in Polish law should be related to the purpose of Article 992 KC. This article reads: "when establishing an inheritance share constituting the basis for calculating the compulsory portion, unworthy heirs and heirs who have rejected the inheritance are taken into account, whereas heirs who have waived their inheritance or have been disinherited are not taken into account." Thus, heirs who have renounced their inheritance are not included when counting the inheritance part, which leads to the fact that the global amount of the compulsory portion does not decrease, because only one of heirs drops out of the group, and this results in an increase in the compulsory portion of another entitled person. The views expressed in the literature indicate, not without criticism, that the criterion of division used by the legislator in Article 992 KC is the testator's knowledge.[17] Disinherited and renounced heirs are not taken into account, because the testator himself disinherits or concludes an agreement to renounce the inheritance. In turn, the testator cannot predict which of the heirs will reject the inheritance, or which will be considered unworthy. However, due to the lack of an explicit regulation of the admissibility of the agreement to renounce the right to a compulsory portion in the Civil Code, there is also no reference to this category of heirs (persons waiving the right to a compulsory portion) in the catalogue of Article 992 KC. In view of the legislator's silence, one may assume that heirs who have renounced only the right to a compulsory portion are not covered by the exemption from the Civil Code (Article 992 KC), and are therefore taken into account when calculating the compulsory portion due to other heirs.[18] There are no "shifts" in terms of the size of the shares of the remaining heirs, there is no

must state whether and what other dispositions *mortis causa* of the testator exist, as well as providing the information specified in § 2354 section 1 subsections 1, 5 and 2.

17 See B. Kordasiewicz, in: *System prawa prywatnego,* vol. 10, 2015, p. 1076 and the literature cited there.

18 Article 992 KC is not supposed to be changed in the upcoming amendment of the KC (see footnote 4 above), as we read in the justification of the amendment: "A person who waives the right to a compulsory portion is taken into account when calculating the legitim of other entitled persons. This has the effect that limiting the waiver only to the compulsory portion excludes the waiver's share, but does not result in the emergence of new persons entitled to the compulsory portion. The fundamental difference between a waiver of inheritance and a waiver of the right to a compulsory portion, illustrating its economic sense, is that the person renouncing the inheritance is not taken into account when determining the inheritance part, which is the basis for determining the compulsory portion." See the Justification of the draft Act on Family Foundation, p. 53.

increase in them. This leads to an increase in the freedom of testation by the value of a compulsory portion as it reduces the debt burden of the inheritance to cover claims for a compulsory portion. On the other hand, it may influence the other heirs (third parties), as will be discussed below.

When it comes to the German regulation, it expressly provides for the norm of § 2310 BGB, which states: "When calculating the compulsory portion, the heirs who are unworthy, excluded from inheritance by virtue of the will, as well as those who have rejected the inheritance are taken into account. Those who have renounced inheritance from intestate succession are not included." Like under Polish law, any heirs who are excluded from inheritance by concluding an agreement on the waiver of inheritance (*Erbverzicht*) are not taken into account.[19] This provision applies regardless of whether compensation (*Abfindung*) has been paid for the renunciation of inheritance, and in what amount. As in Polish law, the renunciation of inheritance is beneficial for the remaining beneficiaries of the compulsory portion, because their statutory inheritance, and thus the amount of the compulsory portion, increases accordingly. In the event of only a partial renunciation of inheritance, the surrender is only partially taken into account when calculating the compulsory portion in favour of the remaining beneficiaries of the compulsory portion. If the renunciation of inheritance is compensated by an inheritance claim (*Vermachtnisanspruch*), the increase in the compulsory portion of the other heirs entitled to the compulsory portion may lead to an unintended reduction of the inheritance claim pursuant to § 2318 section 1, in which case the waiver is not counted.[20] Incidentally, it is worth adding that the admissibility of a partial renunciation of inheritance also does not arise directly from the provisions of the KC. The Supreme Court commented on this issue in its ruling of 21 April 2004 in the case III CK 353/02[21], stating that it is admissible to renounce the inheritance of a fractional part of the inheritance, as the Civil Code does not prohibit the conclusion of such an agreement.[22]

As for heirs who have merely renounced the right to a compulsory portion (§ 2346 section 2 BGB), they are taken into account when calculating the compulsory portion. As indicated in the doctrine, the purpose of this form of regulation is to extend the freedom of testation (*Verfugungsfreihet des Erblassers*).[23]

19 BGH judgment of 3 December 2008 – IV ZR 58/07 = BGH ZEV 2009, 77 (78); OLG Köln ZEV 2004, 155 (156).

20 See C.T. Ebenroth, *Erbrecht*, München 1992, Rn. 366.

21 LEX No 585802.

22 In the literature, as in the case of the admissibility of concluding an agreement for the renunciation of a compulsory portion, one can find various positions. Critically, for example, see W. Borysiak, in: K. Osajda (ed.), *Komentarz KC*, vol. IVA, 2019, pt. 49–59, Legalis, and the literature given there.

23 See the justification of the judgment and the literature given there, especially K.W. Lange, in: *Münchener Kommentar*, vol. 11, 2020, § 2310, pt. 7–9.

These heirs are also included in cases where they have been disinherited. A waiver limited to a compulsory portion only results in the fact that the right to a compulsory portion does not arise, but the statutory right of inheritance remains unaffected.[24] The waiver of the compulsory portion does not, therefore, affect the statutory right to an inheritance. This corresponds to the wording of § 2310 sentence 2, which is due to the death fiction of § 2346 section 1 sentence 2 (the renouncing person is treated as if they are no longer alive at the time of the devolution of the inheritance). In the case of renouncing an inheritance that includes the compulsory portion, the renunciation will have to be taken into account, contrary to the wording of point 2, because otherwise the weight of the compulsory portion could possibly exceed half of the value of the estate.

The problem comes down to the correct interpretation of the norm of Article 992 KC. According to the prevailing view in the literature, whereby, since this provision does not provide for the renunciation of the compulsory portion, the person who renounced it should be taken into account when calculating the inheritance share constituting the basis for calculating the compulsory portion, which in the future will result in the fact that the share of the remaining entitled persons will not increase.[25] Such an interpretation can be seen as questionable, as it introduces a dissonance in terms of the uniform nature of the renunciation agreement. Given the view expressed in the ruling of the Supreme Court, an agreement on the renunciation of the compulsory portion is treated as an agreement for the renunciation of inheritance. In this context, the surrender of the compulsory portion may be an unnecessary institution, since it will generally lead to the effect expected by the testator only in a situation where all the entitled persons renounce their compulsory portion. For this reason, the regulation of Polish law should be assessed as requiring clarification with regard to the method of calculating the amount of the compulsory portion in the event of its renunciation. Therefore, it is not correct *de lege lata* (assuming the admissibility of the waiver of the right to a compulsory portion itself) that the waiver of the right to a compulsory portion, as it was not explicitly mentioned in the catalogue of Article 992 KC, must be treated differently from the waiver of the right to an inheritance. Relying on the arguments of the Supreme Court (whereby the right to a compulsory portion is a derivative of the right to an inheritance) would lead to different conclusions. In that case, the person renouncing the right to a compulsory portion should be treated in the same way as the one who is renouncing the right to an inheritance. This reasoning is flawed. It should rather be assumed that a result of renouncing the compulsory portion should be the reduction of the

24 See K.W. Lange, in: *Münchener Kommentar*, vol. 11, 2020, § 2310, pt. 7–9.

25 For more on this subject, see B. Kordasiewicz, in: *System prawa prywatnego*, vol. 10, 2015, pp. 1075–1076.

global value of everyone's compulsory portion (by eliminating the compulsory portion of the person who has renounced it). Therefore, while sharing the opinion on the admissibility of concluding agreements for the renunciation of the *de lege lata* compulsory portion under Polish law, it should be noted that the accompanying doubts, and in particular the unclear criterion of the division of Article 992 KC, should be clarified.[26]

The issue of possible harm to third parties as a result of concluding an agreement on the waiver of a compulsory portion can be viewed from two perspectives: *in abstracto* and *in concreto*. In a broad sense, the method of determining the circle of heirs should be taken into account and analysed from the perspective of assessing whether the *de lege lata* compulsory portion renunciation agreement may adversely affect the situation of third parties (in the commented case: the other heirs). As stated above, an agreement for the renunciation of a compulsory portion does not lead to an increase in the compulsory portion of the other entitled persons (as in the case of an agreement on the renunciation of inheritance), and therefore leads to an effect other than the waiver of inheritance, which may then affect the situation of third parties. There are opinions[27] stating that the conclusion of an agreement on renouncing the right to a compulsory portion may be directed against third parties not participating in the agreement, and even raise suspicions of collusion between the party surrendering a compulsory portion and the testator, especially in the event that the agreement on the renunciation of a compulsory portion was for consideration. In that case the renouncer would obtain both his share of the inheritance and the equivalent for renunciation, and this could cause confusion for the remaining heirs.[28] This argumentation fails in light of the German regulations, where there are practically no free of charge contracts for the renunciation of inheritance or a compulsory portion,[29] but – due to the transparent and literal regulation of a contract on the renunciation of the compulsory portion, and the way the inheritance share is counted, the consequences of waiving the compulsory portion are clear and predictable.

26 Under the ruling of the Decree on Succession Law of 1946 (which explicitly allowed for the waiver of the compulsory portion) its Article 157 read: "When designating the inheritance part, which is the basis for determining the compulsory portion, the statutory heirs who have waived the right to inherit or are unworthy and the necessary heirs who have been disinherited are not taken into account, while statutory heirs who rejected the inheritance and necessary heirs who have waived only the right to a compulsory portion are taken into account."

27 This argument is often raised by opponents of recognising an agreement to renounce a compulsory share as admissible under Polish law. See T. Justyński, *Glosa…*, p. 7.

28 See T. Justyński, *Glosa…*, p. 7.

29 More on the subject can be found, for example, in J. Pisuliński, *Zrzeczenie się dziedziczenia w prawie niemieckim*, Rejent 1999, No 12, pp. 76 et sq.

Referring it to a specific factual state, when deciding whether the contract could cause harm to third parties (e. g. a social welfare agency), the Federal Court of Justice did not find grounds to state that the conclusion of an agreement to renounce a compulsory portion by a person using social assistance is contrary to morality. In the justification of the judgment, it was presented how this view has evolved over time.[30] In the earlier literature, it was assumed that contracts on renouncing an inheritance, especially those made without consideration, were contrary to morality and therefore invalid. At that time, the courts applied the jurisprudence on the resignation from matrimonial maintenance as being contrary to good morals. The currently prevailing view goes against the thesis that it is contrary to morality: "The waiver of a compulsory portion by the recipient of the benefit is not an example of a 'legally inadmissible contract at the expense of a third party' – as the claimant believes – because the renunciation of inheritance does not impose any contractual obligations on the social insurer."

In the justification we also find reference to applying the principle of the subordination (subsidiarity) of social assistance,[31] whereby anyone may apply for state aid to the extent that they are unable to cover expenses. It has been noted that the structures of civil law may contradict this principle of subsidiarity if they are aimed at meeting the needs of a given person.[32] There is no legal basis in the SGB to limit the inheritance rights of people with disabilities to legally admissible tools. In that case, the BGB pointed out that 'As a rule, everyone is free to decide whether they wish to become someone else's heir or otherwise obtain an inheritance. In this context, from the law of inheritance within the meaning of Article 14 section 1 German Basic Law (*Grundgesetz*) its opposite should also be derived in the sense of a "negative freedom from inheritance." Thus, anyone entitled under the compulsory portion has the right to renounce it, not only on the basis of the guarantee of the autonomy of will in Article 2 section 1 *Grundgesetz*, but also because of the basic assumptions of the freedom of inheritance. The principle of the subsidiarity of social assistance does not give the authorities the power to limit private autonomy or negative freedom of inheritance as defined in § 138 section 1 BGB.

Finally, as the BGH pointed out, the case law of the XII Civil Chamber regarding exemption from the maintenance obligation between spouses is not applicable to the case by analogy. The BGH's case law on the ineffectiveness of waiving alimony/maintenance in marriage and divorce agreements, which are

30 See the justification of the judgment and the literature given there.

31 Nachrangprinzip der öffentlichen Hilfe, § 2 Sozialgesetzbuch XII.

32 However, for example, the rejection of an inheritance by a disabled child (declared by the guardian) is incompatible with the principle of subsidiarity – it cannot be approved by the guardianship court ("it would be contrary to good practice and ordinance at the expense of the general public").

unfavourable to the social assistance provider – cannot be transferred to agreements for the renunciation of a compulsory portion. When the maintenance is waived, the entitled person already has a subjective right and they resign from an already existing source of income and subsistence, while the person entitled to a compulsory portion gives up only the chance to receive an income before the inheritance is opened.

It can be assumed that the Polish court, when examining a similar case, would also not look for analogies to situations in which maintenance claims were waived. It is clear from the statements of the Supreme Court that the claims for a compulsory portion do not relate to those of a maintenance nature.[33] It is also likely (though remembering that the acceptability of renouncing a compulsory portion is ambiguous under Polish law) that the court would not see an infringement of third party rights here, on the basis of Article 58 § 2 KC, i. e. perceived as contrary to the principles of social coexistence and not valid, as the waiver of a compulsory portion does not impose any contractual obligations on a third party.

Both of the analysed judgments emphasise the aspect of the freedom of testation. The justification of the resolution of the Supreme Court explicitly states that the prohibition on agreements on renouncing a compulsory portion would violate this freedom. In the facts on which the analysed German ruling is based, the defendant (the father) indicated the purpose of the agreement to renounce the compulsory portion, which is to preserve the parents' property in full until the death of the other parent.[34] It is worth considering at this point whether there are other instruments by which similar effects could be achieved.

First, this goal could not be achieved by appointing one person to the inheritance. Like under Polish law (Article 991 KC), the testator's descendants, his spouse and parents are entitled to claim a compulsory portion (§ 2303 BGB). On the basis of the facts that were the subject of the Polish Supreme Court's decision in 2017 case[35], the testator's will was to transfer the enterprise to only one of the sons. If he appointed only one son as the heir, the other son, even though he would not be appointed to the inheritance, would be entitled to a compulsory portion in the amount of half of the inheritance share (i. e. in the simplest variant up to one-quarter of the value of the enterprise), which could even lead to the

---

33 See for example: resolution of SN of 13 February 1975, III CZP 91/74, OSNC 1976, No 1, item 6; judgment of SA in Katowice of 23 January 2014, V ACa 742/13, LEX No 1439043.

34 Another example of a practical usage of the right to a compulsory portion (given by M. Pazdan, in: K. Pietrzykowski (ed.), *Komentarz KC,* vol. II, 2011, p. 1272) could be the situation where the testator has made gifts of significant value during his lifetime, and the beneficiaries of the gifts would be obliged to satisfy the claim for a compulsory portion (i. e. a property as part of inheritance).

35 Judgment of SN of 17 March 2017, III CZP 110/16, OSNC 2017, No 12, item 134.

collapse of the enterprise, if the heir wanted to satisfy a claim for a compulsory portion from his assets.

Second, in this case, the application of the agreement on the renunciation of inheritance (explicitly permitted in Article 1047 KC) would also not lead to the intended result, because – due to the method of counting the inheritance share stipulated in Article 992 KC – it results in an increase in the amount of the compulsory portion of other entitled persons, which could also cause a significant burden on the enterprise. In addition, the solution proposed in the literature, according to which, in the current legal status, the effects of renouncing the right to a compulsory portion can be achieved by concluding an inheritance waiver agreement (which has an effect only in terms of statutory inheritance), and then being appointed to the estate in a will, also cannot be treated as an alternative. In this case, the heir would not regain the right to the lost compulsory portion concluded in the inheritance renunciation agreement.[36] However, this solution still does not give the testator the freedom to dispose of their property. One should not lose sight of the other heirs entitled to a compulsory portion -- namely that their share increases due to the other person renouncing their share of the inheritance, while the renouncement of the compulsory portion gives the testator more freedom (e.g. other heirs can inherit the property remaining after the donations made by the descendent). Looking for other possible replacement-solutions, the BGH indicates in the justification that a similar goal cannot be achieved, for example, through a *Pflchtteilssanktion-klausel* – a penal ordinance for demanding a compulsory portion.[37] This, in turn, has no equivalent in Polish inheritance law.

III. Summary

The issue in question can also be seen in a broader context, taking into account the purpose of the legal institution of a compulsory portion. It should therefore be considered acceptable to conclude a *pactum de non petendo* under which the future holder of a compulsory portion undertakes not to pursue a claim for a compulsory portion, and – due to the prohibition under Article 1047 KC – such an agreement would be concluded with the testator, essentially for the benefit of a third party.[38] One could also rely on the institution of a testamentary order or

36 The view expressed by E. Skowrońska-Bocian, *Komentarz KC*, 2011, p. 284.

37 See Senate judgments of 8 December 2004 and 19 October 2005.

38 In this respect, compare the judgment of SA in Krakow of 30 December 2011 (I ACa 1244/2011, Lexis.pl) in which the court stated that the situation where the holder of a compulsory portion undertakes never to pursue any claims in this respect in the future, "can only be assessed on the basis of the provisions governing the issue of contracts relating to inheritance

legacy (Articles 968–981 KC), formulated under an appropriate term or condition.

(Article 1047 KC et seq.), including provisions relating to the form of a legal transaction. In such a situation, the final determination of whether and in what amount the entitled person is entitled to a compulsory portion, should be made taking into account the principles of community life."

Wojciech Bańczyk / Katarzyna Południak-Gierz

§ 14 – A contract in favour of a third-party post-mortem and the applicability of inheritance law

Comparative conclusion
German law explicitly regulates and allows donations post-mortem (after death) as well as contracts in favour of a third-party post-mortem. The issue is that in the case of such contracts, it is not clear whether general civil law provisions (e. g. relating to a mistake) or specific inheritance law provisions should be applied. Additionally, doubts are raised as to what extent a legal act after death may be revoked on grounds that would be characteristic of inheritance law, but not to the general part of civil law. Similar problems arise under Polish law, which additionally lacks any express regulation of donations post-mortem and contracts in favour of a third-party post-mortem, and which allows only for a limited range of contractual freedom post-mortem.

I. Analysis of an example case under German law

According to the BGH judgment of 26 November 2003 in case IV ZR 438/02,[1] the claimant, who is a co-heir (with a one-third share) after the deceased based on a will from 5 June 1996, demanded payment of DM 52,317.67 from the defendant (who was also co-heir after the deceased in a similar share and the executor of the will). This sum equals one-third of the value of securities *(Sparbriefe)* reflecting assets in a bank savings account *(Sparkasse)* that create a substantial part of the estate. The securities were also listed and divided among co-heirs in the will. The defendant claims that, based on the statement of the deceased (namely: a *Sparkasse* form from 25 March 1996, filled-in and signed by the deceased by hand), those securities should be handed over to the defendant *(den Beklagten begünstigt hatte)*, if the defendant survives the deceased *(sofern der Beklagte die Erblasserin überleben werde)*.

The claimant and the third co-heir claimed that the deceased made the statement from 25 March 1996 due to a mistake. In their opinion, this statement was only intended as a power of attorney for the defendant to operate the savings

1 BGHZ 157, 79.

account for the deceased, including as an executor of the will she drafted shortly after. They claimed that the statement from 25 March 1996 was not aimed at granting a free gratuitous personal benefit to the defendant. Thus, they made statements of avoidance *(Anfechtung)* in accordance with § 2078 BGB to void the statement from 25 March 1996 of its legal consequences. Furthermore, they underlined that the fact that a will was made later, in which the same objects (namely: the securities) are disposed of, should be interpreted as revoking *(widerrufs)* the earlier contract in favour of the third party (if it all was concluded). The defendant challenged this manner of reasoning, claiming that he is the only one who has the right to the securities.

The primary concern is the admissibility and nature of legal acts post-mortem. At the same time, it must be noted that the legal question that appears in this case is whether a contract in favour of a third-party post-mortem *(Vertrag zugunsten Dritter auf den Todesfall)* was concluded. Such agreements are, in principle, admissible under German law based on §§ 328 and 331 BGB. In addition, the case refers to the position of a contract post-mortem versus the system of inheritance law *(Erbrecht)*.

There are a number of contractual arrangements *inter vivos* (among the living, in German: *unter Lebenden*, in Polish: *między żyjącymi*) that have a particular effect of creating a post-mortem succession. Firstly, there is a contract for the benefit of a third party where the performance for the third party is supposed to take place after the death of the contracting party (§§ 328 and 331 BGB). Secondly, there is a promise of a donation *mortis causa (Schenkungsversprechen von Todes wegen*, in the event of death*)* based on § 2301 section 1 sentence 1 BGB and the donation post-mortem *(Schenkung auf den Todesfall*, after death*)* based on § 2301 section 2 BGB. These institutions produce different effects than the typical inheritance law succession mechanisms *(Erbfolge)*[2] and were designed to function outside *(außerhalb)* of the inheritance law.[3] However, they influence the post-mortem succession and so are commonly referred to as specific succession measures *(Sonderrechtsnachfolge)*.[4]

These three instruments differ from one another when it comes to their premises and legal consequences.

A promise of a donation *mortis causa* (§ 2301 section 1 sentence 1 BGB) is a promise of gratuitous performance to be made if the beneficiary survives the donor. This "survival condition" is not a condition in the meaning of the general

2 D. Leipold, in: *Münchener Kommentar*, vol. 9, 2010, § 1922, pt. 193.

3 B. Müller-Christmann, in: W. Hau, R. Poseck (eds.), *BeckOK BGB*, 2020, § 1922, pt. 23; similarly, that the instrument is independent from inheritance law (erbrechtsunabhängig) – K. Muscheler, *Universalsukzession und Vonselbsterwerb*, Tübingen 2002, p. 61.

4 K. Muscheler, *Universalsukzession …*, p. 61; B. Müller-Christmann, in: W. Hau, R. Poseck (eds.), *BeckOK BGB*, 2020, § 1922, pt. 23.

part of civil law (§ 158 BGB). Under the latter provision, a legal act made under a condition is seen as already executed (and binds the parties, granting them some rights based on the fact of the execution of the act), whereas the full effectiveness of the acquisition of rights specified in that act remains uncertain. In contrast, in the case of the "survival condition", not only is the effective acquisition of any right uncertain as long as the parties stay alive, but also the donor is not bound by that legal act during their lifetime, and no rights are obtained by the beneficiary (under § 1923 section 1 BGB, only a person who is alive at the time of the devolution of an inheritance may be an heir).[5] Thus, the donor is free to withhold his promise at any time while still alive, without worrying about the consequences of such an action (and prior promise). While the donor lives, the position of the beneficiary is not yet legally protected, and the beneficiary may only hope for a chance *(Hoffnung, Chance)* to receive the promised donation.[6] Such promises are, therefore, similar to the disposition *mortis causa (Verfügung von Todes wegen)*.[7] As a result, these contracts are governed by inheritance law rules on dispositions *mortis causa* (§ 2301 section 1 sentence 1 BGB).

By contrast, a donation post-mortem (§ 2301 section 2 BGB) is already performed *(vollgezogen)* during the lifetime of the parties, but the effects related to its performance (economic effectiveness) appear at the moment of the donor's death. This means that it is the donor, and not his post-mortem successor, who diminishes his lifetime property *(Vermögensopfer)*.[8] This takes place when the donation contract is executed *inter vivos* on the condition (§ 158 BGB) that the donor dies before the beneficiary, or it is stipulated that the effectiveness of the donation appears at the time (§ 163 BGB) of the donor's death.[9] In such cases, the beneficiary acquires the first rights already at the time of concluding the contract. From this moment on, the parties are bound by the contract. It is often also agreed (though not unanimously[10]) that the property of the donor becomes diminished already then, namely when the donor starts bearing any costs of a right that – after death – will be transferred to the beneficiary. In practice, in order to make a donation post-mortem, the donor may issue a power of attorney to make the donation to the prospective beneficiary. Such a donation might be aimed to be performed after the death of the donor[11] (by this, the formless

5 H.-J. Musielak, in: *Münchener Kommentar*, vol. 9, 2010, § 2301, pt. 10.
6 M. Harder, *Zuwendungen unter Lebenden auf den Todesfall*, Berlin 1968, p. 98.
7 M. Harder, *Zuwendungen …*, p. 33.
8 H.-J. Musielak, in: *Münchener Kommentar*, vol. 9, 2010, § 2301, pt. 2.
9 H. Brox, W.-D. Walker, *Erbrecht*, Köln 2009, pp. 413–415.
10 Against e.g. R. Kanzleiter in: *Staudingers Kommentar*, vol. 5, 2006, § 2301, pt. 24.
11 H. Brox, W.-D. Walker, *Erbrecht…*, p. 418; F. Wieacker, *Zur lebzeitigen Zuwendung auf den Todesfall*, in: H.C. Nipperdey (ed.), *Festschrift für Heinrich Lehmann zum 80. Geburtstag*, Berlin 1956, p. 279.

donation contract may be cured, § 518 section 2 BGB). The donor may also prepare the offer of donation, including an offer made by the donor upon the assumption that the offer should not be directed to the beneficiary during the donor's life and should still be effective after the death of the donor as the offering party (§§ 130 section 2 and 153 BGB).[12] In any case, the performance (regardless of how it is understood)[13] of such a donation during the lifetime of the donor makes it a donation *inter vivos* (§ 2301 section 2 BGB).

In addition to the discussion on § 2301 BGB, it is vital to properly contextualise the contract in favour of the third-party post-mortem (§§ 328 and 331 BGB). This institution is based on a regular contract in favour of a third-party (§ 328 BGB). However, under the contract in favour of a third party post-mortem, the promisor *(Versprechende)* and promisee (*Versprechensempfänger*) undertake a contract *inter vivos (Deckungsverhältnis)*, based on which it is the duty of the promisor to make the donation in favour of the third party after the death of the promisee (§ 331 section 1 BGB). This contract *inter vivos* gives grounds for the promisor's performance in favour of the third party. Once the promisee dies, the third party may demand performance directly from the promisor, e.g. to transfer to them a particular right (within *Vollzugsverhältnis)*. If there was no relation between the third party and the promisor, the third party would not be entitled to the transferred right (this performance, if carried out, would lead to an unjustified enrichment at the expense of the promisor[14]).

The last legal relation that needs to be tackled in the case of contracts for a third party is the one between the promisee and the third party *(Valutaverhältnis)*. It is the reason for the promisor's performance to the third party. This also grounds the promisee's performance in favour of the third party, but only in the relation between the third party and the promisee. If the relation between the promisee and the third party does not exist, the third party would still be entitled to the performance from the promisor (in *Vollzugsverhältnis*), but such performance would lead to an unjustified enrichment at the expense of the promisee.[15] *Valutaverhältnis* may be diverse in nature. It can stem from, for instance, a

---

12 Judgment of Bundesgerichtshof from 19 October 1983, IVa ZR 71/82, NJW 1984, 480; Judgment of Bundesgerichtshof from 30 January 2018, X ZR 119/15, FamRZ 2018, 854; P. Gottwald, in: *Münchener Kommentar*, vol. 5, 2009, § 331, pt. 9; D. Grüneberg, in: *Palandt BGB Kommentar*, 2016, § 331, pt. 5.

13 The concept of performance *(vollziehen)* is reffered to as one of the most disputed matters in the legal writing on BGB (*eine der kompliziertesten und erbittertsten Streitfragen des BGB)*. G. Boehmer, *Grundlagen des bürgerlichen Rechtsordnung*, Tübingen 1952, p. 82.

14 W. Fikentscher, A. Heinemann, *Schuldrecht*, Berlin 2006, p. 156–157; D. Medicus, S. Lorenz, *Schuldrecht I, Allgemeiner Teil*, München 2010, p. 388.

15 H. Brox, W.-D. Walker, *Erbrecht …*, p. 424; P. Gottwald, in: *Münchener Kommentar*, vol. 5, 2009, § 328, pt. 29; D. Grüneberg, in: *Palandt BGB Kommentar*, 2016, Einführung vor § 328, pt. 4.

donation *inter vivos* as specified § 2301 section 2 BGB[16] or a promise of donation *mortis causa* referred to in § 2301 section 1 sentence 1 BGB. It can also be the result of an inheritance law benefit,[17] e.g. as a legacy *per damnationem*[18] (§ 1939 BGB) or as alimony support.[19]

At the same time, the three instruments shape the post-mortem succession, fulfilling functions that are typical for inheritance law institutions. For example, they serve to order the legal relations in the event of death,[20] especially by providing help, alimony or any other gratuitous support after the death of the disposing party[21] delivered to a beneficiary based on a non-formalised legal act.[22] They are even referred to as substitutes of a will *(Testamentersatz)*[23] or a surrogate form of legacy by vindication (*Surrogationsform des Vindikationslegat*)[24] which is lacking in the German law system.

The court in the analysed case had to decide what the legal characteristics of the act undertaken by the deceased on 25 March 1996 were. According to the defendant, it should be considered a contract in favour a third-party (namely, the defendant). Its *Valutaverhältnis* was supposedly the donation of assets, which would grant the defendant the possibility to use the assets to his own benefit. By contrast, the claimant claimed that the *Valutaverhältnis* regarded only a mandate contract *(Auftrag)* or some other arrangement whereby the defendant was supposed to take care of the interests *(Geschäftsbesorgung)* of the deceased, including his bank assets. The court underlined that, in order to adjudicate this matter, the actual content of the arrangement among the deceased, the defendant and the *Sparkasse* needs to be ascertained in the evidentiary proceedings.[25]

During an assessment on when the donation contract was established, two further issues arise. Both refer to the applicability of specific inheritance law

16 H. Brox, W.-D. Walker, *Erbrecht* …, p. 425; P. Gottwald, in: *Münchener Kommentar*, vol. 5, 2009, § 331, pt. 9; D. Grüneberg, in: *Palandt BGB Kommentar*, 2016, § 331, pt. 3; H. Lange, K. Küchinke, *Erbrecht* …, München 2001, p. 754; D. Medicus, R. Stürner, in: H. Prütting, G. Wegen, W. Weinreich (eds.), *Bürgerliches Gesetzbuch. Kommentar*, Köln 2014, § 331, pt. 6–7.

17 H. Brox, W.-D. Walker, *Erbrecht* …, p. 424; P. Gottwald, in: *Münchener Kommentar*, vol. 5, 2009, § 331, No 11; D. Grüneberg in: *Palandt BGB Kommentar*, 2016, § 331, No 5; H. Lange, K. Küchinke, *Erbrecht* …, p. 753.

18 M. Harder, *Zuwendungen* …, p. 152.

19 P. Gottwald, in: *Münchener Kommentar*, vol. 5, 2009, § 331, No 3.

20 H. Brox, W.-D. Walker, *Erbrecht* …, p. 412.

21 W. Bańczyk, *Der Vertrag zugunsten Dritter auf den Todesfall im polnischen Recht. Die Zulassung der Lösung aus § 331 BGB kraft Vertragsfreiheit*, OER 2017, No 2, p. 165.

22 G. Boehmer, *Grundlagen* …, p. 83; H. Brox, W.-D. Walker, *Erbrecht* …, p. 412; T. Kipp, H. Coing, *Erbrecht*, Tübingen 1960, p. 339.

23 G. Boehmer, *Grundlagen* …, p. 82.

24 K. Muscheler, *Universalsukzession* …, p. 101.

25 Judgment IV ZR 438/02, pt. 1.c.

provisions to the instruments from §§ 2301 section 1 sentence 1, 2301 section 2 and of 328 and 331 BGB, being legal acts *inter vivos*. Otherwise, general civil law provisions may apply.

Firstly, it needs to be examined whether the inheritance law provision of § 2078 BGB could apply to a mistake by the promisee in *Valutaverhältnis* of the contract in favour of a third-party post-mortem instead of the general civil law provisions of §§ 119 and 122 BGB. In cases where a contract of donation was concluded, rather than a contract of mandate, it should be examined whether the conditions for applying the rules on defects in consent were fulfilled. In this context, establishing what the actual intent of the deceased is crucial.[26]

The scope of situations where avoidance based on the defect of consent is allowed under § 2078 BGB (governing disposing *mortis causa* under mistake) is broader than under § 119 BGB (governing a mistake of the party to a legal act in general). However, under § 2078 BGB the scope of mistakes that allow for the legal act in question to be voided is broader than under the general rule of § 119 BGB, e.g. under § 2078 BGB the mistake in motivation is legally relevant *(Motivirrtum)*.[27]

Additionally, § 122 section 1 BGB states that, if the declaration was to be made to another person, the declarant must pay damages to this person, or pay for the damage that the other or the third party suffered as a result of relying on the validity of a defective declaration. The application of § 122 BGB is, however, explicitly excluded when it was a disposition *mortis causa* that was defective (see § 2078 section 3 BGB).

In the case analysed here, the court was of opinion that both *Deckungsverhältnis* and *Valutaverhältnis* are legal acts *inter vivos*.[28] As it is necessary to protect the counterparties *(Vertragspartners)* of the donor, the list of avoidance reasons should not be broadened as in § 2078 BGB. The court therefore concluded that only § 119 BGB was applicable in the case.[29] At the same time, opposing views are also presented in the legal literature. The court's reasoning sometimes is criticised,[30] with claims that § 2078 BGB should have been applied instead.[31]

The *Deckungsverhältnis* is, without a doubt, a legal act *inter vivos*. When it comes to *Valutaverhältnis*, there can be some dispute. However, in this particular situation, the defendant knew about the transfer of assets in his favour already

26 Judgment IV ZR 438/02, pt. 1.c.
27 T. Hoeren, in: R. Schulze (ed.), *BGB Kommentar*, 2021, § 2078, pt. 1.
28 Judgment IV ZR 438/02, pt. 3.a.
29 Judgment IV ZR 438/02, pt. 3.a.
30 T. Barnert, *BGH, 26.11.2003 – IV ZR 438/02, Verträge zugunsten Dritter auf den Todesfall*, JZ 2004, No 10, pp. 521–522.
31 D. Leipold, in: *Münchener Kommentar*, vol. 9, 2010, § 2078, pt. 18.

before the death of the deceased. He was also aware when this transfer to the benefit of the defendant was supposed to take place. The legal act (regardless of whether it is considered a donation or not) was executed between the parties as a legal act *inter vivos*. The fact that the donation was to be performed, making it valid under § 518 section 2 BGB (a donation *inter vivos* that was invalid due to the lack of form), after the death of the disposing party, through the acquisition of the right by the beneficiary "from himself" *(Von-Selbst-Erwerb)* based on a power of attorney in favour of the beneficiary himself does not change the nature of the legal act.[32] The fact that the disposing party did not experience the actual economic burden of the donation *inter vivos* does not affect the nature of this legal act, performed according to § 2301 section 2 BGB.

Still, the statement of the deceased creating the *Valutaverhältnis* may be avoided if made under the influence of a defect of consent. A statement of avoidance must be delivered by all the heirs,[33] not necessarily acting at the same time *(gleichzeitig)*.[34] The defendant (who is also a co-heir), against whose personal interest the avoidance would be, is not entitled to express his statement in this matter.[35] All the other demands (listed under the general civil law provision) for the avoidance of statements due to defect of consent apply.

Finally, it needs to be considered whether a will (as a later act *mortis causa*) explicitly referring to the subject of an earlier contract in favour of the third-party post-mortem may revoke that contract. This question was raised by the defendant, who argued that a concluded contract *inter vivos* cannot be revoked. This matter was disregarded by the court.

Another issue is that the beneficiary has not yet acquired any rights, even though the donation has already been performed in the sense of § 2301 section 2 BGB (e.g. the offer of the donation post-mortem was made by the donor, but has not yet been delivered by the beneficiary). The offer could be revoked as long as the revocation reaches the beneficiary no later than the offer itself).[36] In the analysed case, the beneficiary undeniably received the offer of donation (and the donation contract was even concluded), and so the donation may not be revoked.

32 No 1.b of the justification of the analysed judgment. The judgment cites prior judicature of BGH in this context.

33 The judgment cites prior judicature of BGH in this context.

34 Judgment IV ZR 438/02, pt. 3.b.

35 Judgment IV ZR 438/02, pt. 3.b.

36 Judgment of Bundesgerichtshof from 30 January 2018, X ZR 119/15, NJW-RR 2018, 518.

II. Consideration of the problem presented in the German case and its comparison with Polish law

Answering these questions under Polish law would be problematic as there is no regulation comparable to §§ 331 and 2301 BGB. Nevertheless, the provisions of the general part of civil law and the principle of freedom of contract (Article 353^1 KC) may justify the admissibility of donations post-mortem or contracts in favour of a third-party post-mortem. Still, this does not mean that they reach the same legal character as in German law, where this instrument has an express legal regulation.

At the same time, most of the doctrine[37] and the Supreme Court case-law (including the 2013 resolution)[38] agrees that a donation post-mortem is allowed under Polish law. Adding the condition that the donor must die before the beneficiary (Article 89 KC) to the regular donation contract, or specifying that the contract becomes effective at the time of the donor's death (Article 116 KC)

---

37 W. Bańczyk, *Glosa do uchwały Sądu Najwyższego z dnia 13 grudnia 2013 r., III CZP 79/13,* in: F. Zoll, S. Daniluk (eds.), *Prawo cywilne. Glosy,* Warszawa 2016, p. 129–130; A. Bieranowski, *Darowizna własności nieruchomości na wypadek śmierci,* in: A. Dańko-Roesler, A. Oleszko, R. Pastuszko (eds.), *Rozprawy z prawa prywatnego oraz notarialnego. Księga pamiątkowa dedykowana Profesorowi Maksymilianowi Pazdanowi,* Warszawa 2014, p. 38–39; W. Borysiak, in: K. Osajda, W. Borysiak (eds.) *Komentarz KC,* 2020, ed. 26, Article 1047, pt. 49.1, Legalis; E. Drozd, *Darowizna na wypadek śmierci,* Rejent 1992, No 5, p. 80; Z. Gawlik, in: A. Kidyba (ed.), *Komentarz KC,* vol. III (zobowiązania, część szczególna), 2014, Article 888, pt. 13, LEX; J. Górecki, *Umowa darowizny na wypadek śmierci,* Rejent 2006, No 2, p. 35; A. Kubas, *Recenzja: L. Stecki, Umowa darowizny,* NP 1974, No 10, p. 1370; A. Janas, in: M. Habdas, M. Fras (eds.), *Komentarz KC,* vol. V, 2018, Article 888, pt. 9, LEX; B. Kucia, in: M. Habdas, M. Fras (eds.), *Komentarz KC,* vol. VI, 2019, Article 941, pt. 20, LEX; P. Kübler, *Darowizna mortis causa,* in: P. Stec, M. Załucki (eds.), *Wokół rekodyfikacji prawa cywilnego. Prace jubileuszowe,* Kraków 2015, p. 382; J. Masiubański, *Glosa do uchwały Sądu Najwyższego z dnia 13 grudnia 2013 r., III CZP 79/13,* Rejent 2014, No 12, p. 121–123; D. Mróz-Krysta, *Glosa do uchwały Sądu Najwyższego z dnia 13 grudnia 2013 r., III CZP 79/13,* 2015, pt. 3, LEX; M. Niedośpiał, *Darowizna na wypadek śmierci,* PiP 1987, No 11, p. 53; K. Osajda, *Darowizna mortis causa de lege lata,* in: T. Ereciński, J. Gudowski, M. Pazdan (eds.), *Ius est a iustitia appelatum. Księga jubileuszowa dedykowana Profesorowi Tadeuszowi Wiśniewskiemu,* Warszawa 2017, p. 914; M. Pazdan, in: *System prawa prywatnego,* vol. 10, 2015, p. 1134; G. Wolak, *Glosa do uchwały Sądu Najwyższego z dnia 13 grudnia 2013 r., III CZP 79/13,* Rejent 2014, No 7, p. 117; L. Zabielski, *Donatio mortis causa. Lex abrogatae,* in: M. Pecyna, J. Pisuliński, M. Podrecka (eds.), *Rozprawy cywilistyczne. Księga pamiątkowa dedykowana Profesorowi Edwardowi Drozdowi,* Warszawa 2013, p. 459; P. Zakrzewski, *Umowa darowizny na wypadek śmierci w prawie holenderskim, niemieckim i polskim,* in: A. Olejniczak, J. Haberko, A. Pyrzyńska, D. Sokołowska (eds.), *Współczesne problemy prawa zobowiązań,* Warszawa 2015, p. 752; J. Zawadzka, *Uwagi o czynnościach prawnych mortis causa,* in: B. Jelonek-Jarco, R. Kos, J. Zawadzka (eds.), *Usus magister est optimus. Rozprawy prawnicze ofiarowane Profesorowi Andrzejowi Kubasowi,* Warszawa 2016, p. 280, 291.

38 Resolution of SN of 13 December 2013, III CZP 79/13, OSNC 2014, No 10, item 98, p. 9; a similar earlier judgment of SN of 6 May 2004, III CK 511/02, Legalis 123625.

regardless of whether the beneficiary survives the donor, does not change the legal character of the donation contract and it remains a legal act *inter vivos.* This suggests that the traditional terminology, namely "donation *mortis causa*" *(donation* in the event of death, *darowizna na wypadek śmierci)* is misleading and should be changed to "donation post-mortem" (after death, *w razie śmierci).*[39]

The admissibility of such contracts derives from the general possibility to create legal relations that are conditional or become effective when the time comes. The condition of the survival or specification of the time of death should not be treated differently. The position of a beneficiary who obtains a legally secured position and rights based on a concluded contract during the life of the donor (even if the contract did not yet bring about its main economic effect – the transfer of the donated right is conditional or postponed) is different from the position of the beneficiary of an act *mortis causa.* Articles 941 and 1047 KC limit the ways in which *mortis causa* effects can be adapted to instruments provided in the inheritance law or instruments introduced by specific legal provisions outside the inheritance law, e.g. as non-probate transfers *mortis causa.*[40]

At the same time, a donation cannot be made after the death of the donor (with the effect of restoring its validity, Article 890 § 1 sentence 2 KC),[41] including via a power of attorney or by formulating an offer of donation that is to be made (passed on) to the beneficiary after the donor's death (although, according to Article 62 KC, in principle a declaration of intent to be made to another person does not lose its legal effect due to the fact that the declarant dies before it reaches the addressee). In such situations, the beneficiary does not obtain a legally secured position or a right before the death of the donor. However, the rules on protection of legal acts post-mortem in Polish law[42] apply only to those legal acts that grant a legally secured position to then beneficiary already during the lifetime of the donor. Donations post-mortem are allowed because, in general, legal acts whose full effectiveness depends on the fulfilment of a condition or the passing of time can be made. Nevertheless, it is not allowed to create effects that fully resemble the effects of legal acts *mortis causa* outside the inheritance law regime. If the aim of a particular donation post-mortem is to bypass the in-

39 W. Bańczyk, *Glosa…*, p. 128; W. Borysiak, in: ed. K. Osajda, W. Borysiak (eds.) *Komentarz KC*, 2020, Article 1047, pt. 49.1, Legalis; K. Osajda, in: K. Osajda, W. Borysiak (eds.), *Komentarz KC*, 2020, ed. 26, Article 941, pt. 10, Legalis; G. Wolak, *Glosa…*, p. 126.

40 W. Bańczyk, *Pozaspadkowe sposoby kształtowania następstwa na wypadek śmierci – o przełamaniu monopolu prawa spadkowego*, Kraków 2021 (unpublished doctoral thesis), pp. 381–382.

41 E. Drozd, *Darowizna…*, p. 87; J. Górecki, *Umowa…*, p. 42.

42 W. Bańczyk, *Pozaspadkowe …*, p. 968.

heritance law provisions, that contract would be invalid (according to Article 58 § 1 KC, an act in law that is designed to circumvent statutory law will be invalid).

For a donation post-mortem to be valid, the donor's declaration must made in the form of a notarial deed (Article 890 § 1 sentence 1KC). The reason behind this formal requirement in the case of donations is to ensure that the donor is aware of the legal and economic consequences of the legal act being performed and makes the decision to benefit the other after some consideration. However, a contract of donation concluded without observing that form becomes valid if the promised performance has been made (Article 890 § 1 sentence 2 KC). If a person concluded an even informal donation contract and then performed it, it can be assumed that they understood the meaning of the legal act in question as they made the actual transfer of the assets themselves. This means that an informal donation post-mortem must be made during the lifetime of the donor, since only then will this fulfil the affirmative and protective function of form of the missing notarial deed.[43] The actual transfer of the donation itself may take place after the death of the donor (due to a condition or a specification of time) as long as the activity understood as performance of the donation took place while the donor was still alive (Article 890 § 1 sentence 2 KC), but without making the donation itself. In the case of donating movables, it is difficult to give an example of a behaviour that could be interpreted as making the donation under Article 890 § 1 sentence 2 KC without the actual transfer of the donated thing.[44] By contrast, when donations of rights are considered, e.g. handing-over the documents referring to the security,[45] or granting a power of attorney to use the assets on a savings account to the attorney's own benefit,[46] it can be understood as making the donation. This can be illustrated with the following example: a contract of donation of rights from a bank account is concluded orally. The parties specify that the contract should become fully effective once the donor dies – only then will the rights to the bank account be transferred to the beneficiary. In principle, this contract is invalid due to the lack of form. However, the donor gives the beneficiary the login and password to that account, and by doing so makes the donation contract, which becomes valid (Article 890 § 1 sentence 2 KC). In any case, because of the term specified in the contract, the rights from that bank account will be transferred to the beneficiary at the moment of the donor's death.

43 M. Grochowski, in: K. Osajda, W. Borysiak (eds.), *Komentarz KC*, 2020, ed. 26, Article 890, pt. 20–22, 56, Legalis.

44 W. Bańczyk, *Pozaspadkowe …*, p. 968.

45 K. Zawada, *Forma przelewu*, Rejent 1992, No 5, pp. 20–22.

46 Judgment of SA in Katowice from 8 November 2017, I ACa 242/17, Legalis No 1683219; judgment of SA in Białystok from 8 June 2016, I ACa 118/16, Legalis No 1473072.

Nevertheless, some legal scholars[47] challenge the admissibility of donations post-mortem under Polish law. They question its character as a legal act among the living,[48] or claim that this modification of the typical donation contract would be too far-reaching.[49] It should also be noted that the introduction of a similar instrument has been proposed twice (see legislative drafts in 2009 and 2011). The initiatives were rejected, from which one may draw the conclusion that donations post-mortem are forbidden under Polish law.[50] More generally, it can suggest that the matter of the admissibility of donations post-mortem should be decided by the legislature and not the judiciary.[51]

Surprisingly, far fewer doubts emerge regarding the admissibility of a post-mortem contract in favour of a third party under Polish law. Most legal scholars agree that such contracts can be concluded, justifying their opinion with arguments similar to those presented during the discussion on the donation post-mortem.[52] However, there are some scholars who refrain from addressing the admissibility of a donation post-mortem, but who expressly accept the admis-

47 M. Bajerski, *Glosa do uchwały Sądu Najwyższego z dnia 13 grudnia 2013 r., III CZP 79/13*, PP UW 2016, No 1, p. 253; T. Justyński, *Glosa do uchwały Sądu Najwyższego z dnia 13 grudnia 2013 r., III CZP 79/13*, OSP 2014, No 11, p. 1273; P. Księżak, *Glosa do uchwały Sądu Najwyższego z dnia 13 grudnia 2013 r., III CZP 79/13*, PiP 2015, No 10, p. 124; I. Mazurkiewicz, *Glosa do uchwały Sądu Najwyższego z dnia 13 grudnia 2013 r., III CZP 79/13*, Pal. 2015, No 11–12, p. 152; J. Ciszewski, J. Knabe, in: J. Ciszewski, P. Nazaruk (eds.), *Komentarz KC*, 2019, Article 1047, pt. 4, LEX; T. Justyński, *Uwagi w sprawie prawnej dopuszczalności zawierania umów darowizny ze skutkiem mortis causa*, PS 2015, No 4, p. 7; J. Kremis, J. Kuźmicka-Sulikowska, in: E. Gniewek, P. Machnikowski (eds.), *Komentarz KC*, 2017, Article 941 pt. 2; R. Niemotko, *Sankcja nieważności umów o spadek po osobie żyjącej*, in: P. Stec, M. Załucki (eds.), *Wokół rekodyfikacji prawa cywilnego. Prace jubileuszowe*, Kraków 2015, p. 404; E. Niezbecka, in: A. Kidyba (ed.), *Komentarz KC*, vol. IV, 2015, Article 941, pt. 2, LEX; E. Skowrońska-Bocian, J. Wierciński, in: J. Gudowski (ed.), *Komentarz KC*, vol. VI, 2017, Article 941, pt. 8, LEX; T. Sokołowski, in: M. Gutowski (ed.), *Komentarz KC*, vol. II, 2019, Article 941, pt. 33, Legalis.

48 T. Justyński, *Uwagi…*, p. 12.

49 P. Księżak, *Glosa…*, p. 125.

50 M. Bajerski, *Glosa…*, p. 252; P. Księżak, Glosa …, p. 126.

51 F. Longchamps de Bérier, *Z uwag do metodologii nauki prawa prywatnego: argumenty historyczny, dogmatyczny i prawnoporównawczy na przykładzie darowizny na wypadek śmierci oraz zapisu windykacyjnego*, in: A. Wudarski (ed.), *Polska komparatystyka prawa. Prawo obce w doktrynie prawa polskiego*, Warszawa 2016, p. 305; J. Rudnicki, *Dekodyfikacja prawa cywilnego w Polsce*, Bielsko-Biała 2018, p. 161.

52 W. Bańczyk, *Der Vertrag…*, p. 176; M. Bednarek, in: *System prawa prywatnego*, vol. 5, 2013, p. 1055; W. Borysiak, *Dziedziczenie. Konstrukcja prawna i ochrona*, Warszawa 2013, p. 291; A. Kubas, *Umowa na rzecz osoby trzeciej*, ZNUJ 1976, No 78, p. 86; P. Machnikowski, in: E. Gniewek, P. Machnikowski (eds.), *Komentarz KC*, 2017, Article 393, pt. 13, Legalis; A. Olejniczak, in: A. Kidyba (ed.), *Komentarz KC*, vol. III (zobowiązania część ogólna) 2014, Article 393, pt. 4, LEX; E. Skowrońska-Bocian, *Prawo spadkowe*, Warszawa 2016, p. 75; Z. Radwański, in: *System prawa cywilnego*, vol. III, part 1, 1976, p. 444; K. Osajda, in: ed. K. Osajda, W. Borysiak (eds.), Komentarz KC, 2020, ed. 26, Article 941, pt. 24, Legalis; G. Wolak, *Glosa…*, p. 128.

sibility of a post-mortem contract in favour of a third party.[53] This inconsistency in reasoning is not justified. If a two-party relation of a certain content and aim is forbidden, the fact that a third party becomes involved into this contractual relation should not have any impact on the legal assessment of the admissibility of the arrangement.[54]

A contract in favour of a third-party post-mortem may only be admissible and fully effective in Polish law when the relation between the promisee and the third party (*Valutaverhältnis*) is valid. In German law, a contract in favour of a third-party post-mortem itself is explicitly regulated by law, and so is the transfer to a third person after the death of the promisee. Consequently, there are various manners of shaping the relation between the promisee and the third party *(Valutaverhältnis*). By contrast, under Polish law, the *Valutaverhältnis* may only stem from a donation post-mortem in its admissible format. Such a donation post-mortem must grant a beneficiary either a legally secured position or a right already during the lifetime of the donor.[55]

If the discussed situation was analysed from a Polish law perspective, the contract in favour of the third-party post-mortem would be admissible only if the relation between the deceased and the defendant stemmed from a contract of donation. The fact that the beneficiary (defendant) was informed about his future benefit already during the lifetime of the donor and then became able to perform the legal acts necessary to obtain the benefit (he was granted power of attorney) means that the contract of donation of the rights to the savings account was concluded and made. Anyway, the donation contract was not in the form required under Article 890 § 2 KC. At the same time, the transfer of rights itself could have and was performed after the donor's death which cured such invalid donation under Article 890 § 1 sentence 2 KC. In conclusion, under Polish law, the relation in *Valutaverhältnis* would be admissible, the contract in favour of the third party would become fully effective once the donor was still alive, and there would be the proper *causa* for keeping the benefit acquired on its basis.

In the Polish doctrine, there is a view that general civil law provisions on the defect of consent (in particular Articles 84 and 88 KC) should apply in the case of a donation post-mortem[56] instead of an inheritance law provision (namely Ar-

53 M. Rzewuski, *Darowizna na wypadek śmierci*, in: A. Olejniczak, J. Haberko, A. Pyrzyńska, D. Sokołowska (eds.), *Współczesne problemy prawa zobowiązań*, Warszawa 2015, p. 632; E. Skowrońska-Bocian, *Prawo…*, p. 75.

54 W. Bańczyk, *Der Vertrag …*, p. 176.

55 W. Bańczyk, *Der Vertrag …*, p. 176.

56 W. Bańczyk, *Pozaspadkowe …*, p. 930; M. Kołodzińska, *Czy instytucja zapisu windykacyjnego może skutecznie zastąpić darowiznę na wypadek śmierci? Uwagi wynikające z praktyki notarialnej*, PS 2012, No 11–12, p. 108; Ł. Mleko, *Darowizna na wypadek śmierci. Rozważania na tle projektowanych rozwiązań legislacyjnych*, KPP 2010, No 4, p. 1060; also M. Bajerski, *Glosa …*, p. 249 (being against the admissibility of donation post-mortem).

ticle 945 KC). The justification was that this was necessary to protect third persons and the safety of the exchange.[57] This reasoning is convincing also if the need to balance the interests of the parties to the donation contract is considered. By contrast, if inheritance law rules on defect of consent were to apply, one party would be better protected at the expense of the other.[58] This should not be allowed, especially when it is taken into consideration that a legal act made due to a defect of consent may be voided by the heirs after the death of the party whose declaration was defective.[59]

Under Polish law, making a will should not affect a prior donation post-mortem.[60] Nevertheless, a donation post-mortem, like every other contract, is generally irrevocable. Consequently, it may not be revoked by a later act *mortis causa,* e. g. making a will after concluding a donation contract. However, revoking the offer of donation post-mortem may be effective if the revocation is delivered to the beneficiary before the offer (Article 61 sentence 2 KC). Still, this would be an exception, i. e. if the offer was intended to be delivered during the lifetime of the donor, but the donor died before delivery took place, the offer can be considered revoked if the offeror made an act *mortis causa* whereby it is clear that their intention was to revoke the prior made but undelivered offer, and then delivered the revocation.

III. Summary

A contract in favour of a third party post-mortem may be valid and effective under Polish law if the relation between the promisee and the third party (*Valutaverhältnis*) is not forbidden by law. Thus, *Valutaverhältnis* may arise from a valid donation post-mortem, provided that this donation is a legal act made among the living. Hence, both a contract in favour of the third party post-mortem and a donation post-mortem are admissible based on freedom of contract. These contracts may be concluded on the condition that they become fully effective at the moment specified in the contract (including where there is a survival condition, or the contract becomes fully effective at the time of the donor's death). However, it is not possible to shape these contracts to becoming similar to acts *mortis causa:* in which the beneficiary acquires no rights during the life of the donor.

57 Ł. Mleko, *Darowizna* …, p. 1060.
58 W. Bańczyk, *Pozaspadkowe* …, p. 930.
59 Judgment of SN of 27 April 1979, III CRN 56/79, OSNCP 1979, No 12, item 244; P. Księżak, *Prawo* …, p. 69.
60 W. Bańczyk, *Pozaspadkowe* …, p. 1033.

In German law, a contract in favour of a third-party post-mortem and a donation post-mortem are explicitly regulated (§§ 2301, 331 and 328 BGB). These contracts may become effective without the need of formalities as regarding dispositions *mortis causa* once they are performed (§ 2301 section 2 BGB). The performance might be carried out, for example, based on a power of attorney.

Both legal systems should not allow inheritance law provisions to apply to legal acts *inter vivos*, especially when voiding legal acts due to the defects of consent is considered. Both parties to contracts *inter vivos* should be protected equally, and if the inheritance law provisions were to be applied, the deceased would be protected at the expense of the other party involved. This does not preclude the application of inheritance law provisions in other situations, when the particular values protected by the analysed institution from the perspective of the legal act *inter vivos* (but post-mortem) and *mortis causa* are the same.

In addition, since a legal act among the living produces legal effects from the moment it is taken, it should not be revocable unless specified otherwise. In particular, a will should not revoke contracts among the living that were concluded by the deceased, since the counterparty's trust should be protected.

Wojciech Bańczyk / Katarzyna Południak-Gierz

§ 15 – Revocation of the power of attorney to make a donation after the death of the donor

Comparative conclusion
German law allows for a power of attorney to become effective after the death of the principal, allowing the attorney to make a donation after the death of the donor. Granting such a power of attorney may serve as making a donation after death, to which the rules on donations *inter vivos* apply (§ 2301 section 2 BGB). At the same time, such a power of attorney may be revoked by an heir after the death of the principal by a conscious legal act. Polish law also allows for the solution of a power of attorney and its revocability, but it has a different legal frame allowing for donations after death which are only possible based on freedom of contract, rather than express admissibility.

I. Analysis of an example case under German law

According to the BGH verdict of 29 November 1994 in case XI ZR 175/93,[1] the deceased owned some securities. After his death, his wife (the claimant) was found to be his sole heir, even though the deceased lived with another woman (the defendant). The deceased handed over the securities to his aunt, along with instructions that they should be passed to the defendant in the event of his death. Shortly after he died, the claimant invited some people (including the defendant and the deceased's aunt) to the deceased's apartment and announced that she is searching for the securities. The aunt did not react to this information, but later handed over the securities to the defendant in line with the deceased's instructions. As soon as the claimant discovered what had happened with the securities, she demanded their return, claiming that they were part of the deceased's estate. The defendant denied this, claiming that the securities were given to her as an effective donation *(wirksame Schenkung)*.

The first issue is whether an heir may revoke a power of attorney granted by the deceased without knowing about it. The court underlined that the claimant's behaviour by searching for the securities in the presence of the person in pos-

1 NJW 1995, 953.

session of such securities (the aunt of the deceased) could not be interpreted as revoking the power of attorney stating that the aunt had to make the donation to the defendant.

In German law, there is no particular provision regarding the duration of a power of attorney after the death of the principal. There is, however, a provision on mandate, whereby in the event of any doubt, a mandate does not expire at the time of death of the mandator (§ 672 section 1 BGB). On this basis, legal scholars argue that a power of attorney should also not expire upon the death of the principal.[2] It is even underlined that § 672 section 1 BGB implies that a power of attorney does not expire at the event of death of the principal.[3] Furthermore, sometimes it is expressly stated in the content of the power of attorney that it should continue after the death of the principal, creating what is known as a trans-mortem power of attorney *(transmortale Vollmacht)*.[4]

However, the unrestricted revocability of a power of attorney is considered a principle (§ 168 section 2 BGB). Accordingly, if the power of attorney continues after death of the principal,[5] the heir should have the possibility to revoke it as they see fit.

Still, the power of attorney did not cover the activity of the attorney both during lifetime of the principal and after his death, as a typical trans-mortem power of attorney does. On the contrary, the activity of the attorney in the analysed case was supposed to initiate only after the death of the principal. Granting such a post-mortem power of attorney *(postmortale Vollmacht)* is allowed, since it is similar in construction to a trans-mortem power of attorney.[6]

The court did not focus on the fact that the aim of the power of attorney was to bind the attorney and the heirs of the principal after the death of the principal. According to the court there were no doubts as to whether it was allowed under German law, and subsequently, this matter did not require further analysis for the court.

Subsequently, the court focused on investigating whether it is possible to revoke a power of attorney through an action made – here, searching for the securities – without the intention to produce this legal effect. The court established that it is not impossible for a certain action that is not intended to be a

2 H. Brox, W.-D. Walker, *Allgemeiner Teil des BGB*, München 2010, p. 236; B. Frensch, in: H. Prütting, G. Wegen, W. Weinreich (eds.), *Bürgerliches Gesetzbuch. Kommentar*, Köln 2014, § 168, p. 262; H. Kötz, *Vertragsrecht*, Tübingen 2010, p. 180; M. Martinek, in: *Staudingers Kommentar*, vol. 2, 2006, § 672, p. 322; D. Medicus, S. Lorenz, *Schuldrecht II, Besonderer Teil*, München 2010, p. 281; E. Schilken, in: *Staudingers Kommentar*, vol. 1, 2004 p. 138; K.-H. Schramm, in: *Münchener Kommentar*, vol. 1, 2006, § 168, p. 2101.

3 B. Frensch, in: ed. H. Prütting, G. Wegen, W. Weinreich (eds.), *Bürgerliches......*, § 168, p. 262.

4 J. Ellenberg, in: Palandt *BGB Kommentar*,2018, § 168, p. 194.

5 D. Kurze, in: W. Burandt, D. Rojahn (eds.), *Erbrecht*, 2019, § 168, pt. 17.

6 K.-H. Schramm, in: *Münchener Kommentar*, vol. 1, 2006, § 168, p. 2108.

statement of intent to produce the legal effects of such a statement of intent. Such an action would produce legal effects of a statement of intent only if it would be reasonably understood as a statement of intent. The reason for this is that the legal system aims to protect the legitimate expectations and trust of anyone receiving a communication that can reasonably be interpreted as a statement of intent, despite the actual intent of the person making the declaration. The core idea behind this theory is that the legal consequences of a statement of intent where there was no intention to produce the legal effects on the side of person making the declaration may arise if it is necessary to protect trust of the recipient of the communication. From this, the court concluded that if the potential legal effect of such a communication is detrimental to the recipient, the behaviour should not give rise to effects of a statement of intent.

A subsequent issue concerns a contract in favour of a third party that is supposed to be performed after death in the context of a revoked power of attorney to make a donation after the death of the donor. Thus, in the event that there was a contract concluded between the deceased (the creditor) and his aunt (the debtor), where the contract was in favour of a third party (the defendant) and was supposed to be carried out after the death of the creditor.[7] The *Deckungsverhältnis* (the original bond between the debtor and the creditor from which the obligation arises) here was a kind-of-mandate contract between the deceased and his aunt based on which the securities were supposed to be kept until the death of the creditor and then transferred to the defendant. The *Vollzugsverhältnis* (the bond between the debtor and the third party) entitled the third party (the defendant) to claim the securities. However, during the lifetime of the deceased, the defendant only barely knew that the aunt of the deceased was supposed to hand the securities over to her. Thus, there was no valid *Valutaverhältnis* between the defendant and the creditor before his death – the deceased (creditor) made an offer of donation that was supposed to be delivered to the defendant after the death of the deceased by his aunt, most likely along with the parallel transfer of securities.

German case law and legal scholars agree that it is sufficient if the *Valutaverhältnis* arises from a donation contract if the offer of donation was presented to the prospective beneficiary after the death of the donor[8] and validated later on by performance (as in § 518 section 2 BGB) made by a person acting based on a

7 Discussed in details in this monograph in § 14.

8 Judgment of Bundesgerichtshof from 19 October 1983, IVa ZR 71/82, NJW 1984, 480; BGH judgment of 30 January 2018, X ZR 119/15, FamRZ 2018, 854; P. Gottwald, in: *Münchener Kommentar*, vol. 5, 2009, § 331, No 9; D. Grüneberg, in: *Palandt BGB Kommentar*, 2016, § 331, No 5.

power of attorney granted by the donor.[9] Such a power of attorney – if formulated as revocable – could be revoked at any time by the heir of the donor.

A vital issue that, according to the court, needs to be verified is whether the donation was performed *(vollgezogen)* before the death of the donor with the consequences as of § 2301 section 2 BGB. If this is the case, the performance would be understood as an action generating costs for the donor while still alive *(Vermögensopfer)*.[10] This would justify the application of § 2301 section 2 BGB and the rules on donations *inter vivos* (including § 518 section 2 BGB, which states that a defect in form is remedied by rendering the performance promised). The donor issuing a power of attorney to make a donation after the death of the donor is sometimes interpreted as performance in the meaning of § 2301 section 2 BGB.[11] Hence, the contract from which the relationship between the defendant and the creditor arose *(Valutaverhältnis)* was valid (§ 518 section 2 BGB) based on rules on donations *inter vivos* (§ 2301 section 2 BGB). However, if the donation of the securities in the case was not considered as performed during the life of the donor, the *Valutaverhältnis* (namely: the promise of the donation *mortis causa*) would be examined in light of the rules on dispositions *mortis causa* (§ 2301 section 1 BGB). The *Valutaverhältnis* would then be invalid in this case.

II. Consideration of the problem presented in the German case and its comparison with Polish law

As above, firstly, it needs to be resolved whether an heir can revoke a power of attorney granted by the deceased even without knowing about it. Under Polish law, there is a general rule that powers of attorney expire with the death of the principal. A power of attorney may continue after the death the principal only exceptionally if such continuation is explicitly stipulated in the power of attorney and is justified by the contents of the legal relationship on which the power of attorney is based (Article 101 § 2 KC). The doctrine provides examples of such reasons, e.g. in order to finalise the affairs of the deceased,[12] to prevent the heirs

9 H. Brox, W.-D. Walker, *Erbrecht*, Köln 2009, p. 418; F. Wieacker, *Zur lebzeitigen Zuwendung auf den Todesfall*, in: H.C. Nipperdey (ed.), *Festschrift für Heinrich Lehmann zum 80. Geburtstag*, Berlin 1956, p. 279.

10 H.-J. Musielak, in: *Münchener Kommentar*, vol. 9, 2010, § 2301, pt. 2.

11 H. Brox, W.-D. Walker, *Erbrecht …*, p. 418; F. Wieacker, *Zur lebzeitigen …*, p. 279. However, a contrary opinion can be found in the doctrine e.g. R. Kanzleiter, in: *Staudingers Kommentar*, vol. 5, 2006, § 2301, pt. 24.

12 J. Ciszewski, *Kilka uwag o pełnomocnictwie nieodwołalnym i niegasnącym ze śmiercią mocodawcy*, GSP 2005, Vol. XIV, p. 798.

from incurring losses,[13] or even to continue running the undertakings of the deceased to the benefit of the market exchange in general,[14] even if it is against the will of their heirs.[15]

Such rationales, however, rarely appear if the power of attorney is granted only to act after the death of the principal (post-mortem). The admissibility of a post-mortem power of attorney is questioned in Polish law. It is underlined that the exception provided in Article 101 § 2 KC allows only for extending the power of attorney for a period after the death of the principal, but it does not allow a power of attorney that starts to act from the moment of the principal's death onwards.[16] However, this manner of reasoning can be challenged. The power of attorney may be granted for a specified period of time or under a condition.[17] Therefore, it might become effective only upon the principal's death and continue afterwards based on Article 101 § 2 KC allowing for the extension of a power of attorney after the death of the principal (regardless of whether the power of attorney came into effect during the life of the principal).[18] After all, under both Polish and German law, the legal construction of a post-mortem and trans-mortem power of attorney is the same.

In conclusion, granting a post-mortem power of attorney is not forbidden under Polish law. However, this does not mean that such a power of attorney is always valid. Article 101 § 2 KC still applies and – consequently – the validity of such a power of attorney depends on whether the content of the underlying relation justifies the continuation of the power of attorney after the principal's death.

It is unclear whether the power of attorney granted to the aunt of the deceased in this situation would be valid under Polish law. The issue is that the performance of the donation after the death of the donor does not make the donation valid; therefore, the act to be undertaken by the aunt of the deceased (making the donation) is not effective (as explained in detail below). This does not mean that the mandate to undertake a legally ineffective activity is invalid *per se*. The issue is that the context of the underlying legal relation aims clearly at evading succession law and is an unauthorised diminishment of the estate. This is what makes the analysed mandate invalid. Consequently, the post-mortem power of attorney

---

13 Judgment of SN of 21 January 2015, IV CSK 252/14, LEX No 1604782.

14 P. Księżak, *Prawo spadkowe*, Warszawa 2017, p. 311; M. Smyk, *Pełnomocnictwo według kodeksu cywilnego*, Warszawa 2010, p. 365.

15 W. Robaczyński, in: P. Księżak, M. Pyziak-Szafnicka (eds.), *Komentarz KC*, 2014, Article 101, pt. 8.

16 P. Księżak, *Prawo…*, p. 312; M. Smyk, *Pełnomocnictwo…*, p. 372.

17 Judgment of SN of 8 May 2001, IV CKN 354/00, LEX No 52538.

18 W. Bańczyk, *Der Auftrag und die damit verbundene Vollmacht nach dem Tod der Parteien. Weiterbestehen im Todesfall im polnischen und deutschen Rechtssystem*, OER 2018, No 2, p. 152.

given to the aunt of the deceased as in the analysed case is ineffective under Polish law. By contrast, a regular mandate (and the resulting post-mortem power of attorney) granted to manage the affairs continuing after death of the principal would be valid.

As a matter of principle, every power of attorney is revocable (Article 101 § 1 KC). This means that a power of attorney exceeding the lifetime of the principal may be revoked by the heirs of the principal.[19]

Under Polish law, a behaviour not intended to produce legal effects may produce them when justified by the trust of the other exchange participants. This comes from the application of the "trust theory" *(teoria zaufania)* that allows a communication that is not intended to create legal effects to be understood as a statement of intent whenever it is reasonably understood as such by the recipient.[20] The power of attorney in this situation would not be revoked under Polish law, not because legal effects cannot be produced without any intention to do so (because they can), but because the attribution of legal effects to the activity not intending them is only possible if it is in the interest of their recipient, and not to their detriment. Thus, the reasons behind the conclusion that the power of attorney was not revoked are similar in both legal systems.

When it comes to the admissibility of a contract in favour of a third-party post-mortem in the context of a revoked power of attorney to make a donation after the death of the donor, Polish law would reject the admissibility of *Valutaverhältnis* as shaped in the analysed case. Simple information about the intended donation cannot be considered as performance demanded by Article 890 § 1 sentence 2 KC, and the donation post-mortem will be invalid due to form deficiency. At the same time, under Polish law it is not possible to perform a donation after the death of the donor with the effect of curing the invalidity of the contract. It is also not possible to make an offer of donation to another party after the death of the donor, including with the use of a power of attorney. *Valutaverhältnis,* being the donor's offer to make a donation in favour of the beneficiary, consciously undelivered to the recipient along with a power of attorney to make such a donation only after the death of the donor, fully resembles the effects of the donor's legal act *mortis causa.*[21] At the same time, Polish law – without explicitly recognising donations post-mortem (such contracts are admissible because of the freedom of contract principle) – allows for such a donation to be made only

19 W. Kaliński, F. Zoll, *Pełnomocnictwo nie gasnące mimo śmierci mocodawcy,* Rejent 1994, No 3, p. 90.

20 U. Ernst, A. Rachwał, F. Zoll, *Prawo cywilne. Część ogólna,* Warszawa 2011, pp. 69–70; K. Południak-Gierz, *Defects of Consent in Consumer E-Commerce from the Polish Law Perspective,* Göttingen 2021, pp. 98–99; K. Mularski, Z. Radwański, in: *System prawa prywatnego,* vol. 2, 2019, pp. 37–38.

21 Discussed in details in this monograph in § 14.

because the beneficiary acquires some rights (from the already concluded, binding contract) before the donor's death.

III. Summary

Both Polish and German law allow for a power of attorney to continue after the death of the principal. In Polish law, this construction is explicitly referred to in Article 101 § 2 KC (as an exception to a general rule); whereas under German law the rule is formulated through jurisprudence and the doctrine based on the provisions on a mandate after the death of the mandator, which – in principle – allow for the continuation of a legal relation as a rule. In addition, granting a power of attorney to act only the after death of the principal is, as a rule, allowed under German law. Under Polish law, the validity of a power of attorney granted to act only after the principal's death depends also on the content of the underlying legal relation.

Nevertheless, under Polish law, a power of attorney could not be used to submit an offer of a donation to the beneficiary, or to make such a donation by performance after the donor's death. Otherwise, it would be possible to circumvent the inheritance law by achieving the effects of a legal act *mortis causa* outside the system of inheritance law. The availability of the donation post-mortem in Polish law depends on whether the donation contract produced legal effects during the life of the donor (certain rights are acquired by the beneficiary at the time of concluding a contract). By contrast, under German law, where a donation post-mortem, to which the rules on donations *inter vivos* apply, is admissible only upon the premise of its performance (§ 2301 section 2 BGB); the acquisition of the right by the beneficiary during the life of the donor is not necessary. The delivery of the offer of donation and a power of attorney to make the donation – both only after death of the donor – may produce the legal effects of a donation post-mortem in German law.

Witold Borysiak

§ 16 – The right to demand the return of the object of the donation after the donor's death, on account of the donor's hardship

Comparative conclusion

German and Polish law both recognise the right of a donor who is in hardship to demand either the revocation of the donation or the return of the donated object, or even to have the donee pay maintenance to the donor. This right expires in both countries if not asserted before the death of the donor. However, if a third party provided the donor with maintenance before their death, then recourse claims that passed to the third party during the donor's lifetime may be asserted against the liable person (e.g. donee) also after the donor's death. In such a situation, German law holds that there is no confusion of debt and claims even if the person obliged to return the object of the donation to the third party is the donee who is the donor's heir.

I. Analysis of an example case under German law

The right to demand the return of an object of donation was considered by the Federal Court of Justice in case IV ZR 212/94 of 14 June 1995.[1] In 1983, the donor (the future testator) transferred ownership of his property to the donee (the future defendant and co-heir) and his wife (the future co-heir), but continued to use the property. The donee undertook to provide care and additional maintenance to the donor.[2] On the same day, the donor designated the defendant and his wife in his will to inherit (each half of the estate). From May 1990 until his death in April 1991, the donor received social assistance from a social welfare institution (the future claimant) in the form of the institution bearing the costs of his care and maintenance in a nursing home. After deducting the deceased's own contribution from the general costs of care and maintenance, the outstanding amount of social assistance provided to him amounted to DM 7809.

1 NJW 1995, No 35, pp. 2287–2289.

2 This agreement was similar in its content to the Polish life tenancy agreement (see Articles 908–916 KC).

After the donor's death, the social welfare institution, claiming reimbursement of the expenses incurred for his maintenance, demanded that the donee return the object of the donation (*Rückforderung*). The basis for the demand to return the donation was § 528 section 1 sentence 1 BGB in conjunction with § 90 BSHG.[3] The first of these provisions governs a demand for the return of the object of a donation because of the donor's hardship. It states in the first section that if a donor, after making a donation, cannot cover their own maintenance costs to the extent corresponding to his reasonable needs in a given situation and fulfil the statutory obligations of supporting his relatives, spouse, life partner or previous spouse or life partner, he may demand that the donee return the object of the donation under the provisions on the restitution of unjust enrichment.[4] The provision states that § 760 BGB applies to the obligation of the donee, § 1613 BGB applies to the obligation of supporting relatives and that, in the event of the donor's death, § 1615 BGB also applies accordingly.[5] At the same time, the second section of § 528 BGB stipulates that, if there are several donees, the earlier donee is obliged only in as far as the later donee is not burdened with this obligation.

The other provision providing the basis for a third party to demand the return of a donated object by the donee was § 90 BSHG.[6] Section 1 of this provision stipulated that, if a social welfare recipient (*Hilfeempfänger*), is entitled to a claim against another person who is not providing care, then the social welfare institution may notify that other person, in writing, about the transfer of the claim (*Übergang*) to the institution up to the amount of the expenses (*Aufwendungen*) that the institution has incurred due to the social welfare recipient. The transfer of this claim to the relevant institution may also occur due to its expenses granted – along with the assistance provided to the social welfare recipient – for the maintenance costs of their spouse and their underage unmarried children. The transfer of the claim is not prevented by the fact that the claim in question cannot be transferred, pledged or seized in the course of bailiff enforcement. At the same time, section 2 of § 90 BSHG stated that: written notification (*die schriftliche*

3 Bundessozialhilfegesetz (BSHG) in der Fassung der Bekanntmachung vom 23. März 1994 (BGBl. I S. 646, 2975), zuletzt geändert durch Art. 4 des Gesetzes zur Familienförderung vom 22. Dezember 1999 (BGBl. I S. 2552). This provision was in force from 1962 until 2004. The regulation was replaced by: Sozialgesetzbuch (SGB) Zwölftes Buch (XII) – Sozialhilfe (as a result of the entry into force of Gesetz zur Einordnung des Sozialhilferechts in das Sozialgesetzbuch vom 27. Dezember 2003 (BGBl. I S. 3022)) – see comments further below.

4 The donee can avoid the return by paying a sum of money needed to support the donor.

5 This provision is important insofar as it stipulates that a maintenance claim extinguishes upon the death of the beneficiary or the debtor, unless it concerns the fulfilment or compensation of damage due to the non-fulfilment for a past period of time, or such prepaid benefits that are due at the time of the beneficiary's or the debtor's death. In the event of the beneficiary's death, the debtor should bear the funeral costs if the payment cannot be obtained from the heirs.

6 It was regulated in Chapter 5 of this law entitled "Obligations of third parties" (*Verpflichtungen anderer*) and entitled "Passing of claims" (*Übergang von Ansprüchen*).

Anzeige) has the effect of transferring the entitlement for the period for which the beneficiary was granted social assistance on a continuous basis.

The claimant argued that, although the transfer of the property to the donee was partially gratuitous, it was still a 'mixed donation' (*gemischte Schenkung*),[7] and thus under § 90 BSHG, the claims that a person in hardship would have against third parties were transferred to the social welfare institution. Since the donor's income was not sufficient to cover the costs of his care in the social welfare home and he remained in debt, he would have a claim against the donee for the return of the object of the donation under § 528 BGB. This claim could also pass to the welfare institution after the death of the donor (testator).

The defendant argued that the claim for the return of the object of the donation due to the donor's hardship expired at the moment of his death, as it was strictly personal in nature, and any claim for the return of the object of the donation in the case under consideration expired at the moment of the donor's death due to confusion. The value of the benefits that the defendant and his wife provided to the donor exceeded the value of the donation, so the condition of enrichment was not fulfilled on their part.

In light of the parties' positions, the issue to be resolved was whether the claim for the return of the object of the donation on the ground of hardship could be transferred if it had not been raised by the donor himself during his lifetime, and whether such a claim could be asserted under a special provision by a third party after the donor's death. The courts hearing the case also examined the question of whether the existence of the claim would be affected by the fact that it would have been made by the donor, while the person against whom it was to be brought subsequently became the heir.

The court of first instance – the Regional Court (*Landgericht*) – dismissed the claim for payment. The Higher Regional Court (*Oberlandesgericht*) then rejected the claimant's appeal. The claimant's cassation was successful and led to the annulment of the decision of the court of second instance. The case was referred back to this court for reconsideration. This is because the BGH concluded that, if the donor had benefited from social assistance prior to his death, the claim under § 528 BGB (for the return of the object of the donation due to hardship) not only does not expire with the donor's death, but due to the obligation to reimburse the costs of social assistance to the institution providing such assistance, which continues to exist even after the donor's death, the claim does not expire as a result of confusion, even if the donee is the donor's heir. Returning the case for reconsideration, the BGH also ordered the court of second instance to ascertain the nature of the donation made to the donee.

7 The equivalent of this German construct is the Polish concept of *negotium mixtum cum donatione*.

It is interesting to trace the reasoning that led to this ruling. In German law, until the BGH ruling, it was disputed whether a donor's claim for the return of the object of a donation due to hardship under § 528 BGB in conjunction with § 1922 section 1 BGB[8] passes to the heirs. This was particularly the case if the donor had received social assistance during their lifetime and had not brought an action for the return of the donation before their death.[9] This issue was only settled by the BGH when it stated that, to the extent that the claim under § 528 BGB includes the reimbursement of social assistance costs, it is heritable.

The BGH stated that a claim under § 528 BGB can be raised after the donor's death if, firstly, it has passed to the social welfare institution and, secondly, if it was asserted against the donee before the donor's death. The donor's heir, in turn, may assert a claim for return of the donation under § 528 BGB if the donor asserted the claim before their death and a third person was making expenses for the donor's maintenance before their death. However, if no one paid the costs of supporting the donor in hardship and the donor himself did not bring an action for the return of the object of the donation, their heirs can no longer do so. The BGH also emphasised that, even if the donor in hardship received means of maintenance from the donee in a grossly inadequate amount in relation to their needs, this should not have any influence on their 'restraint' in obtaining such assistance from a third party, including accepting assistance from the relevant social welfare institution. The social welfare institution, in turn, is entitled to a claim for the return of the object of the donation (*Rückforderungsanspruch*) in the amount of the benefits provided to the donor, which can be raised against the donee also against the donor's will.

The BGH stated that § 90 BSHG gives the social welfare institution that has incurred expenses on the maintenance of a person in need a legal instrument in the form of the possibility to assume the position of a creditor towards that person. Thus, it may enforce the legal obligations of other entities on whom it was incumbent, in a given situation, to provide the necessary assistance to a person in hardship and who failed to do so. The purpose of § 90 BSHG is to give the social welfare institution the opportunity to be in the position it would have been in if the person in hardship had asserted a claim against its debtor in due time. This right exists in substantive law and 'lasts' as long as the social assistance is provided to a given person. A claim for the reimbursement of expenses incurred by

8 The Polish equivalent of this provision is Article 922 KC.

9 Against such heredity were: OLG in Düsseldorf in its judgment of 24 May 1984, 18 U 220/83, the OLG in Stuttgart in its judgment of 22 September 1984, 12 W 27/84 and the OLG in Frankfurt in its judgment of 1 December 1993. In favour of heredity was, among others, the judgment OLG in Karlsruhe of 18 March 1994, 15 U 251/93. In German literature, see C. Brähler-Boyan, H. Mann, *Zur Überleitung des Rückforderungsanspruchs des verarmten Schenkers auf den Sozialhilfeträgers*, NJW 1995, No 29, pp. 1866–1871.

such an institution for a person in hardship does not, therefore, arise at the time when that person requests reimbursement, but exists in substantive law from the time the expenses begin to be provided. A written notification of the transfer of the claim for the reimbursement of expenses (*Überleitungsanzeige*) is only an administrative act that has private law effects and clarifies and individualises the obligation to reimburse the benefit, which is also possible after the death of the person who is the social welfare beneficiary in a given case.

The BGH also stated that donations made by the donor are subject to reimbursement to the extent of the social welfare benefits provided to the donor within the limits of the liability under § 528 BGB. Such an obligation of the donee to return the object of the donation exists irrespective of the donor's intent. The liability of the donee under § 528 BGB (at least to the extent of the social assistance benefits provided to the donor), cannot depend on whether, firstly, the donor is still alive, secondly, whether the donor's claim has been formally transferred to the social assistance institution, or thirdly, whether the donor's claim was asserted in court before the donor's death. However, the BGH also stated that the timing of the written notification to the donee on the transfer of the entitlement to the social welfare institution may sometimes be important. For example, it may be relevant with regard to the good faith of the donee in the context of the regulation of unjust enrichment, e.g. § 818 section 3 BGB.[10] It also protects the legitimate trust of the donee in the existence of such a donation.

A question arose in the case as to whether a claim for the reimbursement of an expended amount that had not expired at the time of the donor's death, nonetheless, expires in a situation where the person liable (i.e. the donee) has become the donor's heir (co-heir). The BGH held that, after the donor's death, the rights of the social welfare institution towards the donee who is the heir may be raised on general principles (if they have not expired already on another basis). In the BGH's view, in the factual situation examined, nothing changed in this respect from the fact that, at the time when the donee received from the social welfare institution a notice of transfer of the claim to the social welfare institution, the division of the estate between the donee and his spouse had not yet taken place (which could potentially affect the assessment as to whether confusion had occurred). The BGH noted that the merger of claim and debt in one hand should indeed result in the extinguishment of the obligation. However, this rule is not explicitly laid down anywhere in German law, nor is it logically necessary (*weder gesetzlich vorgeschrieben noch logisch zwingend*). The claim in question should remain in force if this would affect the 'state of interests' (*Interessenlage*) of the legal subjects, e.g. in the form of rights of a third person. Admittedly, the provisions of the BGB relating to succession law often accept the fiction of the non-

10 Article 409 KC may be regarded as the equivalent of such a regulation in Polish law.

expiry of a certain right as a result of confusion (e.g. in the provisions concerning liability for inheritance debts). However, this does not justify the conclusion that, without the existence of this fiction, a given claim should be extinguished in each case. In the BGH's view, the right to the reimbursement of a welfare benefit of the donor cannot expire to the detriment of a third party, even if the donee has become the donor's heir. Similarly, a donor cannot waive a claim under § 528 BGB to the detriment of a social welfare institution.

This ruling was subsequently endorsed by the German doctrine.[11] The approval also covered issues related to the potential application of the institution of confusion in the described situations.[12] In particular, the need to protect the interests of the social welfare institution as a third party was highlighted.[13] This also did not change after the repeal of the BSHG and its replacement by the new social welfare law of 27 December 2003 (the SGB XII).[14] The new § 93 of the SGB XII[15] in fact contains a similar regulation as § 90 of the BSHG.[16]

II. Consideration of the problem presented in the German case and its comparison with Polish law

An analysis of Polish legal regulations in relation to the BGH ruling should be conducted along two lines. First it is necessary to identify the position of Polish law as regards the most similar regulations relating to the possibility of revoking a donation.

The first provision governing these issues is Article 896 KC. It states that a donor may revoke a donation that has not yet been executed if, after the conclusion of the agreement, their financial status has changed to such an extent that

11 See C. Brähler-Boyan, H. Mann, *Zur Überleitung…*, pp. 1866–1871; D. Zeranski, *Die postmortale Überleitung des Rückforderungsanspruchs des verarmten Schenkers durch den Sozialhilfeträger*, NJW 1998, No 35, pp. 2574–2576; D. Zeranski, *Der Rückforderungsanspruch des verarmten Schenkers. Überleitbarkeit, Abtretbarkeit, Verpfändbarkeit, Pfändbarkeit und Vererblichkeit des Rechts aus § 528 Absatz 1 Satz 1 BGB*, Berlin 1998, pp. 110–138; H. Lange, K. Kuchinke, *Erbrecht. Ein Lehrbuch*, München 2001, p. 94; L. Kunz, in: G. Otte (ed.), *Staudingers Kommentar*, vol. 5, 2017, § 1922, pt. 559; J. Koch, in: *Münchener Kommentar*, vol. 4, 2019, § 528, pt. 12–15; D. Leipold, in: *Münchener Kommentar*, vol. 11, 2020, § 1922, pt. 50; F. Zwißler, in: W. Burandt, D. Rojahn (ed.), *Erbrecht*, 2019, § 528, pt. 3 and 19. See also H. Kollhosser, *Der Rückforderungsanspruch des verarmten Schenkers aus § 528 Abs. 1 Satz 1 BGB – Entstehung, Fortbestand, Vererblichkeit, Pfändbarkeit*, ZEV 2001, No 8, pp. 289–293.

12 D. Leipold, in: *Münchener Kommentar*, vol. 11, 2020, § 1922, pt. 188; R. Fetzer, in: W. Krüger (ed.), *Münchener Kommentar*, vol. 3, 2019, Introduction to § 362, pt. 4.

13 See J. Koch, in: *Münchener Kommentar*, vol. 4, 2019, § 528, pt. 16.

14 This issue is currently regulated by Sozialgesetzbuch (SGB) Zwölftes Buch (XII) – Sozialhilfe.

15 Also entitled *Übergang von Ansprüchen*.

16 L. Kunz, in: *Staudingers Kommentar*, vol. 5, 2017, § 1922, pt. 559.

the execution of the donation could not take place without detriment to their own maintenance for their justified needs, or without detriment to their statutory maintenance obligations.

It is generally accepted in the doctrine and case law that the right to revoke a donation not yet executed by the donor (Article 896 KC) is not heritable and it is not part of the estate. Neither the persons to whom the donor was obliged to provide maintenance nor the donor's heirs are entitled to this right, as it 'takes into account the personal interest of the donor'. This is because it is a right strictly connected with the deceased person. This view is clearly dominant in the doctrine.[17] In case law, this issue arose in the judgment of the Supreme Court of 3 April 2014, V CSK 289/13.[18] In the facts of the judgment, a donation was made by the spouses in respect of an object included in their statutory joint property, but one of them died before the donation was executed, and before it was revoked. The court held that the other spouse may revoke the donation only with respect to their share in the object of the donation (as a result of the transformation, at the time of the spouse's death, of the statutory marital joint property existing between them into a fractional property). The ruling assumed that the right to revoke a donation not yet executed, for the reasons specified in Article 896 KC, is a strictly personal right of the donor, related to their situation arising after the conclusion of the donation agreement and before its execution, as a result of which the execution of the donation cannot take place without detriment to their own maintenance for their justified needs or detriment to their statutory maintenance obligations. In the event of the donor's death, the donor's personal right does not pass to their heirs. This ruling has been endorsed by the doctrine.[19]

---

17 L. Stecki, *Odwołanie darowizny przez spadkobierców darczyńcy*, NP 1973, No 9, pp. 1304–1305; M. Sychowicz, in: *Praktyczny komentarz z orzecznictwem. Kodeks cywilny. Tom II, art. 353–1088*, Warszawa 2005, Article 922, pt. 80; S. Dmowski, in: G. Bieniek (ed.), *Komentarz KC*, book 3, vol. 2, 2011, Article 896, pt. 2; L. Stecki, in: *System prawa prywatnego*, vol. 7, 2011, p. 353, pt. 93; W. Borysiak, *Dziedziczenie. Konstrukcja prawna i ochrona*, Warszawa 2013, p. 186; E. Niezbecka, in: A. Kidyba (ed.), *Komentarz KC*, vol. IV, 2015, Article 922, pt. 29; B. Lackoroński, in: K. Osajda (ed.), *Komentarz KC*, vol. IIIB, 2017, Article 896, pt. 7; E. Skowrońska-Bocian, J. Wierciński, in: J. Gudowski (ed.), *Komentarz KC*, vol. VI, 2017, Article 922, pt. 63; M. Bączyk, L. Stecki, in: *System prawa prywatnego*, vol. 7, 2018, p. 386, pt. 109; J. Jezioro, in: E. Gniewek, P. Machnikowski (eds.), *Komentarz KC*, 2021, Article 896, pt. 8; M. Safjan, in: K. Pietrzykowski (ed.), *Komentarz KC*, vol. II, 2021, Article 896, pt. 1; M. Zelek, in: M. Gutowski (ed.), *Komentarz KC*, vol. III, 2022, Article 922, pt. 12 and 18. Vaguely R. Trzaskowski, in: J. Gudowski (ed.), *Komentarz KC*, vol. V, 2018, Article 896, pt 14.

18 OSNC-ZD 2015, no C, item 32.

19 M. Bączyk, L. Stecki, in: *System prawa prywatnego*, vol. 7, 2018, p. 386, pt. 109; R. Trzaskowski, in: J. Gudowski (ed.), *Komentarz KC*, vol. V, 2018, Article 896, pt. 14; W. Borysiak, in: K. Osajda (ed.), *Komentarz KC*, vol. IVA, 2019, Article 922, pt. 175.1.; M. Safjan, in: K. Pietrzykowski (ed.), *Komentarz*, vol. II, 2021, Article 896, pt. 1.

This position has been reiterated in further case law.[20] In the decision of the Supreme Court of 5 June 2018, IV CSK 27/18,[21] it was also stated that the right to revoke a donation not yet executed, for the reasons specified in Article 896 KC, is a strictly personal right of the donor, related to their situation arising already after the conclusion of the donation agreement and before its execution, as a result of which the execution of the donation cannot take place without detriment to their own maintenance for their justified needs or detriment to their statutory maintenance obligations. The Supreme Court confirmed that in the event of the donor's death, the donor's personal entitlement does not pass to their heirs.

However, the doctrine clarifies the views expressed in case law that heirs have the right to revoke a donation when, after the donor's death, the conditions for revocation are met, i. e., their financial status does not allow them to execute the donation without detriment to the satisfaction of their justified needs or without detriment to their statutory maintenance obligations.[22]

The second basis governing the revocation of a donation – similar to the German regulation – is Article 897 KC. It stipulates that if, after the execution of the donation, the donor falls into hardship, the donee is obliged, within the limits of the existing enrichment, to provide the donor with the means they lack for the satisfaction of their justified needs, or to fulfil their statutory maintenance obligations. However, the donee may exempt themselves from this obligation by reimbursing the donor the value of the donation.

Against the background of this provision, it is also accepted in the doctrine that the right to demand that the donor be provided with means of maintenance on account of their hardship does not form part of the donor's estate.[23] This also

20 For example, the judgment of the Administrative Court in Wrocław of 21 February 2013, I ACa 61/13, Legalis, held that: "The right to revoke a donation under Article 896 of the Civil Code is available only to the donor. Their heirs cannot exercise this right." Likewise, the decision of SN of 5 June 2018, IV CSK 27/18, LEX No 2509658.

21 LEX No 2509658.

22 R. Trzaskowski, in: J. Gudowski (ed.), *Komentarz KC*, vol. V, 2018, Article 896, pt. 14. This author – seemingly erroneously – referred to L. Stecki, in: J. Rajski (ed.), *System prawa prywatnego*, vol. 7, 2011, p. 353. In the opposite direction: S. Dmowski, in: G. Bieniek (ed.), *Komentarz KC*, book 3, vol. 2, 2011, Article 896, pt. 2.

23 S. Rejman, in: Z. Resich et al. (eds.), *Komentarz KC*, vol. 2, 1972, p. 1743; S. Dmowski, in: G. Bieniek (ed.), *Komentarz KC*, book 3, vol. 2, 2011, Article 897, pt. 4; L. Stecki, in: *System prawa prywatnego*, vol. 7, 2011, p. 348; Z. Gawlik, in: A. Kidyba (ed.), *Komentarz KC*, vol III (zobowiązania, część szczególna), 2014, Article 897, pt. 9; P. Księżak, *Prawo spadkowe*, Warszawa 2017, p. 70; R. Trzaskowski, in: J. Gudowski (ed.), *Komentarz KC*, vol. V, 2018, Article 897, pt. 15; W. Borysiak, in: K. Osajda (ed.), *Komentarz KC*, vol. IVA, 2019, Article 922, pt. 428.

consequently means that this obligation expires upon the donor's death (just as it would expire when hardship ceases).[24]

After the donor's death, it is also possible for the donor's heirs to revoke the donation due to gross ingratitude displayed by the donee (Articles 898–899 KC). The donor's heirs may revoke the donation due to gross ingratitude of the donee only if, at the time of death, the donor was entitled to revoke the donation (which applies to the cases described in this chapter) or if the donee intentionally deprived the donor of life or intentionally caused the health disorder that led to the donor's death (Article 899 § 2 KC). The donee's failure to provide maintenance to the donor during their lifetime may be deemed to be such gross ingratitude according to Article 898 § 1 KC.

Nevertheless, in Polish law problems may arise in a situation where the donee's death occurs before the donation is revoked by the donor's heirs. This is because there are doubts about the possibility to revoke a donation on the grounds of the gross ingratitude of the donee after the donee's death. Initially, the Supreme Court judgment of 6 July 1972, II CR 52/72,[25] held that: "The death of the donee does not prevent the exercise of the donor's right to revoke a donation in relation to the heirs of the donee if the one-year period stipulated in Article 899 § 3 KC has not yet expired. The provision of Article 899 § 2 KC, limiting the rights of the donor's heirs, does not change the legal situation of the donee's heirs." However, a later ruling of the Supreme Court of 7 November 2002, II CKN 1395/00[26] stated that the donor or their heirs cannot revoke a donation after the death of the donee, even if the time limit specified in Article 899 § 3 KC has not yet expired, and the reason for the revocation can be the gross ingratitude of the donee, but not of their heirs. This view has met with both approval[27] and criticism[28] in the doctrine.

24 On the other hand, the obligation to provide for the donor's maintenance, which under Article 897 KC rested with their testator, passes to the heirs of the donee, up to the value of the donation – S. Rejman, in: Z. Resich et al. (eds.), *Komentarz KC*, vol. 2, 1972, p. 1743; S. Dmowski, in: G. Bieniek (ed.), *Komentarz KC*, book 3, vol. 2, 2011, Article 897, pt. 4; L. Stecki, in: *System prawa prywatnego*, vol. 7, 2011, p. 348; Z. Gawlik, in: A. Kidyba (ed.), *Komentarz KC*, vol. 3 (zobowiązania, część szczególna), 2014, Article 897, pt. 9; R. Trzaskowski, in: J. Gudowski (ed.), *Komentarz KC*, vol. 5, 2018, Article 897, pt. 16; W. Borysiak, in: K. Osajda (ed.), *Komentarz KC*, vol. IVA, 2019, Article. 922, pt. 428; M. Safjan, in: K. Pietrzykowski (ed.), *Komentarz KC*, vol. II, 2021, Article 897, pt. 6.

25 OSPiKA 1973, No 3, item 57.

26 OSNC 2004, No 3, item 43 with the critical glosses of M. Warciński (Pal. 2004, No 11–12, pp. 273–278) and M. Niedośpiał (NPN 2005, No 2, pp. 63–71).

27 W. Czachórski, A. Brzozowski, M. Safjan, E. Skowrońska-Bocian, *Zobowiązania. Zarys wykładu*, Warszawa 2009, pp. 554 and 555; S. Solarski, *Odwołanie darowizny*, Warszawa 2020, p. 213; M. Tenenbaum-Kulig, *Recenzja: Szymon Solarski, Odwołanie darowizny, Warszawa 2020*, FP 2021, No 2, p. 108; M. Safjan, in: K. Pietrzykowski (ed.), *Komentarz KC*, vol. II, 2021, Article 898, pt. 8 and Article 899, pt. 10; K. Mularski, in: M. Gutowski (ed.), *Komentarz KC*, vol. III, 2022, Article 898, pt. 27; R. Trzaskowski, in: J. Gudowski (ed.), *Komentarz KC*, vol. V, 2018, Article 898, No 14.

The first judgment is supported by the fact that not only are the deceased's rights and obligations inherited, but also the legal position in which the deceased is at the time of death. The donee's heirs acquire this legal position in which the donee is at the time of death. If the donee commits acts of gross ingratitude towards the donor, the donor becomes entitled to revoke the donation. This creates a legal position in which the donee is 'subject to the competence' of the donor. The relevant legal effects are the same for the donee's heirs as they would have been for the donee had the donee been alive. Therefore, in the time limit specified in Article 899 § 3 KC, the donor's heirs can revoke a donation after the donee's death (claiming the object of the donation from the donee's heirs) on the grounds of the gross ingratitude of the donee towards the donor before the donor's death.[29]

At the same time, there is no provision in Polish law that could be regarded as an equivalent of § 90 BSHG. Nevertheless, general provisions may perform similar functions. Pursuant to Article 518 § 1 point 4 KC, a third party that repays the creditor acquires the repaid claim up to the amount of the payment made, if specific provisions so provide. The regulation of Article 122[1] Code of Obligations in the wording in force from 1 October 1950[30] until the entry into force of the Civil Code (on 1 January 1965) may be regarded as their historical model. This provision stated: 'Whoever provides another with means of maintenance or upbringing without being obliged to do so, or is obliged to do so only secondarily, he acquires by law their claim against the person on whom the maintenance obligation rests.'[31] Such subrogation to the rights of a satisfied creditor is now also stipulated in Article 140 § 1 KRO. It states that a person who provides another with means of maintenance or upbringing without being obliged to do so, or who is obliged to do so because it would be impossible or excessively difficult for the beneficiary to obtain timely maintenance from a person obliged in the closer or the same order, may

28 See in more detail: W. Borysiak, *Dziedziczenie…*, pp. 149–152; M. Królikowski, *Możliwość odwołania darowizny po śmierci obdarowanego*, Mon. Praw. 2017, No 24, p. 1323–1325; M. Kaliński, in: A. Brzozowski, J. Jastrzębski, M. Kaliński, W. Kocot, E. Skowrońska-Bocian, *Zobowiązania – część szczegółowa*, Warszawa 2017, p. 417; P. Księżak, *Prawo…*, p. 70; E. Skowrońska-Bocian, J. Wierciński, in: J. Gudowski (ed.), *Komentarz KC*, vol. VI, 2017, Article 922, pt. 64; W. Borysiak, in: K. Osajda (ed.), *Komentarz KC*, vol. IVA, 2019, Article 922, pt. 430–435; J. Kuźmicka-Sulikowska, in: E. Gniewek, P. Machnikowski (ed.), *Komentarz KC*, 2021, Article 922, pt. 23.

29 W. Borysiak, *Dziedziczenie…*, pp. 151–152.

30 The provision was added to the Code of Obligations by the Act of 27 June 1950 – provisions on the introduction of the Family Code (Journal of Laws No 34, item 309).

31 Prior to the introduction of this article into the Code of Obligations, recourse claims by a person who provided a child with maintenance without being obliged to do so were based on Article 117 of the Code of Obligations – see SN judgment of 6 April 1949, C. 405/48, Państwo i Prawo 1949, No 12, p. 125. See K. Lipiński, in: W. Święcicki (ed.), *Prawo cywilne z orzecznictwem, literatura i przepisami związkowymi. Tom I*, Warszawa 1958, p. 210.

demand reimbursement from the person who should have provided such means. This would therefore also consequently apply to the donee who is obliged to provide maintenance to the donor in hardship. As stated in the justification of the Supreme Court's judgment of 24 February 1999, III CZ 179/98[32], a recourse claim arises from the very fact of providing the beneficiary with means of maintenance or upbringing instead of the debtor. At the same time, such a recourse claim remains closely connected with the scope of the debtor's maintenance obligation, since the recourse claim against the debtor depends on the existence and scope of their maintenance obligation. A recourse claim may only be asserted against the person who is actually obliged to provide maintenance to the beneficiary. It is undisputed in the doctrine that the right to claim repayment and the corresponding obligation to reimburse payments made under the terms of Article 140 of the Polish Family and Guardianship Code pass to the heirs, as they are not maintenance payments.[33]

A specific provision with the closest purpose to § 90 BSHG in German law is Article 27 APEM. It stipulates in section 1 that the maintenance debtor is obliged to reimburse the competent authority of the creditor the amount of the benefits paid from the maintenance fund to the entitled person, together with statutory interest for a delay. Such receivables due from the maintenance debtor by virtue of benefits paid from the maintenance fund are recoverable with interest through judicial enforcement under the provisions on the enforcement of maintenance benefits. If, in turn, enforcement proceedings are conducted with a view to satisfying the claim of a person entitled by virtue of maintenance, the competent authority of the creditor that has paid benefits from the maintenance fund will join these proceedings. The body that joins the enforcement proceedings has the same rights as the creditor entitled by virtue of maintenance (Article 27 section 3a APEM). Furthermore, Article 27 section 7 APEM states that the competent authority of the creditor should provide the maintenance debtor, if the debtor's address is known, with information about granting benefits from the maintenance fund to the entitled person, along with the obligation to return these receivables with interest, as well as information on the amount of liabilities of the maintenance debtor towards the State Treasury on this account. The competent authority of the creditor attaches to the application for the initiation of enforcement proceedings, or joining enforcement proceedings, the final decision to grant benefits from the maintenance fund to the entitled person. Recovery is conducted on the basis of the decision without the need to append it with an enforcement clause (Article 27 section 8a APEM).

32 OSP 2000, no 7, item 114.

33 See T. Smyczyński, *Glosa do postanowienia SN z 24. 2. 1999 r., III CZ 179/98*, OSP 2000, No 7–8, item 114, p. 382; J. Pietrzykowski, K. Pietrzykowski, in: K. Pietrzykowski (ed.), *Komentarz KRO*, 2021, Article 140, pt. 1; W. Borysiak, in: K. Osajda (ed.), *Komentarz KC*, vol. IVA, 2019, Article 922, pt. 463.2.

The doctrine notes the similarity of the described regulation to Article 140 KRO, with all its consequences.[34] However, against the background of the previous wording of the APEM, an individual view has been expressed that 'maintenance debts' of a given debtor, for whom maintenance was paid by the maintenance fund, are not inherited by the debtor's descendants.[35] This is because benefits paid from the maintenance fund to the entitled person, together with statutory interest, were recoverable pursuant to the provisions of the Act on Enforcement Proceedings in Administration of 17 June 1966 (EPA), taking into account the provisions of the APEM. In accordance with Article 59 § 1 point 4[36] (formerly Article 59 § 1 point 6) of the EPA, enforcement proceedings are discontinued in the event of the death of the debtor, if the obligation is strictly connected with the deceased person. Since the obligation to reimburse benefits to the maintenance fund resulted from an administrative decision at that time, this obligation was considered as strictly connected with the debtor, the result being that, upon the debtor's death, enforcement proceedings would become pointless and should be discontinued, and the heirs of the maintenance debtor would not be liable for debts to the maintenance fund.[37] After the entry into force of the Act on Amendments to the Act on Assistance to Persons Entitled to Maintenance, the Act on Pensions from the Social Insurance Fund and the Act on Family Benefits of 24 July 2015,[38] receivables falling from the maintenance debtor by virtue of benefits paid from the maintenance fund are recoverable with interest by court enforcement under the provisions on the enforcement of maintenance. This means that, since claims for reimbursement of these receivables are of a civil and financial nature, under Article 922 § 1 KC, they pass *de lege lata* to the debtor's heirs.

34 E. Tomaszewska, *Ustawa o pomocy osobom uprawnionym do alimentów. Komentarz*, LEX/el. 2019, Article 27, pt. 1. See also A. Korcz-Maciejko, in: A. Brzeźna, M. Gajda-Durlik, A. Korcz-Maciejko, *Ustawa o pomocy osobom uprawnionym do alimentów. Komentarz*, Warszawa 2019, Article 27, pt. 3.

35 A. Król, *Czy długi alimentacyjne osoby zobowiązanej do płacenia alimentów (zobowiązany nie płacił, płacił za niego fundusz alimentacyjny) wobec funduszu alimentacyjnego przechodzą po śmierci zobowiązanego w drodze dziedziczenia na jego zstępnych? Jeżeli nie, to jaka jest tego podstawa prawna?*, Lex No 122042.

36 This provision states: "Enforcement proceedings will be partially or completely discontinued in the event of the debtor's death when the obligation: (a) is strictly connected with the debtor, (b) is not strictly connected with the debtor and enforcement is conducted exclusively from a property right that has expired due to the debtor's death."

37 See A. Król, *Czy długi…*, Lex No 122042; M. Rzewuski, in: J.M. Łukasiewicz, I. Ramus (ed.), *Prawo alimentacyjne. Zagadnienia materialne*, Toruń 2015, chapter VII, pt. 6.

38 Journal of Laws of 2015, item 1302.

Witold Borysiak

§ 17 – Succession of economic aspects of image rights after the death of the rights holder

Comparative conclusion

According to the current view in German law, the property elements of the general right of personality do not expire at the death of the right holder, but pass on to their heirs. This applies in particular to image rights, which are often used in practice for commercial purposes, as well as to the rights to a name. With regard to Polish law, the matter of succession to the right to a person's image (or the economic aspects thereof), as well as to the further exercise of this right after the death of the right holder, is the subject of numerous controversies in the literature. That said, the views are very similar to those presented in German legal theory and case law.

I. Analysis of an example case under German law

The state of facts to which the judgment of 1 December 1999 in case I ZR 49/97[1] pertains is the following. Marlene Dietrich died in 1992. Shortly after her death (in 1993), the defendant registered the trademark 'Marlene', which covered, among other things, the production and performance of theatre and film works. He produced a musical about Dietrich's life and work (titled *Sag mir, wo die Blumen sind*), which did not enjoy great success. In consideration for promoting the musical, the defendant entered into a contract authorising, among others, the Fiat car manufacturer to produce a special model of Lancia with the 'Marlene' trademark, Marlene Dietrich's image based on a photo from 1930, and a facsimile of her signature (*Marlene*). The defendant concluded similar contracts for the use of Marlene Dietrich's name and image with several other businesses. For instance, in consideration for the delivery of make-up supplies, the programme for the musical included a two-page advertisement of cosmetics by Ellen Betrix under the slogan 'Marlene-Look', using Marlene Dietrich's image. In addition, the defendant manufactured promotional materials (phone cards, mugs, T-shirts, watches and badges) as well as postcards depicting the image of Marlene

1 NJW 2000, No 30, pp. 2195–2201.

Dietrich along with the title of the musical. The merchandise was sold in front of the theatre.

The claimant – actress Maria Riva – was Marlene Dietrich's only child and heiress. She demanded from the defendant, among others, relief consisting in the defendant ceasing to use the image, name and signature of Marlene Dietrich in connection with her person, life and work for the purposes of advertisement and product labelling, and ceasing to place her image on objects distributed for commercial purposes. Alternatively, she demanded that the defendant cease activities resulting in third parties becoming authorised to use Marlene Dietrich's image as described above. In addition, the claimant demanded that the defendant make a declaration that he would: first, remedy all damage sustained by the claimant as a result of his actions; second, remedy all damage the claimant would sustain in the future on that account; third, surrender the enrichment he had gained as a result of his actions. Moreover, she demanded information about the benefits he had gained up until then from the advertising contracts and the sale of promotional merchandise.

The claimant's fundamental assertions were that: following her mother's death, the claimant was entitled to the protection of her general right of personality (*das allgemeine Persönlichkeitsrecht*). She could therefore assert claims (including claims for damages) on account of an infringement of that right on her own behalf and as the executor of her mother's will. The basis for the claimant's claim for damages was § 823 section 1 BGB,[2] which stipulates the following: 'A person who, intentionally or negligently, unlawfully injures the life, body, health, freedom, property or other right of another person is liable to make compensation to the other party for the damage arising from this.' The legal grounds for the demand to surrender benefits was § 812 section 1 BGB,[3] which provides that a person who obtains something as a result of the performance of another person, or otherwise at their expense, without legal grounds for doing so is under a duty to make restitution to them. This duty also exists if the legal grounds later lapse or if the result intended to be achieved by those efforts in accordance with the contents of the legal transaction does not occur. The demand for the cessation of the infringement of the right to the name of the late Marlene Dietrich, in turn, was based on § 12 BGB,[4] which stipulates: 'If the right of a person to use a name is disputed by another person, or if the interest of the person entitled to the name is injured by the unauthorised use of the same name by another person, the person entitled may require the other to remove the infringement. If further infringements are to be feared, the person entitled may seek an injunction.'

2 Titled *Schadensersatzpflicht* – Liability in damages.
3 Titled *Harausgabeanspruch* – Claim for restitution.
4 Titled *Namensrecht* – Right to a name.

Further grounds for the demand for the protection of image rights was the regulation under the Act on Copyright in Works of Graphic Art and Photography of 9 January 1907 (KUG). Pursuant to § 22 KUG, an image may be disseminated or published only subject to the consent of the depicted person. If there is any doubt, it is assumed that consent was given if the depicted person was remunerated for the use of their likeness. After the death of the depicted person, dissemination or publication require the consent of their family members for a period of up to 10 years. Family members within the meaning of the provision are the surviving spouse[5] and the children of the depicted person, and if there is no spouse[6] or children, then the parents of the depicted person. At the time when the judgment was entered, the matter was also regulated by § 23 KUG. Pursuant to section 1, no consent required under § 22 is necessary with regard to the dissemination and display of: (1) images in the field of contemporary history; (2) pictures in which the person appears only in addition to a landscape or another location; (3) pictures of gatherings, marches and similar events in which the depicted person participated; (4) portraits that have not been made to order, provided that their dissemination or display serves a higher artistic interest. Pursuant to § 23 section 2 KUG, the consent does not cover a dissemination and display that infringes the legitimate interest of the depicted person or, if the person is deceased, of their next of kin.

The defendant argued that, first, the alleged infringement of Marlene Dietrich's personality rights by the advertising campaign carried out in connection with the musical was subject to the defendant's artistic freedom, and second, that the alleged infringement of personality rights after the death of the right holder could not be grounds for the complainant raising any claims, as the right protected non-property interests.

In terms of the state of facts covered by the discussed judgment, the courts had to decide whether the general right of personality was exclusively a non-property and inalienable personal right, or whether it covered property rights as well, which could be part of the right holder's estate subject to inheritance. At the same time, they had to adjudicate whether it was possible to grant damages for an infringement of those rights if the infringement took place after the right holder's death.

Under German law – before the judgment was entered – since the decision of the BGH of 8 May 1956, I ZR 62/54[7] (the *Paul Dahlke* judgment), both legal theory and case law had admitted the possibility not only of asserting injunction claims

5 In 2001, after the judgment was issued, the provision was supplemented with the expression 'or life partner'.
6 In 2001, after the judgment was issued, the provision was supplemented to cover the possibility of not having a life partner.
7 NJW 1956, pp. 1554 et seq.

related to image, but also to granting the entitled person remuneration reflecting the market value of the use of the image. This had become common practice in situations involving the use of an image for advertising purposes without a contractual basis. However, this concerned the images of living people only. Then, in the BGH judgment of 20 March 1968, I ZR 44/66,[8] and in the BVerfG judgment of 24 February 1971, 1 BvR 435/68[9] (the '*Mephisto*' judgments), it was accepted that the general right of personality enjoyed protection also after the right holder's death (known as *postmortaler Persönlichkeitsschutz*). The underlying concept was that certain aspects of human dignity did not expire with the person's demise. The issue, however, continued to be a subject of dispute among legal scholars.[10]

The Regional Court (*Landgericht*) in Berlin, which heard the matter at first instance, admitted the request for relief (in the form of an injunction to cease the infringement) and dismissed the remaining requests. Then the Higher Regional Court (*Oberlandesgericht*) dismissed the appeal made by both parties, admitting only an alternative request of the complainant for injunctive relief to protect her interests against infringements by third parties. The cassation brought by the complainant was successful and resulted in the judgment entered at second instance being reversed, as the BGH ruled that the purpose underlying the general right of personality and its specific manifestations, such as the right to protection of one's image and the right to one's name, is to protect not only an individual's non-property (ideal – *ideellen*), but also property (commercial – *kommerzieller*) rights. If such property elements of personality rights are intentionally infringed through the unauthorised use of an image, a name or other characteristic elements of the right of personality (*Persönlichkeitsmerkmale*), then, irrespective of the degree of the infringement, the personality rights holder has a claim for damages. At the same time, the BGH indicated that the economic elements of the general right of personality continue to exist after the right holder's death for as long as their non-property rights enjoy protection. The relevant entitlements pass to the heirs of the personality rights holder and may be exercised by them in accordance with the deceased person's express or presumed will.

It is interesting to examine the argumentation that led the BGH to this ruling. The court found that the defendant had used Marlene Dietrich's name and image for commercial purposes without proper authorisation. Thus, he had infringed both her image rights and her right to her name, and both these rights are explicitly stipulated in legislation (§ 12 BGB and § 22 and 23 KUG). The image

8 NJW 1968, pp. 1773 et seq.

9 NJW 1971, pp. 1645 et seq.

10 See subject literature and case law discussed by H-P. Götting, *Persönlichkeitsrechte als Vermögensrechte*, Tübingen 1995.

rights and the right to a name are the 'legal manifestations' of the general right of personality, which comprehensively protects each person's right to respect for their dignity and the development of their personality (Articles 1 and 2 section 1 Grundgesetz).

The general right of personality is classified as 'another right' within the meaning of § 823 section 1 BGB and is known as a 'framework right'. Its purpose is primarily to protect a person's intangible interests, so that if their right is intentionally infringed, they can assert claims for not only the cessation, withdrawal and return of benefits, but also for compensation. This only concerns situations where the infringement is grave or the culpability on the side of the infringing party is considerable, and the loss sustained by the aggrieved party cannot be satisfactorily remedied in any other way.

The BGH found that the general right of personality is a 'highly personal' right (*ein höchstpersönliches Recht*) that is inalienable and non-descendible. Only in exceptional instances does the case law admit the posthumous protection of personality (*postmortalen Persönlichkeitsschutzes*) through which the deceased person's life's work is protected against wilful and gross distortions. The exercise of this 'right' of the deceased is entrusted to a person appointed for that purpose during the former's life or, as auxiliary solution, to their next of kin. In practice, the protection is ineffective when the heirs of a well-known person oppose the commercial use of the deceased person's image, name or other elements of the general right of personality (*sonstiger Persönlichkeitsmerkmale*) in an advertisement by asserting claims based on unjust enrichment (§ 812 section 1 sentence 1 BGB) or claims for damages (§ 823 section 1 BGB). In order to prevent third parties from becoming enriched free of charge by using the image, name or other elements of the general right of personality of a deceased person, German scholars began to lean towards the view about the (fully or partly) descendible character of personality rights.

The BGH shared this view, finding that the complainant could claim for damages for the infringement of her mother's general right of personality, which had passed to the heiress after the mother's death. It found that elements of the general right of personality, such as the name and image in the case of well-known people have considerable economic value (*ein erheblicher wirtschaftlicher Wert*), because they are used in advertising under what is known as image transfer. The BGH explained that this practice was nowadays so widely acknowledged by the legal system that the contemporary general right of personality covered both non-property and property components (*Bestandteile*).

The general right of personality is 'highly personal' by nature and therefore not descendible to the extent in which it serves to protect the non-property interests of an individual. On the other hand, the image and name of an individual are subject to commercialisation to a substantive degree. As a result, they should be deemed alienable and descendible with regard to their property aspects. When it comes to the period of protection, the BGH cited § 22 KUG and ruled that it lasted for 10 years from the right holder's death.

For these reasons, the BGH adjudicated that the defendant was liable for damages under § 823 section 1 in conjunction with § 276 BGB for the unlawful and culpable use of Marlene Dietrich's image and name for commercial purposes without the complainant's consent. It decided further that the defendant could not plead a defence under § 23 KUG, because in publishing Marlene Dietrich's image, he had carried out exclusively commercial objectives that do not enjoy protection under the cited provision. The damages the complainant could demand from the defendant exceeded the scope of damages set out in § 252 BGB[11] in conjunction with § 259 BGB,[12] because it covers compensation for lost profits as well as the return of benefits obtained by the defendant, or payment of an appropriate licence fee under § 97 of the German Act on Copyright and Related Rights.[13]

It is appropriate to briefly discuss the further development of German case law and legal theory in this area, as the judgment discussed above may be considered a cornerstone. The reasoning presented in the judgment was confirmed that very same day in the judgment of the BGH of 1 December 1999, I ZR 226/97 (known as *Blue Angel – Der blaue Engel*).[14] This case also concerns the late Marlene Dietrich and both cases had many similarities.[15] Here, too, the court ruled that the constitution-enshrined general right of personality could serve as protection of the right holder's property rights, and that such property elements of personality rights were descendible. The constitutionality of the BGH's decision, in turn, was confirmed by the judgment of the Federal Constitutional Court of 22 August 2006, 1 BvR 1168/04,[16] in which it was even emphasised that the decision had improved the protection of human dignity. In addition, the Federal Constitutional Court confirmed that the personal entitlement possessing a property value

11 The provision regulates the compensation of damage consisting in lost profits.

12 With regard to the duty to render account for management related to earnings or expenses.

13 *Urheberrechtsgesetz* – UrhRG of 9 September 1965 (BGBl. I S. 1273 et seq.).

14 NJW 2000, No 30, pp. 2201–2202.

15 The state of facts to which the judgment of 1 December 1999 in case I ZR 226/97 pertains was as follows. Toshiba advertised its new photocopier with a slogan referring to the film 'Blue Angel' and a picture of the actress styled as Marlene Dietrich, in the characteristic pose she used to adopt when singing the song 'Falling in Love Again (Can't Help It)' (*Ich bin von Kopf bis Fuß auf Liebe eingestellt*). The advertisement was published in 1993, within 10 years after her death. Marlene Dietrich's daughter brought claims for damages, demanding remuneration for the use of her mother's likeness for publicity. The lower courts dismissed the claim for damages, arguing that after the death of the portrayed person, her relatives can only demand an injunction against the use of her image, whereas purely financial interests are not protected.

16 NJW 2006, No 47, pp. 3409–3411.

to use for commercial purposes the attributes of personality in the form of image was descendible and expired within the time limit set by the provisions of law. In this case, the BGH's interpretation had not been an instance of unlawful judicial law-making but had taken into consideration contemporary reality involving the commercial use of personal interests. These judicial decisions were widely discussed also in Polish subject literature.[17]

The judgment of the BGH – despite the occasional critical opinion pointing out that it caused an erosion in the general right of personality[18] – generally met with approval among German legal scholars.[19] Currently, the descendibility of the property aspects of the general right of personality with regard to the name and image is widely accepted.[20] These rights can be protected with claims for damages under general provisions[21] and entail an obligation to pay an appropriate licence fee for the commercial use of an image.[22]

II. Consideration of the problem presented in the German case and its comparison with Polish law

Under Polish law, Article 81 section 1 Copyrights Law provides that the dissemination of an image requires the consent of the depicted person. If no explicit reservation is made, consent is not required when the person received agreed

17 T. Grzeszak, *Dziedziczenie prawa do wizerunku w Niemczech*, Mon. Praw. 2006, No 24, pp. 1312–1313; J. Balcarczyk, *Prawo do wizerunku i jego komercjalizacja*, Warszawa 2009, pp. 216–218; T. Grzeszak, in: M. Namysłowska (ed.), *Reklama. Aspekty prawne*, Warszawa 2012, pp. 681–684; A. Pązik, *Prawo do wizerunku w obliczu zmian*, ZNUJ PPWI 2010, No 1, pp. 145–147.

18 See H. Schack, *Anmerkung zu BGH Urteil von 1. 12. 1999*, JZ 2000, No 21, pp. 1056–1062; K-N. Peifer, *Individualitat im Zivilrecht, Der Schutz persönlicher, gegenständlicher und wettbewerbsrechtlicher Individualität im Persönlichkeitsrecht, Immaterialgüterrecht und Recht der Unternehmen*, Tübingen 2001, pp. 145 et seq.; A. Peukert, *Güterzuordnung als Rechtsprinzip*, Tübingen 2008, pp. 173 et seq.

19 See mostly R. Rixecker, in: C. Schubert (ed.), *Münchener Kommentar*, vol. 1, 2018, Anhang zu § 12. Das Allgemeine Persönlichkeitsrecht (AllgPersönlR), pt. 58–59.

20 In case law, see e. g. judgment of the BGH of 5 October 2006, I ZR 277/03, NJW 2007, pp. 684 et seq. (*Kinski-klaus.de*); judgment of the BGH of 16 September 2008, VI ZR 244/07, NJW 2009, pp. 751 et seq. (*Das Theaterstück – Ehrensache*) with remarks by C. Ahrens, *Anmerkung zu BGH Urteil von 16. 9. 2008, VI ZR 244/07*, JZ 2009, No 4, pp. 212–216; in literature, see for many others: L. Kunz, [w:] *Staudingers Kommentar*, vol. 5, 2017, § 1922, pt. 303–305; G. Wagner, in: *Münchener Kommentar*, vol. 7, 2020, § 823, pt. 422, and D. Leipold, in: *Münchener Kommentar*, vol. 11, 2020, § 1922, pt. 166.

21 See, along with many others, G. Wagner, in: *Münchener Kommentar*, vol. 7, 2020, § 823, pt. 418, and judgment of the BGH of 31 May 2012, I ZR 234/10, NJW 2013, pp. 793 et seq. (*Playboy am Sonntag*).

22 See correspondingly judgment of the BGH of 26 October 2006, I ZR 182/04, NJW 2007, pp. 689 et seq. (*Oscar Lafontaine*).

consideration for having their likeness taken. Consent to the dissemination of an image is not required only if: it depicts a well-known person and the image was taken in connection with them appearing in their public capacity, especially if performing their political, social or professional functions, or if the depicted person is only a detail of a whole such as a gathering, a landscape, or a public event.

Image rights, in the context of their commercial use, come under the Polish doctrine of civil law as: (1) a highly personal non-property right;[23] (2) a mixed personal and property right;[24] (3) a property right in an intangible interest in the form of image (known as *rem in personam*, a right in person);[25] and (4) a personal interest with a certain property aspect (a personal right possessing a property value) – known as a commercial image.[26] The matter has not been fully resolved by case law, although the opinion prevails that an image is an intangible asset that may be subject to commercial transactions.[27]

The posthumous protection of image is set out in Article 83 Copyright Law. It provides that Article 78 section 1 Copyright Law applies accordingly to claims of the right holder in instances when the image of a person is disseminated, and that such claims may be asserted no later than twenty years from the demise of that person. The referenced Article 78 Copyright Law (concerning the protection of property personal interests) stipulates that a person whose image was endangered by the actions of another may demand that such actions be discontinued. In the event of an infringement, they are also entitled to demand that the person committing the infringement perform actions necessary to remove its effects, in particular that the person make a public declaration of appropriate form and substance. If the infringement was intentional, the court may grant the aggrieved party a suitable amount of money as compensation for harm, or may – at the request of the aggrieved party – order that the wrongdoer donate a suitable amount of money to a charitable cause specified by the right holder.

In Polish law, there are some doubts about the scope of people entitled to the posthumous protection of their image. Article 83 Copyright Law does not specify what people are entitled to such protection, causing controversy among legal scholars.[28] Theoretically, those could be: (1) heirs of the depicted person (as-

23 A. Matlak, *Cywilnoprawna ochrona wizerunku*, KPP 2004, No 2, p. 326; A. Pązik, *Prawo…*, p. 127 et seq.; A. Pązik, *Komentarz do ustawy o prawie autorskim i prawach pokrewnych*, in: R. Markiewicz (ed.), *Ustawy autorskie. Komentarze. Tom II*, Warszawa 2021, Article 81, pt. 30.

24 J. Barta, R. Markiewicz, *Wokół prawa do wizerunku*, ZNUJ PWiOWI 2002, vol. 80, pp. 25–27; P. Ślęzak, *Komercyjne wykorzystanie wizerunku*, ZNUJ PPWI 2019, No 4, pp. 45–46.

25 T. Grzeszak, in: *System prawa prywatnego*, vol. 13, 2017, pp. 800–802.

26 J. Balcarczyk, *Prawo…*, pp. 70 et seq. and p. 277.

27 See the judgment of SN of 20 May 2004, II CK 330/03, LEX No 686639.

28 For various theories presented in subject literature, see J. Barta, R. Markiewicz in: J. Barta, R. Markiewicz (ed.), *Prawo autorskie i prawa pokrewne. Komentarz*, Warszawa 2011, pp. 525–

suming that such a right is hereditable);[29] (2) the people listed in Article 78 section 2 Copyright Law;[30] (3) the people specified in Article 82 Copyright Law.[31] Furthermore, there are controversies regarding the legal qualification of image rights. It is namely disputed whether it is a right owned by the potential right holders that emerges by operation of law (at the death of the depicted person), or whether it is a right that passes to them by way of succession.[32] In addition, it is disputed to what extent such people may determine the scope of disseminating the image after the right holder's death, and especially the extent to which they should declare the deceased person's actual or presumed intention.

Most legal scholars represent the opinion that, upon a person's death, their capacity as a legal subject ends and the subjective rights that protect their personal interests are not part of the estate.[33] Thus, a person's image rights – being an individual's personal interest – do not pass to other individuals, and the personal subjective right that protects it is non-hereditable. In that situation, the claims granted by the Copyright Law would amount to claims owned by the persons

---

527, 532; T. Grzeszak, in: *System prawa prywatnego*, vol. 13, 2017, pp. 829–833; M. Markiewicz, *Komentarz do ustawy o prawie autorskim i prawach pokrewnych*, in: R. Markiewicz (ed.), *Ustawy autorskie. Komentarze. Tom II*, Warszawa 2021, Article 83, pt. 2.

29 This view is supported by T. Grzeszak, in: *System prawa prywatnego*, vol. 13, 2017, pp. 831–832; A. Urbański, in: W. Machała, R. Sarbiński (ed.), *Prawo autorskie i prawa pokrewne. Komentarz*, Warszawa 2019, Article 83, pt. 3; A. Nowak-Gruca, *Użytkownik forever off. Wybrane problemy cyfrowego "życia po życiu" związane z ochroną wizerunku i korespondencji*, ZNUJ 2020, No 1, p. 139. The theory is rejected by M. Markiewicz, *Komentarz do ustawy o prawie autorskim i prawach pokrewnych*, in: R. Markiewicz (ed.), *Ustawy autorskie. Komentarze. Tom II*, Warszawa 2021, Article 83, No 3.

30 The provision stipulates that: 'Unless the author expressly wished otherwise, after their death, a complaint for the protection of the deceased person's moral rights may be brought by their spouse, and if there is none, then successively by: their descendants, parents, siblings, and descendants of siblings'. The provision is further clarified by sub-section 3, which provides for the following: 'Unless the author expressly wished otherwise, the persons listed in sub-section 2 are entitled in the same order to exercise the deceased author's moral rights.'

31 The provision pertains to the protection of the right to correspondence and stipulates that unless the addressee of correspondence expressly wished otherwise, the dissemination of correspondence within twenty years of their death requires the consent of the spouse, and if there is none, then successively their descendants, parents, or siblings. This view is most common among legal scholars – e.g. J. Mazurkiewicz, *Non omnis moriar. Ochrona dóbr osobistych zmarłego w prawie polskim*, Wrocław 2010, pp. 416–417; P. Ślęzak, *Ustawa o prawie autorskim i prawach pokrewnych. Komentarz*, Warszawa 2017, Article 83, No 5; K. Bojańczyk, in: W. Machała, R. Sarbiński (ed.), *Prawo autorskie i prawa pokrewne. Komentarz*, Warszawa 2019, Article 81, No 53.

32 For various theories presented in the subject literature, see T. Grzeszak, in: *System prawa prywatnego*, vol. 13, 2017, pp. 829–833; K. Bojańczyk, in: W. Machała, R. Sarbiński (ed.), *Prawo…*, Article 81, No 50–53, and M. Markiewicz, *Komentarz…*, Article 83, No 2.

33 A. Matlak, *Cywilnoprawna…*, p. 326; J. Balcarczyk, *Prawo…*, pp. 191–192, 284–291 and 330; W. Borysiak, *Dziedziczenie…*, pp. 179–180; P. Księżak, in: M. Pyziak-Szafnicka, P. Księżak (eds.), *Komentarz KC*, 2014, Article 23, pt. 15.

listed in the act. However, this matter is subject to numerous controversies, with contrary views being expressed as well.[34] A typical example of such an interpretation may be the decision of the Administrative Court in Warsaw of 7 January 2015 – I ACz 2501/14.[35] The statement of grounds for this says that: 'Personal interests are closely related to the subject that enjoys protection; they emerge and end along with that subject. They cannot pass to other subjects by way of juridical acts or succession. Legal capacity is granted exclusively to existing people and therefore there is no such thing as the personal interests of deceased persons.' It was highlighted in the decision that Article 83 in conjunction with Article 78 section 1 Copyright Law provides no basis for substituting for a deceased person as complainant in an action for non-property protection of image rights, but is grounds for asserting their own claim within 20 years of the person's demise.

To sum up, it ought to be noted that, depending on the view as to the legal nature of image rights, the protection of that right after the right holder's death will take a different shape. If the right to decide about the dissemination of an image is considered a property right in an intangible interest in the form of an image,this right passes to the heirs under general provisions.[36] This stance appears to be closest to the opinions expressed in German case law and subject literature. At the same time, it has been argued that, after the expiry of the twenty-year period of protection and of property rights in the dissemination of an image, a prohibition on using it could be based on the right to the protection of the veneration of the dead, provided that the dissemination in a given situation infringes the personal interests of the deceased person's next of kin.[37]

In the analysed state of facts, the instrument of the right to the protection of the veneration of the dead could be applied under Polish law directly as well. The protection of the personal interest consisting in the veneration of the dead is enjoyed by the person's next of kin when the actions of a third party lack respect for the deceased person's life and work and are an insult to that memory.[38] Another situation is when the use of the deceased person's image is defective. The object of protection in this case is not the deceased person's own personal interest, but a separate personal interest owned by their next of kin. In that event,

34 An example could be the opinion expressed by J. Mazurkiewicz (*Non omnis…*, pp. 367 et seq.), who argues that posthumous protection of the right to image covers the rights owned by the deceased, and their next of kin exercise them on the deceased person's behalf.

35 LEX No 1744683.

36 T. Grzeszak, in: *System prawa prywatnego*, vol. 13, 2017, pp. 831–832.

37 T. Grzeszak, in: *System prawa prywatnego*, vol. 13, 2017, pp. 832–833.

38 See the judgment of SN of 12 June 1968, I CR 252/68, OSNC 1970, No 1, item 18, where the thesis is supported that: 'The emotional sphere related to the veneration of a relation's memory may be subject to legal protection under Articles 23 and 24 of the Civil Code.' See, for many others, P. Księżak, in: M. Pyziak-Szafnicka, P. Księżak (eds.), *Komentarz KC*, 2014, Article 23, pt. 89–97.

the deceased is only a point of reference for the feelings of the living, who base their own self-esteem on the sense of pride in their family members. Thus, enabling the next of kin to assert claims to discontinue the tarnishing of the reputation of the deceased in fact serves to protect their next of kin's own interests.[39]

39 T. Grzeszak, *Dobro osobiste jako dobro zindywidualizowane*, PS 2018, No 4, pp. 33–34.

Witold Borysiak

§ 18 – Succession of claims for compensation for property damage resulting from the death of a business owner

Comparative conclusion
Under both German and Polish law, claims for compensation resulting from the death of a business owner, and the related inability of the heirs to implement previously assumed economic plans are not inherited. The only exception constitutes a situation in which third party compensation claims against the deceased arose before their death. For example, if the deceased dies shortly after a traffic accident, and the heirs do not then collect machines that the deceased had ordered, due to the inability to use them, the heirs cannot then claim damages against the perpetrator of the accident that covers a claim against them from the suppliers of the machines.

I. Analysis of an example case under German law

This issue was the subject of court proceedings and the BGH judgment of 20 February 1962 in case VI ZR 65/61.[1]

On 18 May 1957, the defendant caused a traffic accident as a result of which the deceased was mortally wounded and died four hours later. The only heirs of the deceased were his wife and daughter from his first marriage (each inheriting 1/2 of the estate). The deceased also appointed the executor of the will.

The deceased was a businessman running a chocolate factory with his second wife. At the time of the accident, he was building his own production facility.[2] Before his death, he ordered machines worth approximately DM 900,000, which were to be delivered by the end of May 1957; the deceased had already made the advance payment (from 20 to 30% of the total price). The indicated order also included machines commissioned from two different companies worth approximately DM 332,000 (for which the deceased paid an advance of DM 75,000).

After the deceased's death, the executor and the heirs jointly agreed not to carry out the deceased's plans and so cancelled the orders. The suppliers were

1 NJW 1962, No 20, pp. 911–912.
2 The building shell had already been erected.

able to find other buyers for some of the machines, but demanded almost DM 61,000 (deducted from the advance payments) as lost profit, including their sales representative's commission fee, which had already been paid. In the course of the negotiations, the heirs found themselves partially obliged to pay the compensation (the amount that was not subject to dispute was DM 10,000).

The claimant – the executor of the will, acting on behalf of the heirs – demanded that the defendant pay damages up to the amount of the obligation to return the amount that was not subject to dispute (DM 10,000). In the claimant's opinion, the new factory was so personally adapted to the deceased himself that, as a consequence of his injuries and subsequent death as a result of the accident, it became unfeasible. At the same time, as a result of the accident, the deceased could not fulfil his contractual obligations towards suppliers, and his property was burdened with the obligation to pay compensation. In this way, the claimant perceived the damage not only in the form of the damage caused to the deceased in connection with the death, but the damage can be linked to the accident (which led to the heirs inheriting the deceased's claim for compensation, which can be brought against the perpetrator of the accident). The claimant considered subsequent agreements between the heirs and suppliers as measures aimed at reducing and settling the damage.

The claimant indicated § 1922 section 1 BGB[3] – according to which, upon the death of a natural person (opening the succession), their property (estate) is transferred as a whole to one or more people (the heirs) – in accordance with § 249 BGB.[4] The last provision in the first section indicates that the person who is obliged to repair the damage is obliged to restore the existing condition to what would have existed if the facts giving rise to compensation for damage had not occurred, and in the second section it stipulates that, if the obligation to repair the damage results from causing damage to a person or property, the entitled party may demand, instead of the restoration of the previous condition, the payment of a relevant amount of money.

During the trial, the defendant pointed out that an obligation to pay compensation to the supplier only became justified after the death of the deceased and was a result of the heirs' free decision to withdraw from the project and not to collect the ordered machines from the suppliers. Moreover, he pointed out that neither the injuries of the deceased in the accident nor his subsequent death prevented the performance of agreements previously concluded with the suppliers. Moreover, there was no point before the deceased's death when he could claim damages from the perpetrator of the accident. Hence, the deceased had no

3 Entitled *Gesamtrechtsnachfolge* (Universal Succession).

4 Entitled *Art und Umfang des Schadensersatzes* (Nature and scope of the obligation to compensate for the damage).

claim against the perpetrator of the accident that could be transferred to the heirs. He also indicated that the claimant directs against the perpetrator of the accident third party claims that do not have causal relationship with the causative event.

In the course of the pending proceedings, several problems emerged that needed to be resolved. It was necessary to decide whether the deceased was obliged to pay compensation to the suppliers before his death, or whether there existed a 'legal position' at the time that justified the payment of such compensation. Moreover, it had to be decided whether, before the deceased's death, there existed a pecuniary claim for damages that the deceased could have brought against the perpetrator of the damage, and whether such a claim could have been inherited by the heirs.

The court (*Landgericht*) in Darmstadt upheld the claimant's claim. Subsequently, the Supreme appellate court (*Oberlandesgericht*) in Frankfurt am Main allowed the defendant's appeal and dismissed the claim. The subsequent complaint in cassation was dismissed (rejected) and did not lead to the revocation of the judgment of the second instance court. The BGH decided that if the deceased died shortly after a traffic accident, leading to his heirs not collecting the machines he had ordered, due to their inability to use them, they could not then claim compensation from the perpetrator of the accident covering the supplier's claims for compensation against them.

It is interesting to follow the subsequent motives of the BGH's argumentation. It pointed out that the property of the deceased, which after his death passes to the heirs under § 1922 BGB, includes the property connected with the entire legal relationships (*wertbezogenen Rechtsverhältnisse*) of the deceased at the time of the death. This also includes the rights and obligations that arise after the estate was opened from the legal position in which the deceased was at that moment. In particular, under § 1967 section 2 BGB,[5] the heirs are liable for debts arising after the death of the deceased, even if the deceased only created the situation leading to debt – for example, by a tort – but the consequences that caused the debt arose directly only after the succession was opened. However, this rule does not apply in the opposite case, when a tort was committed against the deceased, causing damage to his former property only after the succession was opened. This

5 This provision indicates that the deceased's obligations include, in addition to the deceased's debts, debts relating to the heirs, in particular debts due to compulsory portions, bequests and orders. A comparison of § 1967 section 1 in connection with § 1967 section 2 and § 1968 BGB confirms that, in German law, the heirs are responsible for the inheritance obligations (*Nachlassverbindlichkeiten*), which include not only the deceased's obligations, but also other obligations imposed on the heirs from the moment the estate was opened, in the form of debts resulting from bequests, orders or the deceased's funeral costs (cf. A. Stein, in: *Soergel BGB Kommentar: Erbrecht 1*, vol. 21, 2002, pp. 278 et seq.).

damage is not incurred by the deceased personally, so it cannot be transferred to their heirs.

BGH emphasised that the obligation to pay damages resulting from torts is limited by exceptions set out in the legal provisions and in court judgments. Such limitations may, in practice, violate the principle of universal succession in the law of succession. The provisions of public insurance law may be considered as such an exception,[6] but they were not applicable to the considered case, even by analogy. In the period from the accident until the death, the deceased was not entitled to bring any claim against the perpetrator of the damage. During this period, irrespective of the triggering event, the suppliers would not be able to pursue any claims for damages against the deceased. The deceased neither refused to accept the ordered machines, nor terminated the agreements concluded pursuant to § 649 BGB.[7] The mere fact of the accident, when objectively assessing all the circumstances of the case, did not lead to any change in the agreements concluded so far. There is also no evidence to suppose that the deceased's performance (in the form of paying the price of the goods or remuneration for the service rendered) could have become objectively impossible. As for possible obligations to cooperate (*Mitwirkungspflichten* – e.g. in the form of taking receipt of goods), they were not 'strictly related to a given person' (*höchstpersönlich*) and therefore could still be fulfilled by a statutory representative of the business owner with the authority to do so.

According to the BGH, the claimant indicated the alleged inability to perform the agreement only due to the inability to achieve the objective pursued by the deceased. However, the view that should be shared in this case is that, already at the time of the accident, it was clear that the business owner would not be able to implement the project himself. It can also be assumed that the heirs would not be able to continue the work he started. In no regard does this have any direct retroactive effect on concluded agreements, which can still be performed (regardless of whether the provisions on the contract of sale or specific work contract work apply to them).

BGH also indicated that failure to achieve the objective pursued by the deceased by purchasing or ordering machinery took place only within the scope of the economic risk he had previously assumed. In the circumstances of the case, there is no information that the suppliers in any way 'participated in the implementation or determination of this objective', including, in particular, making the existence or wording of the agreements conditional on the fact that the

6 They provide for the acquisition by operation of law by a public insurer of claims that the aggrieved party would have against the perpetrator, for which the public insurer is obliged to provide benefits.

7 Its Polish counterpart is Article 644 KC, which allows an agreement to be terminated at any time without giving a reason for the termination.

business owner (as the buyer or ordering party) still sought to achieve the objective at the time of delivery of the machines.

Negotiations and settlements between the suppliers and the heirs were necessary in order to induce the suppliers to give up their right to perform the agreement. The suppliers' claim for damages, which the claimant wanted to be partially compensated by the perpetrator of the damage, was based only on these arrangements. This factual state did not develop until after the succession opened (though for reasons that can be defined as objectively significant).

If the deceased himself was faced with the need to pay the suppliers compensation for a failure to collect the machines, then it would be necessary to take into account the succession of the claim for its return that the deceased would have against the perpetrator due to causing the accident (as is the case with, for example, hospital treatment costs). In this case, however, the current effects on the heirs' property occurred only after the victim's death and are only an indirect consequence of the damage resulting from his injuries. This assessment is not altered by the fact that, from the moment of the incident, the deceased's property was already burdened with the expectation (*Erwartung*) or even the certainty (*Gewißheit*) that the suppliers would be granted compensation.

A potentially imaginable reduction in property prior to the actual occurrence of an expense that was still undefined at a specific point in time, would not *per se* constitute legal grounds for the deceased's claim against the defendant for damages.

Potential compensation claimed from the perpetrator of the damage could include: (1) expenditure incurred for releasing the deceased from an already existing claim, or (2) the reimbursement of expenses made to satisfy it. As these circumstances occurred only after the death of the injured party, the claim for damages was included in his property at the time the succession was opened. Otherwise, it should be assumed, for example, that the property of the deceased at the time of the accident would already have been reduced by the expected profits from the operation of the new factory. The mere expectation of the occurrence of damage does not justify any compensation claims that may be inherited, because the damage related to the accident did not materialise (*die Verwirklichung*) and concretise (*die Konkretisierung*) during the deceased's lifetime.

This ruling was approved in the German doctrine.[8] It was emphasised that each time it was necessary to examine whether the deceased had the right to bring his own claim for damages against the infringing party during his lifetime, or

8 D. Leipold, in: *Münchener Kommentar*, vol. 11, 2020, § 1922, No 75; N. Preuß, in: B. Gsell, W. Krüger, S. Lorenz, Ch. Reymann (eds.), H. Müller-Engels (editor of the part), *Beck-online Grosskommentar*, (stand 1.11.2020), § 1922, pt. 210.2; J. Eichelberger, in: B. Gsell, W. Krüger, S. Lorenz, Ch. Reymann (eds.), A. Spickhoff (editor of the part), *Beck-online Grosskommentar*, (stand 1.12.2020), § 844, pt. 23.

whether the possible damage was incurred only by the heirs.[9] The heirs may only make those claims for damages against the perpetrator of the deceased's death that the deceased could have pursued during his lifetime, even if the effects of the event causing the loss continued to affect his property (i.e. the estate) after the deceased's death.[10] In this respect, the German doctrine points to the heredity of legal positions (*die schwebenden Rechtslagen*).[11] Therefore, if the violation of the legal interests of the deceased occurs during his lifetime, even if the damage in this respect arises only after the death of the deceased, the heirs will still have a claim for compensation against the perpetrator.[12] Nevertheless, the services provided by suppliers which became redundant as a result of the deceased's death, are not the 'loss of the deceased' nor are any claims for damages against his heirs in this respect,[13] as the suppliers are a third party to the perpetrator of the damage (the deceased's death), to whom he is not responsible.[14]

In the German doctrine, since the BGB first came into force, numerous disputes have arisen as to whether liability for inheritance debts is a consequence of the transfer of assets and liabilities to the heirs (§ 1922 BGB) or merely a consequence of the transfer of assets and the express indication to this in the act itself (§ 1967 BGB). However, the first view clearly prevails in the most recent doctrine, according to which the estate includes both the rights and obligations of the deceased.[15] The indicated judgment confirms this direction of interpretation.

II. Consideration of the problem presented in the German case and its comparison with Polish law

The basic provision regulating the inheritance of the deceased's rights and obligations in Polish law is Article 922 KC. It indicates in § 1 that the property rights and obligations of the deceased pass upon death to one or more entities, pursuant to the provisions of Book IV of the Civil Code (the 'law of succession'). At the same time, it indicates in § 2 that the rights and obligations of the deceased

9 J. Eichelberger, in: B. Gsell…, § 844, pt. 23. See also D. Leipold, in: *Münchener Kommentar,* vol. 11, 2020, § 1922, pt. 74.

10 J. Eichelberger, in: B. Gsell…, § 844, pt. 23.

11 D. Leipold, in: *Münchener Kommentar,* vol. 11, 2020, § 1922, pt. 75.

12 D. Leipold, in: *Münchener Kommentar,* vol. 11, 2020, § 1922, pt. 74.

13 N. Preuß, in: B. Gsell…, § 1922, pt. 210.2.

14 D. Leipold, in: *Münchener Kommentar,* vol. 11, 2020, § 1922, pt. 74; in the same direction G. Spindler, in: B. Gsell, W. Krüger, S. Lorenz, Ch. Reymann (eds.), A. Spickhoff (editor of the part), *Beck-online Grosskommentar,* (stand 1.11.2020), § 823, pt. 103.

15 Cf. L. Claussen, *Gesamtnachfolge und Teilnachfolge,* Baden-Baden 1995, pp. 43–44; K. Muscheler, *Universalsukzession und Vonselbsterwerb,* Tübingen 2002, pp. 12–13; T. Kipp, H. Coing, *Erbrecht. Ein Lehrbuch,* Tübingen 1990, pp. 501–502 and literature cited there.

that are strictly personal do not belong to the estate, and that those rights are transferred to the designated entities at the time of death, regardless of whether they are heirs or not. The provisions of Article 922 § 3 KC decide that estate debts also include the costs of inheritance proceedings, the obligation to satisfy claims for a compulsory portion and the obligation to perform ordinary bequests and deceased's orders, as well as other obligations provided for in the provisions of Book IV of the Polish Civil Code.

In Polish law, claims for damages (regardless of whether they arise from the provisions of tort law or contract law) are inherited on general terms.[16] The heirs are subject to claims and obligations for compensation, e. g. for compensation for property damage resulting from destruction or damage to someone else's property, an infringement of personal rights or the non-performance or improper performance of an obligation. A claim for damages is transferred to the heirs of the injured party, and the obligation to compensate for it is transferred to the heirs of the perpetrator. Such claims are transferred to the heirs of the entitled party regardless of the nature of the obligation that has not been performed, the source of the obligation, and whether the rights and obligations resulting from a specific agreement were closely related to the parties.[17]

In principle, in Polish law expectancy rights are also basically subject to succession.[18] However, this refers only to those that have the nature of subjective property rights and that themselves precede the acquisition of subjective rights that could be the subject of succession.[19]

Contrary to the literal wording of Article 922 KC, it should be indicated that, not only the deceased's rights and obligations are inherited, but also the legal position they were in at the time of their death.[20] This is irrespective of whether

16 J. Gwiazdomorski, *Dziedziczność roszczenia z art. 446 § 3 k.c.?*, NP 1972, No 6, p. 873; W. Borysiak, *Dziedziczenie. Konstrukcja prawna i ochrona*, Warszawa 2013, p. 136; W. Borysiak, in: K. Osajda (ed.), *Komentarz KC*, vol. IVA, 2019, Article 922, pt. 314.

17 J. Gwiazdomorski, *Dziedziczność…*, pp. 873–874; E. Skowrońska-Bocian, J. Wierciński, in: J. Gudowski (ed.), *Komentarz KC*, vol. VI, 2017, Article 922, pt. 48; W. Borysiak, in: K. Osajda (ed.), *Komentarz KC*, vol. IVA, 2019, Article 922, pt. 390; M. Pazdan, in: K. Pietrzykowski (ed.), *Komentarz KC*, vol. II, 2021, Article 922, pt. 26.

18 J. Kuropatwiński, *Ekspektatywa powstania wierzytelności w polskim prawie cywilnym*, Bydgoszcz 2006, p. 99.

19 W. Borysiak, in: K. Osajda (ed.), *Komentarz KC*, vol. IVA, 2019, Article 922, pt. 316; M. Zelek, in: M. Gutowski (ed.), *Komentarz KC*, vol. III, 2022, Article 922, pt. 15.

20 A. Ohanowicz, *Glosa do uchwały SN z 21 listopada 1956 r., 4 CO 16/56*, NP 1957, No 10, p. 127; S. Wójcik, *Czy posiadanie jest dziedziczne?* in: W. Osuchowski, M. Sośniak, B. Walaszek (ed.), *Rozprawy prawnicze. Księga pamiątkowa dla uczczenia pracy naukowej K. Przybyłowskiego*, Kraków–Warszawa 1964, p. 525; S. Rejman, *Glosa do wyroku SN z 26 marca 1965 r., III CR 28/65*, NP 1966, No 5, p. 672; J. Gwiazdomorski, *Prawo spadkowe w zarysie*, 1968, pp. 50–51; J. Pietrzykowski, in: Z. Resich et al. (eds.), *Komentarz KC*, vol. 3, 1972, p. 1819; L. Stecki, *Odwołanie darowizny przez spadkobierców darczyńcy*, NP 1973, No 9, p. 1311; B. Gawlik, *Procedura zawierania umowy na tle ogólnych przepisów prawa cywilnego (art. 66–72 k.c.)*, Kraków 1977,

the legal position is favourable to the heirs (e.g. prescription periods run for their benefit) or may cause their assets to be diminished (e.g. prescription, limitation or termination periods run against them).[21] This also applies to legal situations related to compensation law, which is clearly visible especially in a situation where, in certain factual circumstances before the deceased's death, some of the conditions for the liability in tort were fulfilled, but not all.[22]

Legal positions constitute factual circumstances governed by the hypothesis of legal norms in which the deceased remained at the time of his death, and which resulted or could have resulted in legal consequences specified in these norms. Therefore, if the specific factual circumstances that affected the deceased at the time of death were defined by the hypotheses of legal norms through the legal facts specified therein, and the facts have already occurred, then the legal effects which the disposition of such norms determined, after the death of the deceased, will be determined in the same way to the heirs. In other words, the legal effects of the legal facts set out in the hypotheses of the legal norms will be the same for the heirs as they would have been for the deceased if they had lived.[23]

III. Summary

It can be assumed that the indicated facts would be resolved in the same way under Polish law pursuant to Article 922 KC, as it was resolved under German law. In the factual state of the judgment of the BGH of 20 February 1962, VI ZR 65/61, it could not be asserted that the legal situation had arisen before the deceased's death, which could, consequently result in claims that could be in-

p. 131; S. Wójcik, *Ochrona interesów jednostki w polskim prawie spadkowym w zakresie powołania do dziedziczenia*, ZNUJ. Pr. Praw. 1981, No 98, p. 171; J. Gwiazdomorski, *Prawo spadkowe w zarysie* [updated by A. Mączyński], Warszawa 1990, pp. 45–46; M. Niedośpiał, *Glosa do postanowienia SN z 28 kwietnia 1999 r., I CKU 105/98*, Mon. Praw. 2001, No 6, p. 365; M. Niedośpiał, *Glosa do wyroku SN z 7 listopada 2002 r., II CKN 1395/00*, NPN 2005, No 2, p. 70; J. St. Piątowski, A. Kawałko, H. Witczak, in: *System prawa prywatnego*, vol. 10, 2015, p. 126–127; similar: the substantiation of the resolution of the seven-judge panel of SN of 16 March 1970, III CZP 112/69, OSNC 1971, No 1, item 1.

21 W. Borysiak, *Dziedziczenie…*, pp. 142–154; W. Borysiak, in: K. Osajda (ed.), *Komentarz KC*, vol. IV A 2019, Article 922, pt. 323–330; P. Księżak, *Prawo…*, p. 66.

22 An illustrative example is the judgment of the Swiss TFS of 6 December 1977, BGE 103 (1977), vol. II, item 54, pp. 330–339, where the deceased committed suicide by unscrewing the gas valve in the apartment she rented. A gas explosion took place after her death caused by gas poisoning and led to the destruction of the entire building. The court had no doubts that the legal effects of the deceased's unlawful and culpable behaviour passed on to her heirs, despite the fact that the damage itself occurred after her death, so all the conditions for liability for damages actually materialised on the side of the heirs (cf. W. Borysiak, in: K. Osajda (ed.), *Komentarz KC*, vol. IV A, 2019, Article 922, pt. 326.1).

23 W. Borysiak, *Dziedziczenie…*, pp. 146–148.

herited by the heirs. Nor could it be assumed that there was any expectancy right on his side. These claims arose only after the deceased's death as a result of the activities of his heirs. The situation related to the business owner's plans to expand the factory was a factual situation, not a legal situation – it was not directly determined by any hypotheses of legal norms. It was also not included in the agreement concluded with suppliers (e.g. in the form of a condition), so that these plans would gain legal significance. It is also difficult to conclude that, at the time of the deceased's death, the performance became impossible in a legal sense (cf. Article 475 and Article 495 KC). The heirs could have received the ordered performance at any time.

In such a situation, the provisions of Article 639 KC apply, according to which the ordering party may not refuse to pay the remuneration despite the failure to deliver the work if the contractor was ready to perform it but encountered an obstacle for reasons attributable to the ordering party (in this case, the ordering party may deduct the amount that the contractor saved due to not having to perform the work). It cannot be considered that there was an obstacle on the part of the ordering party within the meaning of Article 639 KC. In such a situation, Article 645 KC regarding a specific work contract also would not apply.

Mikołaj Pietrzyk

§ 19 – The management of a commercial enterprise as a component of succession assets

Comparative conclusion
The legal position of the executor of the will under Polish and German law is very different. In particular, the text examines the rights of the executor of a will in terms of managing a commercial enterprise as a component of succession assets. It also focuses on the heir's potential ability to prevent the executor of a will from performing their duties in accordance with the testator's dispositions. Considerations are based on the factual circumstances presented in the BGH case No IV ZR 130/53.

I. Analysis of an example case under German law

The initial aim of this study is to compare the institutions of Polish and German law applicable to the management of an enterprise after the owner's death in light of the ruling of the German Federal Court of Justice of 18 January 1954 in case No IV ZR 130/53.[1]

In particular, I will address the rights of an executor of a will, the legal nature of this institution and the scope and type of liability of heirs for the actions of the executor. In addition, taking into account the German factual circumstances, I will pay special attention to the possibility of limiting or even denying the rights of an executor by the heirs in conflict situations under Polish law.

A comparison of the institution that is the subject of this study against the background of the facts assessed by the German court is intended to serve as a proposal for a decision that a Polish court could adopt on the basis of the Polish legal system. This is the basic aim of this study. An attempt to find a solution against the background of Polish law will also allow for an answer to the question whether Polish law in this respect is functional and whether it handles the problem more efficiently than under German law.

1 NJW 1954, 636.

The factual basis and argumentation of the BGH was as follows. On 14 January 1947, the business owner Walter B. died. In his public will, he named his daughter, born in 1939, as his sole heir, limiting his wife's succession to the mandatory part. The succession assets included a commercial enterprise. The executor of the will, appointed by the testator, was to manage the business until his daughter reached the age of 25. The executor's period of activity was thus to last until 1964, i.e. 17 years after the owner's death. The daughter of the deceased, represented by a statutory representative, entered in the register as owner of the company, demanded that the company be transferred to her and that the executor be dismissed. In this context, on 18 January 1954 the BGH adjudicated in case at hand.

The heiress, as the claimant, argued that such a long period of management of the enterprise was not within the rights of the executor. As the basis for handing over the enterprise, she referred to § 2217 BGB, which provides that an executor of a will is obliged, at the request of the heir, to hand over inheritance items that are evidently unnecessary for the performance of their duties. She also argued that her liability for the commitments made by the executor of the will as part of the management of the enterprise was subject to the limits of liability for the succession debts under the inheritance. The heir considered it unacceptable that she should be liable with all her assets for the debts of the enterprise managed by the executor, while she had no supervisory powers and only the right to information.

However, the BGH did not share this argumentation. In the justification of the ruling, it stated that the unlimited liability of the owner of a registered enterprise is necessary to conduct business activity and is one of the guarantees of business transactions, according to § 25 and § 27 HGB. It decided that these provisions constitute *a lex specialis* in relation to the inheritance law regulations, limiting the liability of heirs for the succession debts.

The court's reasoning was enhanced by the fact that the claimant had previously consented to being entered as the owner of the enterprise in the register. It is from the fact that the heir is disclosed in the register as the owner that her personal liability arises. As a result, the actions of the executor of the will have direct consequences for her. The BGH therefore assumed that the executor of the will who manages an enterprise, acts as a representative of the owner, and therefore on their behalf and for their account (direct representative).

Such a solution creates a special and unprecedented situation, as the represented person has no legal means to supervise (control) the actions taken by the representative, who can perform any actions (including free of charge dispositions and actions exceeding the scope of ordinary management) at their own discretion, often for a very long period. In accordance with the regulation in § 2210 BGB, the management of an executor can last up to 30 years from the opening of the succession. However, this duration may also be longer if the testator indicates that the management is to continue until the death of the executor or the heir, or until a specific condition relating to one of these persons is fulfilled.

The heir is therefore not in a position to limit their liability unless they reject the estate connected with the testator's disposition, which is the subject of the discussion above. It must not be forgotten, however, that the heir is entitled to claim compensation from the executor of the will under the general rules of civil law. However, this is a secondary issue and does not constitute the subject of this study.

The court went on to argue that, in addition to acting as the heir's attorney-in-fact, i. e. on their behalf and for their account, the executor of a will may also act as the heir's trustee on their own behalf (and be liable for their own actions). It is up to the executor to decide how to act, unless the testator's will indicates otherwise.[2] In the analysed case, the executor chose the first course of action.

It should be considered how the relevant legal problems would be resolved under Polish law. As a preliminary remark, it is worth noting that there are two institutions in the national legal order that are applicable to the management of an estate, and more precisely, of an inherited business. First, there is the institution of an executor of a will, which exists in most legal orders, including German law. Second, there is the institution of a succession manager, who manages the enterprise in succession – an institution that is unknown in German law.

As a side note, it should be concluded that the BGH ruling leaves a lot of ambiguity as to the facts, especially as to the type (form) of activity conducted by the business. Therefore, translating the above circumstances into national law, I will consider the issue from the perspective of both a sole proprietorship and a partnership.

II. Consideration of the problem presented in the German case and its comparison with Polish law

The institution of an executor of a will in the Polish legal order is regulated in Articles 986–990[1] KC in fairly general terms, particularly in comparison with German law. In the literature, however, it is generally assumed that the position of an executor is similar under both laws.[3] In light of the further discussion, this assertion may seem doubtful. Due to the aim of this study, I will focus mainly on

2 NJW 1954, 636.

3 K. Peroń, *Zarząd spadkiem w systemach prawnych kręgu germańskiego*, Rejent 2006, No 2, pp. 149–161.

the characteristics of the legal regulations pertaining to the facts forming the basis of the BGH ruling in question. In my view, this is sufficient to demonstrate the fundamental differences in the position of the executor in the two legal orders.

The Polish legislator – similarly to the German legislator – has assumed that a testator may appoint an executor of a will to administer the entire estate, or an organised part or specified component thereof (Article 986^1 KC), or the subject of an absolute legacy until the subject is taken in possession by the person to whom the thing was left by way of the absolute legacy (Article 990^1 KC). Such an organised property, as part of the estate, is typically an enterprise or shares in an enterprise.

In general, the obligations and powers of an executor of a will are defined by the norms of Article 988 KC. This provision stipulates that the executor should administer the estate, repay succession debts, and then hand the estate over to the heirs in accordance with both the testator's intentions and the law. The provision also stipulates that this handover must be done immediately after the estate has been partitioned. An executor of a will is also obliged to hand over to the person to whom a thing was left in an absolute legacy, the subject of that legacy.

An executor of a will may, according to the intentions of the testator, exercise their function by merely supervising the dispositions in the will, or by carrying out those dispositions through administering the estate.[4] The mere supervision of the execution of the dispositions in the will is much less effective. There is no doubt that an executor of a will is independent of the heirs in the administration of the estate and that the heirs are excluded from such administration. As regards the national regulations, this is the unanimous conclusion in legal scholarship.[5]

In German law, this issue is regulated *expressis verbis* by the legislator in § 2211 BGB. It is not possible to exercise administration with regard to the same estate by different people exercising it in a different manner at the same time.[6] In many cases, the performance of dispositions in the will is against the interests of the heirs, which is why an executor of a will must be completely independent. The executor then hands over the estate to the heirs only once they have performed

4 J. Gwiazdomorski, Prawo spadkowe w zarysie, 1985, pp. 252–254.

5 G. Wolak, in: M. Załucki (ed.) *Komentarz KC,* 2020, Article 988, pt. 6, Legalis.

6 It should be noted, however, that such a situation may arise if the testator has appointed two or more executors and they have different visions about performing the dispositions in the will. The Polish legislator, unlike the German legislator, has not ruled on what to do in such circumstances. The provision of § 2224 BGB provides that such a conflict is resolved by the probate court, though this provision is dispositive.

their obligations. There is no uniform view as to whether an executor is the (dependent) possessor or holder of the estate.[7]

Since the legislator does not specify to what extent an executor of a will is entitled to administer the estate, it seems right to assume that it concerns both matters of ordinary administration and matters beyond the scope of ordinary administration.[8]

In addition, the content of Article 988 § 1 KC also raises two serious doubts. First, a fundamental question arises as to what is meant by the obligation to hand over the estate to the heirs in accordance with the testator's will. It is possible to construct at least three interpretative hypotheses with regard to this wording. First, it may equate to the legislator authorising the executor of the will to share the estate according to the testator's intentions. Second, it may involve the handover of the assets of the estate irrespective of issues related to property rights. Third, it may mean that the testator's instructions on how the assets of the estate are to be distributed are merely guidelines for the executor of the will, who cooperates with the heirs in preparing the partitioning agreement or applying for the partitioning of the estate. In German law, there is no doubt about the executor's right to partition the estate.[9]

Polish legal scholarship, however, is not in favour of this solution and rather unanimously rejects the possibility of partitioning the estate in the will, or partitioning the estate by an executor of the will. It is assumed that Article 1037 § 1 KC allows for the partitioning of the estate only at the request of any of the heirs, or under an agreement between all the heirs. Moreover, it is argued that, traditionally, the partitioning of a right or estate is different from acts of administration.[10]

A second kind of doubt arises as to whether or not Article 988 KC provides the heirs with an indirect possibility of removing an executor from performing their duties. This may be important in cases where the execution of dispositions in the will significantly contradicts the interests of the heirs, or where the testator entrusts an executor of the will with the administration for a longer period. This is because an executor of a will is obliged to hand over the estate to the heirs immediately after the estate has been partitioned. It is not difficult to imagine a situation in which the heirs, in order to take possession of the estate, partition it under a contract, thereby forcing the executor to hand over the assets under administration before they have had time to comply with the obligations imposed by the testator. Another doubt concerns the issue of what should happen if there

7 J. Kuźmicka-Sulikowska, in: E. Gniewek, P. Machnikowski (eds.), *Komentarz KC*, 2019, Article 988, pt. 2, Legalis.

8 *Ibidem.*

9 K. Peroń, *Zarząd…*, pp. 149–161; §2204 of the BGB explicitly allows for such a possibility.

10 S. Wójcik, F. Zoll, in: *System prawa prywatnego*, vol. 10, 2015, p. 498.

is only one heir and the estate is not partitioned. It seems that in such a situation, the executor of the will is obliged to hand over the estate once the decision ascertaining the acquisition of the estate has become final, as the estate is portioned only if there is more than one heir. The powers of an executor after the handover of the estate to the eligible person are very limited. They may, for example, claim the performance of an instruction (Article 985 KC), or – as already mentioned – supervise the performance of further testamentary dispositions, since they have been deprived of the control over the estate (they cannot administer it).

The provisions regulating the powers and obligations of an executor of a will concerning the administration of the estate are dispositive in nature, so the testator is free to vary the consequences arising therefrom. It should be stressed, however, that the testator cannot entrust an executor of a will with this function after the partitioning of the estate. Both the wording of the provision and the explanatory memorandum to the draft amendment of the regulations concerning an executor of a will of 29 April 2010[11] support the idea that the administration of the estate by an executor may not continue after the partitioning of the estate. This is not the case under German law, where § 2209 BGB allows the testator to entrust an executor of the will with the administration of the estate, its part or a specific component, even after all the tasks entrusted to them have been performed (including, for instance, the partitioning of the estate).

In Polish law, the function of an executor of a will terminates by operation of law upon their death, the loss of full capacity to legal acts, or the performance of all the testamentary dispositions. Article 990 KC allows the executor of a will to be dismissed for important reasons by a court at the request of an interested person, including the executor themselves. A similar solution has been adopted in German law, with the difference that an executor may terminate their functions at any time by making a declaration of intent before a probate court. It should be noted that the Polish legislator does not impose a time limit on exercising the functions of an executor and leaves this matter to the testator's discretion.[12] The need to regulate this matter was raised by legal scholarship as early as at the drafting stage of the Civil Code, under the provisions of the 1946 Decree on Succession Law.[13] Therefore, it is worth considering whether the recent amendment of the regulations on an executor of a will partly fulfils this proposal by

11 The explanatory memorandum to the bill amending the Civil Code and certain other acts, 29 April 2010, p. 7: http://orka.sejm.gov.pl/Druki6ka.nsf/0/B8E1284ED95F193BC125771A003CC47E/$file/3018.pdf.

12 M. Pazdan, *Zarządca sukcesyjny a wykonawca testamentu*, in: A. Dańko-Roesler, M. Leśniak, M. Skory, B. Sołtys (eds.), *Ius es tars boni et aequi. Księga pamiątkowa dedykowana profesorowi Józefowi Frąckowiakowi*, Wrocław 2018, p. 892.

13 B. Walaszek, *Stanowisko prawne wykonawcy testamentu*, NP 1959, No 4, p. 435.

recognising the partitioning of an estate as the final moment of an executor exercising administrative rights. § 2210 BGB sets a 30-year time limit as a general rule, but, as mentioned above, the testator may decide that an executor will carry out his function until the fulfilment of a condition linked either to the heir or to the executor.

With regard to claims between an executor of a will and the heirs, the legislator has decided to apply the provisions on mandate against remuneration.[14] Therefore, the provisions on mandate apply, i.e. Article 734 et.seq. KC. Particularly significant here are the regulations adopted in the following Articles: Article 735 KC regarding the remuneration due to the mandatary; Article 740 KC regarding the possibility to demand a report on the administration of the estate; as well as Articles 741 and 742 KC the regarding statutory interest and claims of the executor against the heirs.[15]

The most controversial issue is the legal nature of the position of an executor of a will, as the legislator has not made an unequivocal statement on this subject. It is also difficult to reach an unambiguous conclusion on the basis of the provisions that define the legal position of an executor in a comprehensive manner. There is considerable divergence in the views regarding the legal position of an executor. Some authors classify the executor as a representative of the testator or the heirs.[16] However, this is not the dominant view. The vast majority of legal scholars reject it.[17] In support of the position adopting the concept of representation, an argument is made for the admissibility of a power of attorney that does not terminate upon death and for the possibility of the analogous application of these provisions to the position of an executor of a will. In opposition to this view, it is rightly argued that the nature of a power of attorney is contradicted by the fact that it cannot be revoked, either by the deceased testator or by the heirs.[18]

However, in the German regulations, the BGH allowed the executor to act as the attorney-in-fact in the discussed case. The court held that the executor could act as the heirs' representative, on their behalf and for their account. The second solution adopted by the BGH, consisting in the executor of the will acting as a trustee, is also incompatible with the Polish legal order. In the Polish legal system, this would lead to the possibility of circumventing the regulation of Article 964

14 Article 989 KC.
15 M. Pazdan, in: K. Pietrzykowski, *Komentarz KC*, vol. II, 2021, Article 989, pt. 2, Legalis.
16 M. Planiol, *Podręcznik prawa cywilnego [O darowiznach i testamentach]*, translated by: A. Słomiński, Warszawa 1922, p. 133 et seq.
17 S. Wójcik, F. Zoll, in: *System prawa prywatnego*, vol. 10, 2015, p. 498.
18 B. Walaszek, *Krytyczny przegląd teorii dotyczących stanowiska prawnego wykonawcy testamentu*, ZNUJ. Pr. Praw. 1959, No 6, p. 175.

KC, under which the application of fiduciary substitution is prohibited under Polish inheritance law.

There are also views inspired by German concepts, whereby the executor of a will is a representative or an authority of the estate, as a quasi-legal entity. Adopting such a concept under Polish law would be inadmissible, as argued by B. Walaszek, due to the closed catalogue of legal entities adopted by the Polish legislator.[19]

According to another view, the theory of a private office or authority should be applied to the institution of an executor by reference to the legal position of an insolvency administrator.[20] This concept, referring to the position of an insolvency administrator, does not explain much, as the legal position of an insolvency administrator itself is quite controversial. As regards the status of this entity, many different concepts are also adopted and the theory of this authority is itself inconsistent.[21] In addition, Article 160 of the Insolvency Law explicitly indicates that an insolvency administrator acts in their own name, for the account of the insolvent party, and is therefore an indirect substitute and not an authority. The theory of a private office, on the other hand, is firmly established in German scholarship (*Amtstheorie*) derived from § 2202 BGB, which uses the term "*das Amt Testamentsvollstreckers*" (the office of an executor).

In Polish scholarship, the most commonly accepted view regarding the legal nature of an executor (and the correct one in my view) is that of an indirect substitute. Depending on the approach taken by individual authors, an executor acts as an indirect substitute for the heirs, or acts in their own name, but for the account of others (without specifying for whose account) or in their own name, but not for their account (even more generally).[22] An argument raised against the idea of regarding an executor as an indirect substitute is that the interests of the executor are excessively violated. The violation consists in the fact that the executor is personally liable without limitation when assuming the obligations, and is only entitled to the reimbursement of expenses from the heirs. The heirs, in turn, could invoke limitations on liability for succession debts in connection with accepting the estate with the benefit of inventory, and the executor of the will might not receive full compensation for expenses incurred in administering the estate. In my opinion, this claim is incorrect, as the liability of an executor is limited by Article 837 KC. It follows from this provision that an executor of a will

19 *Ibidem.*

20 S. Wójcik, F. Zoll, in: *System prawa prywatnego,* vol. 10, 2015, p. 498.

21 The diversity and non-uniformity of concepts concerning the legal nature of the position of an insolvency administrator is presented in detail by P. Feliga, *Stanowisko prawne syndyka w procesie dotyczącym masy upadłości,* Warszawa 2013, pp. 31–48.

22 J. Kuźmicka-Sulikowska, in: E. Gniewek, P. Machnikowski (eds.), *Komentarz KC,* 2019, Article 988, pt. 2, Legalis.

may limit their liability to the assets entrusted to them. This limitation does not, of course, apply to claims for compensation by the heirs under Article 989 KC.

There is also another institution in the Polish legal system that allows the management of a commercial enterprise as a component of succession assets – the succession manager. This institution raises fewer doubts than the institution of an executor of a will. It is also much more comprehensively regulated. It constitutes an alternative to the institution of an executor of a will with regard to the management of an enterprise in the estate. Succession management was introduced by the Act on the Succession Management of a Natural Person's Enterprise of 5 July 2018 (ZSPOF). As in the case of an executor of a will, I will focus on the regulations relevant to the discussed factual situation.

A succession manager may be appointed during the lifetime of a business owner conducting business activity entered in the CEIDG,[23] or after their death by a spouse who is the co-owner of the enterprise, a heir or a legacy beneficiary, and with the consent of people who are jointly entitled to 85% of the share in the inherited enterprise. A succession manager must consent to the appointment and be entered in the CEIDG. They are obliged to run the enterprise, authorised to perform judicial and extrajudicial acts (Article 18 ZSPOF) and perform acts within the scope of ordinary management. Performing acts exceeding the scope of ordinary management requires the consent of all the owners of the inherited enterprise, and in their absence, requires the court's approval (Article 22 ZSPOF). A succession manager acts on their own behalf for the account of the owners of the enterprise in the estate (Article 21 ZSPOF). He or she is not personally liable for the obligations incurred, but only liable for compensation to the owners of the enterprise for the improper performance of his or her duties (Article 33 ZSPOF).

The reasons for the expiry of succession management, which are relevant for this study, include the acquisition of an enterprise by a single person as a result of: the ruling on the confirmation of the estate acquisition becoming final, the registration of a deed of succession certification (in the case of only one heir) or the partitioning of the estate, as well as at the end of a two-year period from the business owner's death, though this may be extended by a court for up to five years for important reasons (Article 60 ZSPOF).

The introduction of the institution of a succession manager does not exclude the appointment of an executor of the will whose competences would correspond to those of a succession manager.[24] The testator is entirely free to choose the institution they wish to use.

---

23 The CEIDG is a central register of entrepreneurs who are natural persons (i. e. self-employed persons, partners of civil partnership enterprises); register contains information about the business owner, the office address, the profile of the business activity etc.

24 M. Pazdan, *Zarządca…*, p. 893.

Having described of the institution of an executor of a will and a succession manger against the background of Polish law, it is necessary to look at the factual situation in the BGH judgment in question in light of this description.

Let us consider how the factual circumstances presented in the BGH case No IV ZR 130/53 would be treated under Polish legal system. I will discuss two situations, First, a situation in which a deceased business owner had sole proprietorship entered in the CEIDG. I will then discuss a situation in which the business owner was a partner in a general partnership. These two situations correspond most closely to the German factual situation under discussion.

In the first case, the business owner, wishing to ensure the continuity of the enterprise, could appoint a succession manager or an executor. With regard to each of these institutions, the question is whether, as in German law, they could entrust either of them with the management of the enterprise for a period of 17 years, i. e., until the daughter, who is the heir, reaches the age of 25.

In the case of a succession manager this is not allowed. The ZSPOF specifies a maximum period of two years after the business owner's death during which the succession manager may perform the function. The court could extend this time to five years for important reasons. The literature unanimously states that an important reason may include the minority of the owner of the enterprise,[25] so it would not be controversial for the court to apply the maximum five-year period to the facts in question. Issues concerning liability for obligations of an enterprise in the estate managed by a succession manager are precisely regulated by the ZSPOF. There is no doubt that it is borne by the owners of the enterprise jointly (in the discussed case by the sole owner) and not by the manager. It is a special kind of indirect substitution, in which the substitute acts on their own behalf, but the obligations incurred are not their own. It should be emphasised that in this case the liability of the owners of an enterprise in the estate is unlimited and concern only obligations connected with its operation, thus occurring after the business owner's death. The owners are liable under the general rules of inheritance law for previous obligations relating to the running of the enterprise which arose before the opening of the succession and for succession debts.[26]

Summing up, if the institution of a succession manager was applied to the facts that the German court adjudicated on, it would not be possible for the manager to perform the function for more than five years, and the owners of the enterprise would be liable without limitation for the liabilities incurred. It should also be added that anyone who is entitled to more than half of the shares in the enterprise

25 J. Bieluk, *Ustawa o zarządzie sukcesyjnym przedsiębiorstwem osoby fizycznej. Komentarz*, Warszawa 2019, Article 59, pt. 1, Legalis.

26 *Ibidem*; this follows directly from the explanatory memorandum to the draft Act on the Succession Management of a Natural Person's Enterprise (p. 55).

may, at their discretion, dismiss the succession manager.[27] The dispute before the BGH in the discussed case, therefore, would probably never arise on the basis of regulations concerning a succession manager in Polish law.

The situation would be somewhat different if the business owner appointed an executor in his will to manage the enterprise. An executor is not limited in time in performing the function and therefore nothing prevents the testator from entrusting the executor with the management of the enterprise for a longer period. The rules of the liability of the executor and heirs are also different. The executor of a will, as a classic indirect substitute, in the absence of a regulation analogous to Article 33 ZSPOF, incurs their own liabilities and is entitled to be released from them by the heirs. An analogous construction is adopted here to that in the case of a mandatary, when they act as an indirect substitute (*cf.* Article 740 *in fine* KC). However, it should be remembered that the liability of an executor for obligations connected with the management of an enterprise is limited to the assets entrusted to them, pursuant to Article 837 KPC.

The liability of heirs is similar to that in the case of succession management, i. e., obligations incurred prior to the testator's death constitute succession debts, and they are liable, albeit indirectly but without limitation, for the obligations incurred by the executor of the will, within the scope of the enterprise management exercised. What is different, however, is the scope of the executor's powers. They are entitled, unless the testator's will says otherwise, to perform acts exceeding the scope of ordinary management without the need to obtain anyone's consent. It is therefore possible *de jure* for an executor of a will to manage an enterprise for a period of more than 10 years. In practice, however, this is only possible with the concerted cooperation of the heirs. The heirs have a number of ways of preventing an executor of the will from managing the enterprise, in particular through the prior partitioning of the estate and thus forcing the executor to hand over the estate. Another possibility is the appointment of a succession manager. Under Article 24 ZSPOF, if an executor of a will has been appointed and succession management was established after the business owner's death, the executor of the will has no competence to manage the enterprise in the estate.[28] In addition, the heirs may also apply to a court for the dismissal of the executor for important reasons.

It is therefore justified to conclude that, in light of the Polish regulations concerning an executor of a will, the BGH ruling would be invalid. First, because it is quite unanimously and correctly assumed that an executor is an indirect substitute (and thus cannot be either a trustee or a representative, as discussed

27 Article 55 ZSPOF.
28 J. Bieluk, *Ustawa…*, Article 59, pt. 1, Legalis.

above). Secondly, the heirs have a number of legal means to deprive an executor of the will of the capacity to manage the enterprise.

It seems that the situation is similar if the testator were a partner in a general partnership and appointed an executor to manage the rights of the partner, assuming, of course, that the partnership agreement allows for the succession of these rights. The same arguments can be raised with regard to an executor managing an enterprise in the estate, notwithstanding doubts as to the nature of the succession of the partner's rights in partnerships, which are not, however, the subject of this article.

III. Summary

The differences between the Polish and German legal systems stem from fundamental differences in the assumptions concerning the entire system of inheritance law in both systems, as well as from the different distribution of burdens as regards the interests of a testator and the heirs. It seems that the interest and intention of a testator have more weight under German law than under Polish law. One may cite examples, already referred to above, according to which it is possible, under German law, to stipulate in the will how the assets of the estate are to be distributed, and to entrust an executor of the will with the management of the estate even after all the entrusted tasks have been performed, regardless of whether or not the estate has been partitioned. The testator is free to choose an executor of the will himself or to leave the choice to another person or to the court. In addition, it should be noted that the testator is entitled to conclude agreements concerning succession to a greater extent than under Polish law (limited to Article 1047 KC) or to draw up joint wills. Even at a cursory glance, German law recognises the very wide freedom of a testator to decide what will happen to the estate after their death, and in what manner. It should also be noted that, in a way, the legal position of an executor is an emanation and extension of the testator's rights. It is therefore very much in the spirit of the German system of inheritance law to *de facto* force the heirs to continue the activity of the enterprise managed by an executor. In the absence of consent to such a state of affairs, the heirs are left only with the rejection of the estate. The German regulation concerning an executor reflects an interesting remark made by B. Walaszek, according to which the raison d'être of an executor is based on the exact execution of the testator's will, even if that goes against the wishes (and sometimes the interest) of the heirs.[29] Thus, the extremely strong position of an executor in German law is due to the strong position of a testator.

29 B. Walaszek, *Krytyczny...*, p. 175.

The intention of the Polish legislator was different. Weighing the interests of a testator and the heirs, it seems that – in the analysed area – it has given primacy to the latter. Unlike the German legislator, it has reserved the manner of partitioning the estate for the heirs only. The autonomy of the heirs as to whether and how they intend to partition the estate has prevailed over the testator's intention, which also affects the rights of an executor of a will. The assumption that the handover of succession property by the executor is to take place immediately after the partitioning of the estate also precludes the executor from administering the estate after this event. The essential feature of an executor of a will, as indicated by B. Walaszek, was thus significantly limited. One might venture a claim that the Polish regulations reduce the executor to an assistant, who is dealing with the formalities of succession. One should consider whether this regulation of the institution of an executor is not at the root of the fact that in Poland this is a rather dead institution that is very rarely established in practice.

In view of the remarks above, it would not be possible under Polish law to reach a decision similar to that made by the German Federal Court of Justice in the discussed case. The testator's rights do not go so far as to force the heirs to continue the activity of the enterprise managed by the executor of the will. Whether and how the enterprise activity is continued depends on the heirs.

As a side note, I would like to add that, with regard to the discussed issue, a draft regulation on a family foundation that is currently being prepared by the Ministry of Economic Development, Labour and Technology may be of interest. This institution is intended to be a solution allowing for a new way of inheriting enterprises.

Bibliography

Ahrens C., *Anmerkung zu BGH Urteil von 16. 9. 2008, VI ZR 244/07*, JZ 2009, No 4.

Anders M., in: Anders M., Gehle B. (eds.), *Beck'sche Kurzkommentare. Zivilprozessordnung mit GVG und Nebengesetzen*, München 2022.

Bajerski M., *Glosa do uchwały Sądu Najwyższego z dnia 13 grudnia 2013 r., III CZP 79/13*, PP UW 2016, No 1.

Balcarczyk J., *Prawo do wizerunku i jego komercjalizacja*, Warszawa 2009.

Ballhaus W., in: Johannesen K. H., Alff R., Ballhaus W., Weber R., Dunz W. (eds.), *Das bürgerliche Gesetzbuch: mit besonderer Berücksichtigung der Rechtsprechung des Reichsgerichts und des Bundesgerichtshofes: Kommentar*, Berlin 1974.

Bańczyk W., *Der Auftrag und die damit verbundene Vollmacht nach dem Tod der Parteien. Weiterbestehen im Todesfall im polnischen und deutschen Rechtssystem*, OER 2018, No 2.

Bańczyk W., *Der Vertrag zugunsten Dritter auf den Todesfall im polnischen Recht. Die Zulassung der Lösung aus § 331 BGB kraft Vertragsfreiheit*, OER 2017, No 2.

Bańczyk W., *Glosa do uchwały Sądu Najwyższego z dnia 13 grudnia 2013 r., III CZP 79/13* in: Zoll F., Daniluk S. (eds.), *Prawo cywilne. Glosy*, Warszawa 2016.

Bańczyk W., *Granice uwzględniania woli testatora z zaburzeniami psychicznymi w polskim prawie spadkowym*, Białostockie Studia Prawnicze 2017, No 4.

Bańczyk W., *Pozaspadkowe sposoby kształtowania następstwa na wypadek śmierci – o przełamaniu monopolu prawa spadkowego*, Kraków 2021 (unpublished doctoral thesis).

Barnert T., *BGH, 26. 11. 2003 – IV ZR 438/02, Verträge zugunsten Dritter auf den Todesfall*, JZ 2004, No 10.

Barta J., Markiewicz R. (eds.), *Prawo autorskie i prawa pokrewne. Komentarz*, Warszawa 2011.

Barta J., Markiewicz R., *Wokół prawa do wizerunku*, ZNUJ PWiOWI 2002, vol. 80.

Baziński A., *Prawo spadkowe*, Łódź 1948.

Bednarek M., in: Łętowska E. (ed.), *System prawa prywatnego. Tom 5. Prawo zobowiązań – część ogólna*, Warszawa 2013.

Bender P., *Glosa do uchwały Sądu Najwyższego z dnia 17 marca 2017 r., III CZP 110/16, OSNC 2017/12/134*, Rejent 2018, No 5.

Bieluk J., *Ustawa o zarządzie sukcesyjnym przedsiębiorstwem osoby fizycznej. Komentarz*, Warszawa 2019.

Bieranowski A., *Darowizna własności nieruchomości na wypadek śmierci*, in: Dańko-Roesler A., Oleszko A., Pastuszko R. (eds.), *Rozprawy z prawa prywatnego oraz nota-*

rialnego. Księga pamiątkowa dedykowana Profesorowi Maksymilianowi Pazdanowi, Warszawa 2014.

Biernat J., *Umowa o zbycie spadku w polskim prawie spadkowym*, Warszawa 2021.

Biernat J., *Z problematyki tzw. testamentu działowego w polskim prawie spadkowym*, PS 2005, No 4.

Błahuta F., in: Resich Z., Ignatowicz J., Pietrzykowski J., Bielski J.I. (eds.), *Kodeks cywilny. Komentarz, Tom 3*, Warszawa 1972.

Błaszczak Ł., Ludwik M., *Sądownictwo polubowne (Arbitraż)*, Warszawa 2007.

Bławat M., *Konwersja nieważnych czynności prawnych*, Warszawa 2019.

Boehmer G., *Grundlagen der bürgerlichen Rechtsordnung*, Tübingen 1952.

Bojańczyk K., in: Machała W., Sarbiński R. (eds.), *Prawo autorskie i prawa pokrewne. Komentarz*, Warszawa 2019.

Borysiak W., *Dziedziczenie. Konstrukcja prawna i ochrona*, Warszawa 2013.

Borysiak W., in: Osajda K. (ed.), *Kodeks cywilny. Komentarz, Tom 3*, Warszawa 2013, Legalis.

Borysiak W., in: Osajda K. (ed.), *Kodeks cywilny. Komentarz. Spadki. Tom IVA*, Warszawa 2019, Legalis.

Borysiak W., in: Osajda K., Borysiak W. (eds.), *Kodeks cywilny. Komentarz*, Warszawa 2021, Legalis.

Borysiak W., *Konstrukcja czynności prawnych mortis causa*, PP UW 2006, No 2.

Brähler-Boyan C., Mann H., *Zur Überleitung des Rückforderungsanspruchs des verarmten Schenkers auf den Sozialhilfeträgers*, NJW 1995, No 29.

Brox H., Walker W.-D., *Allgemeiner Teil des BGB*, München 2010.

Brox H., Walker W.-D., *Erbrecht*, Köln 2009.

Budniak-Rogala A., *Charakter prawny zapisu na sąd polubowny w postępowaniu cywilnym*, Wrocław 2015.

Cahill D., Connery N., Kennedy T., Power V., *European Law*, Oxford 2011.

Chojnowski W., *Prawo spadkowe*, Warszawa 1951.

Ciszewski J., *Kilka uwag o pełnomocnictwie nieodwołalnym i niegasnącym ze śmiercią mocodawcy*, GSP 2005, Vol. XIV.

Ciszewski J., Knabe J., in: Ciszewski J., Nazaruk P. (eds.), *Kodeks cywilny. Komentarz*, Warszawa 2019, LEX.

Claussen L., *Gesamtnachfolge und Teilnachfolge*, Baden-Baden 1995.

Collins L. (ed.), *Dicey, Morris and Collins on the Conflict of Laws*, London 2006.

Czachórski W., Brzozowski A., Safjan M., Skowrońska-Bocian E., *Zobowiązania. Zarys wykładu*, Warszawa 2009.

Czubayko U., in: Burandt W., Rojahn D. (eds.), *Becks'che Kurz Kommentare, Erbrecht*, München 2022, Beck online.

Damrau J., *Bürgerliches Gesetzbuch*, Band 9, Erbrecht, Stuttgart-Berlin-Köln 1992.

Damrau J., in: Damrau J. (ed.), *Soergel Kommentar. Bürgerliches Gesetzbuch mit Einführungsgesetz und Nebengesetzen: BGB*, Band 23: Erbrecht 3 §§ 2274–2385 BGB, Stuttgart 2002.

Denkinger M., *Europäisches Erbkollisionsrecht-Einheit Trotz Vielfalt?*, Köln 2009.

Dmowski S., in: Bieniek G. (ed.), *Komentarz do kodeksu cywilnego, Księga trzecia. Zobowiązania tom 2*, Warszawa 2011.

Doliwa A., *Umowy dotyczące spadku*, SPP 2008, No 1.

Drozd E., *Darowizna na wypadek śmierci*, Rejent 1992, No 1.
Duda A., *Wspólny małżeński testament w prawie niemieckim*, Jurysta 2004, No 4.
Dyoniak A., *Dziedziczenie testamentowe rozwiedzionego małżonka*, RPEiS 1988, No 3.
Dyszlewska-Tarnawska A., in: Habdas M., Fras M. (eds.), *Kodeks cywilny. Komentarz. Tom VI. Spadki (art. 922–1087)*, Warszawa 2019, LEX.
Ebenroth C.T., *Erbrecht*, München 1992.
Eccher B., in: Schwimann M. (ed.), *Praxiskommentar zum Allgemeinen Bürgerlichen Gesetzbuch, Band* 3, Wien 1989.
Eichelberger J., in: Gsell B., Krüger W., Lorenz S., Reymann Ch. (eds.), Spickhoff A. (editor of the part), *Beck-online Grosskommentar*, (stand 1.12.2020).
Ellenberg J., in: Brudermüller G. et al., *Palandt Bürgerliches Gesetzbuch. Beck'sche Kurz-Kommentare*, München 2018.
Ernst U., Rachwał A., Zoll F., *Prawo cywilne. Część ogólna*, Warszawa 2011.
Feliga P., *Stanowisko prawne syndyka w procesie dotyczącym masy upadłości*, Warszawa 2013.
Felski T., *Wpływ woli testatora na sposób podziału majątku spadkowego*, Pal. 1994, No 12.
Fierich F. K., *Rzut oka na najważniejsze zadania prac kodyfikacyjnych. Wykład wygłoszony w Warszawie przy inauguracji Komisji Kodyfikacyjnej d. 10 listopada 1919 r.*, Przegląd Prawa i Administracji 1919, year XLIV.
Fikentscher W., Heinemann A., *Schuldrecht*, Berlin 2006.
Flume W., *Allgemeiner Teil des bürgerlichen Rechts. Zweiter Band. Das Rechtsgeschäft*, Berlin-Heidelberg 1992.
Franusz A., *Arbitraż testamentowy jako specyficzna forma zapisu na sąd polubowny*, in: Olszewski J. (ed.), *Arbitraż i mediacja. III Ogólnopolska Konferencja Naukowa. Nałęczów Zdrój 8–10 Maja 2009*, Rzeszów 2009.
Fries M., Schulze R., in: Schulze R. (ed.), *Bürgerliches Gesetzbuch. Handkommentar*, Baden-Baden 2021.
Gandor K., *Konwersja nieważnych czynności prawnych*, SC 1963, vol. IV.
Gawlik B., *Procedura zawierania umowy na tle ogólnych przepisów prawa cywilnego (art. 66–72 k.c.)*, Kraków 1977.
Gawlik Z., in: Kidyba A. (ed.), *Kodeks cywilny. Komentarz, Tom III. Zobowiązania – część szczególna*, 2014, LEX.
Gehrlein M., in: Hau W., Poseck R. (eds.), *BeckOK BGB (Beck'sche Online-Kommentare)*, München 2021.
Gniewek E., in: Gniewek E. (ed.), *System prawa prywatnego. Tom 3. Prawo rzeczowe*, Warszawa 2020.
Górecki J., *Umowa darowizny na wypadek śmierci*, Rejent 2006, No 2.
Górecki J., *Nieruchomość jako składnik spadku – uwagi na tle Rozporządzenia Parlamentu Europejskiego i Rady (UE) nr 650/2012*, in: Dańko-Roesler A., Oleszko A., Pastuszko R. (eds.), *Rozprawy z prawa prywatnego oraz notarialnego. Księga pamiątkowa dedykowana Profesorowi Maksymilianowi Pazdanowi*, Warszawa 2014.
Górecki J., *Umowa zrzeczenia się dziedziczenia*, Rejent 2020, No 12.
Górska K., in: Gniewek E., Machnikowski P. (eds.), *Kodeks cywilny. Komentarz*, Warszawa 2021, Legalis.
Gottwald P., in: Krüger W. (ed.) *Münchener Kommentar zum Bürgerlichen Gesetzbuch. Band 2: Schuldrecht Allgemeiner Teil (§§ 241–432)*, München 2007.

Gottwald P., in: Habersack M., *Münchener Kommentar zum Bürgerlichen Gesetzbuch, Band 5, Schuldrecht, Besonderer Teil III, Allgemeiner Teil §§ 705–853*, München 2009.

Götting H-P., *Persönlichkeitsrechte als Vermögensrechte*, Tübingen 1995.

Grochowski M., *Artykuł 210 § 1 k.c. - jako regulacja dyspozytywna*, Pal. 2017, No 1–2.

Große-Boymann T., in: Burandt W., Rojahn D. (eds.), *Becks'che Kurz Kommentare, Erbrecht*, München 2022, Beck online.

Grüneberg D., in: Brudermüller G. et al., *Palandt Bürgerliches Gesetzbuch. Beck'sche Kurz-Kommentare.* München 2016.

Grzeszak T., *Dziedziczenie prawa do wizerunku w Niemczech*, Mon. Praw. 2006, No 24.

Grzeszak T., *Czy wolno w reklamie wywołać skojarzenie z konkretną osobą?*, in: Namysłowska M. (ed.), *Reklama. Aspekty prawne*, Warszawa 2012.

Grzeszak T., in: Barta J. (ed.), *System prawa prywatnego. Tom 13. Prawo autorskie*, Warszawa 2017.

Grzeszak T., *Dobro osobiste jako dobro zindywidualizowane*, PS 2018, No 4.

Gschnitzer F., Faistenberger Ch., *Österreichisches Erbrecht*, Wien–New York 1983.

Gwiazdomorski J., *Prawo spadkowe*, Warszawa 1959.

Gwiazdomorski J., *Prawo spadkowe w zarysie*, Warszawa 1968.

Gwiazdomorski J., *Dziedziczność roszczenia z art. 446 § 3 k.c.?*, NP 1972, No 6.

Gwiazdomorski J., *Wykładnia przepisów o testamencie na tle uchwały składu siedmiu sędziów Sądu Najwyższego*, NP 1973, No 6.

Gwiazdomorski J., *Prawo spadkowe w zarysie*, Warszawa 1985.

Gwiazdomorski J., *Prawo spadkowe w zarysie* [updated by A. Mączyński], Warszawa 1990.

Hans W., *Umowy dotyczące spadku*, NP 1967, No 2.

Harder M., *Zuwendungen unter Lebenden auf den Todesfall*, Berlin 1968.

Hoeren T., in: Schulze R. (ed.), *Bürgerliches Gesetzbuch. Handkommentar*, Baden-Baden 2021.

Horn C.-H., Kroiß L., *Testamentsauslegung. Strategien bei unklaren letztwilligen Verfügungen*, München 2019.

Hosemann G., *Von den Bedenken gegen das Testieren "im stillen Kämmerlein" - Die Geschichte des eigenhändigen Testaments in Deutschland, dargestellt aus Anlass des 200. Geburtstags des Badischen Landrechts*, RNotZ 2010, No 10.

Ignatowicz J., in: Resich Z., Ignatowicz J., Pietrzykowski J., Bielski J.I. (eds.), *Kodeks cywilny. Komentarz. Tom 1*, Warszawa 1972.

Ihering von R., *Walka o prawo*, transl. by A. Matakiewicz, Lwów 1875.

Janas A., in: Habdas M., Fras M. (eds.), *Kodeks cywilny. Komentarz. Tom V. Zobowiązania. Część szczegółowa (art. 765–921[16])*, Warszawa 2018, LEX.

Jagielska M., Macierzyńska-Franaszczyk E., Rott-Pietrzyk E., Zoll F., Żmij G. (eds), *Limits of harmonisation and convergence. Dissimilarities within Similarities of Polish and German Contract Law*, Warszawa 2018.

Jasiakiewicz T., *Glosa do uchwały Sądu Najwyższego z dnia 17 marca 2017 r., III CZP 110/16, OSNC 2017/12/134*, OSP 2018, No 9, item 86.

Jasiakiewicz T., *Testament wspólny jako przedmiot regulacji w prawie polskim i niemieckim*, Toruń 2018.

Jezioro J., in: Gniewek E., Machnikowski P. (eds.), *Kodeks cywilny. Komentarz*, Warszawa 2021, Legalis.

Justyński T., *Glosa do uchwały Sądu Najwyższego z dnia 13 grudnia 2013 r., III CZP 79/13*, OSP 2014, No 11.

Justyński T., *Glosa do uchwały Sądu Najwyższego z dnia 17 marca 2017 r., III CZP 110/16, OSNC 2017/12/134*, OSP 2018, No 11, item 109.

Justyński T., *Uwagi w sprawie prawnej dopuszczalności zawierania umów darowizny ze skutkiem mortis causa*, PS 2015, No 4.

Kaliński M., in: Brzozowski A., Jastrzębski J., Kaliński M., Kocot W., Skowrońska-Bocian E., *Zobowiązania – część szczegółowa*, Warszawa 2017.

Kaliński W., Zoll F., *Pełnomocnictwo nie gasnące mimo śmierci mocodawcy*, Rejent 1994, No 3.

Kanzleiter R., in: Otte G. (ed.), *J. von Staudingers Kommentar zum Bürgerlichen Gesetzbuch, Buch 5, Erbrecht, §§ 2265–2338*, Berlin 2006.

Kanzleiter R., *Das Berliner Testament: immer aktuell und fast immer ergänzungsbedürftig*, ZEV 2014, No 5.

Kanzleiter R., *Empfiehlt es sich, das privatschriftliche gemeinschaftliche Testament abzuschaffen?*, ZEV 2011, No 1.

Kanzleiter R., *Verwirkungsklausel zu Lasten eines Erben, dem ein belasteter Erbteil in Höhe des Pflichtteils (oder weniger) zugewendet ist?*, DNotZ 1993, No 12.

Karaszewski G., in: Balwicka-Szczyrba M., Sylwestrzak A. (eds.), *Kodeks cywilny. Komentarz*, Warszawa 2022, LEX.

Kipp T., Coing H., *Erbrecht*, Tübingen 1960.

Kipp T., Coing H., *Erbrecht. Ein Lehrbuch*, Tübingen 1990.

Klyta W., *Testamenty wspólne*, Rejent 2006, No 2.

Knabe J., in: Ciszewski J., Nazaruk P. (eds.) *Kodeks cywilny. Komentarz*, Warszawa 2022, LEX.

Koch J., in: Westermann H.P. (ed.), *Münchener Kommentar zum Bürgerlichen Gesetzbuch, Band 4. Schuldrecht – Besonderer Teil I §§ 433–534, Finanzierungsleasing, CISG*, München 2019.

Kociucki L., in: Osajda K., Domański M., Słyk J. (eds.), Kodeks rodzinny i opiekuńczy. Komentarz, Warszawa 2020, Legalis.

Kollhosser H., *Der Rückforderungsanspruch des verarmten Schenkers aus § 528 Abs. 1 Satz 1 BGB – Entstehung, Fortbestand, Vererblichkeit, Pfändbarkeit*, ZEV 2001, No 8.

Kołodzińska M., *Czy instytucja zapisu windykacyjnego może skutecznie zastąpić darowiznę na wypadek śmierci? Uwagi wynikające z praktyki notarialnej*, PS 2012, No 11–12.

Komarowska M., *Dopuszczalność umowy zrzeczenia się zachowku. Glosa do uchwały SN z dnia 17 marca 2017 r.*, Białostockie Studia Prawnicze 2017, No 4.

Korcz-Maciejko A., in: Brzeźna A., Gajda-Durlik M., Korcz-Maciejko A., *Ustawa o pomocy osobom uprawnionym do alimentów. Komentarz*, Warszawa 2019.

Kordasiewicz B., in: Kordasiewicz B. (ed.), *System prawa prywatnego. Tom 10. Prawo spadkowe*, Warszawa 2015.

Kosik J., in: Piątowski J.St. (ed.), *System prawa cywilnego. Tom IV. Prawo spadkowe*, Wrocław 1986.

Kozak I., *Umowa o zrzeczenie się dziedziczenia*, PS 2004, No 11–12.

Kötz H., *Vertragsrecht*, Tübingen 2010.

Kremis J., in: Gniewek E. (ed.), *Kodeks cywilny. Komentarz*, Warszawa 2011, Legalis.

Kremis J., in: Gniewek E., Machnikowski P. (eds.), *Kodeks cywilny. Komentarz,* Warszawa 2016, Legalis.

Kremis J., Kuźmicka-Sulikowska J., in: Gniewek E., Machnikowski P. (eds.), *Kodeks cywilny. Komentarz,* Warszawa 2017, Legalis.

Kroppenberg I., *Ist unser Erbrecht noch zeitgemäß? Überlegungen zum zivilrechtlichen Gutachten des 68. Deutschen Juristentags in Berlin,* NJW 2010, No 36.

Król A., *Czy długi alimentacyjne osoby zobowiązanej do płacenia alimentów (zobowiązany nie płacił, płacił za niego fundusz alimentacyjny) wobec funduszu alimentacyjnego przechodzą po śmierci zobowiązanego w drodze dziedziczenia na jego zstępnych? Jeżeli nie, to jaka jest tego podstawa prawna?,* Lex No 122042.

Królikowski M., *Możliwość odwołania darowizny po śmierci obdarowanego,* Mon. Praw. 2017, No 24.

Krziskowska K., Łobos-Kotowska D., Stańko M., in: Habdas M., Fras M. (eds.), *Kodeks cywilny. Komentarz. Tom II. Własność i inne prawa rzeczowe (art. 126–352),* Warszawa 2018, LEX.

Księżak P., *Żądanie wykonania polecenia,* PS 2006, No 4.

Księżak P., *Zachowek w polskim prawie spadkowym,* Warszawa 2010.

Księżak P., *Zapis windykacyjny,* Warszawa 2012.

Księżak P., in: Osajda K. (ed.), *Kodeks cywilny. Komentarz. Tom II. Własność i inne prawa rzeczowe,* Warszawa 2017, Legalis.

Księżak P., in: Osajda K., Borysiak W. (eds.), *Kodeks cywilny. Komentarz,* Warszawa 2020, ed. 26, Legalis.

Księżak P., *Glosa do uchwały Sądu Najwyższego z dnia 17 marca 2017 r., III CZP 110/16, OSNC 2017/12/134,* Rejent 2017, No 9.

Księżak P., *Prawo spadkowe,* Warszawa 2017.

Kubas A., *Recenzja: L. Stecki, Umowa darowizny,* NP 1974, No 10.

Kubas A., *Umowa na rzecz osoby trzeciej,* ZNUJ 1976, No 78.

Kucia B., *Oświadczenie o przyjęciu lub odrzuceniu spadku w imieniu małoletniego,* in: Fras M., Ślęzak P. (eds.), *Prawo prywatne wobec wyzwań współczesności. Księga pamiątkowa dedykowana Profesorowi Leszkowi Ogiegle,* Warszawa 2017.

Kucia B., in: Habdas M., Fras M. (eds.), *Kodeks cywilny. Komentarz. Tom VI. Spadki (art. 922–1087),* Warszawa 2019, LEX.

Kulski R., *Umowy procesowe w postępowaniu cywilnym,* Warszawa 2006.

Kunz L., in: Otte G. (ed.), *J. von Staudingers Kommentar zum Bürgerlichen Gesetzbuch mit Einführungsgesetz und Nebengesetzen. Buch 5, Erbrecht. Einleitung zum Erbrecht; §§ 1922–1966 (Erbfolge),* Berlin 2017.

Kuropatwiński J., *Ekspektatywa powstania wierzytelności w polskim prawie cywilnym,* Bydgoszcz 2006.

Kurowski W., Zrałek J., *Związanie osoby trzeciej skutkami zapisu na sąd polubowny (głos w dyskusji na przykładzie dłużników solidarnych),* in: Dańko-Roesler A., Oleszko A., Pastuszko R. (eds.), *Rozprawy z prawa prywatnego i notarialnego. Księga pamiątkowa dedykowana Profesorowi Maksymilianowi Pazdanowi,* Warszawa 2014.

Kuźmicka-Sulikowska J., in: Gniewek E., Machnikowski P. (eds.), *Kodeks cywilny. Komentarz,* Warszawa 2021, Legalis.

Kübler P., *Darowizna mortis causa* in: Stec P., Załucki M. (eds.), *Wokół rekodyfikacji prawa cywilnego. Prace jubileuszowe,* Kraków 2015.

Lackoroński B., in: Osajda K. (ed.), *Kodeks cywilny. Komentarz. Tom IIIB. Zobowiązania. Część szczegółowa,* Warszawa 2017, Legalis.

Lagarde P., in: Bergquist U., Damascelli D., Frimston R., Lagarde P., Odersky F., Reinhartz B., *EU Regulation on Succession and Wills. Commentary,* Köln 2015.

Lange K.W., in: Kessal-Wulf S. (ed.), *Münchener Kommentar zum Bürgerlichen Gesetzbuch: BGB. Band 11: Erbrecht, §§ 1922–2385, §§ 27–36 BeurkG,* München 2020.

Lange O., Kuchinke L., *Erbrecht. Ein Lehrbuch,* München 2001.

Leipold D., in: Schlichting G. (ed.), *Münchener Kommentar zum Bürgerlichen Gesetzbuch. Erbrecht: §§ 1922–2385, §§ 27–35 BeurkG, Band 9,* München 2010.

Leipold D., in: Kessal-Wulf S., Fest T. (eds.), *Münchener Kommentar zum Bürgerlichen Gesetzbuch: BGB. Band 11: Erbrecht, §§ 1922–2385, §§ 27–36 BeurkG,* München 2022.

Lewaszkiewicz-Petrykowska B., *Wady oświadczenia woli przy sporządzaniu testamentu,* in: Kordasiewicz B., Łętowska E. (eds.), *Prace z prawa cywilnego wydane dla uczczenia pracy naukowej Profesora Józefa Stanisława Piątowskiego,* Wrocław 1985.

Lisiewski M., *Ograniczone prawa spadkowe* DPP 1947, No 8.

Litzenburger W., in: Hau W., Poseck R. (eds.), *BeckOK BGB (Beck'sche Online-Kommentare),* München 2021.

Litzenburger W., in: Hau W., Poseck R. (eds.), *BeckOK BGB (Beck'sche Online-Kommentare),* München 2022.

Longchamps de Bérier F., *Z uwag do metodologii nauki prawa prywatnego: argumenty historyczny, dogmatyczny i prawnoporównawczy na przykładzie darowizny na wypadek śmierci oraz zapisu windykacyjnego,* in: Wudarski A. (ed.), *Polska komparatystyka prawa. Prawo obce w doktrynie prawa polskiego,* Warszawa 2016.

Longchamps de Berier R., *Zobowiązania,* Lwów 1938.

Lübbert F., *Verwirkung der Schlußerbfolge durch Geltendmachung des Pflichtteils,* NJW 1988, No 43.

Markiewicz M., *Komentarz do ustawy o prawie autorskim i prawach pokrewnych,* in: Markiewicz R. (ed.), *Ustawy autorskie. Komentarze. Tom II,* Warszawa 2021.

Martinek M., in: Reuter D. (ed.), *J. von Staudingers Kommentar zum Bürgerlichen Gesetzbuch mit Einführungsgesetz und Nebengesetzen. Buch 2, Recht der Schuldverhältnisse §§ 657–704 (Geschäftsbesorgung),* Berlin 2006.

Masiubański J., *Glosa do uchwały Sądu Najwyższego z dnia 13 grudnia 2013 r., III CZP 79/13,* Rejent 2014, No 12.

Matlak A., *Cywilnoprawna ochrona wizerunku,* KPP 2004, No 2.

Mazurkiewicz I., *Glosa do uchwały Sądu Najwyższego z dnia 13 grudnia 2013 r., III CZP 79/13,* Pal. 2015, No 11–12.

Mazurkiewicz J., *Non omnis moriar. Ochrona dóbr osobistych zmarłego w prawie polskim,* Wrocław 2010.

Mączyński A., *Dziedziczenie testamentowe w prawie prywatnym międzynarodowym,* Warszawa-Kraków 1976.

Mączyński A., *Glosa do uchwały SN z 22 marca 1971 r. III CZP 91/70,* OSPiKA 1972, No 2, item 26.

Medicus D., Lorenz S., *Schuldrecht I, Allgemeiner Teil,* München 2010.

Medicus D., Lorenz S., *Schuldrecht II, Besonderer Teil,* München 2010.

Medicus D., Stürner R., in: Prütting H., Wegen G., Weinreich W. (eds.), *Bürgerliches Gesetzbuch. Kommentar,* Köln 2014.

Mleko Ł., *Darowizna na wypadek śmierci. Rozważania na tle projektowanych rozwiązań legislacyjnych*, KPP 2010, No 4.
Mróz-Krysta D., *Glosa do uchwały Sądu Najwyższego z dnia 13 grudnia 2013 r., III CZP 79/ 13*, Lex 2015.
Mularski K., in: Gutowski M. (ed.), *Kodeks cywilny. Komentarz. Tom III. Art. 627–1088*, Warszawa 2019, Legalis.
Mularski K., in: Gutowski M. (ed.), *Kodeks cywilny. Komentarz. Tom III. Art. 627–1088*, Warszawa 2022, Legalis.
Muscheler K., *Erbrecht. Band I*, Tübingen 2010.
Muscheler K., *Erbrecht. Band II*, Tübingen 2010.
Muscheler K., *Universalsukzession und Vonselbsterwerb*, Tübingen 2002.
Musielak H.-J., in: Schlichting G. (ed.), *Münchener Kommentar zum Bürgerlichen Gesetzbuch. Erbrecht: §§ 1922–2385, §§ 27–35 BeurkG, Band 9*, München 2010.
Müller-Engels G., in: Burandt W., Rojahn D. (eds.), *Becks'che Kurz Kommentare, Erbrecht*, München 2019, Beck online.
Müller-Christmann B., in: Hau W., Poseck R. (eds.), *BeckOK BGB (Beck'sche Online-Kommentare)*, München 2020.
Niedośpiał M., *Darowizna na wypadek śmierci*, PiP 1987, No 11.
Niedośpiał M., *Testament. Zagadnienia ogólne testamentu w polskim prawie cywilnym*, Kraków-Poznań 1993.
Niedośpiał M., *Czynności prawa spadkowego*, Przegląd Prawa i Administracji 1995, No XXXIII.
Niedośpiał M., *Glosa do postanowienia SN z 28 kwietnia 1999 r., I CKU 105/98*, Mon. Praw. 2001, No 6.
Niedośpiał M., *Swoboda testowania*, Bielsko-Biała 2004.
Niedośpiał M., *Glosa do wyroku Sądu Najwyższego z dnia 7 listopada 2002 r., II CKN 1395/ 00, OSNC 2004, Nr 3, poz. 43*, NPN 2005, No 2.
Niemotko R., *Sankcja nieważności umów o spadek po osobie żyjącej*, in: Stec P., Załucki M. (eds.), *Wokół rekodyfikacji prawa cywilnego. Prace jubileuszowe*, Kraków 2015.
Niezbecka E., in: Kidyba A. (ed.), *Kodeks cywilny. Komentarz, Tom IV. Spadki*, Warszawa 2012, LEX.
Niezbecka E., in: Kidyba A. (ed.), *Kodeks cywilny. Komentarz. Tom IV. Spadki*, Warszawa 2015, LEX.
Nordmeier C.F., *Zulässigkeit und Bindungswirkung gemeinschaftlicher Testamente im Internationalen Privatrecht*, Tübingen 2008.
Nowak-Gruca A., *Użytkownik forever off. Wybrane problemy cyfrowego "życia po życiu" związane z ochroną wizerunku i korespondencji*, ZNUJ 2020, No 1.
Ohanowicz A., *Glosa do uchwały SN z 21 listopada 1956 r., 4 CO 16/56*, NP 1957, No 10.
Ohanowicz A., *Recenzja: J. Gwiazdomorski, Prawo spadkowe, Warszawa 1959*, RPEiS 1959, year XXI, No 3.
Olejniczak A., in: Kidyba A. (ed.), *Kodeks cywilny. Komentarz. Tom III. Zobowiązania – część ogólna*, 2014, LEX.
Oleszko A., *Umowy dotyczące spadku w praktyce notarialnej*, NP 1977, No 6.
Osajda K., *Testamenty wspólne*, Warszawa 2005.

Osajda K., *Darowizna mortis causa de lege lata* in: Ereciński T., Gudowski J., Pazdan M. (eds.), *Ius est a iustitia appelatum. Księga jubileuszowa dedykowana Profesorowi Tadeuszowi Wiśniewskiemu*, Warszawa 2017.

Osajda K., in: Osajda K. (ed.), *Kodeks cywilny. Komentarz. Spadki. Tom IVA*, Warszawa 2019, Legalis.

Osajda K., in: Osajda K., Borysiak W. (eds.), *Kodeks cywilny. Komentarz,* Warszawa 2020, ed. 26, Legalis.

Osajda K., Grzegorczyk K., in: Osajda K., Borysiak W. (eds.), *Kodeks cywilny. Komentarz,* Warszawa 2022, Legalis.

Pacocha M., *Związanie podmiotów trzecich umową arbitrażową*, Warszawa 2019 (unpublished doctoral thesis), available at: https://www.wpia.uw.edu.pl/uploads/media/5ee21d2dc7731/zwiazanie-podmiotow-trzecich-umowa-arbitrazowa.pdf?v1 [last access: 17.12.2021].

Pająk-Kozub A., *Testamenty wspólne w prawie polskim – uwagi de lege lata i de lege ferenda*, in: Fras M., Ślęzak P. (eds.), *Prawo prywatne wobec wyzwań współczesności. Księga pamiątkowa dedykowana Profesorowi Leszkowi Ogiegle*, Warszawa 2017.

Paluch A., *Captatoria conditio: meaning and admissibility in the light of freedom of testation. Analysis of selected legislations of Western European countries*, Acta Iuris Stetinensis 2020, No 4.

Paluch A., *Gewährleistung oder Beschränkung der Testierfreiheit – Über die Unzulässigkeit der gemeinschaftlichen Testamente im polnischen Erbrecht*, OER 2016, No 2.

Paluch A., *Granice swobody rozrządzania majątkiem na wypadek śmierci w prawie polskim*, Warszawa 2021.

Pazdan M., *Umowa o zrzeczenie się dziedziczenia w polskim prawie prywatnym międzynarodowym,* NP 1975, No 5.

Pazdan M., *Umowa o zrzeczenie się dziedziczenia w polskim prawie spadkowym,* Rejent 1997, No 4.

Pazdan M., *Bezskuteczność lub nieważność zapisu na sąd polubowny w prawie polskim* in: Nowaczyk P., Pieckowski S., Poczobut J., Szumański A., Tynel A. (eds.), *Międzynarodowy i krajowy arbitraż handlowy u progu XXI wieku. Księga pamiątkowa dedykowana doktorowi habilitowanemu Tadeuszowi Szurskiemu,* Warszawa 2008.

Pazdan M, in: Pietrzykowski K. (ed.), *Kodeks cywilny. Tom II. Komentarz do art. 450-1088,* Warszawa 2011, Legalis.

Pazdan M, in: Pietrzykowski K. (ed.), *Kodeks cywilny. Tom II. Komentarz do art. 450-1088. Przepisy wprowadzające,* Warszawa 2015, Legalis.

Pazdan M., *Statut spadkowy w świetle rozporządzenia spadkowego*, in: Pazdan M., Górecki J. (eds.), *Nowe europejskie prawo spadkowe*, Warszawa 2015.

Pazdan M., *Wybrane projektowane zmiany w prawie spadkowym*, in: *Nowy kodeks cywilny odpowiedzią na wyzwania współczesności – konferencja naukowa (Warszawa, 10 April 2015)*, Warszawa 2015.

Pazdan M., *Zarządca sukcesyjny a wykonawca testamentu*, in: Dańko-Roesler A., Leśniak M., Skory M., Sołtys B. (eds.), *Ius es tars boni et aequi. Księga pamiątkowa dedykowana profesorowi Józefowi Frąckowiakowi*, Wrocław 2018.

Pazdan M, in: Pietrzykowski K. (ed.), *Kodeks cywilny. Tom I. Komentarz do art. 1-449[10]*, Warszawa 2020, Legalis.

Pazdan M., in: Pietrzykowski K. (ed.), *Kodeks cywilny. Tom II. Komentarz do art. 450-1088. Przepisy wprowadzające,* Warszawa 2021, Legalis.

Pązik A., *Komentarz do ustawy o prawie autorskim i prawach pokrewnych* in: Markiewicz R. (ed.), *Ustawy autorskie. Komentarze. Tom II*, Warszawa 2021.

Pązik A., *Prawo do wizerunku w obliczu zmian*, ZNUJ PPWI 2010, No 1.

Peifer K-N., *Individualitat im Zivilrecht, Der Schutz persönlicher, gegenständlicher und wettbewerbsrechtlicher Individualität im Persönlichkeitsrecht, Immaterialgüterrecht und Recht der Unternehmen,* Tübingen 2001.

Peroń K., *Zarząd spadkiem w systemach prawnych kręgu germańskiego*, Rejent 2006, No 2.

Peukert A., *Güterzuordnung als Rechtsprinzip*, Tübingen 2008.

Piątowski J.St., Kordasiewicz B., *Prawo spadkowe*, Warszawa 2003.

Piątowski J.St., Kordasiewicz B., *Prawo spadkowe*, Warszawa 2011.

Pietrzykowski J., in: Resich Z., Ignatowicz J., Pietrzykowski J., Bielski J.I. (eds.), *Kodeks cywilny. Komentarz, Tom 3,* Warszawa 1972.

Pietrzykowski K., in: Pietrzykowski K. (ed.), *Kodeks rodzinny i opiekuńczy. Komentarz,* Warszawa 2021, Legalis.

Pionkowski J., *Nieważność testamentów osób wykazujących zaburzenia psychiczne*, NP 1963, No 2.

Pisuliński J., *Zrzeczenie się dziedziczenia w prawie niemieckim,* Rejent 1999, No 12.

Pisuliński J., *Umowa zrzeczenia się dziedziczenia na korzyść określonej osoby,* in: Jelonek-Jarco B., Kos R., Zawadzka J. (eds.), *Usus magister est Optimus. Rozprawy prawnicze ofiarowane profesorowi Andrzejowi Kubasowi,* Warszawa 2016.

Planiol M., *Podręcznik prawa cywilnego [O darowiznach i testamentach],* translated by: A. Słomiński, Warszawa 1922.

Południak-Gierz K., *Defects of Consent in Consumer E-Commerce from the Polish Law Perspective*, Göttingen 2021.

Potrzobowski K., Żywicki W., *Sądownictwo polubowne,* Warszawa 1961.

Preuß N., in: Gsell B., Krüger W., Lorenz S., Reymann Ch. (eds.), Müller-Engels H. (editor of the part), *Beck-online Grosskommentar*, (stand 1.11.2020).

Przybyłowski K., *Niedopuszczalność wspólnych testamentów*, SC 1963, vol. IV.

Radwański Z., in: Radwański Z. (ed.), *System prawa cywilnego. Tom III. Część 1. Zobowiązania – część ogólna,* Wrocław 1976.

Radwański Z., in: Grzybowski S. (ed.), *System prawa cywilnego. Tom I. Część ogólna,* Wrocław 1985.

Radwański Z., *Wykładnia oświadczeń woli składanych indywidualnym adresatom,* Wrocław 1992.

Radwański Z., *Wykładnia testamentów,* KPP 1993, No 1.

Radwański Z., Gutowski M., in: Radwański Z., Olejniczak A. (eds.), *Prawo cywilne – część ogólna. System Prawa Prywatnego, Warszawa* 2019.

Radwański Z., Mularski K., in: Radwański Z., Olejniczak A. (eds.), *System prawa prywatnego. Tom 2, Prawo cywilne – część ogólna,* Warszawa 2019.

Rejman S., *Glosa do wyroku SN z 26 marca 1965 r., III CR 28/65*, NP 1966, No 5.

Reimann W., *Das Schicksal letztwilliger Zuwendungen an Schwiegerkinder nach Ehescheidung,* ZEV 2011, No 12.

Rejman S., in: Resich Z., Ignatowicz J., Pietrzykowski J., Bielski J.I. (eds.), *Kodeks cywilny. Komentarz, Tom 2,* Warszawa 1972.

Rixecker R., in: Schubert C. (ed.), *Münchener Kommentar zum Bürgerlichen Gesetzbuch, Band 1. Allgemeiner Teil §§ 1–240, AllgPersönlR, ProstG, AGG,* München 2018.
Robaczyński W., in: Księżak P., Pyziak-Szafnicka M. (eds.), *Kodeks cywilny. Komentarz. Część ogólna,* Warszawa 2014.
Rott-Pietrzyk E., *Umowa o zrzeczenie się dziedziczenia – uwagi de lege lata i de lege ferenda,* Rejent 2006, No 3.
Rudnicki J., *Dekodyfikacja prawa cywilnego w Polsce,* Bielsko-Biała 2018.
Ruhwinkel S., Fetzer R., in: Krüger W. (ed.) *Münchener Kommentar zum Bürgerlichen Gesetzbuch., Band 3: Schuldrecht – Allgemeiner Teil II (§§ 311–432),* München 2019.
Rzewuski M., in: Łukasiewicz J.M., Ramus I. (eds.), *Prawo alimentacyjne. Zagadnienia materialne,* Toruń 2015.
Rzewuski M., *Darowizna na wypadek śmierci* in: Olejniczak A., Haberko J., Pyrzyńska A., Sokołowska D. (eds.), *Współczesne problemy prawa zobowiązań,* Warszawa 2015.
Rzewuski M., *Wykładnia testamentu a okoliczności zewnętrzne towarzyszące testowaniu,* PS 2015, No 1.
Safjan M., in: Pietrzykowski K. (ed.), *Kodeks cywilny. Tom II. Komentarz do art. 450–1088. Przepisy wprowadzają ce,* Warszawa 2021, Legalis.
Säcker F.J., Rixecker R., in: Säcker F.J. (ed.), *Münchener Kommentar zum Bürgerlichen Gesetzbuch. Allgemeiner Teil. Band 1,* München 2006.
Schack H., *Anmerkung zu BGH Urteil von 1. 12. 1999,* JZ 2000, No 21.
Schilken E., in: Gursky K.-H., Habermann N. (eds.), *J. von Staudingers Kommentar zum Bürgerlichen Gesetzbuch mit Einführungsgesetz und Nebengesetzen. Buch 1, Allgemeiner Teil §§ 164–240,* Berlin 2004.
Schlitt G., *Das Erbrecht in der Ehekrise,* ZEV 2011, No 12.
Schmitz W., *Das Problem der Beschränkung der Testierfreiheit,* Berlin 1936.
Schotten G., in: Otte G. (ed.), *J. von Staudingers Kommentar zum Bürgerlichen Gesetzbuch mit Einführungsgesetz und Nebengesetzen, Buch 5, Erbrecht §§ 2346–2385 (Erbverzicht, Erbschein, Erbschaftskauf),* Berlin 2010.
Schuhmann M., in: Burandt W., Rojahn D. (eds.), *Beck'sche Kurz-Kommentare, Erbrecht,* München 2022, Beck online.
Siedlecki W., *Glosa do orzeczenia Sądu Najwyższego z dnia 18 sierpnia 1964 r., III CR 87/63,* OSPiKA 1965, No 9, item 200.
Simon U., in: Westermann H.P. et al. (eds.), *Erman Bürgerliches Gesetzbuch. Band 2,* Köln 2014.
Skowrońska E., *Glosa do uchwały Sądu Najwyższego z 5. 02. 1993 r., III CZP 10/93,* OSP 1994, No 5, item 83.
Skowrońska E., *Z problematyki powołania spadkobiercy w testamencie,* Pal. 1993, No 1–2.
Skowrońska-Bocian E., *Testament w prawie polskim,* Warszawa 2004.
Skowrońska-Bocian E., *Komentarz do Kodeksu cywilnego. Księga czwarta. Spadki,* Warszawa 2011, LEX.
Skowrońska-Bocian E., *Prawo spadkowe,* Warszawa 2016.
Skowrońska-Bocian E., Warciński M., in: Pietrzykowski K. (ed.), *Kodeks cywilny. Tom I. Komentarz do art. 1-449[10],* Warszawa 2018, Legalis.
Skowrońska-Bocian E., Wierciński J., in: Gudowski J. (ed.), *Kodeks cywilny. Komentarz. Tom VI. Spadki,* Warszawa 2017, LEX.

Smyczyński T., *Glosa do postanowienia SN z 24. 2. 1999 r., III CZ 179/98*, OSP 2000, No 7–8, item 114.

Smyk M., *Pełnomocnictwo według kodeksu cywilnego*, Warszawa 2010.

Sokołowski T., in: Gutowski M. (ed.), *Kodeks cywilny. Komentarz. Tom II. Art. 353–626*, Warszawa 2019, Legalis.

Solarski S., *Odwołanie darowizny*, Warszawa 2020.

Spindler G., in: Gsell B., Krüger W., Lorenz S., Reymann Ch. (eds.), Spickhoff A. (editor of the part), *Beck-online Grosskommentar*, (stand 1. 11. 2020).

Stadler A., in: Stürner R. (ed.), *Jauernig Bürgerliches Gesetzbuch mit ROM-I-VO, Rom-II-VO, Rom-III-VO, EG-UnthVO/HUntProt und EuErbVO. Kommentar*, München 2021.

Stasiński Z. (ed.), *Orzecznictwo Sądu Apelacyjnego w Poznaniu w Sprawach Cywilnych, Zażaleniowych za Lata 1920–1937*, Self-published 1937.

Stecki L., *Odwołanie darowizny przez spadkobierców darczyńcy*, NP 1973, No 9.

Stecki L., in: Winiarz J. (ed.), *Kodeks cywilny z komentarzem*, Warszawa 1980.

Stecki L., in: Rajski J. (ed.), *System prawa prywatnego. Tom 7. Zobowiązania – część szczegółowa*, Warszawa 2011.

Stecki L., Bączyk M., in: Rajski J. (ed.), *System Prawa Prywatnego. Tom 7. Zobowiązania – część szczegółowa*, Warszawa 2018.

Stein A., in: Damrau J. (ed.), *Soergel Kommentar zum Bürgerlichen Gesetzbuch. Band 21. Erbrecht 1, §§ 1922–2063*, Stuttgart–Berlin–Köln–Mainz 2002.

Stempniak A., *Autonomia i integracja postępowań działowych w prawie polskim*, Warszawa 2017.

Sticherling P., in: Kessal-Wulf S., (ed.) *Münchener Kommentar zum Bürgerlichen Gesetzbuch: BGB. Band 11: Erbrecht, §§ 1922–2385, §§ 27–36 BeurkG*, München 2020.

Strobel B., *Bedarf das gemeinschaftliche Testament des deutschen BGB einer Reform?*, AcP 2021, vol. 221, No 3.

Stürner R. (ed.), *Jauernig BGB: Bürgerliches Gesetzbuch Kommentar mit ROM-I-VO, Rom-II-VO, Rom-III-VO, EG-UnthVO/HUntProt und EuErbVO*, München 2021.

Stürner R., in: Stürner R. (ed.), *Jauernig Bürgerliches Gesetzbuch mit ROM-I-VO, Rom-II-VO, Rom-III-VO, EG-UnthVO/HUntProt und EuErbVO. Kommentar*, München 2021.

Suliński G., *Osoba trzecia w arbitrażu handlowym*, Warszawa 2018.

Swaczyna B., *Warunkowe czynności prawne*, Warszawa 2012.

Sychowicz M., in: *Praktyczny komentarz z orzecznictwem. Kodeks cywilny. Tom II, art. 353-1088*, Warszawa 2005.

Sylwestrzak A., in: Balwicka-Szczyrba M., Sylwestrzak A. (eds.), *Kodeks cywilny. Komentarz*, Warszawa 2022, LEX.

Szadkowski K., in: Gutowski M. (ed.), *Kodeks cywilny. Komentarz. Tom I. Art. 1–352*, Warszawa 2021, Legalis.

Szpyt K., in: Załucki M. (ed.), *Kodeks cywilny. Komentarz*, Warszawa 2023, Legalis.

Ślęzak P., *Ustawa o prawie autorskim i prawach pokrewnych. Komentarz*, Warszawa 2017.

Ślęzak P., *Komercyjne wykorzystanie wizerunku*, ZNUJ PPWI 2019, No 4.

Święcicki W. (ed.), *Prawo cywilne z orzecznictwem, literatura i przepisami związkowymi. Tom I*, Warszawa 1958.

Tappmeier K., *Erbeinsetzung und Bezugsberechtigung des Ehegatten aus einer Kapitallebensversicherung nach Scheidung der Ehe*, DNotZ 1987, No 12.

Tenenbaum-Kulig M., *Recenzja: Szymon Solarski, Odwołanie darowizny, Warszawa 2020*, FP 2021, No 2.

Tiedtke K., *Die Umdeutung eines Vermächtnisses in ein Rechtsgeschäft unter Lebenden*, NJW 1978, No 51.

Till E., *Prawo prywatne austryackie, tom VI, Wykład Austr. Prawa Spadkowego*, Lwów 1904.

Tomaszewska E., *Ustawa o pomocy osobom uprawnionym do alimentów. Komentarz*, LEX/el. 2019.

Trzaskowski R., in: Gudowski J. (ed.), *Kodeks cywilny. Komentarz. Tom V. Zobowiązania. Część szczegółowa*, Warszawa 2018.

Urbański A., in: Machała W., Sarbiński R. (eds.), *Prawo autorskie i prawa pokrewne. Komentarz*, Warszawa 2019.

Wacke A., *Rechtsfolgen testamentarischer Verwirkungsklauseln Anwachsung oder Ersatzerbschaft?*, DNotZ 1990, No 7.

Wagner G., in: Habersack M. (ed.), *Münchener Kommentar zum Bürgerlichen Gesetzbuch, Band 7. Schuldrecht – Besonderer Teil IV §§ 705–853, Partnerschaftsgesellschaftsgesetz, Produkthaftungsgesetz*, München 2020.

Walaszek B., *Krytyczny przegląd teorii dotyczących stanowiska prawnego wykonawcy testamentu*, ZNUJ. Pr. Praw. 1959, No 6.

Walaszek B., *Stanowisko prawne wykonawcy testamentu*, NP 1959, No 4.

Walker J., *Halsbury's Laws of Canada. Conflict of Laws*, Markham 2011.

Warciński M., *Glosa do wyroku Sądu Najwyższego z dnia 7 listopada 2002 r., II CKN 1395/00, OSNC 2004, Nr 3, poz. 43*, Pal. 2004, No 11–12.

Wąsiewicz A., *Powstanie, istota i zniesienie współwłasności ułamkowej*, Poznań 1965.

Weckbach T., *Die Bindugswirkung von Erbteilungsverboten*, Berlin 1987.

Wegerhoff S., in: Kessal-Wulf S. (ed.), *Münchener Kommentar zum Bürgerlichen Gesetzbuch: BGB. Band 11: Erbrecht, §§ 1922–2385, §§ 27–36 BeurkG*, München 2020.

Wegerhoff S., in: Kessal-Wulf S., Fest T. (eds.), *Münchener Kommentar zum Bürgerlichen Gesetzbuch: BGB. Band 11: Erbrecht, §§ 1922–2385, §§ 27–36 BeurkG*, München 2022.

Weitz K., *Jurysdykcja krajowa w sprawach spadkowych w świetle rozporządzenia spadkowego*, in: Pazdan M., Górecki J. (eds.), *Nowe europejskie prawo spadkowe*, Warszawa 2015.

Welser R., *Der Erbrechts-Kommentar §§ 531–824 ABGB*, Wien 2019.

Werner O., in: Otte G. (ed.), *J. von Staudingers Kommentar zum Bürgerlichen Gesetzbuch mit Einführungsgesetz und Nebengesetzen, Buch 5, Erbrecht §§ 1967–2063*, Berlin 2002.

Wieacker F., *Zur lebzeitigen Zuwendung auf den Todesfall*, in: Nipperdey H.C. (ed.), *Festschrift für Heinrich Lehmann zum 80. Geburtstag*, Berlin 1956.

Wierciński J., *Brak świadomości albo swobody przy sporządzaniu testamentu*, Warszawa 2013.

Wiśniewski R., *Charakter dyspozycji wkładem oszczędnościowym w myśl art. 37 Prawa bankowego*, NP 1983, No 7–8.

Wolak G., *Glosa do uchwały Sądu Najwyższego z dnia 13 grudnia 2013 r., III CZP 79/13*, Rejent 2014, No 7.

Wolak A., *Umowa zrzeczenia się dziedziczenia w polskim prawie cywilnym*, Warszawa 2016.

Wolak G., in: Habdas M., Fras M. (eds.), *Kodeks cywilny. Komentarz. Tom VI. Spadki (art. 922–1087)*, Warszawa 2019, LEX.

Wolak G., in: Załucki M. (ed.), *Kodeks cywilny. Komentarz,* Warszawa 2020, Legalis.

Wójcik S., *Czy posiadanie jest dziedziczne?* in: Osuchowski W., Sośniak M., Walaszek B. (eds.), *Rozprawy prawnicze. Księga pamiątkowa dla uczczenia pracy naukowej K. Przybyłowskiego,* Kraków–Warszawa 1964.

Wójcik S., *Ochrona interesów jednostki w polskim prawie spadkowym w zakresie powołania do dziedziczenia,* ZNUJ. Pr. Praw. 1981, No 98.

Wójcik S., in: Piątowski J.St. (ed.), *System prawa cywilnego. Tom IV. Prawo spadkowe,* Wrocław 1986.

Wójcik S., Zoll F., *Testament,* SPP 2006, No 2.

Wójcik S., Zoll F., in: Kordasiewicz B. (ed.), *System prawa prywatnego. Tom 10. Prawo spadkowe,* Warszawa 2009, 2013, 2015.

Wrześniewski P., *Charakter prawny zapisu na sąd polubowny,* Warszawa 2010.

Wysocka-Bar A., *Jurysdykcja krajowa sądów polskich a kolizyjna jednolitość spadku,* PWPMEiP 2016, vol. XIV.

Wysocka-Bar A., *Prawo właściwe dla dziedziczenia według unijnego rozporządzenia dotyczącego spraw spadkowych,* KPP 2012, No 4.

Zabielski L., *Donatio mortis causa. Lex abrogatae,* in: Pecyna M., Pisuliński J., Podrecka M. (eds.), *Rozprawy cywilistyczne. Księga pamiątkowa dedykowana Profesorowi Edwardowi Drozdowi,* Warszawa 2013.

Zakrzewski P., *Umowa darowizny na wypadek śmierci w prawie holenderskim, niemieckim i polskim,* in: Olejniczak A., Haberko J., Pyrzyńska A., Sokołowska D. (eds.), *Współczesne problemy prawa zobowiązań,* Warszawa 2015.

Żarnowiec Ł., *Odwołanie testamentu w polskim prawie spadkowym,* Rej. 2011, No 12.

Zawada K., *Forma przelewu,* Rejent 1992, No 5.

Zawadzka J., *Uwagi o czynnościach prawnych mortis causa,* in: Jelonek-Jarco B., Kos R., Zawadzka J. (eds.), *Usus magister est optimus. Rozprawy prawnicze ofiarowane Profesorowi Andrzejowi Kubasowi,* Warszawa 2016.

Zawadzka J., *Warunek w prawie cywilnym,* Warszawa 2012.

Zeranski D., *Die postmortale Überleitung des Rückforderungsanspruchs des verarmten Schenkers durch den Sozialhilfeträger,* NJW 1998, No 35.

Zeranski D., *Der Rückforderungsanspruch des verarmten Schenkers. Überleitbarkeit, Abtretbarkeit, Verpfändbarkeit, Pfändbarkeit und Vererblichkeit des Rechts aus § 528 Absatz 1 Satz 1 BGB,* Berlin 1998.

Zelek M., in: Gutowski M. (ed.), *Kodeks cywilny. Komentarz. Tom III. Art. 627-1088,* Warszawa 2022, Legalis.

Zimmer M., *Anmerkung zu BGH, Urteil vom 3.12.2008 –IV ZR 58/07,* NJW 2009, 1146.

Zimmermann R., *Kulturelle Prägung des Erbrechts?,* JZ 2016, No 7.

Zimmermann R., *Testamentsformen: "Willkür" oder Ausdruck einer Rechtskultur?,* RabelsZ 2012, vol. 76.

Zoll F., *Czy odwołalność testamentu zawsze powinna być nieograniczona?,* in: Pecyna M., Pisuliński J., Podrecka M. (eds.), *Rozprawy cywilistyczne. Księga pamiątkowa dedykowana Profesorowi Edwardowi Drozdowi,* Warszawa 2013.

Zoll F., *Intestate Succession in Poland,* in: Reid K.G.C., De Waal M.J., Zimmermann R. (eds.), *Intestate Succession,* Oxford 2015.

Zoll F., Szpunar A., *Prawo cywilne w zarysie,* Kraków 1948.

Zwißler F., in: Burandt W., Rojahn D. (eds.), *Beck'sche Kurz-Kommentare, Erbrecht*, München 2019, Beck online.

List of Authors

Wojciech Bańczyk – Doctor of law (*cum laude*), is an assistant at the Chair of Civil Law, Jagiellonian University in Krakow (JU) and an attorney-at-law in Krakow. He teaches civil law and sustainable development law at JU. A co-director of the American Law Program by The Catholic University of America in Washington D.C. and JU. Winner of the first prize in the contest of the General Counsel to the Republic of Poland for the best master theses on court law. A member of the European Society of Comparative Legal History, the European Law Institute and others. Awarded scholarships by the German Academic Exchange Service (DAAD) and the Foundation of Polish Science (FNP). Co-investigator and principal researcher of the Polish National Science Centre (NCN) grants, co-researcher of the Polish-German Academic Foundation (DPWS) grants. Author of contributions on contract law, succession law, ownership law, comparative law and legal history, for example in Brill, Springer, ZEuP.

Witold Borysiak – Doctor of law (*cum laude*), assistant professor at the University of Warsaw, Faculty of Law and Administration and at the Institute of Justice. A former member of the Working Group on Succession Law of the Polish Civil Law Codification Commission. He has been a visiting scholar at many scientific Institutes and universities worldwide, including the Max-Planck-Institut für ausländisches und internationales Privatrecht in Hamburg, the Swiss Institute of Comparative Law in Lausanne, the Institute for European Tort Law in Vienna and at the University of Geneva's Faculty of Law (SCIEX scholarship). His main areas of interest are comparative private law, succession law, the law of obligations, family law, medical law and European legal tradition. He is the author of numerous publications, including co-authorship of the System of the Polish Private Law and System of the Polish Medical Law, as well as commentaries on the Polish Constitution, the Civil Code and the Family and Guardianship Code.

Paulina Gwoździewicz-Matan – Doctor of law, assistant professor at the University of Silesia in Katowice at the Faculty of Law and Administration. She is an attorney-at-law specialising in civil and intellectual property law, the author of publications on art and cultural property law, intellectual property law and civil law, a speaker at many conferences, seminars and trainings.

Wojciech Klyta – Doctor hab. in law, associate professor at the Faculty of Law and Administration at the University of Silesia in Katowice, lecturer in private international law and an expert in commercial arbitration. He publishes in the field of international and comparative company law, international insolvency law, international succession law and international traffic accidents.

Bartosz Kucia – Doctor of law (*cum laude*), assistant professor at the Faculty of Law and Administration at the University of Silesia in Katowice, attorney-at-law specialising in commercial and inheritance law, author of publications on domestic, comparative and international succession law, including commentaries on Polish law. The particular fields of his research are the administration of estate and succession law in *common law* countries, and their correlation with inheritance law and procedure in the countries of continental Europe.

Małgorzata Lubelska-Sazanów – Doctor of law, researcher based at the University of Silesia. She studied law in Katowice and in Vienna and has an LLM degree from University of California, Davis. She performed her doctoral dissertation in form of a co-tutelle at the University of Silesia and the University of Osnabrück. Her main research interest refers to the position of animals in private law, EU regulations regarding animal welfare and contract law. She has been awarded numerous scholarships, including from the Max Planck Institute, DAAD, and the Foundation for Polish Science. The author of numerous publications in the field of Private Law and Animal Law, including "Animals as specific objects of obligations", V&R Unipress, 2020.

Elwira Macierzyńska-Franaszczyk – Doctor of law (*cum laude*), MBA, lawyer, assistant professor at the Civil Law Department at Kozminski University in Warsaw; research assistant at the European Legal Studies Institute at the University of Osnabrück. Former member of the working group on Service Contracts of the Codification Commission on Civil Law at the Polish Ministry of Justice. Member of the European Law Institute, Vienna. She specialises in Polish and European private law, consumer and e-commerce law, law of new technologies and private international law. The author of numerous publications.

Mikołaj Pietrzyk – A student in the Doctoral School at the University of Silesia in Katowice. His scientific interests and publications focus on the philosophy of law, private law, statutory interpretation, and the relations between courts and lawmakers.

Katarzyna Południak-Gierz – Doctor of law, assistant professor at the Civil Law Department, Faculty of Law and Administration at the Jagiellonian University of Krakow. A member of the European Law Institute in Vienna. Her scientific interests focus on the interplay between private law and technology. She researches private law reaction towards use of personalisation techniques in consumer contracts and the possibility of using granularity to increase the ecological efficiency of sales law.

Ewa Rott-Pietrzyk – Professor dr hab., working at the Institute of Legal Sciences, Faculty of Law and Administration at the University of Silesia in Katowice, a lecturer in private law, and an expert in contract law and an arbitrator. Coordinator and member of many national and international projects (e.g. member of the Research Group on EC Private Law – Acquis Group), including coordination in projects financed by Deutsch-Polnische Wissenschaftsstiftung. Former member of the working group on general part of civil law of the Codification Commission on Civil Law at the Polish Ministry of Justice and author of the project on commercial agency contract (which has been in force since 2000). The author of several dozen studies on private law and private international law (mainly in general private law institutions, contract law, including commercial intermediary agreements), Chinese law, and comparative law, published in Polish and foreign sources.

Fryderyk Zoll – Professor dr hab., doctor honoris causa of the National Economic University of Ternopil, professor at the Civil Law Department, Faculty of Law and Administration at the Jagiellonian University in Krakow and at the European Legal Studies Institute at the University of Osnabrück. He has experience as a leading researcher of numerous grant projects on private law and civil procedure. He is a member numerous associations connected with private law as well as the legal education and justice system. A former member of the Executive Committee of the European Law Institute, of the Common Frame of Reference and Committee of Acquis Group drafting teams, as well as of the Codification Commission at the Polish Ministry of Justice. His scientific interests focus mostly on European private law, consumer law, comparative law, public interference with private law (e.g. ecology), and independence of judiciary.

Aneta Żuradzka – Doctoral student and academic teacher at the Faculty of Law and Administration of the University of Silesia in Katowice. The author of publications in the field of civil law, including inheritance law and private international law, as well as pharmaceutical law. An attorney-at-law registered on the list of attorneys-at-law of the Katowice Bar Association of Attorneys-at-Law. She provides legal assistance in the field of civil law and proceedings, pharmaceutical law, individual and collective labour law, personal data protection law. A speaker at conferences and seminars, and active as a trainer.